THE PASTORAL EPISTLES

In the church tradition, three letters, now known as the Pastoral Epistles, are attributed to the apostle Paul. They are unlike any other letters by Paul. They are written to two of his closest companions, Timothy and Titus, and they instruct those two leaders how to lead gathered Christians in Ephesus and in Crete. The letters contain plenty of instruction for how church leaders at that time, and in those places, were to function. In this commentary, Scot McKnight seeks to explain the major themes of the Pastoral Epistles – church order, false teaching, and failing Christians – and their foundational vision for how Christians could make a good impression in public life. These three brief letters express a view of how Christians were to live in the Roman Empire in a way that does not offend public sensibilities. They prescribe a way of public behavior best translated as "civilized religion."

SCOT MCKNIGHT is Professor of New Testament at Northern Seminary and author of numerous publications on the New Testament.

NEW CAMBRIDGE BIBLE COMMENTARY

GENERAL EDITOR: Ben Witherington III
HEBREW BIBLE/OLD TESTAMENT EDITOR: Bill T. Arnold

EDITORIAL BOARD
Bill T. Arnold, *Asbury Theological Seminary*
† James D. G. Dunn, *University of Durham*
Michael V. Fox, *University of Wisconsin-Madison*
Robert P. Gordon, *University of Cambridge*
Judith M. Gundry, *Yale University*

The New Cambridge Bible Commentary (NCBC) aims to elucidate the Hebrew and Christian Scriptures for a wide range of intellectually curious individuals. While building on the work and reputation of the Cambridge Bible Commentary popular in the 1960s and 1970s, the NCBC takes advantage of many of the rewards provided by scholarly research over the last four decades. Volumes utilize recent gains in rhetorical criticism, social scientific study of the Scriptures, narrative criticism, and other developing disciplines to exploit the growing advances in biblical studies. Accessible jargon-free commentary, an annotated "Suggested Readings" list, and the entire New Revised Standard Version (NRSV) text under discussion are the hallmarks of all volumes in the series.

PUBLISHED VOLUMES IN THE SERIES
The Pastoral Epistles, Scot McKnight
The Book of Lamentations, Joshua Berman
Hosea, Joel, and Amos, Graham Hamborg
1 Peter, Ruth Anne Reese
Ephesians, David A. deSilva
Philippians, Michael F. Bird and Nijay K. Gupta
Acts, Craig S. Keener
The Gospel of Luke, Amy-Jill Levine and Ben Witherington III
Galatians, Craig S. Keener
Mark, Darrell Bock
Psalms, Walter Brueggemann and William H. Bellinger, Jr.
Matthew, Craig A. Evans
Genesis, Bill T. Arnold
The Gospel of John, Jerome H. Neyrey
Exodus, Carol Meyers
1–2 Corinthians, Craig S. Keener
James and Jude, William F. Brosend II
Judges and Ruth, Victor H. Matthews
Revelation, Ben Witherington III

The Pastoral Epistles

Scot McKnight
Northern Seminary

Shaftesbury Road, Cambridge CB2 8EA, United Kingdom

One Liberty Plaza, 20th Floor, New York, NY 10006, USA

477 Williamstown Road, Port Melbourne, VIC 3207, Australia

314–321, 3rd Floor, Plot 3, Splendor Forum, Jasola District Centre, New Delhi – 110025, India

103 Penang Road, #05-06/07, Visioncrest Commercial, Singapore 238467

Cambridge University Press is part of Cambridge University Press & Assessment, a department of the University of Cambridge.

We share the University's mission to contribute to society through the pursuit of education, learning and research at the highest international levels of excellence.

www.cambridge.org
Information on this title: www.cambridge.org/9781107138797

DOI: 10.1017/9781316481677

© Scot McKnight 2023

This publication is in copyright. Subject to statutory exception and to the provisions of relevant collective licensing agreements, no reproduction of any part may take place without the written permission of Cambridge University Press & Assessment.

First published 2023

A catalogue record for this publication is available from the British Library.

Library of Congress Cataloging-in-Publication Data
NAMES: McKnight, Scot, author.
TITLE: The Pastoral Epistles / Scot McKnight, Northern Seminary.
DESCRIPTION: Cambridge, United Kingdom ; New York, NY, USA : Cambridge University Press, 2023. | Series: New Cambridge Bible commentary | Includes bibliographical references and index.
IDENTIFIERS: LCCN 2022057097 (print) | LCCN 2022057098 (ebook) | ISBN 9781107138797 (hardback) | ISBN 9781316503591 (paperback) | ISBN 9781316481677 (ebook)
SUBJECTS: LCSH: Bible. Pastoral Epistles–Commentaries.
CLASSIFICATION: LCC BS2735.53 .M39 2023 (print) | LCC BS2735.53 (ebook) | DDC 227/.8307–dc23/eng/20230523
LC record available at https://lccn.loc.gov/2022057097
LC ebook record available at https://lccn.loc.gov/2022057098

ISBN 978-1-107-13879-7 Hardback
ISBN 978-1-316-50359-1 Paperback

Cambridge University Press & Assessment has no responsibility for the persistence or accuracy of URLs for external or third-party internet websites referred to in this publication and does not guarantee that any content on such websites is, or will remain, accurate or appropriate.

Contents

Acknowledgments	*page* xi
List of Abbreviations	xii
1 INTRODUCTION	1
The Pastorals and the Life of Paul	2
Authorship	4
The Opponents in the Pastoral Epistles	10
The Theology of the Pastoral Epistles	12
A Sketch of Timothy's Life	13
A Sketch of Titus' Life	14
The Structure of the Pastoral Epistles	15
2 COMMENTARY ON 1 TIMOTHY	18
1:1–2 Apostle to Pastor of Pastors	19
1:3–7 Pastoring People in the Faith	21
Problems at Ephesus	23
A Closer Look: The False Teachers and Their Teachings	25
Responding to the Problems at Ephesus	25
1:8–11 The Purpose of the Law	28
1:12–17 The Apostle as Example	31
Noteworthy Uses of "Faithful" (*pistos*) in the Pastoral Epistles	34
1:18–20 A Faithfulness for Timothy	36
Timothy	36
Hymenaeus and Alexander	37
2:1–7 Teaching People to Pray	38
A Closer Look: On *Civilized Piety*	43
2:8–15 Order in the Assemblies	44
For Men	47
For Women	48

A Closer Look: Perictione I on the Harmonious Woman (fourth to third century BCE; perhaps the author is Plato's mother)	48
A Closer Look: Melissa to Clearte	49
A Controversial Passage: A Recent Approach	51
Another Approach	53
A Closer Look: Comparing 1 Corinthians 14:34–35 and 1 Timothy 2:11–12	56
A Closer Look: Jewish and Christian Texts (from Gathergood)	61
3:1–7 Bishops	62
A Closer Look: What Do We (Not) Know?	65
A Closer Look: Virtues and Vices in the Greco-Roman World	66
3:8–13 Deacons	71
3:14–16 Reason for the Letter	75
If I Am Delayed	76
The Mystery of Our Religion	77
4:1–5 Signs of the Time	79
The Times	80
The Manifestations	81
4:6–10 A Good Servant of Christ	83
A Closer Look: *Kalos* in the Pastoral Epistles	84
4:11–16 Ministry of Teaching	88
A Closer Look: Age	89
5:1–16 Older Folks and Widows	92
Older Folks	93
Widows	94
Real Widows (5:3, 5–6, 9–10)	95
Family Support for Widows (5:4, 7–8)	98
Younger Widows (5:11–15)	99
Christian Support for Relatives Who Are Widows (5:16)	101
A Closer Look: Crucial NT References to Widows	102
5:17–25 Some Church Instructions	102
Remuneration	103
Respect	105
Correction	105
Ordination	106
Wine	107
General Instruction	107
6:1–2a Instructions for Slaves	108
6:2b–10 For Timothy	110
General Exhortation	111
The Importance of Defending Apostolic Teaching	112
Material Contentment	114

Contents ix

6:11–16 Final Words for Timothy	116
6:17–19 Final Words about the Wealthy	120
6:20–21 Yet More Final Words for Timothy	124
3 COMMENTARY ON 2 TIMOTHY	126
1:1–2 The Apostle to Pastor of Pastors	126
1:3–7 The Apostle Prays for Timothy	128
1:8–14 Timothy and the Apostle	131
The Gospel	133
The Apostle and Timothy	135
1:15–18 Reception and Response	137
2:1–7 Metaphors of Morality	139
2:8–13 The Gospel in Confessional Lines	143
The Gospel Articulated	144
The Gospel and Suffering	145
A Sure Saying	146
2:14–26 Five Commands	148
Remind	149
Do Your Best	150
Avoid Profane Chatter	150
Shun Youthful Passions	152
Pursue Righteousness, Etc.	153
Have Nothing to Do with Controversies	154
3:1–9 Analysis of Apostasy	155
A Vice List for Ephesus	156
A Closer Look: Character in Theophrastus of Eresos	158
A Closer Look: Virtues of Aristotle	158
3:10–17 A Charge for Timothy	163
The Apostle's Example	164
A Principle for Ministry	165
The Reason for the Principle	166
Instructions for Timothy's Behavior	166
The Foundation for the Instructions	167
4:1–5 A Charge Continued	170
Some Instructions for Pastors	171
Some More Instructions for Pastors	173
4:6–18 Personal Details	174
The Apostle Facing Death	176
The Apostle Reflecting on Faithfulness	177
4:19–22 Letter Ending	180

4 COMMENTARY ON TITUS	183
1:1–4 The Apostle to Titus for the Assemblies in Crete	183
Servant and Apostle	184
True Son	186
1:5–9 Pastors for the People	186
The Plan	187
The List	189
1:10–16 Troublemakers on Crete	192
The Troublemakers	194
Instructions for Titus	196
2:1–10 Instructing the Households	197
Instructions for Titus (2:1, 7–8)	199
Instructions for Older Men (2:2)	200
A Closer Look: What Makes a Person "Old"?	201
Instructions for Older Women (2:3–5)	201
Instructions for Younger Men (2:6–7a)	203
Instructions for Slaves	203
2:11–15 The Household's Redemptive Foundation	204
Foundation of Grace	205
Effects of Grace	206
Time for Grace to Do Its Work	208
Foundation and Effects Restated	209
Summing It All Up	210
3:1–11 Civilized Piety	210
Seven Reminders (3:1–2)	211
Seven Vices (3:3)	213
Redemption in Christ (3:4–8a)	214
Final Instructions (3:8b–11)	217
3:12–15 Final Words	218
Travel Plans	218
One More Instruction	220
Greetings	220
Bibliography	221
Scripture Index	229

Acknowledgments

I am grateful to Ben Witherington for the invitation to write these commentaries on 1 and 2 Timothy and Titus, and for the wisdom he has shared with me over the years, including in the production of this work. I am also grateful to my graduate assistant, Justin K. Gill, without whom this book would still be in the research phase. Justin, a scholar in his own right, was originally slated to be a coauthor, but he has not yet completed his PhD, a requirement for Cambridge University Press. He did prodigious work on some of the footnotes and made suggestions on nearly every page. At times we both know we don't know for sure who had originated a certain idea. We were delayed in the submission of the manuscript because of – what else – COVID-19 but also because Justin moved back to the Ozarks and settled into a new home. Sending off this manuscript to the press will at least slow down our routine discussions about these three wonderful letters.

Two Northern Seminary students helped clean up this manuscript, so I thank pastors Laura Mott Tarro and Cody Matchett.

Abbreviations

Classical sources in Greek or Latin have been cited from the Loeb Classical Library unless otherwise noted.

ASV	American Standard Version (Bible)
BBRSuppl	Bulletin for Biblical Research, Supplements
BDAG	Bauer, Danker, Arndt, and Gingrich, *Greek-English Lexicon of the New Testament and Other Early Christian Literature*
BibSac	*Bibliotheca Sacra*
BNTC	Black's New Testament Commentary
BZNW	Beiheft zur Zeitschrift für die neutestamentliche Wissenschaft
CEB	Common English Bible
CGL	*Cambridge Greek Lexicon*
DLNT	*Dictionary of the Later New Testament*
DPL	Dictionary of Paul and His Letters, ed. Gerald F. Hawthorne and Ralph P. Martin (Downers Grove: IVP, 1993)
ESV	English Standard Version (Bible)
JBL	Journal of Biblical Literature
JSNT	*Journal for the Study of the New Testament*
JSNTSup	Journal for the Study of the New Testament, Supplement Series
JSPL	*Journal for the Study of the Pauline Letters*
LNTS	Library of New Testament Studies
NIBC	New International Bible Commentary
NICNT	New International Commentary on the New Testament
NIGTC	New International Greek Testament Commentary
NIV	New International Bible
NovTSupp	Novum Testamentum, Supplements
NPNF	Nicene and Post-Nicene Fathers

List of Abbreviations

NRSV	New Revised Standard Version (Bible)
NTS	*New Testament Studies*
SBLDS	SBL Dissertation Series
SNTSMS	Society for New Testament Studies, Monograph Series
WBC	Word Biblical Commentary
WUNT	Wissenschaftliche Untersuchungen zum Neuen Testament

1 Introduction

As found in our Bibles, the Pastoral Epistles, 1 and 2 Timothy and Titus (=PEs), were originally sent by the apostle Paul to two of his closest coworkers in the gospel, Timothy and Titus. The letters throw open a window on how churches formed their identities and developed responses to altering circumstances.[1] They are personal letters[2] that have become paradigmatic in the history of the church for pastors, priests, elders, bishops, deacons, ministers, and other church leaders. The letters, however, are as much ecclesial as they are pastoral. The language of these letters to his close coworkers prompts us to focus our attention on the "house" or "household of God," the *oikos/oikonomia theou*.[3]

---

[1] Clarice J. Martin, "1–2 Timothy and Titus (The Pastoral Epistles)," in Brian K. Blount, Cain Hope Felder, Clarice J. Martin, and Emerson B. Powery, eds., *True to Our Native Land: An African American New Testament Commentary* (Minneapolis: Fortress, 2007), 409–436, here pp. 409–410.

[2] A point made by Stanley Porter, *The Apostle Paul: His Life, Thought, and Letters* (Grand Rapids: Eerdmans, 2016), 410–411.

[3] For introductions to the PEs, the following brief list garners our top recommendations: I. Howard Marshall, *The Pastoral Epistles*, ICC (London: T & T Clark, 1999), 1–108; James D. G. Dunn, "The First and Second Letters to Timothy and the Letter to Titus: Introduction, Commentary, and Reflections," in *New Interpreter's Bible: A Commentary 11* (Nashville: Abingdon, 2000), 773–880; Philip H. Towner, *The Letters to Timothy and Titus*, NICNT (Grand Rapids: Eerdmans, 2006), 1–89; Ben W. Witherington III, *Letters and Homilies for Hellenized Christians: A Socio-Rhetorical Commentary on Titus, 1–2 Timothy and 1–3 John* (Downers Grove, IL: IVP Academic, 2006), 23–85; Douglas A. Campbell, *Framing Paul: An Epistolary Biography* (Grand Rapids: Eerdmans, 2014), 339–403; Porter, *Apostle Paul*, 411–431; Annette Bourland Huizenga, *1–2 Timothy, Titus*, Wisdom Commentary 53 (Collegeville: Liturgical Press, 2016), xli–lii; Michael J. Gorman, *Apostle of the Crucified Lord: A Theological Introduction to Paul and His Letters*, 2nd ed. (Grand Rapids: Eerdmans, 2017), 612–659; Christopher R. Hutson, *First and Second Timothy and Titus*, Paideia Commentaries on the New Testament (Grand Rapids: Baker Academic, 2019), 1–21. For a recent sketch of scholarship on the Pastorals, see T. Christopher Hoklotubbe, "The Letters to Timothy and Titus," in Nijay K. Gupta, Erin Heim, and Scot McKnight, eds., *The State of Pauline Studies* (Grand Rapids: Baker Academic, forthcoming), ms pp. 1–23. For a slightly older study,

The PEs are similar enough to categorize them as a corpus,[4] a unit in the Pauline canon of the New Testament. Luke Timothy Johnson's new grouping of the letters of Paul helpfully makes use of the term "cluster" for letters to "Paul's Delegates."[5] He stiff-arms simplistic assignments of these letters to someone other than Paul when he says, "the Pastorals are no closer or more distant from Galatians and Romans as those two letters are to the Thessalonian correspondence."[6] Exaggerations of their differences with the so-called genuine Paulines have been successfully challenged, though this hardly proves Pauline authorship. They are, however, a noticeable cluster, which permits syntheses of the PEs on topics, ecclesial strategies, opponents, and pastoral theology. Yet, each is unlike the others in important respects and thus require to be read separately with integrity. While doing so, overlaps with other clusters in the Pauline correspondence will be often observed.

THE PASTORALS AND THE LIFE OF PAUL

The Acts of the Apostles comes to its end without resolution, at least for the life of Paul. He's in prison preaching the kingdom of God "without hindrance" (Acts 28:31). The trial, anticipated for several chapters, is not reported in Acts. Instead, the message of the gospel goes to the heart of the Empire in Paul's preaching. Then Acts ends, full stop, leaving us with unanswered and sometimes unanswerable questions: Did the trial in Rome lead to an immediate execution? Was the model for Luke's telling of this story of Paul the trial of Jesus so that we are to assume that, like Jesus, Paul

---

Mark Harding, *What Are They Saying about the Pastoral Epistles?* (New York: Paulist, 2001).

[4] Like most conclusions, the corpus idea has also been subjected to intense study. See Jermo van Ness, "The Pastoral Epistles: Common Themes, Individual Compositions? An Introduction to the Quest for the Origin(s) of the Letters to Timothy and Titus," *JSPL* 9 (2019): 6–29; Jens Herzer, "Narration, Genre, and Pseudonymity: Reconsidering the Individuality and the Literary Relationship of the Pastoral Epistles," *JSPL* 9 (2019): 30–51; see too the response to Herzer in Matthijs den Dulk, "Pauline Biography and the Letter to Titus: A Response to Jens Herzer," *JSPL* 9 (2019): 52–61.

[5] Luke Timothy Johnson, *Constructing Paul*, vol. 1, The Canonical Paul (Grand Rapids: Eerdmans, 2020), 85–88. See also Armin D. Baum, "Stylistic Diversity in the *Corpus Ciceronianum* and in the *Corpus Paulinum*: A Comparison and Some Conclusions," *JSPL* 9 (2019): 118–157, and the response by John Percival, "Deciding What Counts: The Difficulties of Comparing Stylistic Diversity. A Response to Armin D. Baum," *JSPL* 9 (2019): 158–166. Percival challenges the adequacy of Baum's methodology.

[6] Johnson, 1:88.

was killed? Or was the case against Paul dropped? Was he released to carry on more mission, perhaps all the way to Spain? Was Acts written up as a kind of defense of the life of Paul before some Roman judge, and now that Luke was done with his account, had he also finished writing about Paul's life? Acts answers none of these questions. Historians, however, have attempted to do so, sometimes with much confidence.

We don't know for sure what happened, or at least we should admit we don't know. There are at least two multilayered options: (1) that Paul died not long after where the account ends, or (2) that Paul was released. If the latter, perhaps he carried on his missionary work in Spain. He told the Romans that was his plan (Rom 15:23–24), and a later pastor in Rome, Clement, confirms this when he says Paul's mission "reached the farthest limits of the west" (*1 Clem* 5:7), in which case Paul may, too, have returned to his former mission churches including Crete and Greece (Corinth) and Asia Minor. Perhaps a trip to Spain was cut short due to a lack of success, or perhaps Clement got it wrong, although I don't find that explanation compelling, since the man has no reason to make things up with an audience that may well have known Paul's life story – and Paul immediately, with a quick nod of thanks to Nero, returned to the scenes of his former mission churches. If Paul did return – and it appears he did – he changed his mind about going to Spain. In Acts 20:25 we read that Paul had told the elders of the southwest corner of Asia Minor (Ephesus, Miletus) "I know that none of you ... will ever see my face again," and in Romans 15:23 he had already made it clear that his mission work was finished in Greece and Asia Minor. Those who read 1 Corinthians 16 and 2 Corinthians 1 carefully will know Paul's travel plans were in flux most of the time.

To gather the widest reach of the evidence, I collect these details from Paul's letters to his coworkers that could then be pressed into service for constructing the life of the apostle Paul that can be gleaned from these letters. Each of the letters claims to be from Paul and sent to one of his closest associations (1 Tim 1:1; 2 Tim 1:1; Titus 1:1).

From *1 Timothy*: (1) with respect to *travel* we read that Paul, in the past, was in Ephesus on his way to Macedonia when he asked Timothy to remain in Ephesus for more careful instruction (1 Tim 1:3), that he hoped to come to Timothy in Ephesus soon (3:14–15); (2) Paul uses his *conversion and call* to support arguments (1:12–16; 2:7); (3) Paul knows about the elders' prophecies over *Timothy* (1:18; 4:14) and knows his age (4:12; cf. 5:1–2) and his health challenges (5:23), and Paul knows (4) about the faith failure of *Hymenaeus and Alexander* (1:20; cf. Acts 19:33–34). Thus, (5) a *close relationship* of Paul to Timothy is emphatic throughout the letter.

From *2 Timothy*: (1) Paul connects himself to his *ancestors* (1:3) and once again recalls his *conversion and calling* (1:11) and during his mission work he taught Timothy (1:13; 2:2; 3:10–11); (2) the closeness of Paul's *relationship* to Timothy is emphatic again (1:2; 2:1); Paul knows his tears (1:4) and the names of his grandmother Lois and his mother Eunice (1:5; 3:14–15), he knows about laying his hands on Timothy for his (prophetic?) gift (1:6), he knows about his suffering (1:8; 2:3; cf. 3:11–12) and his age (2:22); (3) he knows about the faith failure of *Phygelus and Hermogenes* (1:15) and perhaps *Demas* (4:9), and he knows about the faithfulness of *Onesiphorus* to Paul in Rome during his confinement (1:16–18; 2:9) as well as to the gospel work in Ephesus (1:18); (4) he knows too of the faith failure of *Hymenaeus and Philetus* (1:17–18; perhaps 3:8–9; cf. 1 Tim 1:20); (5) Paul's *own life is coming to an end* (4:6–8) and he is (6) increasingly *alone*, as Demas and Crescens and Titus and Tychicus are all gone (4:10, 12) and only Luke remains (4:11); (7) he asks Timothy to *bring Mark* with him when he comes to Rome (4:11, 21), and when he does come, to bring *his cloak and books and parchments* (4:13); (8) *Alexander* is mentioned (4:14–15; cf. 1 Tim 1:20 and Acts 19:33–34), and Timothy is warned about him. A decisively significant element comes now: (9) Paul mentions *a "first defense"* (4:16) when he was abandoned by everyone (cf. 4:10), but that he was *"rescued* from the lion's mouth" (4:17) and thinks the rescue will lead to great ministries (4:18). Also, (10) he mentions *more names*: Prisca and Aquila, Onesiphorus (4:19) and Erastus were left in Corinth and Trophimus in Miletus (4:20), Eubulus, Pudens, Linus, and Claudia send greetings from Rome (4:21), and finally (11), his bigger concern is that Timothy join him in Rome (4:21).

From *Titus*: (1) as is the case of a close relationship with Timothy, the term Paul uses for Titus is *endearing* (1:4) and Paul may see him as a young man too (2:2, 3); (2) Paul has been to *Crete* in ministry and left Titus there to carry on that ministry (1:5); (3) Paul generalizes about his *conversion and calling* (3:3–7); (4) Paul plans to send to Crete *Artemas or Tychicus* (3:12; cf. 2 Tim 4:12) and (5) is in *Nicopolis* when he sends this letter to Titus (3:12), and (6) he wants Titus to commission *Zenas* the lawyer and *Apollos* (3:13).

The density of these personal data, the apparent triviality of some of them, and the coherence of some of the names with the Pauline mission mean the letters strike many readers as either very clever forgeries or genuine letters from Paul.

AUTHORSHIP

If we begin with the earliest evidence after the PEs we land upon Polycarp (*To the Philippians* 4.1; 5.2) and *1 Clement* 2.7; 60.4; 61.2, and both texts know of our PEs (Polycarp knows 1 Tim 6:7, 10 and 3:8–13; Clement of

Rome knows of 1 Tim 1:17; 2:7; and Titus 3:1), which means the PEs are known to them at the turn of the century into the second century CE. Irenaeus stated that Paul wrote 1 Timothy (e.g., *Against Heresies* 1. Preface; see also 1.23.4; 2.14.7; 3.1.1; 4.16.3; 5.17.1). Clement of Alexandria refers to all three PEs (*Stromateis* 1.1, 9, 10; 4.7; *Exhortation* 1). The letters are in the Muratorian Canon. All to say that by the end of the second century these letters are both Pauline and "canonical," Marcion's omission of them being most likely intentional.[7] Towner throws down a challenge at this point: "the evidence of early second-century reception and use (let alone the still earlier attestation possible in the case of *1 Clement*) has not been adequately accounted for by the majority, pseudonymity view."[8] Pauline authorship, then, is not disputed in the early church.[9]

Does this make the PEs Pauline? No, but it tightens the screws on those who deny Pauline authorship. What remains, however, to explain is how these three letters fit into the life of Paul, and their fit is anything but simple. A common explanation is that Paul was not put to death at the hands of Nero but was released, carried on the facts we find in the PEs, was then re-arrested, and from Rome Paul sent these letters later in his life, say in the late 60s. Many have read *1 Clement* 5:6–7 as indicating he believed Paul had gone to the far west on a mission trip, and this could indicate the anticipated trip to Spain. I translate that text as follows:

... becoming a proclaimer in both the East and the West, he received a noble honor for his faith, teaching righteousness for the whole world, coming to the end of the West and witnessing before the governors, so he was released from the world and taken up into the holy place, becoming the greatest paradigm of resilience.

The doubled use of "West," with the second one having the "end of the West," suggests he got to the western end of the Roman Empire. If this reading is accepted, Clement of Rome at the end of the first century believed Paul had gone to Spain. This would require both a release from prison in Rome followed by a second arrest and second imprisonment.

---

[7] Towner, *Timothy and Titus*, 5.
[8] Towner, 6.
[9] The missing seven pages in P46 can be explained in a variety of ways, and so nothing certain can be inferred from the absence of the PEs in P46 (see Towner, *Timothy and Titus*, 6–7). That Paul's name is not mentioned in the earliest patristic citations of the PEs is taken by some to indicate the name was attributed later. See A. Hultgren, "The Pastoral Epistles," in James D. G. Dunn, ed., *The Cambridge Companion to St Paul* (New York: Cambridge University Press, 2003), 141–155, here pp. 141–142. For a sketch of the early textual evidence, see Mounce, *Pastoral Epistles*, lxiv–lxix.

Eusebius knows this too (*Church History* 2.22.2). The church tradition, then, is consistent in a release from Rome, a subsequent arrest, and martyrdom. The evidence of movements and people in the PEs cannot be squared easily with the Book of Acts.[10] If, however, one grants a release, an opening is also given to locate the movements and persons in a life of Paul. Many today are disinclined to trust the early church evidence, but one must at least grant the possibility that a release would open up for the details in the PEs.

Did Paul write the PEs? Let it be said that the cluster-theory of Johnson mentioned above is eminently reasonable and indicative of a number of hands in the Pauline letters.[11] Paul did not physically "write" any of his letters. Each of his letters was the result of conversations with coworkers, with drafts and final drafts, and then – and only then – someone actually putting a quill to parchment.[12] The style differences that are sketched by Johnson indicate that the people who wrote his letters used their own style and even vocabulary. The fundamental implication of such a conclusion is that there is no singular "Pauline style," usually attributed to Galatians, Romans, and the Corinthian letters, against which other letters can be compared.

This does not prove that Paul wrote the PEs, but that conclusion pushes against people who assume Paul could not have written the letters. Their arguments are not only many, but for many they are compelling.[13] Four

---

[10] The "gap theory" has been posed to attribute the actions of the PEs between Acts 19:20 and 19:21 where 19:21's "after these things" could encompass a long stretch of time. Others pose other unknown and unknowable gaps. For a summary, Towner, *Timothy and Titus*, 12–15.

[11] See too Michael Prior, *Paul the Letter-Writer and the Second Letter to Timothy* (JSNTSup 23; Sheffield: Sheffield Academic Press, 1989). 2 Timothy shows signs of co-authorship, a secretary is not likely, and the letter is private – these three factors deserve attention in all discussions of authorship. He argues that neither the fragments hypothesis nor pseudonymity are as conclusive as some believe.

[12] E. Randolph Richards, *The Secretary in the Letters of Paul*, WUNT 2 42 (Tübingen: Mohr Siebeck, 1991); E. Randolph Richards, *Paul and First-Century Letter Writing: Secretaries, Composition and Collection* (Downers Grove, IL: IVP Academic, 2004). Richards has been challenged with respect to Tertius in Rom 16:22 by Alan H. Cadwallader, "Tertius in the Margins: A Critical Appraisal of the Secretary Hypothesis," *NTS* 64 (2018): 378–396.

[13] The now standard study against Pauline authorship is Lewis R. Donelson, *Pseudepigraphy and Ethical Argument in the Pastoral Epistles* (Hermeneutische Untersuchungen zur Theologie 22; Tübingen: Mohr Siebeck, 1986); see also James D. G. Dunn, *Neither Jew nor Greek: A Contested Identity*, Christianity in the Making 3 (Grand Rapids: Eerdmans, 2015), 677–682; Gorman, *Apostle of the Crucified Lord*, 612–615; Lyn M. Kidson, *Persuading Shipwrecked Men: The Rhetorical Strategies of*

Introduction 7

basic arguments have been lodged against Pauline authorship of the PEs.[14] First, the vocabulary of the PEs varies from the other Pauline letters, the vocabulary has glaring absences of typical Pauline words, and it uses different terms for the very same ideas (e.g., *epiphaneia* instead of *parousia*). I don't consider this argument easy or even necessary to counter, though the various authors who actually wrote the letters can explain some of it.[15] Second, the church organization of the PEs shows significant development from what is found in the other Pauline letters, so much so that "early Catholicism" was at the time invoked over the PEs. The assumption was that the earliest churches were charismatic and unstructured, and leaders were organically formed instead of institutionally appointed. The either–or approach here has been questioned on a number of fronts, including the absence of church order in 2 Timothy and the variety of order between 1 and 2 Timothy. The ethic of the PEs, especially as we unfold it as "civilized piety" as brilliantly explained by Christopher Hoklotubbe, is more urbane and socially conscious than the other Pauline letters.[16] Again, this is difficult and unnecessary to counter. Instead, we need to admit this significant difference, which could be explained as a later development in Paul's own mission work as he sought to keep more under the radar of the Roman Empire. We have already touched upon the fourth argument: the non-fit of these letters into the chronology of Paul's life on the basis of either his letters or the Book of Acts, or both.

---

1 Timothy 1, WUNT 2.526 (Tübingen: Mohr Siebeck, 2021). E. P. Sanders might be alone in not only not discussing the PEs but not citing one text at all in his index. See his *Paul: The Apostle's Life, Letters, and Thought* (Minneapolis: Fortress, 2015). German scholarship assumes non-Pauline authorship for the PEs. For a good example, see Oda Wischmeyer, ed., *Paul: Life, Setting, Work, Letters*; trans. Helen S. Heron; rev. trans. Dieter T. Roth (London: T & T Clark, 2012), where the PEs are covered in the "Reception of Paul" (pp. 321–328) as "Trito-Paulines." Another is their absence in Udo Schnelle, *Paulus: Leben und Denken* (Berlin: Walter de Gruyter, 2003).

[14] E. Earle Ellis, "Pastoral Letters," in *DPL*, 659–661. A searching criticism of the method used in adjudicating authorship is found in Johnson, *1–2 Timothy*, 55–90.

[15] Extensive discussion at Mounce, *Pastoral Epistles*, xcix–cxviii.

[16] T. Christopher Hoklotubbe, *Civilized Piety: The Rhetoric of Pietas in the Pastoral Epistles and the Roman Empire* (Waco, TX: Baylor University Press, 2017). For an earlier study, see Reggie M. Kidd, *Wealth and Beneficence in the Pastoral Epistles: A "Bourgeois" Form of Early Christianity?*, SBLDS 122 (Atlanta: Scholars Press, 1990). Essentially, the bourgeois nature of the PEs can be summarized as socially ascendant, culturally accommodative, and unheroically conservative (pp. 9–25). For some this implies distance from Paul who was more critical of any such bourgeois social status and ethic. Kidd concluded there was more in common with the authentic Paulines and the PEs when it came to such factors. The word "bourgeois" carries too much baggage to be historically helpful.

These arguments, as Towner sketches them, formed into a four-legged foundation: the PEs are pseudonymous, they are a unique cluster of letters, they are from the early second century, and the church has now adjusted to life in the empire by learning various forms of compromise and assimilation.[17] Towner, who has spent his academic life studying and publishing about the PEs, has countered these in reasonable and respectable ways. We turn now to his rebuttals.

It remains an important consideration that a community rooted in truthfulness, a community opposing deception and not the least deception at the level of leadership, a community that did not consider pseudonymity acceptable (I'm speaking here of nascent Christianity as is clear in 2 Thess 2:2 and Tertullian, *On Baptism* 17), and that three letters with the level of incidental details we find in the PEs that are not by the author attributed in the opening line (considering these "thats"), that a letter sent in Paul's name by someone who lived two generations after Paul would be given immediate status in the Christian community is most unlikely.[18] Early Christianity shows no acceptance of other texts written in someone else's name.[19] For many it is impossible to distinguish deception from pseudonymity. True enough, but it is a fact that the Jewish community's standards of truth-telling were every bit as strong as very early Christianity's, and that the Jewish community's relatively common form of pseudepigraphy was not done (normally) as forgery, fraudulence, or deception but showed respect and continuity with someone a new author sought to follow.[20] I consider pseudonymity unlikely for the PEs but dismissal of pseudonymity as necessarily fraudulent or forgery overstates the evidence.[21]

---

[17] Towner, *Timothy and Titus*, 15–20.
[18] This challenges the curriculum in schools of someone writing in the name of another as an assignment as proposed by Huizenga, *1–2 Timothy, Titus*, xlvii–xlviii.
[19] Marshall, *Pastoral Epistles*, 92–93; Towner, *Timothy and Titus*, 20–21.
[20] This is the well-known argument of Richard Bauckham. See Richard A. Bauckham, *Jude–2 Peter*, rev. ed., WBC 50 (Grand Rapids: Zondervan Academic, 2014), 158–162. For the viability and early Christian challenges of pseudepigraphal letters and their types, see Richard Bauckham, "Pseudo-Apostolic Letters," *JBL* 107 (1988): 469–494. For more, James D. G. Dunn, "Pseudepigraphy," *DLNT*, 997–984. For a solid response to claims of pseudonymity, Witherington III, *Letters and Homilies for Hellenized Christians*, 23–38.
[21] For a sophisticated approach to what happens rhetorically when an author chooses to write pseudonymously, see now Kidson, *Persuading Shipwrecked Men*, 37–54. An older study of the rhetoric is Mark Harding, *Tradition and Rhetoric in the Pastoral Epistles* (Studies in Biblical Literature 3; New York: Peter Lang, 1998).

Second, Towner offers a fair assessment of an assumption of disjunction in the events and person in Acts and Paul's letters when compared with the PEs. He questions the disjunction on the basis of realistic gaps found both in letters and the Book of Acts. For instance, Luke does not account for all that Paul tells us in 2 Corinthians 11:23–29 about his travels, plots, sufferings, and adventures. Third, Towner questions the literary contradictions and tensions between the genuine Paulines and the PEs. I myself have argued that too many assume a genuine Pauline style in Galatians, Romans, and 1–2 Corinthians and use those criteria as the standard by which they measure all other letters, arguing that letters that don't match that style aren't from Paul. But Paul did not write any of his letters. He had other people write them for him, and we can neither assume the same writer for each letter or that those various authors were not given freedom to express something in their own way. This is not a cop-out but a measured conclusion of how writing occurred for Paul and his coworkers.[22] There is, too, a methodological flaw: what is discontinuous with the supposed genuine Paulines proves pseudonymity and what is continuous proves pseudonymity! That is, if it is discontinuous with Paul it shows he didn't write it, while if it is continuous it shows the author was fabricating.

The logic that concludes in favor of pseudonymity is not as compelling for me as it is for many today, but I contend that there is a pseudonymity for these letters that is neither deceptive nor forgery. I doubt that is the case for these letters, but the case should not be made against pseudonymity on the basis of deception. Rather, it should be rooted in clear literary and historical evidence, which, as indicated above, presents challenges that are not unchallengeable or even undefeatable. Many of the cases for Pauline authorship are erudite and informed. Howard Marshall and his student, Phil Towner, both contend for what they call "allonymity" ("another name"), which is what I have indicated above, that is, for an honest pseudonymous composing of the letters in a way that is expressing only what they thought the deceased Paul would have said. I contend, however, that too much is made of the tension between the PEs and the artificial construct of what is called "genuine" Paulines. The voices of the Pauline letters fall naturally into clusters, and each cluster reflects a given (perhaps more than one) writer (not Paul) whose task it was to give expression to Paul's and his coworkers ideas, as they themselves developed and

---

[22] Scot McKnight, *The Letter to Colossians*, NICNT (Grand Rapids: Eerdmans, 2018), 5–12.

interacted with various churches, and this author wrote from a location that had its own linguistic and ideological context.[23] A letter by the same author from Cenchreae would not sound in all ways like that author's letter from Thessalonica. Towner, however, concedes this: "It is not possible to prove the authenticity of the letters to Timothy and Titus."[24]

If Paul wrote the letters,[25] they are from the 60s and the latest (2 Timothy) from probably 67 CE. If not, they can be dated between the late 60s to the first decade of the second century CE. The order of the letters is disputed, with some today thinking Titus was the first of the PEs.[26] It is reasonable to think 1 Timothy is written from Macedonia (1 Tim 1:3), 2 Timothy from Rome (2 Tim 1:16–17), and Titus from Nicopolis to Crete (Titus 1:5).

THE OPPONENTS IN THE PASTORAL EPISTLES

Opposition to the Pauline mission and the gospel lurks in every chapter and comes to the fore often enough for readers to be unable to avoid pondering who the opposition was and what it taught.[27] So, notice the following: 1 Timothy 1:3–7, 18–20; 4:1–10; 6:2–10, 20–21; and 2 Timothy 2:14–26; 3:1–9; 4:1–5; and Titus 1:9–16; 3:9–11. These descriptions by Paul, whom we designate often in the Commentaries below as the Apostle, were not objective descriptions but often polemical denunciations or pastoral disappointments, and the language Paul uses for these opponents is typical enough that precise identification becomes fraught with weaknesses.[28] We delineate the concerns of the Apostle in six basic categories, though there

---

[23] More than a generation ago a reasonable case was made that Luke was the writer of the PEs; see S. G. Wilson, *Luke and the Pastoral Epistles* (London: SPCK, 1979). This line of thinking has been developed in Witherington, *Letters and Homilies*, who said "the voice is the voice of Paul, but the hand is the hand of Luke" (60).

[24] Towner, *Timothy and Titus*, 26.

[25] One of the more recent defenses of the traditional view is Robert Yarbrough, *The Letters to Timothy and Titus* (Pillar New Testament Commentaries; Grand Rapids: Eerdmans, 2018), 67–90.

[26] Marshall, *Pastoral Epistles*; Witherington III, *Letters and Homilies for Hellenized Christians*, 65–68; Hutson, *1–2 Timothy, Titus*. Gorman thinks 2 Timothy may have been Paul's last letter; cf. *Apostle of the Crucified Lord*, 612.

[27] For a recent sketch, see Dillon T. Thornton, *Hostility in the House of God: An Investigation of the Opponents in 1 and 2 Timothy*, BBRSuppl 15 (Winona Lake: Eisenbrauns, 2016). For his brief summary of the opponents, pp. 264–265.

[28] Robert J. Karris, "The Background and Significance of the Polemic in the Pastoral Epistles," *JBL* 92 (1973): 549–564.

is no solid reason to think there is only one group about whom Paul speaks, and neither can we assume the opponents of 1–2 Timothy are the same as those in Titus, for what happens in Ephesus is not the same as what happens on Crete, though similarities ought not to be pushed aside.

First, there is a solid Jewish/Judean[29] core to some of the opposition, especially in 1 Timothy, which pertains directly to Ephesus.[30] They are (mis)teaching the Torah (1 Tim 1:7, 8–11; Titus 1:10, 14; 3:9). Second, status and wealth drive some of the opponents, and a desire for wealth may well delineate their motive (1 Tim 2:9–15; 6:3–10; Titus 1:11).[31] Third, at work in these false teachings also are features often connected to moral rigors and scrupulosities like celibacy and abstention from food (1 Tim 4:3–5), which could be connected to Jewish food laws (4:7b–8, 10a). Fourth, turning now to the Apostle's evaluations of the opponents, he describes his opponents as moral failures who have rejected their conscience (1 Tim 1:19; 4:1–2; Titus 1:15), which leads to a variant in faith failure (1 Tim 1:3; 4:1–2). This sounds like they were former insiders in the church of Ephesus.[32] Fifth, Paul criticizes their blasphemy and false teachings, using terms like myths and speculations, and their denial of the resurrection (1 Tim 1:4, 6–7, 20; 4:7; 6:4–5, 20–21; 2 Tim 2:14, 16, 18, 23; 4:3–4; Titus 3:9–11). Finally, the impact of the opponents is to lead believers astray (1 Tim 3:6) as a sign of the last times (1 Tim 3:1–5; 4:3–4). Paul has a basket filled with labels for these opponents.[33] Three of the opponents are named: Hymenaeus, Alexander (1 Tim 1:20), and Philetus (2 Tim 2:17), and this indicates most likely that they were formerly connected to the Pauline house churches in Ephesus.

Perceptions of Judaism and Hellenism have often been contained in reified categories but since the 1970s especially these categories have collapsed in favor of nuanced, diverse, and mixed groupings.[34] At one

---

[29] On which now see the paradigm-shifting study by Jason A. Staples, *The Idea of Israel in Second Temple Judaism: A New Theory of People, Exile, and Israelite Identity* (New York: Cambridge University Press, 2021).
[30] On Ephesus, see now esp. Paul Trebilco, *The Early Christians in Ephesus from Paul to Ignatius* (Grand Rapids: Eerdmans, 2007).
[31] Gary G. Hoag, *Wealth in Ancient Ephesus and the First Letter to Timothy: Fresh Insights from Ephesiaca by Xenophon of Ephesus* (Winona Lake: Eisenbrauns, 2015).
[32] Thornton, *Hostility in the House of God*.
[33] Listed at Marshall, *Pastoral Epistles*, 372 n. 32.
[34] I only mention two paradigmatic scholars: Martin Hengel, *Judaism and Hellenism: Studies in Their Encounter in Palestine in the Early Hellenistic Period*, trans. John Bowden, 2 vols. (Philadelphia: Fortress, 1974); E .P. Sanders, *Paul and Palestinian Judaism: A Comparison of Patterns of Religion* (Minneapolis: Fortress, 2017); E. P.

time the quest was to label everything as Gnostic or proto-gnostic and then there was a push to press all oppositions into syncretistic forms of Judaism. There has also been a tendency, now mostly shaken loose, to think of Judaism in rabbinic categories but Judaism's ideas were noticeably diverse in the first century diaspora. The upshot is that we can't identify these opponents with any specific group, but we should instead recognize the diversity of religions in Ephesus, Crete, and admit diverse expressions in each location of both Judaism and nascent Christianity.

Towner again is the benchmark for this discussion; he examines Gnostic and Jewish features of these opponents and their teachings as well as a mixture of those two features along with ascetic elements. But he adds as well the cultural factor of women who are described as disruptive (1 Tim 2:9–10, 15; 5:3–16; Titus 2:1–8) and he then explores "lateral" relationships to Corinth and other Pauline churches.[35] The opponents, at least those mentioned in 1 Timothy, have a Jewish connection, have some kind of sub-Pauline eschatology that denies resurrection and that extended into asceticism, and it seems entirely reasonable that some of the opponents, at least, were formerly connected to the Christian community. Knowing some names strongly indicates their former connection to the churches.

THE THEOLOGY OF THE PASTORAL EPISTLES

The major themes in the PEs are shaped in response to the opponents; they are not expounded in any kind of systematic theology and neither do the PEs articulate theology as one finds in either Galatians or Romans. The themes concern especially church organization, though the charge of early Catholicism of the Tübingen school was overdrawn, salvation in Christ, transformation of the Christians into a publicly respectable "godliness," or "civilized piety," and there is clear teaching on the apocalyptic manifestation of the gospel in Christ, the Holy Spirit, and the importance of Scripture. The Christology of the letters, as Towner has shown, is not identical but they are variations on Christology's centrality. Towner posits

---

Sanders, *Judaism: Practice and Belief, 63 BCE–66 CE* (Minneapolis: Fortress, 2016). Studies since these two scholars have exploded with nuance.

[35] Towner, *Timothy and Titus*, 41–50. The recent study by Dillon Thornton of the opponents in the PEs concludes that the opponents of the Pauline mission arose in the Ephesian churches who had been infected by a greed-based teaching role coming to expression in an exaggerated eschatology that led to their celibacy and disbelief in a future resurrection. See Thornton, *Hostility in the House of God*.

a trajectory from Jesus as human (1 Tim) to Christ as co-Savior (Titus) to the Lord Jesus as the paradigm of suffering and vindication (2 Timothy).[36]

To generalize as much as possible, a particular concern has to do with the theology of human relations; in particular, the claim that the PEs convey a systemic culture in need of being challenged and subverted. Annette Huizenga puts this as crisply as it gets when she says "these letters as a group contain arguably the most sexist, exclusivist, and socially oppressive teachings in the New Testament." She acknowledges that to claim God as the author of the text has more than permitted male domination and violence – they are "troubling texts."[37] Tamez, Martin, and Huizenga remind us that the PEs must not be reified into unchallengeable categories, not least as the letters speak about authority, socioeconomic and household paternalistic structures, slavery, and wealth.[38] I grieve their experiences and so cannot contest their concerns nor the history the impact these texts have inflicted at times on church and society. A tension between a hermeneutic of suspicion and a hermeneutic of context-shaped retrieval will run throughout the Commentary.[39]

A SKETCH OF TIMOTHY'S LIFE

Timothy has often been seen as the shadow behind Paul, but it is wiser to depict the man as an associate apostle. He's more than the student of the Apostle and has grown well beyond being just a young man in need of guidance. He's a mature adult companion and coworker in the Pauline mission who is capable of being on his own when necessary, but is also a man Paul wanted in his immediate circle as often as possible. I imagine him to be Paul's best conversation partner. In what follows I will assume the basic historical value of the statements in Paul's letters, Acts, and the PEs.

Timothy's father was Greek, his mother Jewish, and they lived in Asian Lystra (Acts 16:1; 20:4). He was "discipled" into Torah observance by his

---

[36] Towner, 62–67. For more on the theology of the PEs, I recommend Hoklotubbe, *Civilized Piety*; Gorman, *Apostle of the Crucified Lord*, 612–659.
[37] Huizenga, *1–2 Timothy, Titus*, lii.
[38] Tamez, *Struggles for Power*; Martin, "1–2 Timothy and Titus," 410–11; Huizenga, *1–2 Timothy, Titus*, xli–xliii.
[39] I value the now dated sketch of feminist hermeneutics in A. C. Thiselton, *New Horizons in Hermeneutics* (Grand Rapids: Zondervan, 1992), 411–470, for what I learned about the scope and power of such a hermeneutic.

mother and grandmother (2 Tim 1:5; 3:14–15). Timothy was converted to faith in Jesus as the Messiah through the Pauline mission work in Lystra on Paul's first mission trip, probably in the late 40s or early 50s (Acts 12:25–14:29; see esp. 14:8–21) but, because he was uncircumcised and thus had liminal status, Paul regulated his status by having him circumcised (Acts 16:3). From this point on Timothy not only travelled with Paul on the mission trips but became an associate apostle with Paul (cf. Acts 16:3; 19:22; 20:1–6; 1 Cor 4:17; 16:10–11). He was sent on separate missions by Paul (cf. 1 Thess 3:1–5), and may have been imprisoned (Heb 13:23), with Paul at times (cf. Phil 1:1; 2:19–23). He becomes the leading pastor over the Pauline churches in Ephesus (1 Tim 1:3).

Now some observations: he was probably Paul's closest, dearest friend, or as Paul terms it, sibling/brother (Acts 17:15; 1 Cor 16:10; 2 Tim 4:9, 21). Paul loved Timothy (cf. 1 Cor 4:17; Phm 1), and deemed him faithful (Phil 2:22) and a son (1 Tim 1:2, 18). Paul had prophesied over him (1 Tim 1:18). So close were they that Paul sent him out as his representative (Acts 17:14–5; 18:5; 19:22; 1 Thess 3:1–6; 1 Cor 4:17; 16:10; 2 Cor 1:19; Phil 2:19) and, as representative, he was a reliable witness about Paul (1 Cor 4:17). Timothy should be understood as Paul's theological partner (Phm 1) and that is why he appears as Paul's co-author so often (1 Thess 1:1; 2 Thess 1:1; Col 1:1; Phm 1; 2 Cor 1:1; Rom 16:21; Phil 1:1).[40] His humility seems manifest in the absence of credit given to Timothy for his contribution to the Pauline mission and correspondence. Put differently, it is of no surprise to the careful reader of the Pauline mission for two special letters sent to him to survive in the early Christian canonical process.

A SKETCH OF TITUS' LIFE

Titus, who goes unmentioned in the Book of Acts, can be labeled Paul's reconciling friend.[41] He was Greek and was therefore not required to be

---

[40] In a recent study, Jason A. Myers situates the historical Timothy as a rustic, and that lack of status led Paul to less sophisticated rhetoric in the PEs. See Jason A. Myers, "Rhetoric from the *Rusticas*: In Search of the Historical Timothy and Implications for the Rhetoric of 1–2 Timothy," in Todd D. Still and Jason A. Myers, eds., *Rhetoric, History, and Theology: Interpreting the New Testament* (Lanham, MD: Lexington/Fortress Academic, 2022), 179–200.

[41] In an investigation of 1 and 2 Corinthians, one scholar proposed that Timothy and Titus were the same person, and that Titus was Timothy's own informal self-designation: Richard G. Fellows, "Was Titus Timothy?," *JSNT* 81 (2001): 33–58.

circumcised (Gal 2:3), either upon conversion or under the influence of Jerusalem's pressure. He quickly impressed Saul (who will be called Paul to avoid confusions) and Barnabas as a future leader, and seems to have accompanied them to Jerusalem in a mission to care for the poor (Gal 2:1, 10). In that context he experienced no pressure to be circumcised, and thus knew gentile Christians as unobligated to Torah observance, and he also experienced in the same context a mutuality in mission (Gal 2:9). He probably then returned with Paul to Antioch (Acts 13:1) but we hear nothing about him on either the first or second mission trips. He was part of the third mission trip and the collection for the saints in Jerusalem. We find him in Crete, then Nicopolis, and then on to Dalmatia in the PEs (e.g., 2 Tim 4:10).

His part in reconciliation can be drawn out now. In reading Galatians 2:1–10 we realize he was an ambassador for the Syrian Antioch church's gift for the poor in Jerusalem and becomes, so it appears to me, a "test case" for gentile (non)circumcision. He observes in Jerusalem, at least in Paul's description, a reconciled movement for the gospel. He becomes, perhaps as a result of such experiences in Jerusalem, Paul's Ephesus-based ambassador of reconciliation with the Corinthian house churches. He was a partner in the gospel mission, which involved raising money (2 Cor 8:23), and some have suggested he was the courier of the communications between Paul and Corinth, especially when it came to raising funds (2 Cor 8–9; cf. 2:12–17 and 7:12–23). In all this Paul knew Titus's obvious empathy in pastoral care (cf. 2 Cor 7:15).

In Titus we learn that Paul considers Titus his "loyal child in the faith" (1:4) and that Paul left him in Crete to carry on the Pauline pastoral mission (1:5) as Paul went on to Nicopolis (3:12). Titus is to wait in Crete for Artemas or Tychicus (3:12–13) and then to come to Nicopolis to be with Paul. While in Crete Titus is instructed to show hospitality to Zenas and Apollos (3:13). The letter is an exhortation to Titus to pastor the Christians on Crete, but it involves being (like Timothy) an associate apostle in establishing spiritually capable leaders in the churches (1:5–9) and in teaching a faithful gospel message (cf. 1:10–16) in a way that preserves unity.

THE STRUCTURE OF THE PASTORAL EPISTLES

Some ink has been consumed in drafting various structural proposals for these letters, though no consensus has been achieved as with the letters in

Galatians or Romans. We have followed a more topical approach and used the Commentary itself to make connections. In comparing the relatively unordered PEs to other Pauline letters, A. T. Hanson once said: "The Pastorals are a meandering brook, but a brook which contains unexpected pools of remarkable depth," which he then summarized as "relative incoherence"![42] Ray Van Neste has taken critical responses to Hanson's and Miller's incoherence approach to the next level by proposing a tight cohesion.[43]

There is a tendency in the scholars of many such proposals to become convinced of the structure and then to explain everything in the text through that explanation. But the text is not so cooperative, which reminds me of something a public intellectual once said: "It is we, the bipeds with the fat heads and opposable thumbs, who impose straight lines on nature."[44] The texts we are about to examine are more like nature than we sometimes care to admit. We will let the text flow as it does, drawing connections that make sense on the surface.

This Commentary is not the place to carry on extensive conversations about and with the scholarship on the Pastorals even as it continues at a rapid pace. The original design of the Cambridge Bible Commentaries was for the higher forms of schools and not for the researchers in universities. I have tried to keep that in mind in spite of my joy in reading brilliant scholarship on the PEs. For the freshest survey of the Pastorals see the recent sketches of scholarship below by Hoklotubbe and Kidson.

A word about footnoting. It would have been easy to add hundreds more footnotes. Nearly every exegetical observation could be attached to a rabbit hole of scholarship. I have perhaps too frequently indicated in the notes those scholars with whom I have chosen to interact – especially Marshall, Towner, Huizenga, Knight, Mounce, Johnson, Hoklotubbe, Kidson, Collins, et al. – and I could have cited them, along with others, until the cows come home. Such is the fertility of scholarship today that no one masters any book, and I have isolated myself more with the text and my

---

[42] A. T. Hanson, *Studies in the Pastoral Epistles* (London: SPCK, 1968).
[43] Ray Van Neste, *Cohesion and Structure in the Pastoral Epistles* (JSNTSup 280; London: T & T Clark, 2004). See James D. Miller, *The Pastoral Letters as Composite Documents* (SNTSMS 93; Cambridge: Cambridge University Press, 1997).
[44] Charles Krauthammer, *Things That Matter: Three Decades of Passions, Pastimes and Politics* (New York: Crown Forum, 2013), 118.

favorite studies than with every corner of the library. Hence, while very much appreciated, some Commentaries have not been cited as they could have been. Over and over, I have learned from the major scholarship on the Pastorals and wish here to credit them, all at once, for what I have written.

2 Commentary on 1 Timothy

1 Timothy is a letter written by a pastor of coworkers, namely an apostle, to a "pastor" of bishops and deacons, Timothy, and thus indirectly becomes a pastoral letter for those in pastoral ministry. This letter, along with 2 Timothy and Titus, thus become paradigmatic letters to pastors about pastoring. Letters functioned then (as now) as the presence of the author[1] but Margaret Mitchell made the important point that authors were also envoys and thus at times more than just a presence.[2] Recently a more precise genre for 1 Timothy, that of the administrative letter, has been proposed.[3] Such a proposal implies that this letter was designed for an audience that saw Paul as an official of an institution set in motion by the command of God. Precise identification of the genre of any of the New Testament (NT) letters more or less fits such genre specifications but how that impacts interpretation varies from scholar to scholar. We should be wary about imposing ideal genres on NT letters.

---

[1] Robert W. Funk, "The Apostolic *Parousia*: Form and Significance," in William R. Farmer, C. F. D. Moule, and Richard R. Niebuhr, eds., *Christian History and Interpretation: Studies Presented to John Knox* (Cambridge: Cambridge University Press, 1967), 249–268; John L. White, *Light from Ancient Letters*, Foundations and Facets (Philadelphia: Fortress, 1986); Hans-Josef Klauck, *Ancient Letters and the New Testament: A Guide to Content and Exegesis* (Waco: Baylor University Press, 2006); Richards, *Paul and First-Century Letter Writing*. See also Heinz-Werner Neudorfer, *Der erste Brief des Paulus an Timotheus*, 2nd ed., Historisch-Theologische Auslegung: Neues Testament (Witten: SCM/R. Brockhaus, 2012), 40.

[2] Margaret M. Mitchell, "New Testament Envoys in the Context of Greco-Roman Diplomatic and Epistolary Conventions: The Example of Timothy and Titus," *JBL* 111 (1992): 641–662.

[3] Kidson, *Persuading Shipwrecked Men*, 55–102.

1:1-2 APOSTLE TO PASTOR OF PASTORS

1:1 Paul, an apostle of Christ Jesus by the command of God our Savior and of Christ Jesus our hope,

1:2 To Timothy, my true child in the faith: Grace, mercy, and peace from God the Father and Christ Jesus our Lord.

The letter purports to be from the Apostle Paul[4] (hereafter Apostle), grand missioner to the gentiles and writer of letters in the New Testament. (Our Introduction (Chapter 1) laid out a case for 1 Timothy as "written" by Paul.[5]) As in his other letters, Paul labels himself *apostle*, which is not so much a claim to authority[6] as a self-designation of his calling: he was sent by Christ.[7] His commission is given emphasis here by the claim that his apostleship derived from the *command* of both *God* and *Christ Jesus*, an early intimation of what was later to be the Trinitarian language of Father and Son. As a commissioned pastor the Apostle was a formal representative of God and Christ Jesus to Timothy and through Timothy to the church under his guidance. This sets off a theistic succession system in the early church.[8]

God is declared to be *Savior*, a statement that evokes contrast with the Roman emperor as savior[9] and could thus indicate a willingness by some

---

[4] On his name Paul, which was for some his gentile mission context name, see Martin Hengel, *The Pre-Christian Paul*, trans. John Bowden (Philadelphia: Trinity Press International, 1991), 6-15. It is perhaps his Roman (or gentile) name.

[5] Introduction, section "Authorship."

[6] Ernest Best, "Paul's Apostolic Authority—?," *JSNT* 27 (1986): 3-25. But recent masculinity studies could suggest a "hegemonic gender ideal" of a man in Paul's self-presentation in Titus and 1 Timothy. See Peter-Ben Smit, "Supermen and Sissies: Masculinities in Titus and 1 Timothy," *JSPL* 9 (2019); 62-79. He is challenged successfully by Suzan J. M. Sierksma-Agteres, "Faithfulness as Subhegemonic Antidote to a Precarious Existence: A Response to Peter-Ben Smit," *JSPL* 9 (2019): 80-88.

[7] See Acts 9:1-30. For discussions, see Richard N. Longenecker, ed., *The Road from Damascus: The Impact of Paul's Conversion on His Life, Thought, and Ministry* (Grand Rapids: Eerdmans, 1997). On the meaning of "apostle," see P. W. Barnett, "Apostle," in *DPL* 45-51.

[8] See Perry L. Stepp, *Leadership Succession in the World of the Pauline Circle*, New Testament Monographs 5 (Sheffield: Sheffield Phoenix, 2005). He concludes that succession ensures possession, manner, institutional vitality, realization of an effect, the effect itself, and legitimizes the successor (see pp. 193-197). A variety of terms denote such a process, including tradition and instruction. In the PEs, succession can be found throughout.

[9] The theme of Paul's or the church's relation to the empire and to the emperor can be expressed in three alternatives: accommodation/capitulation, resistance, or negotiation. The term negotiation has been elucidated and demonstrated by Hoklotubbe, *Civilized Piety*, 2017. His view will be assumed as proven throughout this commentary. See also

to confront the powers of Rome.[10] Referring to Christ Jesus as *our hope* evokes the Parousia (Titus 2:13), the completion of redemption and establishing of the kingdom, with an inherent challenge to those who would find some hope in the possessions of status and wealth in this age (1 Tim 6:17). (Christ is also Savior in the Pastorals, most noticeably in 2 Tim 1:10; Titus 1:4; 2:13; 3:6).[11] The word *command* could echo the gentile mission of Paul's calling (Rom 16:26).

The Apostle writes to *Timothy*, Paul's closest associate, whom he calls *my loyal child in the faith*. The term *loyal* can be translated as "true" (ASV, CEB, NIV, ESV) or "genuine." Other NT references can be read as either loyal or true in the sense of genuine,[12] but here the term authorizes Timothy as a genuine representative of the Apostle. The weight of meaning rests on the term *child*. More often than not this term refers to age, that is to a child over against a young man or a mature adult,[13] which leads some to think Timothy was quite young (cf. 1 Tim 4:12, where the word *neotētos* is used). But the Apostle connects *child* to *in the faith* and this suggests Timothy's spiritual parentage[14] and familial intimacy[15] more than his age. Thus, the Apostle evokes a father–son relationship.[16]

As the Apostle's delegate to represent him in Ephesus, Timothy is expected to continue the apostolic ministry by correcting and encouraging the Ephesian leaders. Yet the Apostle does not appoint Timothy to this position in an authoritative manner. As a metaphor of endearment this term indicates the sort of intimate relationship that existed between Paul and Timothy as sage-parent and mentored student. Thus, this kind of sage-mentored relationship sets the stage for Timothy's relationship with the bishops and deacons in Ephesus. As Paul's child he will mentor them into the same kind of sage–child relationship.

Scot McKnight and Joseph B. Modica, eds., *Jesus Is Lord, Caesar Is Not: Evaluating Empire in New Testament Studies* (Downers Grove: IVP Academic, 2013). Empire criticism, when based on perceived insinuations in the text, at times stretches the evidence too far.

[10] Towner, *Timothy and Titus*, 97. Collins suggests Paul's use of "savior" for God indicates a Jewish provenance. See Raymond F. Collins, *I & II Timothy and Titus* (Louisville: Westminster John Knox, 2002), 22.

[11] For discussion of the Christology of the PEs, see Towner, *Timothy and Titus*, 59–68.

[12] 2 Cor 8:8; Phil 4:3; Titus 1:4.

[13] Acts 21:5, 21; 1 Cor 7:14; Eph 6:1, 4; 1 Tim 3:4, 12; 5:4; Titus 1:6.

[14] Gal 4:19, 31; Rom 8:16–17, 21; 9:7; 1 Cor 4:14; Phil 2:15 Eph 5:1, 8.

[15] 1 Thess 2:7, 11; 1 Cor 4:17; 2 Cor 6:13; Phm 10; Phil 2:22; 1 Tim 1:18; 2 Tim 2:1; Titus 1:4.

[16] Kidson, *Persuading Shipwrecked Men*, 97–101.

The common Jewish greeting *peace* and the Greek greeting of *grace*, the combination of which are the typical Pauline greeting (e.g., Rom 1:7; Titus 1:4), find a new term (*mercy*) between them (2 Tim 1:2). These are terms of greeting rather than rich theological propositions even if in the burgeoning Christian movement one can never completely get away from some theological echo in these terms.[17] The source of this triad again is both God and Christ Jesus, to which is added here *our Lord*.

1:3–7 PASTORING PEOPLE IN THE FAITH

Most of Paul's letters begin with a prayer of thanksgiving, though Galatians, 2 Corinthians, and Ephesians diverge from that pattern. 2 Corinthians and Ephesians open with a blessing of God (2 Cor 1:3–7; Eph 1:3–14), while Galatians, 1 Timothy, and Titus burst into the room and immediately get down to business.

1:3 I urge you, as I did when I was on my way to Macedonia, to remain in Ephesus so that you may instruct certain people not to teach any different teachings,

1:4 and not to occupy themselves with myths and endless genealogies that promote speculations rather than the divine training that is known by faith.

1:5 But the aim of such instruction is love that comes from a pure heart, a good conscience, and sincere faith.

1:6 Some people have deviated from these and turned to meaningless talk,

1:7 desiring to be teachers of the law, without understanding either what they are saying or the things about which they make assertions.

At 1 Timothy 1:3–7 the letter's substance officially begins and this is followed in 1:8–11 with a parenthetical observation to clarify what the law is designed to accomplish, a law the Apostle mentions in 1:7. Our outline of 1 Timothy sees a larger section extending from 1:3 to 3:16 and our passage as the first of four parts in a unit about false teachings (1:3–7, 1:8–11, 1:12–17, and 1:18–20).[18]

---

[17] Perhaps there's a liturgical basis for a soteriological triad; see Neudorfer, *1. Timotheus*, 52–53.

[18] 1 Tim 1:3 opens in Greek with *kathos* ("just as") and awaits a completion with an apodosis ("so also"), which never appears. One can suggest it begins irregularly with the *hina* clause in 1:3b, or that it is implied in 1:4, or that it does appear at 1:18 when Paul uses the expected first-person verb (*paratithemai soi*) as well as a noun completion (*ten*

The official beginning of 1 Timothy creates one of the many problems for dating these books since the setting, expressed as *when I was on my way to Macedonia*, can be connected to any number of trips undertaken by Paul. Was he leaving Ephesus and heading north to Macedonia as at Acts 19:21–22? Or was he on the western side of the Aegean Sea, say in Corinth or Athens or farther north in Philippi on his way to Macedonia? And when did he tell Timothy *to remain in Ephesus*, or perhaps to "carry on with the ministry" or "persevere in the task"? Is this a recent request or one more remote in time? Could this be a fiction in order to create an imagined reality? We are not likely to know, though the first of the options (leaving Ephesus, not long ago) is more likely. The evidence can be explained both during Paul's ministry before his imprisonment in Rome, or if a release from that imprisonment occurred, after he got back to the Aegean mission churches.[19]

What matters to the Apostle is Timothy's pastoring the pastors of Ephesus, to be true to the rule of faith because of the emergence of false teachers, as Acts 20:17–38 predicted.[20] Timothy is to *instruct certain people*, and by that Paul means teachers in Ephesus of the various house churches. There is an indication of pastoral responsibility in the term *instruct* (*paraggello*), and as such it is found at 4:11; 5:7; 6:13, 17. Those to be instructed are undefined (*tisin*) but the rest of this letter, not to ignore possible connections in both Titus and 2 Timothy, gives us a sharper profile of *certain people*,[21] and two are named in 1:20 (Hymenaeus [again at 2 Tim 2:17] and Alexander), and a third, Philetus, is named in 2 Tim 2:17. (See "A Closer Look: The False Teachers and Their Teachings" below.)

---

paraggelian) of the verbal beginning at 1:3 (*parakalesa*). One must also consider that it is not unlike Paul to get so wrapped up in his cascading thoughts in 1:3 and following, that he never completes the *kathos*; so Towner, *Timothy and Titus,* 106. See further at Marshall, *Pastoral Epistles,* 362–363.

[19] So Neudorfer, *1. Timotheus,* 56.

[20] On the task for Timothy, see Witherington III, *Letters and Homilies for Hellenized Christians,* 190. Huizenga sees the argument of the Apostle to be *ad hominem* too often; see, for example, *1–2 Timothy, Titus,* 5. One has to wonder *if* the Apostle's perceptions of his opponents are justifiable and, *if so,* whether or not the labeling he uses is *ad hominem* or more a trading in typical polemical, harsh rhetoric.

[21] At times opponents of Paul are not given the status of being named: cf. 1:6, 19; 4:1; 5:15, 24; 6:10, 21. See also, for example, Gal 1:7; 2:12; Rom 3:8.

Problems at Ephesus

The several problems in Ephesus, mentioned by the Apostle when he tries to persuade the mistaken to return to faithfulness, are the intents of this letter.[22] First: there is a *different doctrine* (1:3),[23] which implies the existence of some measure of apostolic faith or perhaps even more the act of a teacher teaching (*didaskalia*) false ideas. If the former, the apostolic instruction was knowingly rejected (cf. 1:10–11; 6:3). Second: the Apostle is concerned with *myths and endless genealogies that promote speculations* (1:4). The terms are sufficiently ambiguous that many people can fill them in as they please,[24] but there are enough clues to lead us to an approximation of what these opponents taught.[25] The false teachers, through their explorations into the Old Testament, have become obsessed (NRSV: *occupy themselves*[26]) with *myths and endless genealogies ... speculations* and so become *teachers of the law* (of Moses). The law features in the Apostle's discussion of the false teachers[27] whose study leads them to focus on *myths* and these *myths* are tied to fruitless or theologically and morally useless *genealogies*. Since the latter term is connected to the study of Old Testament characters like the patriarchs, there would be reason to think the Apostle has in mind midrashic or allegorical readings of Old Testament patriarchal narratives, which readings promote one's philosophy more than perceive the meaning of those texts, something found in abundance in Philo.[28] The Apostle knows that the impact[29] of their readings of the law is *speculations*, or intense debates (NIV: "controversial speculations"; CEB: "guessing games").

Third: his concern is with those who have *deviated from* the apostolic faith and *turned to meaningless talk* (1:6). The movement of the false

---

[22] See especially Kidson, *Persuading Shipwrecked Men*.
[23] The Greek term is *hetero-didaskalein*, and it is natural to connect to it the term *heterodoxy*, or heresy (see 6:3; "who teaches otherwise"). See the discussion in Kidson, *Persuading Shipwrecked Men*, 112–124. She concludes that the emphasis is not the content of teaching, heresy, but more on the act of teaching or instructing a different way of life.
[24] Good examples at Jay Twomey, *The Pastoral Epistles Through the Centuries* (Chichester, UK; Malden, MA.: Wiley-Blackwell, 2008), 19–21.
[25] For a comprehensive sketch, see Thornton, *Hostility in the House of God*.
[26] *Prosechein*: 3:8 (with wine); 4:1 (with "deceitful spirits"); 4:13 (with "public reading of scripture ..." etc.); cf. Titus 1:14.
[27] Hence, the digression at 1:8–11 on the law. One can profitably compare, then, Titus 1:10, 14; 3:9.
[28] Towner, *Timothy and Titus*, 110.
[29] On the term *prosechein*, translated in the NRSV as *promote*, see BDAG, 776.

teachers is doubled; they deviate[30] from the path and they turn aside[31] to speculations. The Apostle's language depicts swerving from the faith in 6:21 and from the resurrection in 2 Timothy 2:10. In 5:15 they turn to "follow Satan," in 6:20 the Apostle wants them to turn away from "profane chatter," and in 2 Timothy 4:4 the Apostle speaks about the time when some will turn away "from listening to the truth and wander away to myths." These are not accidental mistakes or unintentional moves but fully conscious, intentional denials of the apostolic gospel. He describes here both heresy and apostasy.[32] The term "heresy," meaningless talk (cf. Titus 1:10),[33] labels their teachings according to its content and impact. The term *faith* entails trust, trust over time, and obedience, so the term "allegiance" is one of the finest translations for the term.[34]

The fourth problem is those *desiring to be teachers of the law* (1:7). Those uppermost in the Apostle's concerns are Jewish believers who are intensely concerned with the Torah and who want to be known as "teachers of the law," used more positively in Luke 5:17 and Acts 5:34 but pejoratively in 1 Timothy. While it is possible these are gentile Godfearers who want to finish off their conversion by becoming masters of the Torah, it is more likely these are Jewish believers. It is not so much that they want to teach the Torah that concerns the Apostle; it is that their teachings are false. Hence, we agree with Johnson: they are "intellectual imposters."[35]

Fifth: he sweeps away all these aspiring teachers as *without understanding* (1:7). Their desire to teach Torah is overmatched by an ignorance demonstrated both by *what they are saying* (the content of their teaching) and of *the things about which they make assertions* (presumably, the Torah narratives on which they speculate). Behind "make assertions" is the Greek term *diabebaioomai*, and suggests thorough, stubborn, and resolute insistence. The Apostle can also use this term positively in describing what his apostle delegate is to insist on in his instructions: the gospel and its behaviors (cf. Titus 3:8 with 3:1–7).

---

[30] On the term *astocheo*, see 1 Tim 1:6; 6:21; 2 Tim 2:18.
[31] On *turn to*, see other uses in the Pastorals: 1 Tim 5:15; 6:20; 2 Tim 4:4.
[32] Paul uses a number of terms for apostasy: 1 Tim 1:19 ("suffered shipwreck"); 4:1 ("renounce the faith"); 5:15 ("turned away"); 6:10 ("wandered away from the faith"), 21("missed the mark").
[33] Other denunciatory terms include "profane" (1:9), "profane myths and old wives' tales" (4:7), "profane chatter" (6:20), as well as "contradictions" (6:20).
[34] Matthew W. Bates, *Salvation by Allegiance Alone: Rethinking Faith, Works, and the Gospel of Jesus the King* (Grand Rapids: Baker Academic, 2017).
[35] Johnson, *1-2 Timothy*, 166.

> ### A Closer Look: The False Teachers and Their Teachings
>
> Without reciting fully what was said in the Introduction (Chapter 1), the following observations of the "opponents" at 1 Timothy, and the Pastorals in general, include the following: They, or at least some, are Jewish teachers of the law (1:7, with 1:8–11; cf. Titus 1:10, 14; 3:9); they evidently have status based on wealth (1 Tim 6:9–10; cf. Titus 1:11); they are described by the Apostle as both moral failures (1 Tim 1:19; 4:1–2; cf. Titus 1:15), and faith/teaching failures, which is the focus of all three letters (1 Tim 1:3; 4:1–2), and can be described with a number of terms;[36] as false teachers they lead others astray (3:6). Their failure as teachers of the gospel tradition leads them to some moral rigors outside the gospel behaviors, and those rigors include celibacy (4:3) and abstention from certain foods (4:3–5, 7b–8, 10a), and this food issue could be explained as Jewish food laws. The Apostle's pastoral hermeneutic enables him to see his opponents as Satan-shaped instruments in the moral collapse at the end of times (1:20 [cf. 2 Tim 2:26]; 1 Tim 3:1–5; 4:3–4).

Responding to the Problems at Ephesus

The lines between the Apostle's calling, his delegate's calling, and the bishop-elder-deacon's callings in all the Pastorals are blurred, and this is why so many pastors, bishops, and teachers in the history of the church identify themselves with Paul, Timothy, and the various terms in the Pastorals. What the Apostle does, the delegate does, the leaders do, and modern church leaders follow suit. This may not be intended by the text but it is inherent to the reception history of this text. What follows is part of that reception history. The Apostle sets forth the positive side of (all) pastoral teaching: Timothy as the apostolic delegate is to *instruct* them (see 1:3) and he is to maintain the gospel tradition himself and in the leaders at Ephesus. The gospel itself is the core content of the apostolic tradition, and it is the "canon" by which all teachings in the church are to be measured. The intent of the Apostle is to persuade the false teachers to turn from their false teachings back to the apostolic tradition through Timothy.[37]

Here that tradition is a ministry, that is, the *divine training that is known by faith* (1:4). Divine training translates *oikonomia*, which often means

---

[36] On the various terms, see Marshall, *Pastoral Epistles*, 372 n. 32.
[37] See now Kidson, *Persuading Shipwrecked Men*. An older study is by Lewis R. Donelson, *Pseudepigraphy and Ethical Argument in the Pastoral Epistles*, Hermeneutische Untersuchungen zur Theologie 22 (Tübingen: Mohr Siebeck, 2006).

management, appointment, arrangement, ministry, or plan but here has been translated in the NRSV as "training," while the NIV and CEB have "God's work" and "God's way of doing things." A nuanced understanding of this view translates "responsibility" or perhaps "assignment" or "ministry" and has in mind the responsibility of the steward of the household: thus, the *oikonomia* of the one called to manage the *oikonomos*.[38] Hence, as is the case in Titus 1:7, the term *oikonomia* refers to the function of a church leader who can be called "a steward of God." This ministry/responsibility entails either the "faithfulness" (CEB) of the minister or a ministry exercised "in the faith" (which is better than "known by faith" as in NRSV, and "by faith" as in NIV), and here the Apostle circumscribes this ministry and excludes those who operate outside this faith.

If the false teachers promote speculations, *the aim*[39] of faithful gospel ministry, Timothy's specific *aim* as the apostolic delegate to Ephesus is three-fold, each with a modifier: *love that comes from a pure heart, a good conscience, and sincere faith* (1:5). These terms are especially characteristic of pastoral ministries because they are characteristic of all believers (2:15; 4:12). The focus here is on individual virtue, and there are reasons to see these terms primarily in the individual's relation with God, which suggests the first half of the Shema, the historic daily prayer for the observant in the Jewish world (Deut 6:4–9).[40]

Love is everywhere valorized and rarely defined with sufficient rigor, and yet it is the prime virtue of the New Testament (Mark 12:28–32; Gal 5:6, 14, 22; 1 Cor 16:14; Rom 13:9; Col 3:14). Love cannot be defined by opening an English dictionary but instead is best understood by observing the love shown by the God of the Bible (1 John 4:7–10). Thus, love is a rugged, affective commitment to another person (to God, to another) to be present *with* that person, to be an advocate *for* that person, and to mutually be shaped *unto* Christoformity.[41] Genuinely effective gospel teaching

---

[38] Marshall, *Pastoral Epistles*, 367–368. On *oik-* terms, see especially 1 Tim 3:4, 5, 12, 15; 5:4; 2 Tim 1:16; 4:19; Titus 1:11. For ordering or pattern as the idea of *oikonomia*, see Johnson, *1–2 Timothy*, 164; Towner, *Timothy and Titus*, 112–113.

[39] Kidson laments the neglect of the term behind "aim," namely *telos*, which should be seen in the contexts of ancient *paideia*; see Kidson, *Persuading Shipwrecked Men*, 173–175.

[40] Neudorfer, *1. Timotheus*, 63–64. *Contra* Johnson, *1–2 Timothy*, 165, 174–175.

[41] I have essayed this definition in a number of settings, including *Reading Romans Backwards* (Waco: Baylor University Press, 2018). The famous reductions of C. S. Lewis to four terms falls short of this divine panorama of love in the Bible. See C. S. Lewis, *The Four Loves* (New York: Harcourt Brace Jovanovich, 1960). A fresh study

results in that kind of person with that kind of behavior and direction. In the Pastorals love is connected to Christ (1 Tim 1:14; 2 Tim 1:13), is a virtue for all (1 Tim 2:15; Titus 2:2), is a virtue for Timothy (1 Tim 4:12; 6:11; 2 Tim 2:22), is derived from God's Spirit (2 Tim 1:7), and is embodied in the Apostle (2 Tim 3:10). In our passage this kind of love springs from an inner reality of God's redemptive grace, baptism, forgiveness, and sanctification (*from a pure heart*, 1:5). Any kind of teaching not leading to love is not apostolic, as Augustine once famously said.[42]

Good conscience, another expression used often in the Pastorals,[43] reflects the inner reality of a person with its capacity to evaluate truth (1 Tim 3:9; 2 Tim 1:3) and morality, and so guide a person into virtue. Phil Towner appropriately calls it an "organ of decision,"[44] which as the etymology (*syn + eidēsis*) suggests, means a coknowing. The "co" connects a person to God and to a person's community's socialization. In our passage the term "good" means the impact of God's grace on a person as understood in the apostolic teaching that leads believers to evaluate and shape their behaviors in accordance with the gospel – all before God.[45] This ethical dimension of having a *good conscience* bridges the grace of God into the public life of the believer. It becomes the quality that displays the person's citizenship under the rule and reign of Christ Jesus as Lord, which quality of life displays the eschatological hope in Christ Jesus through a way of life formed by the apostolic gospel.[46] Rejection of a gospel-formed conscience shipwrecks one's faith (1:19; 4:2; Titus 1:15). The Apostle's emphasis on God's grace to transform the human conscience into a state of goodness reveals the Christian notion that the conscience alone cannot be counted on to lead people into good or ethical behavior.[47]

Sincere attached to *faith* could be understood as turning faith from the act of believing into the content of what is to be believed (e.g., 1 Tim 3:9,

---

filled with insight is Jon D. Levenson, *The Love of God: Divine Gift, Human Gratitude, and Mutual Faithfulness in Judaism* (Princeton: Princeton University Press, 2016).

[42] *On Christian Doctrine* 1.40.

[43] 1 Tim 1:5, 19; 3:9; 4:2; 2 Tim 1:3; Titus 1:15. Elsewhere in Paul it is used more than a dozen times, including Rom 2:15; 13:5; 1 Cor 10:25–29; 2 Cor 1:12; 5:11. See Marshall, *Pastoral Epistles*, 217–227; Towner, *Timothy and Titus*, 116–119.

[44] Towner, *Timothy and Titus*, 116.

[45] Witherington III, *Letters and Homilies for Hellenized Christians*, 194; Towner, *Timothy and Titus*, 118–119.

[46] Martin Dibelius, and Hans Conzelmann, *The Pastoral Epistles: A Commentary on the Pastoral Epistles*, Hermeneia: A Critical and Historical Commentary on the Bible (Philadelphia: Fortress, 1972), 20.

[47] Witherington III, *Letters and Homilies for Hellenized Christians*, 194.

13; 4:1, 6; 5:8, 12; 6:12, 21),[48] but faith is every bit a subjective, growing reality (1:14, 19; 2:15; 4:12). The emphasis on "sincere" (also 2 Tim 1:5) indicates a faith that begins with trust in Christ's redemption, is not masked behind hidden motives, is shaped by honest verbal confessions, and delivers a life rooted in and reflecting Christ. Surely the focus of a negative modifier – "unhypocritical" (here translated *sincere*) – turns attention on the false teachers whose faith is hypocritical or insincere. The Apostle works backwards through the teachings of those Timothy needs to correct. Their bad ethics unleash bad theology.[49]

Here then the positive over against the negative: false teachers provoke controversies rooted in speculations while the gospel-based teacher promotes love, a good conscience, and a genuine life of faith. The contrast between the two sides serves Paul's rhetoric effectively.[50]

1:8–11 THE PURPOSE OF THE LAW

1:8 Now we know that the law is good, if one uses it legitimately;
9 this means understanding that the law is laid down not for the righteous but for the lawless and disobedient, for the godless and sinful, for the unholy and profane, for those who kill their father or mother, for murderers,
10 the sexually immoral, men who engage in illicit sex, slave traders, liars, perjurers, and whatever else is contrary to the sound teaching **11** that conforms to the glorious gospel of the blessed God, with which I was entrusted.

It was a natural move, perhaps not expected by some readers today, for the Apostle to move from v. 7's *desiring to be teachers of the law* to Paul's theorizing on the purpose of the law, by which he means the Torah of Moses. Vv. 8–11 are a parenthetical clarification and would be a sidebar in modern writing. The paragraph moves through an opening claim (1:8) and a statement on the target audience for the law (1:9–10, that is, sinners), which ends on a general note about *sound teaching* (1:10), which is itself then itself clarified in 1:11.

---

[48] Marshall, *Pastoral Epistles*, 213–217.
[49] Witherington III, *Letters and Homilies for Hellenized Christians*, 193–194.
[50] Kidson, *Persuading Shipwrecked Men*, 178–235.

The pervasive idea here is that the law is designed by God to unmask sinners by revealing their sins. Yet when it says *the law is good*,[51] the term *good* connotes both morally excellent and beautiful, which is a pervasive Hellenistic value (see Rom 7:16).[52] But the law of Moses is only good *if one uses it legitimately*. The weight hangs on this last term, which translates *nomimos*, a term that could be translated "lawfully." The term spins us around: the law is good if used lawfully! The use of the term at 2 Timothy 2:5 – an athlete competing *according to the rules* – clarifies our verse. The law's excellence arises in being observed. Because the Apostle connects ethics to *sound teaching* and to *gospel*, to use the law "legitimately" also requires practicing it through the lens of the gospel.[53] One might argue from this text that the Apostle thinks the law applies to unbelievers while believers (described here as *innocent*) are under the *gospel*. However, a gospel-guided observance of the law promotes the gospel-formed virtue of love (1 Tim 1:5), and reminds of the critique of those *desiring to be teachers of the law* who misuse the law for speculation (e.g., 1 Tim 1:4, 6–7). The Apostle turns to what the Reformation sometimes called the "first use of the law," that is, the law of Moses revealing the will of God and unmasking human sinfulness. So Paul poses two groups, the godless and the *innocent*,[54] and he sees the law revealed especially *for the lawless and disobedient, for the godless and sinful, for the unholy and profane*.

I here provide comments on a few of the terms: *lawless* refers as expected to those who do not observe the law in the Christian sense, while *disobedient (anupotaktos)* labels one who is insubordinate and refuses the authority of God (cf. 2:11; 3:4). To bring into the discussion *those who kill their father or mother* may seem over the top, but since the next term is *murderers* we are required here to view parricide and matricide. *Fornicators* points at either the sexually immoral in general or at those who visit prostitutes, both of which was typical behavior for males in the

---

[51] His "we know" is formulaic: cf. Rom 2:2; 3:9; 8:28.
[52] The term "good" here translates *kalos*, a term characteristic of the PEs: e.g., 1 Tim 1:18; 2:3; 3:1, 7, 13; 4:4, 6; 5:10, 25; 6:12–13, 18–19. See Marshall, *Pastoral Epistles*, 227–229.
[53] Richard B. Hays, *The Moral Vision of the New Testament: Community, Cross, New Creation, A Contemporary Introduction to New Testament Ethics* (San Francisco: HarperOne, 1996).
[54] Translating *dikaios*, a term that means "observant of the will of God" or "one whose behavior accords with Torah," with "innocent" ignores the Jewish context entirely. It means "observant" or "right" or "righteous" here. For a seminal discussion, Benno Przybylski, *Righteousness in Matthew and His World of Thought*, SNTSMS 41 (Cambridge: Cambridge University Press, 1981).

Roman Empire. This is also the case for "males who bed males," or *sodomites*. The Greek term here is *arsenokoitēs* and creates the image of men going to bed with men.[55] Some 30 percent of the Roman Empire population were slaves and many of these were captured in war. When there were no wars one method of acquiring slaves was by kidnapping, and thus the Apostle denounces *slave traders*.[56]

The law is only a partial revelation of Christian virtue. To show the fullness of moral revelation, the Apostle finishes off this listing of vices with *whatever else is contrary to sound teaching*, and *sound teaching* moves readers from the Torah into the ethical imagination of Jesus and the apostles. Each of the PEs uses a similar expression for the theological-ethical teachings of the emerging Christian tradition (cf. 2 Tim 4:3; Titus 1:9). It is a mistake to think of *sound teaching* as abstract theology or philosophy. In the Christian tradition theology is lived theology, and one can infer one's theology from one's life.[57] The vices listed here then are contrary to the law of Moses and even more to the *sound* (moral) *teaching* of the apostles. Why? Because *sound teaching* is about *the glorious gospel of the blessed God*. The Apostle's use of *blessed God* connects to a Hellenistic Jewish expression.[58] Naturally, any teaching from the law must be understood in light of the gospel in order to be *legitimate* and *sound*. Thus, Paul draws into a tight circle here *sound teaching*, the moral imagination, and the *gospel* – defined in 2 Timothy 2:8 and 1 Corinthians 15:1–28. The gospel cannot be restricted to the message of how to get saved, but is the story of Jesus who brings redemption, which is why the four Gospels have the title they do.[59]

This gospel has been, the Apostle claims, *entrusted to me*, which reflects his commissioning by the Lord Jesus to be a missionary to the gentiles with

---

[55] For extensive discussion, William Loader, *The New Testament on Sexuality* (Grand Rapids: Eerdmans, 2012). His discussion of this text is found at pp. 332–334. See also Sanders, *Paul: The Apostle's Life, Letters, and Thought*, 335–373, 727–747.

[56] On slavery, Scot McKnight, *The Letter to Philemon*, NICNT (Grand Rapids: Eerdmans, 2017), 6–29.

[57] See the richly suggestive work of Charles Marsh in the category of "lived theology." Thus, Charles Marsh, Peter Slade, and Sarah Azaransky, eds., *Lived Theology: New Perspectives on Method, Style, and Pedagogy* (New York: Oxford University Press, 2016).

[58] Collins, *1–2 Timothy, Titus*, 34–35.

[59] N. T. Wright, *What Saint Paul Really Said: Was Paul of Tarsus the Real Founder of Christianity?* (Grand Rapids: Eerdmans, 1997); G. N. Stanton, "Paul's Gospel," in James D. G. Dunn, ed., *The Cambridge Companion to St Paul* (Cambridge: Cambridge University Press, 2003), 173–184; Scot McKnight, *The King Jesus Gospel: The Original Good News Revisited*, 2nd edn. (Grand Rapids: Zondervan, 2015).

a message that calls them to the "obedience of faith" (Rom 1:5). His gospel calling entails preservation of that gospel's purity.

1:12–17 THE APOSTLE AS EXAMPLE

1:12 I am grateful to Christ Jesus our Lord, who has strengthened me, because he considered me faithful and appointed me to his service,
13 even though I was formerly a blasphemer, a persecutor, and a man of violence. But I received mercy because I had acted ignorantly in unbelief,
14 and the grace of our Lord overflowed for me with the faith and love that are in Christ Jesus.
15 The saying is sure and worthy of full acceptance: that Christ Jesus came into the world to save sinners – of whom I am the foremost.
16 But for that very reason I received mercy, so that in me, as the foremost, Jesus Christ might display the utmost patience, making me an example to those who would come to believe in him for eternal life.
17 To the King of the ages, immortal, invisible, the only God, be honor and glory forever and ever. Amen.

Having stated that he is an apostle (1:1) and stated the centrality of the gospel (1:11), the Apostle turns to the incongruity of God's grace[60] revealed in his own call to the gentiles (1:12–17). His gratitude (1:12) emerges from his redemption from a sinful, ignorant past (1:13) and then he turns to the bright side of God's call. The Apostle's conversion by grace (1:14) illustrates Christ Jesus' work to save sinners (1:15) but that redemption is aimed at transformation. Paul thus becomes an archetype for saved sinners (1:16) but all the praise goes to God (1:17). This super God saved a super sinner by super grace.

Paul's transformed life was enveloped by God's grace and calling. In fact, the NRSV's *I am grateful* might be translated "I am grace." This is not Paul's typical phrase for thanks (*eucharisteo*) but a more classical expression, *charis*, or "grace" (cf. 2 Tim 1:3; Heb 12:28).[61] This gratitude is to the One who *strengthened* him,[62] namely, *Christ Jesus our Lord*. God's raising up leaders in *service* to his people is a recognizable biblical theme usually

---

[60] Themes of grace here are developed in John M. G. Barclay, *Paul and the Gift* (Grand Rapids: Eerdmans, 2015).
[61] Marshall, *Pastoral Epistles*, 387.
[62] Also at Rom 4:20; Phil 4:13; Eph 6:10 with 2 Tim 2:1; 4:17.

entailing a calling experience, the bestowal of authority, and empowerment by the Holy Spirit.[63]

The Apostle is grateful *because* the Lord *considered me faithful* (1 Cor 4:2; 7:25). This causal expression might evoke the sense that he has earned the apostolic calling, but it is better to think that on the Damascus Road[64] the conversion call of Christ *judged* Paul to be faithful because Paul knew that the One calling the man was powerful enough to empower the man to do what God needed done. Christ *appointed* (so NIV) Paul *to his service*, forming him into an apostle (1 Tim 1:12, 2:7; 2 Tim 1:11).[65] The word "service" translates *diakonia*, from which we get the term "deacon," and is often used by Paul for a gospel-serving ministry. That service is a species of a larger service: all of the redeemed have entered into the Lord's service. Thus, the Apostle considers himself a *diakonos*, a servant (e.g., 1 Cor 3:5), alongside other gospel workers.

It is the Apostle's past (1:13–14) that led to the first term (in Greek) in this paragraph in 1:12: *charis* (NRSV: *grateful*, or "grace"). That past was interrupted by God: *I received mercy*. He was a *blasphemer*, that is, one who insulted the good work of God in Christ; he was a *persecutor*, or chaser-down of believers; he was *a man of violence*, which could be translated as "arrogance" or "hubris" (Greek: *hybris*).[66] Paul's story is told in longer form three times in Acts (9:1–29; 22:3–21; 26:9–20) as well as in Galatians 1:11–24, 1 Corinthians 15:8–11, 2 Corinthians 4:1–6, Romans 1:1–7, and Philippians 3:4–11, each of which fills in the meaning of each of the terms used here (blasphemer, persecutor, man of violence).

There is no hint of excuse when Paul says *I had acted ignorantly in unbelief* (*apistia*, "antifaith" or "without faith"). The Apostle's *ignorance* (NIV) draws on the Jewish distinction between a person who sins intentionally against God, thereby rejecting the mercy of God already revealed to them, and a person who sins unknowingly against God.[67] Paul admits, in a different way, to being filled with zeal yet lacking the knowledge of God's work (Rom 10:2) and so sinning. Through his conversion story the

---

[63] For God's empowering of his servants, Marshall, *Pastoral Epistles*, 388–389. See also *God's Empowering Presence: The Holy Spirit in the Letters of Paul* (Peabody: Hendrickson, 1994).
[64] Longenecker, *The Road from Damascus*.
[65] Towner, *Timothy and Titus*, 137.
[66] For an emphasis on *hubris*, with Paul's former life the paradigm for the false teachers, see Kidson, *Persuading Shipwrecked Men*, 193–217. She offers solid arguments for their primary vice being hubris.
[67] Collins, *1 & 2 Timothy and Titus*, 37–38.

Apostle magnifies God's incongruous *mercy* and grace for sinners, judges the false teachers for their rejection of the revealed gospel (1:3),[68] and encourages the believers of Ephesus to continued faithfulness since they are no longer ignorant and antifaith. This is why Paul uses *formerly* in 1:13: this was how he once was, but he no longer is that way, and neither should the believers in Ephesus be.

This transformation from a faithless sinner, both ignorant and hostile to God's work, into an apostle to the nations is accomplished by the superabundant *grace of our Lord*. By saying "superabundant" I am paraphrasing *overflowed*, which could be rendered "hyper-filling-up." Grace here is an effective redemptive power, and union with Christ is the location of that gracious power.[69] The Apostle's conversion story displays God's superabundant grace toward Paul, in which his ignorance of God's work (the gospel, 1:11) is shattered and his hostility quelled, creating in their place the Apostle's *faith* toward Christ Jesus *and love* for his followers. Faith and love, two central terms to the Christian faith and both in constant need of attentive definitions (see 1:4–5), must not be understood as virtues to be attained by effort but as qualities generated by the grace of being *in Christ Jesus*. Yes, they come into maturity by the habits of the body but they are generated by God. The Apostle here neither denies human responsibility nor gives it more credit than it deserves: his theology of grace knows that God's incongruous, superabundant grace creates an efficacious allegiance and love.

This incongruous nature of God's grace is a distinctive characteristic of Pauline theology, and no passage in the entire collection of Paul's letters – whether one posits this as written by him or not – clarifies God's grace better than 1 Timothy 1:15–16. In support of this conviction about God's grace, the Apostle cites an early Christian theological saying of unknown origin:[70] *Christ Jesus came into the world to save sinners*. The work of Jesus in the world, tied closely with the intention of his incarnation, is often expressed in the NT through the language of "coming", such as "I have come to" and "he came to" (e.g., Mark 2:17; Luke 19:10; John 1:9).

---

[68] Towner, *Timothy and Titus*, 141, 142–143.
[69] James D. G. Dunn, *The Theology of Paul the Apostle* (Grand Rapids: Eerdmans, 1998), 390–412; Grant Macaskill, *Union with Christ in the New Testament* (New York: Oxford University Press, 2018).
[70] For extensive discussion, Marshall, *Pastoral Epistles*, 326–330.

Paul confesses *I am the foremost* (or even "first") of sinners saved by Christ Jesus' coming.[71] Paul calls these words a *saying*, or in Greek a *logos*, a word that is *sure* or better yet *faithful* (*pistos*) (NIV: "trustworthy"; CEB: "reliable"). This word is not only faithful but also *worthy of full acceptance* or "acceptance by all." As such, it is then one of the earliest hints of a catholic, universal faith and thus anticipates the later famous Vincentian canon: "that faith which has been believed everywhere, always and by all."[72] On account of being *the foremost* sinner, he *received mercy* (1:16), and the Apostle divulges here the divine intent of such a rescue operation: *so that . . . Jesus Christ might display the utmost patience.* Jewish faith in the first century generally did not distinguish between purpose and result as much as the philosophical tradition has. In the Jewish tradition whatever resulted was believed to have been purposed and whatever was purposed becomes the result. A careful examination of the Greek terms *hina* and *pros* bears this out.[73]

Noteworthy Uses of "Faithful" (*pistos*) in the Pastoral Epistles

1 Tim. 1:12 I am grateful to Christ Jesus our Lord, who has strengthened me, because he considered me faithful and appointed me to his service,

1 Tim. 1:15 The saying is sure and worthy of full acceptance: that Christ Jesus came into the world to save sinners – of whom I am the foremost.

1 Tim. 3:1 The saying is sure: whoever aspires to the office of bishop desires a noble task.

1 Tim. 4: 9-10 The saying is sure and worthy of full acceptance. For to this end we toil and suffer reproach, because we have our hope set on the living God, who is the Savior of all people, especially of those who believe.

2 Tim. 2:2 and what you have heard from me through many witnesses entrust to faithful people who will be able to teach others as well.

---

[71] For discussion, Marshall, 399–401.
[72] Vincent of Lérins, *Commonitory* 2.6 (NPNF 2.11, p. 132).
[73] For discussions, see Murray J. Harris, *Prepositions and Theology in the Greek New Testament: An Essential Reference Resource for Exegesis* (Grand Rapids: Zondervan, 2012), 193–194.

Commentary on 1 Timothy

2 Tim. 2:11 The saying is sure:
    If we have died with him, we will also live with him;
2 Tim. 2:13 if we are faithless, he remains faithful –
    for he cannot deny himself.
Titus 1:9 holding tightly to the trustworthy word of the teaching, so that he may be able both to exhort with sound instruction and to refute those who contradict it.
Titus 3:8 The saying is sure.
    I desire that you insist on these things, so that those who have come to believe in God may be careful to devote themselves to good works; these things are excellent and profitable to everyone.

Furthermore, God's purpose was to make the Apostle *an example to those who would come to believe*. Education in the Greco-Roman and Jewish world was by emulation more than information.[74] That is, converts to Jesus as Lord would have emerged from a world of emulation and would have expected to find worthy examples in the Christian faith.[75] Paul here becomes a pattern for what is possible for any sinner.[76] The Apostle has also made himself the pastoral standard, revealing how the gospel faith flows from leaders and teachers into their churches by means of imitation and emulation.

Yet the Apostle's use of his testimony and the faithful tradition are not merely rhetorical flourish to make his teaching more encouraging to believers. Paul provides Timothy with his conversion story as the pattern of gospel formation for the churches, thereby creating an ethical rubric by which to compare and admonish the false teachers. Timothy and the churches must take care to follow this faithful example to become renewed in the grace, faith, and love found in Christ Jesus.[77]

---

[74] The Greek term here is *hypotuposis*; see also 2 Tim 1:13.
[75] See the sketch of Victor A. Copan, *Saint Paul as Spiritual Director: An Analysis of the Concept of the Imitation of Paul with Implications and Applications to the Practice of Spiritual Direction*, reprint edn., Paternoster Biblical Monographs (Eugene: Wipf & Stock, 2008), 45–69; Ernest Best, *Paul and His Converts*, The Sprunt Lectures 1985 (Edinburgh: London: T & T Clark, 1988), 59–72; Jason B. Hood, *Imitating God in Christ: Recapturing a Biblical Pattern* (Downers Grove: IVP Academic, 2013). For an older and still valuable study, E. A. Judge, "The Teacher as Moral Exemplar in Paul and in the Inscriptions of Ephesus," in David M. Scholer, ed., *Social Distinctives of the Christians in the First Century: Pivotal Essays by E. A. Judge* (Peabody: Hendrickson, 2008), 175–188.
[76] For analysis of pattern vs. prototype, Marshall, *Pastoral Epistles*, 402–404.
[77] Towner, *Timothy and Titus*, 147–151.

Reflecting on grace, exemplified in his own life, the Apostle is compelled to praise God. His language sounds like a typical Hellenistic Jewish doxology.[78] God is called *King*, cutting into the common exalted honors given to the Roman emperor (who was not called *Rex*), but the term "king" here could be translated "emperor." Unlike Rome's emperor, Paul's God rules *the ages*, is *immortal* and *invisible* and, in the tradition of monotheistic Judaism (e.g., Deut 6:4–9), *the only God*. He alone is worthy to receive praise (1:17).

1:18–20 A FAITHFULNESS FOR TIMOTHY

The Apostle backs up at 1:18 ("command") to where he left off at 1:3 ("command") in his direct teachings to Timothy for a personal word, but also banks off the story of his own transformation (1:12–17). In this new passage the Apostle reminds Timothy that the contents of this letter and its exhortation to enact them are rooted in God's call to Timothy (1:18), which is to be carried out with integrity (1:19a), an integrity not characteristic of some teachers, namely the false teachers in Ephesus named Hymenaeus and Alexander (1:19b–20a), whom Paul has disciplined for the purpose of restoration (1:20b). Timothy in this passage becomes the counter-paradigm to these false teachers and a model for the false teachers.[79]

1:18 This charge I commit to you, Timothy, my child, in accordance with the prophecies made earlier about you, so that by following them you may fight the good fight,
19 having faith and a good conscience. By rejecting conscience, certain persons have suffered shipwreck in the faith;
20 among them are Hymenaeus and Alexander, whom I have turned over to Satan, so that they may be taught not to blaspheme.

Timothy

Timothy, already addressed at 1:2, is again called *my child*, which term is not about his age so much as his intimate sage–student relationship with the Apostle (see more at 1:2; also Gal 4:19). The Apostle's trust in Timothy

---

[78] Others at 6:16 and 2 Tim 4:18. See also, e.g., Gal 1:5; Rom 11:36; 16:27; Eph 3:21. Also, on the characteristic qualities of Hellenistic Jewish doxologies see both Collins, *1 & 2 Timothy and Titus*, 45–47; Towner, *Timothy and Titus*, 152–154.
[79] Kidson, *Persuading Shipwrecked Men*, 236–273.

Commentary on 1 Timothy

makes him a mediator of the Apostle's teaching so he gives him, or "lays down," *this charge*,[80] which refers back to the task of correcting false teachers while perhaps exhorting them to follow the true gospel (cf. 1 Tim 6:20). Yet "charge" is perhaps not as strong as the term the Apostle uses: *parangelia* connotes announcement or command as much – if not more – than the older "instruction" and even "charge"" (cf. 1:5).[81] Noticeably, Timothy's role in mediating the Apostle is *in accordance with the prophecies made earlier*: the laying-on-of-hands ritual that generated that gift is detailed at 4:14, and the content of that prophetic message in 6:11–16.[82]

His charge to Timothy is to *fight the good fight*, language drawn from the world of the military (2 Tim 2:4; used as a similar metaphor at 2 Cor 10:3, and for the moral battle in 1 Pet 2:11[83]). The fight here is for early Christian beliefs about God's redemption in Christ as well as Christian virtue.

Timothy is to fight with integrity, or as put here with some favorite PE terms: *having faith and a good conscience*. The "faith" expresses both allegiance and an early version of what came to be called creeds (1:2, 4), while "conscience" is the inner mind that focuses on the capacity to evaluate truth (1 Tim 3:9; 2 Tim 1:3) and how to live the "good" Christian life (see at 1:5). It is *faith* and *good conscience* that create a contrast between Timothy and these *certain persons* who have begun to teach a different doctrine (1:3, 6).[84]

Hymenaeus and Alexander

As the Apostle began the letter speaking directly to Timothy and then launched into words about the false teachers (1:3–11 and countered with Paul as an example in 1:12–17) so here he launches again from words to Timothy into false teaching, this time giving names and revealing the act of church discipline.

---

[80] On "laying down" (Greek: *paratithemi*), Marshall states this refers to committing something to someone for care. See Marshall, *Pastoral Epistles*, 407.
[81] See BDAG, 760; CGL, 1063.
[82] A prophecy-inspired ordination is described in Acts 13:1–3. Echoes of such an event are seen too at 1 Tim 4:12–16; 2 Tim 1:6.
[83] A synonymous expression is found at 1 Tim 6:12, and one must think too of Eph 6:10–17.
[84] Collins, *1 & 2 Timothy and Titus*, 49; Witherington, *Letters and Homilies for Hellenized Christians*, 209–210.

Those named, *Hymenaeus and Alexander*, have *suffered shipwreck in the faith* (1:19b; perhaps countered with 3:8-9; see also 2 Tim 1:17-18) *by rejecting conscience*.[85] The consciousness and deliberateness of the act is found in *apotheo*, a term that in nautical imagery refers to a castaway but could also suggest "driving away."[86] It is unwise to turn this into a chain reaction: reject faith and one shipwrecks morally, or reject conscience and morality and one wanders theologically. Rather, the two are, as Marshall rightly observes, inseparable (cf. 6:20-21).[87] Theology is as much life as it is thought.

The Apostle's discipline appears to many today as overly dramatic. The Apostle's language is cosmic and spiritual: *I have turned* [them] *over to Satan*, language Paul himself used about the sexually immoral man in Corinth (1 Cor 5:5), where also the goal was restoration in the faith. As well, at 2 Timothy 2:24-26 restoring through correction is an element of the pastoral calling. *Satan*, normally an adversary of the divine, is used to discipline the people of God in this context. The Apostle's language here is different but only in externals. This dramatic act of handing someone over to Satan is neither vindictive nor permanent but rather temporary because its purpose is clear: *so that they may learn not to blaspheme*, or as 2 Timothy 2:25-26 puts it, "that they will repent and come to know the truth, and ... escape from the snare of the devil." The Apostle's intention for this letter is not just to expose false teachers, to name them, or to denounce them, but to restore them to God and to the community of faith.

2:1-7 TEACHING PEOPLE TO PRAY

One gets an impression from *First of all* at 2:1 that this is the official beginning to the proper part of the letter with all of chapter one of First Timothy as a kind of introduction. Having taken care of warning everyone about the false teachers and their teachings (1:3-20), the Apostle's pastoral letter to Timothy for the congregations in Ephesus now turns to prayer in

---

[85] On the false teachers, see Chapter 1, "Introduction," section "The Opponents in the Pastoral Epistles," and "Closer Look: The False Teachers and Their Teaching," at 1:3-8. On Paul's three separate shipwrecks, see 2 Cor 11:25. See for other names at 2 Tim 1:15; 2:17; 4:14; also Acts 18:33. For the possibility that the rejection is again both faith and conscience, see Mounce, *Pastoral Epistles*, 67.

[86] See BDAG, 286.

[87] Marshall, *Pastoral Epistles*, 411-412.

what many assume are ecclesial gatherings.[88] Prayer, in fact, begins a paragraph at 2:1 and 2:8, but the themes shift away from prayer in each paragraph. 1 Timothy 2:1–7, then, begins with a redeemer-sanctioned urging of prayer for all, including political leaders, for the sake of a life free of hassles (2:1–3). God as *Savior* wants all to be saved and this one God has a *mediator* – Jesus – who *gave himself a ransom for all* (2:4–6), and Paul describes himself here as the *herald and apostle* of this mediator in his mission to the *Gentiles* (2:7).

2:1 First of all, then, I urge that supplications, prayers, intercessions, and thanksgivings be made for everyone,
2:2 for kings and all who are in high positions, so that we may lead a quiet and peaceable life in all godliness and dignity.
2:3 This is right and acceptable before God our Savior,
2:4 who desires everyone to be saved and to come to the knowledge of the truth.
2:5 For there is one God; there is also one mediator between God and humankind, Christ Jesus, himself human,
2:6 who gave himself a ransom for all – this was attested at the right time.
2:7 For this I was appointed a herald and an apostle (I am telling the truth, I am not lying), a teacher of the Gentiles in faith and truth.

The Apostle's *First of all* could suggest the importance of prayer for all because either some did not want to pray for all or because some did not accept the Apostle's mission to the gentiles. However, maybe *First of all* is the first piece of instruction in the letter, which would place prayer at the top of the list for congregational life. Or better yet, this is wisdom: the believers must learn to behave with what Chris Hoklotubbe calls "civilized piety" (See "Closer Look" below) and respectable behaviors, and that begins with praying for others. The plea (*urge*: see 1:3; Rom 12:1) is for them to offer *supplications, prayers, intercessions, and thanksgivings*, terms that added together seem to form a torpedo-like synthesis of prayer.[89] Perhaps the terms are more analytical and are thus four distinct modes of prayer. *Supplications* describes requests or petitions while *prayers* is generic, but it should be observed that diaspora synagogues were called *proseuchai*, or places of prayer (Acts 16:13); *intercessions* points to

---

[88] Cynthia Long Westfall, *Paul and Gender: Reclaiming the Apostle's Vision for Men and Women in Christ* (Grand Rapids: Baker Academic, 2016), 286–290.
[89] Marshall, *Pastoral Epistles*, 419.

petitionary prayer, and *thanksgivings* nurtures gratitude – each or all of these are to be given *for everyone*. While at times sacrifices were offered for other nations and their kings in Jerusalem's temple, just as prayers were offered in synagogues (Jer 29:7; *Let Aris* 45), this *for everyone* has the gentile mission in view (2:4–7), and as Marshall observes, it is a polemic against "an exclusive elitist understanding" of which persons constitutes the people of God. It is suggested that such a view is at work in the false teachers.[90]

Praying for *kings and all who are in high positions* became a strategy in the early Christian movement (cf. 1 Pet 2:11–12 with 2:13–17): be good, keep your head down, stay out of trouble, understand how status works, and do good.[91] Which is why the next words are *so that we may lead a quiet and peaceable life in all godliness and dignity*. The terms used here, not least *godliness*, which translates *eusebeia*,[92] describe a pious way of life highly valued in the Roman world and therefore the terms describe social respectability and status.[93] We are inclined to believe civilized piety is a dominating theme in the PEs, and that such a theme opens the door to observe the cultural location of the Pauline mission churches. It is reasonable to think the Apostle is urging the congregations to become socially respectable by connecting their own religious *habitus* with the Roman *habitus*. Such an instruction could suggest a posture of tolerance of others for the sake of being tolerated. Alternatively, it may suggest a subversive approach to gaining a platform, or a position somewhere between the two. Praying for political authorities is not the same as submitting to them as we find elsewhere in the early church (Rom 13:1–7; 1 Pet 2:13–17), though one might think this is a specific example of it.[94] The early Christian prayer *habitus* emerged more likely from a strategy designed to elicit tolerance, perhaps through civilized piety and opportunity for evangelism. That the Apostle refers to *kings* in the plural indicates he's thinking of more than the

---

[90] Marshall, *Pastoral Epistles*, 420. On the distinctiveness of the Christian gentile mission, Scot McKnight, *A Light among the Gentiles: Jewish Missionary Activity in the Second Temple Period* (Minneapolis: Fortress, 1991); Martin Goodman, *Mission and Conversion: Proselytizing in the Religious History of the Roman Empire* (New York: Oxford University Press, 1994); Irina Levinskaya, *The Book of Acts in Its Diaspora Setting*, The Book of Acts in Its First Century Setting 5 (Grand Rapids: Eerdmans, 1996).
[91] Again, Hoklotubbe, *Civilized Piety*.
[92] Beside Hoklotubbe above, see a less likely view in the excursus of Marshall, *Pastoral Epistles*, 135–144.
[93] See Josephus, *B.J.* 1.201, where nearly exact terms are used.
[94] Marshall, *Pastoral Epistles*, 420–421.

Commentary on 1 Timothy 41

Roman emperor, which is made clearer by *all who are in high positions*.[95] What's more, such a prayer *habitus* was a natural development of the Jewish tactic of sacrifices and intercessions for the good of the emperor.[96] Prayers for *all who are in high positions* becomes the Apostle's gospel method of retaining the churches' religious identity while still religiously displaying political loyalty, the piety expected of good citizens. The strategy is to keep the powerful off their back. As the letter unfolds, civilized piety will be shown to be more than prayer as well.

The foundation for praying *for everyone* is that it is *right and acceptable*[97] to *God our Savior* (2:3),[98] an honorific commonly used for the Roman emperor. This Savior God *desires everyone to be saved*, that is, *to come to the knowledge of the truth* (2:4). The desire of God to redeem all, which may have a polemical edge, is a theme in the PEs (2:4, 6; 4:10; Titus 2:11). Would such a polemic be against exclusivism or does it affirm their evangelistic efforts?[99] Is *everyone* to be understood as generic (all sorts of persons) or distributive (every single person)? Is this about a *desire* that must be matched by a human response of faith? The language here and elsewhere does not support a bald universalism at work in the PEs (or in Paul) because to be *saved* here means *to come to the knowledge of the truth*, implying conversion (2:4) as well as the *truth* of the gospel in Jesus Christ, ideas sketched both in 2:3–6 and 3:16.[100] This *knowledge of the truth* is not a simple acknowledgement of past historical events but the recognition of transformed state of reality in God's gospel work that is now embodied in both personal commitment and in the life of the community of faith. Notice, too 1:16's "those who would come to believe" (cf. 3:16) but especially 4:10's "the living God, who is the Savior of all people, especially of those who believe." Hence, it appears this is about God's *desire* and "universal accessibility" but not an affirmation of universalism.[101]

---

[95] Towner, *Timothy and Titus*, 167–169.
[96] Dibelius and Conzelmann, *Pastoral Epistles*, 37–38.
[97] Deut 12:25, 28; 13:19; 21:9; cf. Rom 12:1–2.
[98] 1 Tim 1:1; 4:10; 2 Tim 1:10; Luke 1:47; 2:11; John 4:42; Acts 5:31; 13:23; Eph 5:23; Phil 3:20. Noticeably in the PEs God the Savior is also Christ the Savior.
[99] The exclusivism theme may be present in 1 Tim 1 but it is just as likely to be a carryover from Galatians and Romans; hence, the theme of gentile mission is more likely. For discussion, Marshall, *Pastoral Epistles*, 425–426.
[100] On truth, see Marshall, 122–123.
[101] Marshall, 425–427. Quotation from p. 427. A recent attempt to defend, with fundamentalist vitriol, is David Bentley Hart, *That All Shall Be Saved: Heaven, Hell, and Universal Salvation* (New Haven: Yale University Press, 2019). Universalism's history has been examined in depth by Michael McClymond, *The Devil's Redemption:*

In re-affirming the Jewish creed (Deut 6:4–9) the Apostle says of this Savior that there is *one God* (cf. 1 Cor 8:4–6; Gal 3:20; Rom 3:29–30; Eph 4:4–6).[102] This one God, however, has a *mediator* in Jesus, *himself human*,[103] *who gave himself a ransom for all* (1 Tim 2:5–6). The oneness of God forms into an exclusive sense of redemption whereas polytheism easily becomes pluralism.[104] The agent of redemption, the *one mediator* (cf. also Heb 8:6), is the Jesus whose self-giving[105] life, death, burial, resurrection, and ascension created that redemption as a *ransom*. A *ransom* is a price paid in exchange for – in this case – human redemption (cf. Mark 10:45), and the Apostle has in mind a representative substitution *for all*.[106] Paul's use of *one* for both God and Jesus intuits the monotheistic development of the Jewish creed toward the Christian creed, which declares the Father and the Son's unity of nature.[107] That unity comes to expression in the *ransom*, conveying a cruciform reality to the nature of God.

The Apostle reiterates his calling in 1 Timothy 2:7 (cf. 1:12–17), though here he moves from Paul as example to Paul as *herald*, a word that is cognate with preaching, hence "preacher" or "evangelist" are viable translations.[108] As a *herald*, one who publicly declares a message, *and apostle*, one who is sent on a representative mission,[109] he is also a *teacher* (as at 2 Tim 1:11). The occasional attempt to distinguish these terms into separable offices in the church is unrealistic and mistaken. These various

---

A New History and Interpretation of Christian Universalism (Grand Rapids: Baker Academic, 2018).

[102] Scot McKnight, "Few and Far Between: The Life of a Creed," in Alan J. Avery-Peck, Craig A. Evans, and J. Neusner, eds., *Earliest Christianity within the Boundaries of Judaism: Essays in Honor of Bruce Chilton* (Leiden: E. J. Brill, 2016), 168–186.

[103] This term anchors Jesus into those redeemed: humans. See Rom 5:15 and Phil 2:6–11.

[104] Miroslav Volf and Matthew Croasmun, *For the Life of the World: Theology That Makes a Difference* (Grand Rapids: Brazos, 2019), 85–113.

[105] Towner notes the consistent emphasis of "self-giving" in Pauline ransom soteriology. See Towner, *Timothy and Titus*, 183–185.

[106] For my discussions of atonement theory, Scot McKnight, *Jesus and His Death: Historiography, the Historical Jesus, and Atonement Theory* (Waco: Baylor University Press, 2005); Scot McKnight, *A Community Called Atonement* (Nashville: Abingdon, 2007).

[107] Dibelius and Conzelmann, *Pastoral Epistles*, 1972, 42. It would not fit the passage to separate these "one-ness" creedal statements into two categories. The first part (2:5a) being about the uniqueness of God and the mediator, but only the second part (2:5b), concerning the humanity of the mediator, as being about nature; *contra* Mounce, *Pastoral Epistles*, 87.

[108] So Marshall, *Pastoral Epistles*, 434.

[109] Mounce, *Pastoral Epistles*, 92.

Commentary on 1 Timothy

gifts are for the *Gentiles*, and to be performed *in faith and truth*. The Apostle sees his own calling to bring *the knowledge of truth* to the nations, including their leaders, as a natural desire of the God of Jewish monotheism.[110] There is only *one God* and through his *one mediator*, Jesus Christ, he alone is saving *all*, Jew and Gentile alike, because he is the only God and *Savior* of humanity (cf. 4:10).

The paragraph begins on a theme of prayer and next returns to prayer. Prayer for everyone is because (1) God is one, and (2) God's one mediator, Jesus Christ, has brought redemption, and (3) Paul's mission is to preach that redemption throughout the Roman Empire. For this redemption of the world the congregations are urged to pray.

A Closer Look: On *Civilized Piety*[111]

For many the common usage of the term *piety* refers to the quiet, resolute, and mainly private devotion of a wizened, elderly saint. For others the word conjures up images of rigid and puritanical church life, something akin to the contemporary trope of the Puritans. T. Christopher Hoklotubbe in *Civilized Piety* explains that neither of those two popular definitions are helpful ways of understanding piety in the PEs.

Piety (Latin, *pietas*) was a word packed with political meaning. In Greek, *eusebeia* (piety) meant having the proper reverence for the gods and performing the proper public cultic practices. In Latin, it referred to the affectionate devotion for one's own family, people, and emperor. A fitting modern synonym would be affection for one's homeland with religious connotations. Within the cultural and political melting pot of Asia Minor's Roman Hellenism, piety in Ephesus was the term used for the public performance of socially acceptable allegiance to the emperor, and it was woven into the civic life of the city through public events and religious festivals. Piety, as *public religious civility and social respectability*, became increasingly important under the reign of Augustus. Such devotion displayed belief in Roman exceptionalism and exhibited submission to the emperor's role as high priest. Piety became a way for vassal states and loyal families to participate in the larger sociopolitical family of Rome, in which Caesar was the father of all. This religious affection for one's

---

[110] Knight III, George W. *The Pastoral Epistles*. NIGTC. Grand Rapids: Eerdmans, 199, 120–122, 127.

[111] Hoklotubbe, *Civilized Piety*. I have fleshed out the theme in "*Eusebeia* as Social Respectability: The Public Life of the Christian Pastor," in Todd D. Still and Jason A. Meyers, eds., *Rhetoric, History, and Theology: Interpreting the New Testament* (Lanham: Lexington/Fortress Academic), 157–174.

political leader and country created a distaste for the worship of foreign gods since that deviated allegiance might invoke the anger of the Roman gods.

The PEs navigate and negotiate negative scrutiny by Rome of the congregations by attempting to make Christian religious practices socially respectable in the Roman Empire. The term *eusebeia* was one of their strategic negotiations: the churches are called to a socially respectable way of life, while they knew at the same time that they had radically redefined the term. The Apostle teaches the church of Ephesus to camouflage itself from the hostile gaze of Rome through gestures of piety, specifically through public and communal prayers for political leaders. This was a tactic learned from Jewish communities throughout the Empire. Christian support for Rome included family piety, which was embodied in the ordered lives of wives and children. As Hoklotubbe puts it:

The author of the Pastorals attempts to portray Christians as civilized and exemplary participants within the Roman social order who nevertheless maintained their theological distinctiveness (which, of course, could be considered "countercultural" in its own respect), representing a singular strategic response of what might be considered a "sly civility" along a spectrum of early Christian attempts to negotiate their imperial situation.[112]

The opponents of the Apostle were dangerous precisely because their teachings disrupted the social order that piety called Christians to embody among the Romans, particularly when it came to family order and money, which could draw the unwanted scrutiny of Roman officials. The PEs use of the term *piety*, better yet "civilized piety," reveals the early Christian struggle to be sincere public members of Roman society and the desire to evade a hostile relationship with Roman officials who would demand a public and religious piety toward Rome that the Ephesian church had already given to a different king and kingdom.

2:8–15 ORDER IN THE ASSEMBLIES

The theme of prayer, which began with a noticeable "First of all" at 2:1, continues in this paragraph and, like that previous paragraph (2:1–7), the Apostle wanders from prayer to other concerns.

2:8 I desire, then, that in every place the men should pray, lifting up holy hands without anger or argument,

---

[112] Hoklotubbe, *Civilized Piety*, 216.

Commentary on 1 Timothy 45

9 also that the women should dress themselves in moderate clothing with reverence and self-control, not with their hair braided or with gold, pearls, or expensive clothes,
10 but with good works, as is proper for women who profess reverence for God.
11 Let a woman learn in silence with full submission.
12 I do not permit a woman to teach or to have authority over a man; she is to keep silent.
13 For Adam was formed first, then Eve,
14 and Adam was not deceived, but the woman was deceived and became a transgressor.
15 Yet she will be saved through childbearing, provided they continue in faith and love and holiness, with self-control.

For some this passage is a battleground about women while for others it is a passage that belongs back in places and times when men ran the world. In her outline, Clarice Martin calls these verses "A Patriarchal Family Ethic" and describes the long-term impact of patriarchy.[113] Cynthia Long Westfall says all that needs to be said when it comes how this text has played out:

> Historically, 1 Timothy 2:12 is the primary text that has been used up to the present to ban women from certain activities and functions within the church, regardless of a woman's training, skills, or spiritual gifts. It has provided a lens or exegetical grid through which all other Scripture is applied to women. In traditional interpretation, in fact, obedience to this passage, together with submission, seems to constitute the entire scope of a woman's call.[114]

That this text became both a litmus test of commitment to a biblical way of life as well as the filter through which all activities of women in churches are pressed cannot be disputed. That it also reflects the rise of masculinism among white American evangelical men also cannot be disputed. That it is a "favorite" of feminist hermeneutics is well earned.[115] Our treatment will do its best to begin with what 1 Timothy 2:8–15 meant *then*. It is also important to contain our exegetical findings within the practice of the early

---

[113] "1–2 Timothy and Titus," 421–425.
[114] Westfall, *Paul and Gender*, 279.
[115] See Huizenga, *1–2 Timothy, Titus*, 20–30.

church and within Pauline statements elsewhere,[116] and any theologizing will only appear on top of those conclusions.[117]

In returning back to prayer the Apostle emphasizes that the *men* are to pray in a respectful, noncombative manner (2:8) while the *women* are to dress in a respectful manner (2:9–10). But once again prayer is dropped and the passage moves into women teaching, which itself shifts into a variety of claims anchored in context (2:11–15). It is a contested passage, one of the New Testament's most contested, and that contest is only properly comprehended when the context is respected.[118]

---

[116] Some think this text departs from early Christian practice and even Pauline theology and practice and, as such, departs from the gospel of earliest Christianity. E.g., Elisabeth Schüssler-Fiorenza, *In Memory of Her: A Feminist Theological Reconstruction of Christian Origins* (New York: Crossroad, 1983), 289–291. Our exegesis considers an alternative.

[117] Knowing the danger of turning this footnote into a book, I mention only these: Ben Witherington III, *Women and the Genesis of Christianity*, ed. Ann Witherington (Cambridge: Cambridge University Press, 1990); Ben Witherington III, *Women in the Earliest Churches*, SNTMS 58 (Cambridge: Cambridge University Press, 1991); Craig S. Keener, *Paul, Women, and Wives: Marriage and Women's Ministry in the Letters of Paul* (2nd edn.; Grand Rapids: Baker Academic, 2004); Ronald W. Pierce, Rebecca Merrill Groothuis, and Gordon D. Fee, eds., *Discovering Biblical Equality: Complementarity Without Hierarchy* (3rd edn.; Downers Grove: IVP Academic, 2021); Lynn H. Cohick, *Women in the World of the Earliest Christians: Illuminating Ancient Ways of Life* (Grand Rapids: Baker Academic, 2009); Philip Barton Payne, *Man and Woman, One in Christ: An Exegetical and Theological Study of Paul's Letters* (Grand Rapids: Zondervan, 2009); Westfall, *Paul and Gender*; Lynn H. Cohick and Amy Brown Hughes, *Christian Women in the Patristic World: Their Influence, Authority, and Legacy in the Second through Fifth Centuries* (Grand Rapids: Baker Academic, 2017). The issue for some evangelicals was provoked in 1991 by John Piper and Wayne Grudem, eds., *Recovering Biblical Manhood and Womanhood: A Response to Evangelical Feminism* (Westchester: Crossway, 2012). On the masculinist, militarist movement in the USA, see Emily Suzanne Johnson, *This Is Our Message: Women's Leadership in the New Christian Right* (New York: Oxford University Press, 2019); Kristin Kobes Du Mez, *Jesus and John Wayne: How White Evangelicals Corrupted a Faith and Fractured a Nation* (New York: Liveright, 2020); Beth Allison Barr, *The Making of Biblical Womanhood: How the Subjugation of Women Became Gospel Truth* (Grand Rapids: Brazos, 2021).

[118] Including some of those listed in the previous note, a few with a strong focus on context, see R. T. France, *Women in the Church's Ministry: A Test-Case for Biblical Hermeneutics*, Didsbury Lectures (Eugene: Wipf & Stock, 2004); Richard Clark Kroeger and Catherine Clark Kroeger, *I Suffer Not a Woman: Rethinking 1 Timothy 2:11–15 in Light of Ancient Evidence* (Grand Rapids: Baker Academic, 1998); Tal Ilan, *Jewish Women in Greco-Roman Palestine* (Peabody: Hendrickson, 1996); Tal Ilan, *Integrating Women into Second Temple History* (Peabody: Hendrickson, 2001).

For Men

The opener is strong but the meaning of *I desire*, which translates a term that can mean anything from "I prefer" to "I determine" (5:14), is shaped in sense by context. Other terms in this passage are shaped by the imperative mood (2:11) and the tone of authority to the Apostle's mission (2:7).[119] He wants the men *to pray*, a term wider in sense than the petitions of 2:1-2, *in every place*, an expression that suggests Paul sees this instruction carried out both in homes and in assemblies.[120] There could be a hint (based on Malachi 1:10-11) that *every place* implies the gentile mission (2:7).[121]

Oddly, Paul wants these men to pray in an altogether common manner (*lifting up holy hands*; Ps 28:2; Jas 4:8) and in a special, if not peculiar, mood (*without anger or argument*). The use of *holy* with *hands* turns the act of handwashing (Exod 30:19-21) into a metaphor of being fit to enter into God's presence.[122] The instruction to avoid *anger or argument* seems to imply strife among the males in Ephesus but it can also be taken as a condition for one's prayers being acceptable to God (cf. Jas 1:6-8). Two of Paul's concerns are *anger* (Rom 12:19; Col 3:8; Eph 2:3; 4:31) and *argument* (Rom 14:1; Phil 2:14). It seems more likely this concern is not a theoretical statement about conditions of prayer so much as another reminder about theological errors and affective conditions among some teachers in Ephesus, as we have already seen in 1:3-11. The theme reverberates in the Pastorals often enough that one is on sure ground to see 2:8's language directed at the problem makers (cf. 3:3, 8-9, 11; 5:13; 6:11).[123]

---

[119] Kelly, *Pastoral Epistles*, 65; Knight, *Pastoral Epistles*, 128.
[120] Westfall argues vigorously against 1 Tim 2:1-15 occurring in public or household worship in Westfall, *Paul and Gender*, 286-290. However, that one is not alone is required for 2:9b to make sense, and the women who are learning are also not alone. These considerations, however, are not proof this is an assembly of Christians for worship. For reasons for a corporate assembly, see Mounce, *Pastoral Epistles*, 107-108. Jewish prayers were not restricted to particular places, see Collins, *1 & 2 Timothy and Titus*, 65-66.
[121] Marshall, *Pastoral Epistles*, 444-445.
[122] Towner, *Timothy and Titus*, 201-202.
[123] Towner, 202; Mounce, *Pastoral Epistles*, 105; Witherington, *Letters and Homilies for Hellenized Christians*, 223.

For Women[124]

For some the term *also* ought, continuing 2:8, to imply that the women are *also* being instructed to pray. After all, the shifting from males praying to females dressing would be a bolt out of the blue. Thus, it is suggested Paul means to say, "I desire ... also [for women to pray and in their public worship and prayers to] *dress themselves* [appropriately]."[125] Thus 2:9 is about how women are to dress in these public prayers,[126] and the public deportment of women was hardly only a Jewish or Christian concern; it was an abiding concern about the Pythagorean and Neopythagorean woman philosophers (see Closer Look: Perictione I "On the Harmonious Woman). The concern is direct enough to make us wonder if female dress may somehow embody false teaching or be connected to the Artemis cult.[127]

> **A Closer Look: Perictione I on the Harmonious Woman (fourth to third century BCE; perhaps the author is Plato's mother)**
>
> Therefore a woman will neither cover herself with gold or stone of India or of any other place, nor will she braid her hair with artful device; nor will she anoint herself with Arabian perfume; nor will she put white makeup on her face or rouge her cheeks or darken her brows and lashes or artfully dye her graying hair; nor will she bathe a lot. For by pursuing these things a woman seeks to make a spectacle of female incontinence. The beauty that comes from wisdom and not from these things brings pleasure to women who are well born.[128]

---

[124] In what follows there is no attempt to sketch all views and weigh each issue separately. That would take dozens of pages. In what follows I will explain how I read the text with only side glances at alternatives. For the complementarian take on the passage, see Mounce, *Pastorals*, 94-149, with eight dense pages of bibliography, nearly all of it white evangelical men debating one another.

[125] Ward, *I & II Timothy and Titus*, 50; Witherington, *Letters and Homilies for Hellenized Christians*, 224.

[126] Marshall, *Pastoral Epistles*, 446-448.

[127] For an extensive study of the Artemis cult in Ephesus, see Jerome Murphy-O'Connor, *St. Paul's Ephesus: Texts and Archaeology* (Collegeville: Liturgical, 2008). Two extensive studies connect as much as possible the Artemis cult (Artemis was a virgin, not a fertility or a mother goddess) with what is written in 1 Tim 2; see Sandra L. Glahn, "The Identity of Artemis in First-Century Ephesus," *BibSac* 172 (2015): 316-334; "The First-Century Ephesian Artemis: Ramifications of Her Identity," *BibSac* 172 (2015): 450-469.

[128] From Sarah B. Pomeroy, *Pythagorean Women: Their History and Writings* (Baltimore: Johns Hopkins University Press, 2013), 72. See also "Melissa to Cleareta," pp. 102-103.

Commentary on 1 Timothy

One is led by the concentration of words about respect in the PEs to the conclusion that there was an agglomeration of religion and flouting of wealth among Christians in Ephesus. The language about their clothing urges the women to dress in a manner communicating civilized piety as Christians understood such piety.[129] *Moderate clothing* translates what could be rendered "worldly-fashionable outfits"[130] and thus be an instruction for the Christian women to keep status and social location in mind. As such, their *clothing* ought to be worn with reverence and self-control, again two terms with social location in mind. Behind *reverence* is *aidous* while behind *self-control* is *sōphrosynēs,* terms that could be rendered "with dignity and class" or "with respect," while the second term could be understood as "with prudence" or "good sense" and even "with public self-control" (cf. 2:15).[131] This is not an injunction to look backward nor does it instruct them to be intentional in some form of asceticism, but rather it is about socially respectable clothing. Both culture and social location determine what clothing to wear.[132]

> **A Closer Look: Melissa to Clearte**
>
> Melissa to Clearete, greetings. Of your own desire, it seems to me, you possess most of what is good [or, excellent]. For your zealous [wish] to listen to the topic of [woman's adornment] offers fair hope [that you intend] to perfect yourself in virtue. [It is necessary then] for the moderate and liberal woman to live [with] [her lawful] husband [adorned] with quietness, white and clean in her dress, plain and [not costly], simple and not elaborate [or excessive]. For she must reject [...], and garments shot with purple or gold. For these are used by call-girls in [soliciting] the generality of men, but if she is [attractive] to one man, her own, a woman's ornament is her manners and not her clothing. And a liberal and moderate [or, prudent] woman must seem good-looking to her own husband, but not to the man next door, having her cheeks the blush of modesty rather that of rouge or powder, and good bearing and decency and moderation rather than gold and emerald. For it is not in expenditure on dress and looks that the moderate woman should express

---

[129] See the excellent sketch of evidence in Hutson, *1-2 Timothy, Titus,* 66–71.
[130] Because of the common Pauline use of *kosmos* in a pejorative sense, it is noticeable here that the text uses cognates here twice, with to dress (*kosmeō*) and suitable (*kosmios* as adjective). One might then render it "I want them to face the world in worldly clothing," but here "worldly" does not mean sinful, rebellious, or anti-God.
[131] On *decently,* see Marshall, *Pastoral Epistles,* 182–191.
[132] Clothing was understood to be an external expression of one's own virtuous character, or lack thereof, see Towner, *Timothy and Titus,* 205–206; Collins, *1 & 2 Timothy and Titus,* 66–67.

> her love of the good but in the management and maintenance of her household, and pleasing her own husband, given that he is a moderated man, by fulfilling his wishes. For the husband's will ought to be engraved as law on a decent wife's mind, and she must live by it. And she must consider that the dowry she has brought with her that is best and greatest of all is her good order [*eutaxian*]. And she must believe in the beauty and wealth of the soul rather than in that of money and appearance. As for money and looks, time, envy, illness, and fortune take them away. But adornment of the soul lasts till death with women who possess it.[133]

The Apostle opposes ostentatious displays of wealth by these women: *not with their hair braided, or with gold, pearls, or expensive clothes* (2:9), which language sounds like 6:7–10, 17–19 and 1 Peter 3:3. From an inscription written by a man about his wife at the turn of the first century, the husband of his now-deceased wife after forty-one years of marriage, refers to her in these terms: "As for your domestic virtues, loyalty (to our marriage), obedience, courteousness, easy good-nature, your assiduous wool-working, reverence (for the gods) without superstition, attire not designed for attracting attention, modest refinement – what need have I to make mention of these?"[134]

A Greek novel by Xenophon of Ephesus, which according to some scholars comes from about AD 50, uses some of this language for public worship in the temple of Artemis in Ephesus. The particulars aside, the entire scene was of young women parading through the great city to the temple for worship in erotically charged attire. The novel is called *Anthia and Habrocomes* or by others *Ephesiaca*. I quote some pertinent lines:

Heading the line of girls was Anthia, daughter of Megamedes and Euippe, locals. Anthia's beauty was marvelous and far surpassed the other girls. She was fourteen, her body was blooming with shapeliness, and the adornment of her dress enhanced her grace. Her hair was blonde, mostly loose, only little of it braided, and moving as the breezes took it. Her eyes were vivacious, bright like a beauty's but forbidding like a chaste girl's; her clothing was a belted purple tunic, knee-length and falling loose over the arms, and over it a fawnskin with a quiver attached, arrows [. . .], javelins in hand, dogs following behind (1.2.5–6).

---

[133] S. R. Llewelyn, with R. A. Kearsley, *New Documents Illustrating Early Christianity* 6 (Grand Rapids: Eerdmans, 1992), 18–23 (discussion at that location by E. A. Judge).

[134] G. H. R. Horsley, *New Documents Illustrating Early Christianity* 3 (Grand Rapids: Eerdmans, 1983), 34.

Commentary on 1 Timothy 51

And so when the procession was over, the whole crowd repaired to the shrine for the sacrifice, the order of the procession was dissolved, and men and women, ephebes and girls, gathered in the same spot. There they saw each other. Anthia was captivated by Habrocomes, and Habrocomes was bested by Eros. He kept gazing at the girl and though he tried, he could not take his eyes off her: the god pressed his attack and held him fast. Anthia too was in a bad way, as with eyes wide open she took in Habrocomes' handsomeness as it flowed into her, already putting maidenly decorum out of her mind: for what she said was for Habrocomes to hear, and she uncovered what parts of her body she could for Habrocomes to see. He gave himself over to the sight and fell captive to the god (1.3.1–2).[135]

One may reasonably think the Apostle knows of such public worship events, even if the text is dated later, and that such practices may be making inroads in the Christian assemblies, and that someone needed to step in.[136] So, one reading of this text in context is that it pertains to a stance over against the Artemis cult of Ephesus.[137]

The "attire" of the women shifts therefore from the material to the metaphorical (as it does for Peter in 1 Peter 3:4): the women are to dress up *with good works*, which customarily refers to caring for the poor as well as publicly respectable behaviors.[138] In Pauline theology good works are the result of God's transforming grace that turns humans into active agents of goodness.[139] Such metaphorical attire is determined by what is *proper for women who profess reverence* [or, civilized piety] *for God*. Here *profess* refers to a way of life that is both religiously and socially respectable.[140]

A Controversial Passage: A Recent Approach

A shift occurs in 2:11 to opposing false teaching more directly. Prayer starts the section at 2:1, that prayer life is resumed in 2:8 and probably implied in 2:9, but the conduct of those praying shifts in 2:11 to the

---

[135] LCL (Henderson).
[136] Collins, *1 & 2 Timothy and Titus*, 68; Witherington, *Letters and Homilies for Hellenized Christians*, 224–226.
[137] For but one such approach, Hoag, *Wealth in Ancient Ephesus and the First Letter to Timothy*, 61–99.
[138] Hoklotubbe, *Civilized Piety*, 123.
[139] Bruce W. Longenecker, *Remember the Poor: Paul, Poverty, and the Greco-Roman World* (Grand Rapids: Eerdmans, 2010); Marshall, *Pastoral Epistles*, 227–229.
[140] Towner, *Timothy and Titus*, 209–210.

conduct of women or wives[141] with respect to learning, teaching, and exercising *authority over a man* [or a husband] (2:12). Again, context matters.

A really good example of reading 1 Timothy 2:11–15 in context can be found in the work of Lyn Kidson.[142] Her view does not square with what I have for a long time argued, but I have to admit that when I read her argument it sounds very persuasive to me. Overall, she sees 2:1–15 as an explication of what we are calling "civilized piety" for men and women. Thus, for her there is no significant break at 2:11. Her view can be presented if we begin with Adam and Eve, a married couple. With a married couple in view the man and the woman in 2:11–15 could be a married couple, and when that view is taken, the whole passage takes on a new contextual meaning. So, instead of translating "Let a *woman* learn" it can be translated "Let a *wife* learn." The Greek term for woman and wife is identical; only context permits clarity, which means, too, that "have

---

[141] It is difficult to know from this context if this term means a woman in general (Marshall, *Pastoral Epistles*, 452) or a woman as wife. The shift from plurals in 2:8–10 to a singular woman in 2:11 may be unremarkable, but it is possible that this is one woman teaching one man in private or that it turns in 2:11 to women as wives. See Westfall, *Paul and Gender*, 288–289. Witherington does not believe the shift from plural to singular indicates a sharpening of focus to a subset of women as wives, see Witherington, *Letters and Homilies for Hellenized Christians*, 226 n. 196.

[142] In these citations and in the discussion above I am grateful to Lyn Kidson for her own work, which she has at times forwarded to me, and for clarifications of questions I have addressed to her. I cite bibliography here for the paragraphs sketching Kidson's view: Lyn Kidson, "'Teaching' and Other Persuasions: The Interpretation of Didaskein 'to Teach' in 1 Timothy 2:2," in E. Murphy, and D. Starling, *The Gender Conversation: Evangelical Perspective on Gender, Scripture and the Christian Life* (Macquarie Park/Eugene: Morling Press/Wipf & Stock, 2016), 125–137; Lyn Kidson, "Aussie Men, Roman Men, and Fashioning the Evangelical Man from 1 Timothy 2," in Angela Standhartinger, Eve-Marie Becker, Jens Herzer, and Florian Wilk, eds., *Reading the New Testament in the Manifold Contexts of a Globalized World Exegetical Perspectives*, Neutestamentliche Entwürfe zur Theologie (Outlines in New Testament Theology), (Tübingen: Francke, 2022.) On the Pythagorean women, see Annette Bourland Huizenga, *Moral Education in the Pastoral and Pythagorean Letters: Philosophers of the Household*, NovTSupp 147 (Leiden: Brill, 2013); Pomeroy, *Pythagorean Women*. On the churches as intellectual communities, the classic study is by E. A. Judge, "The Early Christians as a Scholastic Community," *J.Relig.Hist* 1 (1960): 4–15, 125–137; an excellent recent discussion is Kidson, *Persuading Shipwrecked Men*, 14–29. Along this line is Brian J. Wright, *Communal Reading in the Time of Jesus: A Window into Early Christian Reading Practices* (Minneapolis: Fortress, 2017).

Commentary on 1 Timothy

authority over a *man*" is "over a [or her] *husband*." The issue then is between a wife and her husband.

Kidson argues that the term "teach," which refers back to 1:3's false teachings, when combined with "have authority" (translating *authentein*) means "persuade" in a forceful manner. Here's where her view resonates in context. The wife is persuading her husband about a restrained sexual, ascetic life, which is a part of the entire fabric of the false teachers in Ephesus (4:1–3); it gets deeper but entirely reasonable and contextual. First, Kidson joins others in perceiving the churches as an intelligent, almost scholastic organization. Second, this wife echoes a well-known philosophical movement, the Pythagoreans and Neopythagoreans, in which the women were educated and some were even philosophers. They were by and large wealthy, though they eschewed opulent clothing. The lower classes imitated the currents in intellectual movements.

To get back to the Apostle's words in our passage, such a movement of educated, elite women were in need of theological gospel-framed teachings (e.g., 1:10–11) and practicing modesty (2:8–10), which is why the Apostle says they must *learn*. Here's where it gets somewhat persuasive for me. The Adam and Eve imagery, which in many accounts is an ad hoc out of nowhere insertion, resonates the very depth of what the Apostle writes. Adam was formed first (cf. Gen 2:7) to be joined to Eve (1 Tim 2:13), but Eve deceived Adam (2 Cor 11:3). In the world of this letter, the educated wife has the persuasive powers to deceive her husband away from the calling to a good creation and the goodness of a sexual life (1 Tim 4:3–5), bearing children and nurturing them in the faith. The salvation of 2:15 then is a return to the apostolic gospel and thus to being saved from false teachings.

Another Approach

I have indicated that I am not fully persuaded of Kidson's view, but in describing it the view is convincing. However, I here provide a view I have become comfortable with over the last two decades. As Peter exhorts Christian women to avoid ostentatious dress and instead to "wear" what he calls "the inner self with the lasting beauty of a gentle and quiet spirit" (3:4), so the Apostle in 2:11 turns to women learning *in silence* (or quiet). Among some authors the two manners of learning, namely *in silence* and *with full submission*, unfortunately eclipse any attention from the verb *learn*.[143] To *learn* evokes early Christian catechism in the faith, and its form as a noun is "disciple" (*mathētēs, mathētria*).[144] One might then translate the term "Let a woman be discipled ..." It was uncommon for women to be as educated as the men. So the early church's practice of the distribution of spiritual gifts without respect to gender, including gifts of communication like prophecy, created a greater need for women to learn the faith in order to exercise their gifts in accordance with the faith.[145] To learn *in silence* can be read in a number of ways, including a categorical silence in the public, ecclesial setting; it could describe deference, or which is most likely, it refers to a noninterruptive but attentive form of receiving instruction as one finds in Proverbs 1:2-7.[146] To learn in silence and *with full submission* intensifies both the posture of the learning women and the orderliness of catechesis. Listening was the student's first virtue. The term *submission*, which for too many readers implies domination, meant to live with, in, and under the order, or *hypotaxis*, of the day, and the *hypotaxis* at work here is students learning from teachers. The same term in 3:4 refers to a child's "respectful" behavior.[147] Hence, this is more about the posture of a student to a teacher than a woman to a man.[148]

This posture of learning is clarified in 2:12, another verse that has become a flashpoint but which also requires contextual study: *I do not permit a woman to teach or*[149]*to have authority over a man; she is to keep silent*. Silence, which is socially respectable, then frames the nonpermissive

---

[143] In the Pastorals: 1 Tim 5:4, 13; 2 Tim 3:7, 14; Titus 3:14. In Paul, see also Rom 16:17; 1 Cor 4:6; 14:31, 35; Eph 4:20; Phil 4:9, 11; Col 1:7. Learning is the focus rather than the issue of leadership; *contra* Mounce, *Pastoral Epistles*, 117.

[144] All cultures educate through various forms of formation, and the Jewish wisdom tradition is as important here as is the Greco-Roman forms of *paideia*. On women and instruction/learning in Judaism, see Ilan, *Jewish Women*; Ilan, *Integrating*; Cohick, *Women in the World of the Earliest Christians*.

[145] For this passage, see Keener, *Paul, Women, and Wives*, 107–108. See esp. Huizenga, *Moral Education in the Pastoral and Pythagorean Letters*.

[146] Discussions at Marshall, *Pastoral Epistles*, 453; Towner, *Timothy and Titus*, 214; Mounce, *Pastoral Epistles*, 118–119; Witherington, *Letters and Homilies for Hellenized Christians*, 226. On deference, Huizenga, *1–2 Timothy, Titus*, 25–26.

[147] Witherington, *Letters and Homilies for Hellenized Christians*, 226.

[148] Marshall, *Pastoral Epistles*, 454. For the section being set within a traditional household social structure see Towner, *Timothy and Titus*, 192; Collins, *1 & 2 Timothy and Titus*, 69–70.

[149] Much debate surrounds the Greek *oude*, whether it means "or" as in another item (teaching *and* assuming authority), which could then be categorical ("I am not permitting a woman to teach" – a full stop – "or to dominate/etc. a man"), or it means "and" in the sense of a connected item (teaching-assuming authority as a single action). On the latter, Hutson, *1–2 Timothy, Titus*, 75.

Commentary on 1 Timothy

statement before and after. If this letter is Pauline this instruction contradicts what Paul himself permits according to Acts 18:26 when Priscilla is involved in teaching Apollos. What's more, the Spirit-prompted gifts of teaching are distributed to whom the Spirit chooses (1 Cor 12:4–11; Rom 12:7), and it is worth remarking that prophecy and teaching are not without substantive overlap – and women were prophets in the Pauline mission (1 Cor 11:5; Acts 21:9). Titus 2:3 describes women who are good teachers.[150] It is then wisest to limit the nonpermission in 1 Timothy 2:12,[151] and the clue to this limitation is the second term: *to have authority*, yet another flashpoint. But first we need to back up.

Precisely here, context can shape the conversation toward clarity. Who are the women about whom the Apostle is speaking? (We have already discussed above the possibility that they are women echoing the Pythagorean women.) In 1 Timothy 5:13's instructions about young widows we read "Besides that, they learn to be idle, gadding about from house to house; and they are not merely idle, but also gossips and busybodies, saying what they should not say." These seem to be the women about whom the Apostle is speaking in 2:11–15, not women in general, and in 5:11–12 we read that the younger widows, who had been put on the charity roster, were violating their pledge (to celibacy for the list) in wanting to be married, which leads to 5:14's instruction to marry and have children, which then all ties back to 1 Timothy 2:15's concerns about childbirth. We can add to 1 Tim also 4:3–5's teachings of an ascetical nature. The connection then of the young widows of 1 Timothy 4 and 5 to the women of 1 Timothy 2 must be considered carefully. (The presence of Eve as a deceiver in our passage (2:14) suggests that this passage is about false teaching by female teachers.[152])

One more approach to the context of these verses comes from Bruce Winter's recent study of the new Roman women, a liberation-from-tradition type movement that was also characterized by extravagance in clothing.[153] Some interpreters connect a similar liberation theme in

---

[150] For a fuller evaluation of the possible role of women in first century ministry within the cultural world of the Roman Empire see Towner, *Timothy and Titus*, 218–220.
[151] Witherington, *Letters and Homilies for Hellenized Christians*, 226–227.
[152] Proven decisively in Payne, *Man and Woman, One in Christ*, 299–304. See the chart in Payne, p. 300. See too Kidson, *Persuading Shipwrecked Men*.
[153] Bruce W. Winter, *Roman Wives, Roman Widows: The Appearance of New Women and the Pauline Communities* (Grand Rapids: William B. Eerdmans, 2003). For his reading of our passage, pp. 97–122.

Galatians 3:28 and even to 1 Corinthians 11:2–16, to the teaching of women giftedness, and especially to the early Christian teaching of freedom in Christ. The issue became both the influence of such a Roman movement and whether it extended as far as Ephesus. Was it in fact at work in the house churches and among Christians – the presenting problems being seductive dress, extravagant and opulent clothing, and a disrespectful (according to the male patriarchal tradition) behavior with respect to customary male leadership?[154] It is hard to know with confidence.

It has also been suggested that some of the context for our passage has to do with education at home for wives/women who, to repeat, were not usually educated as were (mostly elite) males.[155] This connection can be illustrated by comparing what is said in 1 Corinthians 14:34–35 (whether authentic or not) with what is said in 1 Timothy 2:11–12.[156] Here we emphasize the words in distinct fonts to show the parallels between these passages. The best explanation of these passages then includes the need for women/wives to be educated in order to catch up with men and, one can easily infer, once educated the prohibition of teaching is lifted and the desire to dominate ended.[157]

A Closer Look: Comparing 1 Corinthians 14:34–35 and 1 Timothy 2:11–12

1 Cor 14:34 women should be *silent* in the churches. For they are **not permitted to speak** but should be *subordinate*, as the law also says. 35 If there is something they want to learn, let them ask their husbands at home. For it is shameful for a woman to speak in church.	1 Tim 2:11 Let a woman learn in *silence* with **full submission.** 12 **I do not permit a woman to teach** or to have authority over a man; she is to keep *silent*.

---

[154] A good example, though but one, is Petronius, *Satyricon* 67 (Petronius was Nero's advisor). For a possible reconstruction of the Ephesian context with the New Roman Woman influence, see Towner, *Timothy and Titus*, 196–197.

[155] Keener, *Paul, Women, and Wives*, 101–132.

[156] For analysis of the textual relationship between these verses, see Towner, *Timothy and Titus*, 193–194.

[157] Witherington, *Letters and Homilies for Hellenized Christians*, 232.

We move on *to have authority*, a translation of a highly unusual term, *authentein*.[158] Some take this to mean authority in a positive sense while others think this is a more negative forceful authority in the sense of independent authority, self-assumed authority, seizing control, usurping, and acting violently, coercively, or in a dominating manner.[159] John Chrysostom, to take but one example, told the men not to "be despotic or domineer [*authentein*] the woman" (*Homilies* 10), which by a solid linguistic principle of synonymity, suggests despotic echoes the sense of *authenteō*. The Latin Vulgate translates the term with *dominari*. Westfall has accurately observed that this term is never used in a benevolent, pastoral way, making this observation:

> In the Greek corpus, the verb *authentein* refers to a range of actions that are not restricted to murder or violence. However, the people who are the targets of these actions are harmed, forced against their will (compelled), or at least their self-interest is overridden, because the actions involve the imposition of the subject's will over against the recipient's will, ranging from dishonor to lethal force.[160]

As such this term at least describes in our context a woman overpowering the will of a man.[161] After his exhaustive analysis Philip Payne concluded that the best rendering is that the Apostle is not permitting a woman "to assume authority to teach a man."[162] But Payne is not done: the prohibition, he continues, is about "self-assumed authority," and this is buttressed by the uncommon (and un-Pauline) term (*authentein*) used. Payne has made significant contributions in discussions of this term, but he does not go far enough because the term conveys the sense of coercive force by a leader, in this passage a woman over a man (or as we discussed a wife over her husband in teaching false teachings). Thus, the term refers to something like lording it over someone and the desire to garner more power for oneself (like Matt 20:20) and possibly then to lead people astray.[163]

---

[158] NIV 2011: "assume authority over"; CEB: "to control her husband/a man." For a listing of many of the studies on this term, see Westfall, *Paul and Gender*, 290–291 n. 32. See also Jamin Hübner, "Revisiting *authenteō* in 1 Timothy 2:12: What Do the Extant Data Really Show?," *JSPL* 5 (2015): 41–70, who prefers a meaning of one assuming authority for oneself, to act on one's own authority.

[159] Westfall, 292. For insightful discussions, Marshall, *Pastoral Epistles*, 456–458; Witherington, *Letters and Homilies for Hellenized Christians*, 227–228.

[160] Westfall, *Paul and Gender*, 292. On p. 293 she mentions Chrysostom using this verb for something husbands were not to do to their wives, and suggests it means there "spousal abuse." She also suggested (p. 308) this could include wives choosing to withhold sexual relations with husbands. See also Towner, *Timothy and Titus*, 220–223.

[161] Everywhere present is the issue of translation: women or wives? I'm not persuaded 1 Tim 2:11–15 is about wives vs. women, though 1 Cor 14:34–35, again if authentic, clearly is. For a similar view, see Witherington III, *Women in the Earliest Churches*, 121.

[162] Payne, *Man and Woman, One in Christ*, 361–397, here 395–396.

[163] Cf. Winter, *Roman Wives, Roman Widows*, 116–119.

To bring a theme present in this passage that can get lost in the details about terms, we need to say that *learning* (1 Tim 2:11) the truth of the gospel is the path for these women in avoiding the errors of the opponents in Ephesus, errors that were at work among the young widows, errors that were creeping into their teaching, and thus these words have a specific meaning in a specific context. Specific women were in need of specific learning before they could become teachers.

Interpretive issues tumble out on top of one another in this paragraph. Adam was a routine source of appeal in Jewish literature; Eve not so often.[164] The Apostle's turn to Genesis 2–3[165] and to Eve as deceived (and deceiver?) in vv. 13–14, then, forms an analogy (not so much a proof)[166] and is noteworthy that he begins with primogeniture in creation order: *For Adam was formed first; then Eve*. The inference must be read into the text because it is not explicit: Is the argument that since Adam was first he is to have authority and, since Eve was formed second, she is not to have authority? Is this an argument – so obvious to many male interpreters – grounded in the creational order itself and therefore normative?[167] Or as some have argued, are there voices in Ephesus contending women are prior (Gen 3:20 or 1 Cor 11:12 can be so read) or superior to men so they have authority which the Apostle counters with the order of Genesis? How does this relate to problems appearing elsewhere with women/widows (cf. 1 Tim 1:4; 4:7; 5:13)? Is then v. 14 a second creation account argument: Not only was Adam formed first (and therefore more authoritative) but also that it was Eve, the woman and therefore women in general, who was and is why women are more easily deceived? While *formed* appears to be straight from Genesis 2:7–8, the term at times has had *paideia* connections in the sense of moral and intellectual formation, while it could also be connected to being formed to fit in union with the woman. The *first* with *then* suggests the Apostle appeals to the created order. When tied to Eve's

---

[164] Dennis R. Venema and Scot McKnight, *Adam and the Genome: Reading Scripture after Genetic Science* (Grand Rapids: Brazos, 2017), 147–169. See also John R. Levison, *Portraits of Adam in Early Judaism: From Sirach to 2 Baruch*, Journal for the Study of the Pseudepigrapha, Supplement Series 1 (Sheffield: JSOT Press, 1988); Felipe de Jesús Legarreta-Castillo, *The Figure of Adam in Romans 5 and 1 Corinthians 15: The New Creation and Its Ethical and Social Reconfiguration*, Emerging Scholars (Minneapolis: Fortress, 2014).

[165] On the use of Genesis here, see Towner, *Timothy and Titus*, 225–234.

[166] Witherington III, *Women in the Earliest Churches*, 122.

[167] Mounce, *Pastoral Epistles*, 130; Kelly, *Pastoral Epistles*, 68; Ward, *I & II Timothy and Titus*, 52; Knight, *Pastoral Epistles*, 143.

deception in 2:14, it appears that his argument for catechism in 2:11 is anchored in Genesis.[168] Since none of this is as explicit as all this it is also reasonable to think something is being opposed here. One suggestion is that the young widows and women were teaching false ideas[169] that included either female priority or superiority – so a quick riposte is offered from Genesis 2 – or teaching sexual restraint and asceticism (4:1–3).[170]

The claim that *Adam was not deceived* (cf. Gen 3:13) is quite unusual in a Jewish context where Adam is the moral prototype at times of disobedience(!), so the words of the Apostle here are applicable only to Adam not being the one who *first* fell for the serpent's plot. If Judaism's focus is Adam as the prototypical breaker of the law (cf. Rom 5:12–14), the Apostle here calls Eve the *woman* who was *deceived*,[171] *a transgressor* (1 Tim 2:14), a term that sets up redemption in 2:15 (but more of that in a moment). The argument, perhaps like Sirach 25:24 (see vv. 15–26), could be that women are susceptible to deceit in a way that carries on the deception of Eve. But the pressure comes not from their being female but from their being deceived by false teaching, and the Apostle finds the creation narrative to be a suitable location for his counter argument.[172] Women taught and prophesied and "apostle-d" and "deacon-ed" in the era of Paul and so this cannot be a generalized, universal argument against women teaching or even their susceptibility to deception. Rather, it is a specific problem with a particular counter argument for a specific occasion.[173]

Yet she, namely, the deceived woman Eve and generically the women of 2:9–10 and 2:12 (see "they" in 2:15b), *will be saved*, a term and its cognate used at 1 Timothy 1:15; 2:4; 4:16; 2 Timothy 1:9; 2:10; 3:15; 4:18 and Titus 2:11; 3:5.[174] In all but our passage the term refers to redemption or liberation from sin and death, and God is the Savior in PEs. That it would not mean redemption here seems unlikely even if many nuanced interpretations are on offer, including a woman being rescued from the clutches of the evil one's grip in this false teaching or in temptations, as well as a now growing view that it refers to deliverance in giving birth. If one factors in

---

[168] Witherington, *Letters and Homilies for Hellenized Christians*, 231–232.
[169] Towner, *Timothy and Titus*, 198.
[170] Towner, 232–233.
[171] The verbs for deception shift slightly from *apataō* to *exapataō*, the second of which intensifies the woman's sin.
[172] Towner, *Timothy and Titus*, 231–233.
[173] Marshall, *Pastoral Epistles*, 466; Collins, *1 & 2 Timothy and Titus*, 74–75.
[174] For Savior: 1 Tim 1:1; 2:3; 4:10; 2 Tim 1:10; Titus 1:3–4; 2:10, 13; 3:4, 6.

the contextual theory that some women in Ephesus avoided marriage and taught against it, it might be that the Apostle is saying women can be saved even if they have children in the context of marriage and family life. But there's more to consider here.

What is said next surprises: *through childbearing*.[175] One can doubt this refers to the birth of Jesus by Mary however cryptic and popular this view has been, no matter how central Christ (who is not mentioned in these lines) is for redemption.[176] An allegorical reading is less likely.[177] More likely is the view that the Apostle sees women in Ephesus falling for false teaching. They are exhorted to pull out of some kind of antimarriage movement or perhaps an Artemis cult attraction (cf. Acts 19:23-27) and, as would be the case for most (not all), marry, and in such a family life in a household live in the faith and so find redemption (from the false teachings).[178] One might also ask if this exhortation is an indicator of the practice of abortion, exposure, and infanticide in the Roman Empire, with the Apostle insisting on preserving the infant.[179] Josephus tells his readers Jews prohibited abortion and the woman who does destroy the child is guilty of "infanticide" (*Ag. Ap.* 2.202; translation Barclay). But Emily Gathergood has pulled together Jewish and Christian texts that demonstrate convincingly that *saved through childbearing* is about giving birth to children in a physical sense of salvation (preservation) and that God is the midwife who saves the mother in the process of giving birth, thus reversing the curse (seen in part in 1 Tim 2:13-14) and countering the ascetic

---

[175] For a summary of views, Cohick, *Women in the World of the Earliest Christians*, 138-140. On this term I am especially grateful to Emily Gathergood for sharing with me her Nottingham University PhD dissertation. See her *The Midwifery of God: Tokological Deliverance in 1 Timothy 2:15 in Light of Early Jewish and Christian Readings of Genesis 3:16*.

[176] But see Payne, *Man and Woman, One in Christ*, 417-441; Witherington, *Letters and Homilies for Hellenized Christians*, 230; Linda L. Belleville, "1 Timothy," in *1 Timothy, 2 Timothy, Titus, Hebrews* (ed. P. W. Comfort; Cornerstone Biblical Commentary 17; Carol Stream: Tyndale, 2009), 54-64.

[177] E.g., beside the many early fathers who read the text this way, see also Kenneth L. Waters, "Saved through Childbearing: Virtues as Children in 1 Timothy 2:11-15," *JBL* 123 (2004): 703-735.

[178] See the discussion in Marshall, *Pastoral Epistles*, 468-470.

[179] For discussion of abortion in the Roman world, comparing Roman and Jewish practices and attitudes, see the brief summary of Martin Goodman, *Rome and Jerusalem: The Clash of Ancient Civilizations* (New York: Alfred A. Knopf, 2007), 233-238. Jewish attitudes were almost entirely negative when it came to abortion and especially to infanticide, though some later rabbinic texts provide exceptions (*m. Ohol.* 7:6).

movement at work in Ephesus.[180] The texts Gathergood amassed for her interpretation, not to ignore her facility in multiple languages and in the history of scholarship, persuade me to think salvation here is physical preservation.

> **A Closer Look: Jewish and Christian Texts (from Gathergood)**
>
> **Gen 3:16** To the woman he said,
> "I will greatly increase your pangs in childbearing;
> in pain you shall bring forth children,
> yet your desire shall be for your husband,
> and he shall rule over you."
> **Psalm 22:9-10** Yet it was you who took me from the womb;
> you kept me safe on my mother's breast.
> On you I was cast from my birth,
> and since my mother bore me you have been my God.
> **71:6** Upon you I have leaned from my birth;
> it was you who took me from my mother's womb.
> My praise is continually of you.
> **Job 10:18** "Why did you bring me forth from the womb?
> Would that I had died before any eye had seen me"
> **Isaiah 66:9** Shall I open the womb and not deliver?
> says the LORD;
> shall I, the one who delivers, shut the womb?
> says your God.
>
> *2 Baruch* 72–74 (73:7): Messianic age reversing the curse of Adam's sin in Genesis 3:16. "And women will no longer have pain when they bear, nor will they suffer torment when they yield the fruits of their womb" (trans. Daniel Gurtner).[181]
>
> *Life of Adam and Eve* 25:1-4: "And the Lord turned to me and said: Since you listened to the serpent, and disregarded my commandment, you will be in manifold troubles, and in unendurable pains you will bear children [in many ways]. And in one hour you will come to the birth and lose your life, from your great distress and pangs. But you will confess and say: Lord, Lord, save me, and I will turn no more to the sin of the flesh. Therefore, according to your words I will judge you, because of

---

[180] Gathergood, *Midwifery of God*. See also Glahn, "First-Century Ephesian Artemis," who contends Artemis was perceived in Ephesus as a saving midwife.
[181] Daniel Gurtner, *Second Baruch: A Critical Edition of the Syriac Text, with Greek and Latin Fragments, English Translation, Introduction and Concordances* (Jewish and Christian Texts in Contexts and Related Studies 5; New York: T&T Clark 2009).

> the enmity which the enemy has placed in you; and you will return again to your husband, and he will rule over you."[182]
>
> *Ascension of Isaiah* 11, rooted as it is in Isaiah 66:7–9, and in AscIsa 11 Mary gives birth to Jesus without pain and without a midwife and without losing her virginity. Drawing on Isa this text affirms God as midwife.
>
> *Odes of Solomon* 19:7–8, again a birth without pain or midwife, and a body where God's salvation occurs.
>
> *Protevangelium of James* 11:17–20, where divine activity has shifted from conception to the birthing. Again, no pain, no midwife because God is the midwife.
>
> Latin *Acts of Andrew* 25:1–11, where conversion from the goddess Artemis/Diana to Jesus Christ brings redemption for a woman in childbirth.

What follows is common Christian teaching as well as consistent with what was said above (at 2:9): *provided they[183] continue in faith and love and holiness, with self-control.* Justification was not by works and neither was it without works. Final judgment, as was the case in Judaism, is always connected to how one lived. This snippet in 1 Timothy 2:15 ending as it does with *self-control* then is of a piece with early Christian teaching on perseverance of faith, and here perseverance is once again tied to the civilized piety of Christian women, or more particularly the young widows (cf. 2:9).

3:1–7 BISHOPS

Chapter divisions can be as much a problem as an aid. Is 1 Timothy 3:1–7 simply a random shift to a new topic or are these qualifications for a "bishop" organically connected to the words used for males in 2:8 and to the "man" of 2:12 over whom the woman is not to "teach" or "to have authority"? Does this perhaps suggest the women were only prohibited from instructing overseers (and deacons)? Or has the Apostle been dealing with false teachers and false teaching all along? (Yes.) In which case, is this

---

[182] Johannes Tromp, *The Life of Adam and Eve in Greek: A Critical Edition* (Pseudepigrapha Veteris Testamenti Graece 6; Leiden: Brill, 2005), 150–151. It is noticeable that salvation here is used of the woman, her redemption is connected to repentance, and the salvation itself is preservation of her physical life. For discussion, I am grateful again to Gathergood, *Midwifery of God*.

[183] Why "they" instead of "she" and who is the "they"? Probably faithful women or the wife and the husband (so Westfall, *Paul and Gender*, 311).

list a counter-list to the behaviors and character of the false teachers? (Probably yes.) Is this then, like Titus (cf. 1 Tim 5:22), about appointing bishops and deacons in churches in general?[184] (Yes.)

To make our discussion of the Apostle's instructions on the qualifications for bishops easier on the reader, we have enumerated the qualifications (or qualities, or virtues) and there are fourteen. What the bishop does is not the focus; instead, the focus is the bishop's character, manifested in behaviors. A parallel is found at Titus 1:5–9.

3:1 The saying is sure: whoever aspires to the office of bishop desires a noble task.

2 Now a bishop must be [1] above reproach, [2] married only once, [3] temperate, [4] self-controlled, [5] respectable, [6] hospitable, [7] an apt teacher,

3 [8] not a drunkard, [9] not violent but gentle, [10] not quarrelsome, [11] and not a lover of money.

4 [12] He must manage his own household well, keeping his children submissive and respectful in every way –

5 for if someone does not know how to manage his own household, how can he take care of God's church?

6 [13] He must not be a recent convert, or he may be puffed up with conceit and fall into the condemnation of the devil.

7 [14] Moreover, he must be well thought of by outsiders, so that he may not fall into disgrace and the snare of the devil.

The opening in 3:1 uses a truth-emphasizing (and here forward looking) formula (*The saying is sure*)[185] and then states the *noble task* through its name: *bishop* or perhaps "bishop-ing" or "overseeing" instead of *office of bishop*. Some suggest "supervising/supervisor" as the best translation. This term, as made known years ago by Edwin Hatch and now revived in the work of Alistair Stewart, often referred to the financial administrator of a city.[186] Contrary to his common practice, the Apostle chooses a term (*episkopos*, bishop) from the public sector so one must import at least some of the content of the term to Paul's term. Which is to say that *not a*

---

[184] Marshall, *Pastoral Epistles*, 471–473.
[185] See 1:15; 4:9; 2 Tim 2:11; Tit 3:8. For discussion, Marshall, 326–330.
[186] Edwin Hatch, *The Organization of the Early Christian Churches*, reprint edn., The Bampton Lectures 1880 (Eugene: Wipf & Stock, 1999); Alistair C. Stewart, *The Original Bishops: Office and Order in the First Christian Communities* (Grand Rapids: Baker Academic, 2014).

lover of money suggests the overseer had at least some ministry of oversight in the distribution of funds for the poor in the churches and perhaps society as well. The use of the term *bishop* does not limit oversight to financial administration, but overseeing was a task with a wide range of leading responsibilities, and so carried similarities to leaders in other Second Temple Jewish groups.[187] This *noble task* of oversight was marred by the behavior of the false teachers, tainting anyone who *aspires to the office* or would have to confront their false teaching.

The term *bishop* has become a source of controversy for discussions about church polity because time will reveal that this term was used for higher and higher offices as the church grew bigger and bigger. That is, we will begin to see monarchical bishops who will become church administrators of pastors and churches and dioceses. A *bishop*, or overseer, is found in the New Testament at only a few places, and what we know of the early church is based on what we can see in such texts (Phil 1:1; Titus 1:7; with Acts 1:20; 20:28). The term refers to some recognizable, organized category of ministry in the church in Acts 1:20, 20:28 and 1 Timothy 3:1. The bishop is a spiritual, pastoral, or shepherding task according to Acts 20:28 and 1 Peter 5:2, which in light of 1 Peter 2:25 participates in the ministry of Jesus himself. Pastoral ministry is as varied as it is complicated: those in one's assembly will more or less shape what that pastoral task will involve while the fundamental calling to pastor/overseer will also shape the relationship with the assembly. It will at least involve, from 1 Timothy 3, hospitality, teaching, and taking care of the church folks as well as civil engagement with the public. A term connected to *leading* is present both in 1 Timothy 3:4, 5 (*manage* in the NRSV) and in 1 Thessalonians 5:12–13 (*proistemi*), though in 1 Timothy 3:4, 5 it refers to one's house and by extension shapes what *take care* means in the second half of 3:5.[188]

---

[187] Towner, *Timothy and Titus*, 242–243.
[188] There is a trend among some more anarchic sorts to say leadership was not a part of NT vocabulary. Such anarchy is unmasked by ignorance of what the NT actually says, for the term of that day for leadership is found at Rom 12:8; 1 Thess 5:12; 1 Tim 5:17 (elders "who rule well" or who "lead" well), and it may be used for elders/bishops in Titus 3:8, 14.

> **A Closer Look: What Do We (Not) Know?**
>
> We do not know whether in a given locality (e.g., a town) there was a local congregation, or a set of independent house congregations, or a local congregation that consisted of smaller house congregations, and we do not know whether there was any organization that brought different localities together in larger groupings. Nor again do we know whether a house congregation consisted of one household or several (as in a modern house fellowship, so called because it meets in a house rather than an ecclesiastical building).[189]

A hornet's nest is knocked loose when one asks about the various NT terms. Namely, is the bishop/overseer an "elder" and are there "pastors" (Eph 4:11) or is pastoring one of the functions of bishops and elders? These terms are not defined or delineated with precision in the NT so one is left to see what the texts say and don't say, and do one's best to use the terms responsibly without imposing later ecclesial definitions on the NT church. It is, however, noticeable that the Apostle speaks first to bishops/overseers and does not here call them "elders." The Pastorals use "elder" at 1 Timothy 5:1, 17, 19 and Titus 1:5, which is first of all an age description of sages and advisors (e.g., Acts 2:17) and so becomes an early Christian term for such persons in the assemblies (Acts 11:30; 14:23; 15:2, 4, 6, 22–23; 16:4; 20:17; 21:18; James 5:14; 1 Pet 5:1, 5; 2 John 1; 3 John 1). It is our judgment that a bishop or overseer is more of what we call an office, while an elder is more of a group of wise advisors alongside the bishop. Yet, Titus 1:5 and 1:7 use the terms (apparently) interchangeably. Later Christian usage of these terms builds on what is said in the NT but is not identical (or as restricted of course) to what we find in the NT. What is clear is that the overseer is not to be young (1 Tim 3:6) and thus there is an elderliness in a bishop.

Bishop-ing, then, is a *noble task*, with the word "noble" translating a word that refers to excellence and beauty (*kalos*). It is right and proper for a person to *aspire to*, or to reach for, to extend oneself toward or even to tend toward being a bishop. Such a person *desires* or has a passion for what is noble.[190] Having said that, it is worth observing that wanting, desiring, and aspiring do not a bishop make. What does make an overseer for the Apostle is character and giftedness combining in a context where such a

---

[189] Marshall, *Pastoral Epistles*, 180–181.
[190] The two terms here are synonyms and they are not negative. See Marshall, 476.

person is needed, recognized, and appointed. What makes for a bishop contrasts with typical character traits or virtues in the Greco-Roman world (see Closer Look: Virtues in the Greco-Roman World), and it was not uncommon in that world to sketch the virtue by describing someone with a vice (which is how we ought also to understand vices lists in the NT; e.g., 1 Tim 6:4–5).

> A Closer Look: Virtues and Vices in the Greco-Roman World
>
> Homer, *Iliad* 13.278–286
>
> ... the coward will change color at every touch and turn; he is full of fears, and keeps shifting his weight first on one knee and then on the other; his heart beats fast as he thinks of death, and one can hear the chattering of his teeth; whereas the brave man will not change color nor be frightened on finding himself in ambush, but is all the time longing to go into action.[191]
>
> Semonides of Amorgos, *Poem on Women*, connects the character of some women to various natural phenomena (natural elements, animals, insects), and the poem is a blistering display of vitriol at times.
>
> Herodotus, *Histories*, forms a character portrait of why monarchs ought to be eliminated:
>
> There is no one better than him at welcoming slander, and there is no one more erratic in his behaviour. I mean, if your admiration for him is moderate, he is offended at your lack of total subservience, and if you are totally subservient, he is angry at you as a flatterer. And now I come to the most important problems with monarchy. A monarch subverts a country's ancestral customs, takes women against their will, and kills men without trial.[192]
>
> Plato, *Republic*, writes of four character types behind four inadequate forms of government: The Timarchic Man, the Oligarch, the Democrat, and the Tyrant.[193] Aristotle, who taught and worked alongside Theophrastus, famously matched vices, moderations, and virtues (see below, section "A Closer Look: Virtues of Aristotle"). Less known perhaps is that Aristotle formed a character portrait of old men in ways that we find in more complete form in Theophrastus:

---

[191] Homer, *Iliad* 13.278–286 (LCL, trans. Butler).
[192] Herodotus, *Histories* 3.80.5 (trans. Waterfield and Dewald). Found in Sonia Pertsinidis, *Theophrastus' Characters: A New Introduction*, Routledge Focus on Classical Studies (New York: Routledge, 2018), 31, whose study of Theophrastus includes a survey of the texts in this Closer Look.
[193] Plato, *Republic* 547–566.

Commentary on 1 Timothy

> Owing to their having lived many years and having been more often deceived by others or made more mistakes themselves, and since most human things turn out badly, they are positive about nothing, and in everything they show an excessive lack of energy. They always "think," but "know" nothing; and in their hesitation they always add "perhaps," or "maybe"; all their statements are of this kind, never unqualified.[194]

Numbers [1] through [11] are not expounded as [12] through [14] are, and these last three may be summarized as someone who is a leader, mature, and respectable, while the first eleven are random expressions rooted in the history and wisdom of what makes for good pastoral character and giftedness. ([1] may be more generalizing than the others.) Since most of these are about character, one can suggest that even though Paul does not here use the term, he is describing a person who is (to use the Hebrew term) *Tov*, or someone who is good and marked by goodness. Someone who is *tov* is also overall *above reproach*. As Jesus said, a good heart yields good (Luke 6:45), so this list is the good yield of a good heart. To the degree this list is about character we should avoid turning the items into external lists of qualifications but instead use them as manifestations of character and giftedness for the pastoral work, which means the overseer's behaviors need to reflect the inner work of God's Spirit transforming the person into *tov* (Gal 5:22, which the NRSV translates as "generosity," which is but one manifestation of "goodness"/*tov*). In light of this observation about character, comments on the specific requirements will be limited. Furthermore, since this list is about character, we are led to think a person's character is a presenting factor in leadership decisions. Character precedes gifts, skills, abilities, and education. Perhaps most of all, character mattered more than wealth, which dominated the Ephesian landscape in appointing leaders.[195] In particular, the *absence* of terms connected to benefactions configures this list over against the Ephesian honor society (but cf. 1 Tim 6:2's use of benefaction for masters of slaves). (For the lists of character in Aristotle and Theophrastus, see Titus, section "A Closer Look: Characters in Theophrastus of Eresos.")

---

[194] Aristotle, *Rhetoric* 2.13.1–3 (LCL, trans. Freese).
[195] Hoag, *Wealth in Ancient Ephesus and the First Letter to Timothy*, 100–130.

The early Christian *Didache*'s own requirements for a bishop and deacon are character-based: "who are worthy of the Lord, gentlemen who are not fond of money, who are true and approved" (*Did* 15:10), which leads the author to say such persons are the ones who do the work of prophesying and teaching (15:2).[196]

First: the overseer is assumed to be male but being male may not be required. To be sure, the masculine gender for the nouns (*episkopos, neophyte* in v. 6) as well as *married* [to a woman] *only once* and the house leader do imply a male but one must at least admit that the assumption of a male is not the same as a requirement of a male.

Second: the term "one-woman-man" (or *married only once*; see, too, Tit 1:6) is underdetermined and could refer to being nonpolygamous or not remarried (after a divorce or loss of one's wife) or a married man instead of a single man or a man who is faithful to his wife.[197] If it refers to a nonpolygamous man it may well be a stance in favor of respectability in the Roman Empire because Jewish law permitted polygamy (cf. Josephus, *B.J.* 1.477; *Ant.* 17:14). The virtue of one man with one woman is on full display in the *Laudatio Turiae*, which records a husband's glorious praise of his virtuous wife, often identified as Turia, though the name is generally not accepted as genuine.[198] Praise on a tombstone for a woman included her being *univira*, a "one-man-woman." Martin Goodman, in his expert work on *Rome and Jerusalem*, summarizes Roman marriage laxity with this: "In the late Republic and early empire, divorce was so common among aristocrats that Roman practice appears less like monogamy than serial polygamy, one spouse at a time," but he concedes that the number of divorces have political reasons as well.[199] Though an antipolygamy posture for the overseer is reasonable so too is the view that this speaks of faithfulness. That the Apostle is urging civilized piety, however, suggests that he may have turned to the *univira* ideal for women, in which a woman remained married to one husband and, after his death, was celibate and unmarried. In turning to the *univira* ideal Paul would have been one-upping the Roman ideal by requiring the same for husbands! Both bishops

---

[196] LCL (Ehrman).
[197] For faithfulness, Marshall, *Pastoral Epistles*, 478. For a general overview of options, see Mounce, *Pastoral Epistles*, 170–173.
[198] http://www.u.arizona.edu/~afutrell/survey/laud%20tur.htm
[199] Martin Goodman, *Rome and Jerusalem: The Clash of Ancient Civilizations* (New York: Alfred A. Knopf, 2007), 205.

and deacons would then fufill the ideal of a one-woman-man.[200] However, since the young widows are *permitted* to remarry (cf. 1 Tim 5:11) it seems the Apostle's instructions here are not consistent with the *univira* ideal.

Third: the use of *hospitable* (3:2), in Greek *philoxenon* ("friendship for strangers"), is not simply a term about generosity. Being *hospitable* describes the early Christian habit and character trait of caring also for those itinerant preachers, evangelists, and letter carriers as they practiced their ministry,[201] or in following believers who were fleeing persecution (cf. Rom 12:13).[202]

Fourth: while being an *apt teacher* (3:2) is connected to the role of *bishop* there is an assumption that the person *aspiring to the office of bishop* is already teaching.[203] This allowed for their teaching, both in skill and content, to be evaluated as good and correct, which then counters the false teachers and their teaching (cf. Tit 1:7–9).[204] In this context in 1 Timothy 3 *apt teacher* also indicates, in a similar way as *to teach* in 2:12, that in the Pastorals teaching is not reducible to public speaking but emerges from a good character. The expectation here is more than mere academic capability. This *apt teaching* is the gift of helping fellow believers exemplify and apply the gospel faith to their daily life together as a family and community (Tit 1:9; Eph 4:11–16).[205] All teaching in the world of the Apostle involved emulation as the primary form of instruction.

Fifth: the negations of v. 3 (e.g., *not a drunkard,* etc.) set the bishop apart from common behaviors of Greco-Roman male leaders, or at least from the stereotypes of such leaders. That the person should not be *a drunkard* is stated also in Titus 1:7 about the overseer and is rephrased and emphasized again for deacons in this letter to Timothy (3:8). Such repetition reveals a particular issue in the contexts of the PEs. While rejection of what is *violent* is connected to the raucous behavior of *a drunkard* that hints back to unconverted behavior (1:12–13), the emphasis on *gentle* and as *not quarrelsome* perhaps touches upon men not praying in anger (2:8). Lastly, *not a lover of money* was important for a few reasons: (1) the term "bishop"

---

[200] Lynn H. Cohick, *Women in the World of the Earliest Christians*, 104–105.
[201] Collins, *1 & 2 Timothy and Titus*, 82.
[202] This understanding of hospitality is also reflected in the Apostolic Fathers, in texts cited in some of the commentaries: *1 Clement* 1:2, 10:7–11:1, 12:1–3; Shepherd of Hermas, *Mandates* 8:10; *Similitudes* 9:27.
[203] Towner, *Timothy and Titus*, 244.
[204] Marshall, *Pastoral Epistles*, 478; Dibelius and Conzelmann, *Pastoral Epistles*, 1972, 55.
[205] Ward, *I & II Timothy and Titus*, 56.

was a common title for those with financial responsibilities within a group in some official capacity;[206] (2) Jesus' teachings on the incompatibility of greed with gospel life (Matt 6:24, 13:22; Luke 16:13) and greed is connected to Judas' betrayal (Matt 26:14-16; Mark 14:10-11; Luke 22:3-6; John 12:4-6); (3) greed was a characteristic of the false teachers who were abusing fellow believers (1 Tim 6:10; cf. 5:6; 2 Tim 3:2). The early churches continued to be wary of anyone who sought a profit from being a leader or teacher in a Christian community.[207] These negations show a continued application of the gospel to the situation in Ephesus.

Sixth: the location of the assembly in a household helps explain the orientation of 3:4-5, namely, the importance of a child's faith as an indicator of a father's nurturing of the children into the faith. While converting this into some kind of church law overcooks how the text should be treated, one must appreciate the wisdom at work. A *tov* parent's character will shape the character of a child, so a child's character can function as a barometer of the parent's faith. What seems implicit is that being a household father is connected to being a church bishop, creating an intrinsic and organic link between household and church communal life and structure.[208] Such a calling in the community of faith was structured after the *paterfamilias*, evoking the importance of submission to the leader of the family.[209] Furthermore, the bishop nurtures faithfulness to the gospel through correct teaching as well as skillful admonishment to correct those who have been duped by false teaching or compassionate rebuke for those struggling with sin.

Seventh: immaturity must be avoided because youth makes a person susceptible to the temptations that always accompany leadership, namely, arrogance, power mongering and spiritual abuse. This same word for being *puffed up with conceit* (*tuphōtheis*) is connected to false teachers (6:4; 2 Tim 3:4), reflecting their incorrect and unauthorized teaching and sinful behavior. This conceit could lead one to *fall into the condemnation of the devil* or to *fall into disgrace and the snare of the devil* (3:7) and would carry forward the warning brought to mind by Adam and Eve in 2:13-15. If the *bishop* does not enact the proper gospel-based character on account of his

---

[206] Towner, *Timothy and Titus*, 244-245. See too Stewart, *Original Bishops*.
[207] *Didache* 11:6, 12, 15:1; Polycarp, *To the Philippians* 5:2.
[208] A common connection made in commentaries: see, for examples, Marshall, *Pastoral Epistles*, 479-480; Ward, *I & II Timothy and Titus*, 57. But also see Witherington, *Letters and Homilies for Hellenized Christians*, 233.
[209] Collins, *1 & 2 Timothy and Titus*, 84; Towner, *Timothy and Titus*, 254-255.

naïve state as *a recent convert* then he becomes susceptible to the false teachings being perpetuated in Ephesus. Such naivety allows the devil to strike a decisive blow to *the church of God*.

Eighth: social respectability and civilized piety are a constant theme in the Pastorals (cf. 2:2). What *outsiders* think matters, and always has mattered, and it matters today. The term the Apostle uses here in 3:2 is *kosmion*, translated as "respectable," which was previously used in 2:9 for *suitable clothing* when addressing the women of the assembly. One should consider this term "respectable" to be describing socially respected and socially accommodating and socially gifted relations of the overseer. Being a *tov* bishop extends from one's relation to God to one's family to one's assembly and into the public square. This happens because the character, not just the behaviors or *persona*, is *tov*.

Finally, each item in this list – and the larger picture of character at work – is also expected of nonbishops, nonelders, and nondeacons. These are then common virtues of common followers of Jesus, but virtues expected to be especially expressed and exemplified in those who are church leaders.[210]

3:8–13 DEACONS

We now turn from bishops to deacons, the latter term being a very common Greek term for servant (*diakonos*). A "servant" in New Testament times is used both generally for household servants (Matt 22:13) and in a transferred sense for the general Christian disposition of serving one another (Mark 9:35; 10:35–45). But it was also used for a specific kind of service in a local house church (Phil 1:1) just as it is used by the Apostle for those who were involved with him in gospel ministries (Col 1:7; cf. Acts 6:1–6). As such, in Christian subversion of values of power and honor, a "servant" is an especially "high" calling in the church.[211]

In this passage the term *deacon* refers to a specific function or office in the church alongside that of bishop, but the *deacons* seem to have lacked

---

[210] As Collins points out, "Apart from not being a neophyte, the qualities are those that one would expect to find in anyone who is an upright, responsible, and respectable husband and father." Collins, *1 & 2 Timothy and Titus*, 78. See also, Towner, *Timothy and Titus*, 241.
[211] John N. Collins, *Diakonia: Re-Interpreting the Ancient Sources* (New York: Oxford University Press, 2009).

certain responsibilities such as oversight and teaching.[212] As with bishops, the focus is not so much on tasks as it is mature character. It would be little more than guesswork to try to know specifics with any exactitude about the relationship of the bishop to the deacon in this period. While deacons could have been official representatives of the overseer through particular acts of service to the community, my guess would be they are younger church leaders on the path toward elders and bishops and as such are assistants.[213] (In the translation that follows, we have inserted the numbers.)

3:8 Deacons likewise must be [1] serious, [2] not double-tongued, [3] not indulging in much wine, [4] not greedy for money;
9 [5] they must hold fast to the mystery of the faith with a clear conscience.
10 [6] And let them first be tested; then, if they prove themselves blameless, let them serve as deacons.
11 Women likewise must be [a] serious, [b] not slanderers, but [c] temperate, [d] faithful in all things.
12 Let deacons [7] be married only once, [8] and let them manage their children and their households well;
13 for those who serve well as deacons gain a good standing for themselves and great boldness in the faith that is in Christ Jesus.

In 1 Timothy 3:2 we previously read *Now a bishop <u>must be</u>* and the *must be*, though not explicitly stated, is assumed in 3:8 and is thus translated as such in the NRSV. With bishops there were fourteen items in the list while there are here only seven for deacons. A parenthetical insertion in v. 11 about *women* occurs. Between bishops and deacons there are common qualifications: alcohol abuse is similar because [3] for deacons overlaps with [8] for bishops. Greed is common: [4] for deacons, [11] for bishops. With respect to [5]'s concern for orthodox thinking and teaching, one sees an overlap in the bishops list at [7] and [13]. One might think that once this has been shown to be true of the deacon it is assumed for the bishop, but this is undercut by the once-married requirement which is found in both lists: [7]

---

[212] Marshall believes that "deacons" must be tested because they are to share in the task of teaching, see Marshall, *Pastoral Epistles*, 485, 487–488. Witherington thinks Paul does not indicate any hierarchical authority of the bishop over the deacons; Witherington, *Letters and Homilies for Hellenized Christians*, 240–241.
[213] For a similar assessment see Towner, *Timothy and Titus*, 261–262.

and with bishops at [2], as is the case with house management: [8] with bishops at [12].

To be *serious* (*semnos*), a term found in a register of spiritual reverence, is found elsewhere in the NT at Philippians 4:8 and 1 Timothy 3:11 (for the *women*) as well as for the elderly man at Titus 2:2. It indicates a dignified, pastoral manner of civilized piety. It is possible that [2–4] explicate what *serious* means. As previously discussed, the term *eusebeia* in the PEs indicates civilized piety and *serious* translates a noun that comes from a similar root, so one might think of *serious* in social terms. The term *not double-tongued* points out the kind of duplicity of speech that leads to mistrust of one's words and even cynicism. *Not indulging in much wine* [3] is both a general problem in the Mediterranean cities as well as an indicator that one lacks control (cf. 1 Tim 3:3; Titus 2:3), while [4] *not greedy for money* points at the problem of corrupted motive (Titus 1:7, 11). One's disposition toward money is an indicator of one's godliness (1 Tim 6:3–10), and if we connect the bishop with distribution of funds, and if one makes *deacons* assistants to the bishops, then we could be looking in the term *greedy* at management of the funds of the church more than at one's own funds. If distribution is in mind then we are talking about filching from the funds, an accusation laid at the feet of the false teachers throughout the PEs (1 Tim 6:9–10; cf. 3:3; Titus 1:7).

The *deacons* are to be orthodox in faith: [5] *they must hold fast to the mystery of the faith with a clear conscience*. The term *mystery* is a Pauline favorite for the inclusion of gentiles in the redemption of God in Christ (Eph 3:1–6; Col 1:24–2:5). It does not have to be narrowly focused on gentile inclusion but can also widen out to the express "the fundamental realities of the gospel and of the life of the congregation."[214] This *mystery* is *the faith*,[215] and thus the apostolic, traditional, and redemptive gospel (e.g., 1 Tim 4:6; 6:12, 21). This *mystery of the faith* will be spelled out in 3:16. Integrity, honesty, and transparency are all at work when the Apostle says *with a clear conscience*. One who does not believe in the resurrection of the body of Jesus ought not to confess the Apostles' or the Nicene Creed. The *conscience* was explicated at 1:5 and points as the capacity to evaluate truth (1 Tim 3:9; 2 Tim 1:3) and to discern Christoform morality.[216]

---

[214] Dibelius and Conzelmann, *Pastoral Epistles*, 1972, 58.
[215] Marshall, *Pastoral Epistles*, 213–217, 490–491.
[216] Marshall, 217–227.

A new theme emerges in 1 Timothy 3:10 with [6] *let them first be tested.* This kind of discernment could refer to the deacons' theological fit (as in v. 9) or, which is more likely, to the deacons' character encompassing both theology and behaviors. An emphasis on character helps to explain why they need to be measured as *blameless.* The *blameless*-ness of the deacon is connected to the instruction to *hold fast.* The *first* test is a character of behavior matching belief.

Does an entirely different theme appear at 3:11 when it turns to *Women likewise*? They too are to be marked as *serious, not slanderers, but temperate, faithful in all things,* the last summarizing the first three. Who are these *women*? Are they women *deacons*?[217] Or are they the wives (*gynē* can be translated "wives" or "women") of the men deacons? Appearing as it does between instructions to males this instruction to *women* could indicate "wives" of the deacons. However, (1) the absence of any instructions to the wives of bishops in 3:1–7, (2) the clear use of this term *deacon* for Phoebe in Romans 16:1–2, (3) the use of *likewise*, which parallels 3:8's connection to 3:1, and (4) the absence of an article or pronoun indicating "their wives" suggests women *deacons*. They are faithful to the gospel and thus stand in contrast to women who are not yet or who have not been faithful (cf. 2:9–15; 5:11–13). That the women deacons are to be *serious* indicates the gravity of their ministry. The instructions that follow *serious* parallel what was said to males in 3:8–10: as the males are not to be *double-tongued* or out of control, so the women *deacons* are to be *temperate.* As the males are to be orthodox in faith (3:9–10), so the women are to be *faithful in all things.*

Returning back to the men, the Apostle instructs the deacons to be [7] a "one-woman-man" (cf. 3:2), which is an identical expression to the bishop list and probably best refers to faithfulness to one's wife. Again, the *deacon* is [8] to *manage* (or "lead") one's family.

A summary exhortation completes the list. Those who "deacon" well (excellently, in a civilized manner) will *gain a good standing for themselves* as well as *boldness* (or "frankness") *in the faith.* This is not an eschatological reward at the Day of Judgment but rather recognition in church and society. An "excellent" *standing* suggests passing the test, established as an excellent leader in the church, and having a good public reputation.[218]

---

[217] Marshall, 492–495. Huizenga thinks the women are wives of deacons because she thinks the author's view of women is so negative: see *1–2 Timothy, Titus,* 37.
[218] Marshall, *Pastoral Epistles,* 496; Dibelius and Conzelmann, *Pastoral Epistles,* 1972, 59.

Some think *boldness* indicates confidence in Christ, but the term is commonly used for verbal communication. Thus, a *good standing* gives the *deacon* the opportunity to speak with "frankness" in the sphere of Christ, that is, within the Christian community on matters of *the faith*. The deacons thus become those entrusted with being beacons of the apostolic gospel and publicly recognized for their faithful way of life. This contrasts with the false teachers among the churches of Ephesus.[219]

3:14–16 REASON FOR THE LETTER

This passage, known for its apparent citation of an early Christian creed,[220] sorts out the reason for this letter: until the Apostle arrives this letter will serve the purpose of guidance for Timothy. Letters have always been a substitute presence and as such becomes the Apostle's instructions for life in the church.[221]

3:14 I hope to come to you soon, but I am writing these instructions to you so that,

15 if I am delayed, you may know how one ought to behave in the household of God, which is the church of the living God, the pillar and support of the truth.

16 Without any doubt, the mystery of godliness is great:

He was revealed in flesh,
    vindicated in spirit,
        seen by angels,
proclaimed among gentiles,
    believed in throughout the world,
        taken up in glory.

---

[219] Witherington believes Paul is intentionally putting the false teachers and the misbehaving women of 1 Tim 2 in juxtaposition with the overseers and deacons, including women who correctly hold to "the mystery of the faith"; see Witherington, *Letters and Homilies for Hellenized Christians*, 241–242.

[220] The case that this hymn/creed traveled with the Jewish Christians who moved out of Jerusalem in the persecution of Stephen and took up shop in Syrian Antioch, where Paul picked it up, can be found in R. H. Gundry, "The Form, Meaning, and Background of the Hymn Quoted in 1 Timothy 3:16," in W. Ward Gasque and Ralph P. Martin, eds., Apostolic History and the Gospel: Biblical and Historical Essays Presented to F. F. Bruce on His 60th Birthday (Grand Rapids: Eerdmans, 1970), 203–222.

[221] Collins, *1 & 2 Timothy and Titus*, 101; Towner, *Timothy and Titus*, 272–273.

One could pause for a long talk about the precise referent for *these* in *these instructions* (3:14), but it probably refers to all that has so far been written, especially 2:1–3:13.

If I Am Delayed

Following a personal note to Timothy about possible delay and the function of the letter (3:14a, 15), the Apostle explains the reason for the letter: *so that . . . you may know how one ought to behave in the household of God*. Household suggests both the location of early Christian gatherings as well as a theory of the church as family.[222] *Household* is then defined as *the church of the living God*[223] which is further defined as *the pillar and support of the truth*. The Apostle's intention is to call Timothy, as a leader of the church, to bring the church into a proper communal life of integrity according to the gospel of Christ Jesus both in teaching and practice. The use of the more architectural terms of *pillar* and *support* adds to the family aspect of the *household of God* some temple nuances common to Paul's Jewish theology (Rom 12:1; 1 Cor 2:16–17; Eph 2:19–3:7).[224]

The Apostle's emphasis in this letter up to this point on the church in Ephesus to display civilized piety rules out a sectarian church isolated from culture (cf. 1 Tim 2:1–2). Paul's common tactic of using contemporary political and religious terminology and imagery during his public preaching (Acts 17:6–8; Rom 1:4–5; Phil 2:8–11) would also push against such a Christian isolationist reading. Rather, the Apostle is emphasizing that the Christian's personal integrity comes to expression in an ecclesial *and* public life. This rightly ordered relationship with the world displays the church as the embodiment of God's truth (Eph 3:9–10).[225]

---

[222] Joseph H. Hellerman, *The Ancient Church as Family* (Minneapolis: Fortress, 2001). Debate about the location of early Christians gatherings can be seen in Edward Adams, *The Earliest Christian Meeting Places: Almost Exclusively Houses?*, rev. edn. (New York: Bloomsbury T&T Clark, 2015); Roger W. Gehring, *House Church and Mission: The Importance of Household Structures in Early Christianity* (Peabody: Hendrickson, 2004).

[223] For an extensive excursus, see Marshall, *Pastoral Epistles*, 512–521.

[224] Witherington, *Letters and Homilies for Hellenized Christians*, 245; Knight, *Pastoral Epistles*, 180–182; Mounce, *Pastoral Epistles*, 220, 221–222, 223; Marshall, *Pastoral Epistles*, 507–510, 515. See also the helpful excursus in Collins, *1 & 2 Timothy and Titus*, 102–106. Towner disagrees that there is any temple reference to the phrase, see Towner, *Timothy and Titus*, 274 n. 17.

[225] Witherington, *Letters and Homilies for Hellenized Christians*, 245; Marshall, *Pastoral Epistles*, 503–504, 516.

The Mystery of Our Religion

The Apostle is about to delineate the faith and opens those lines with a summary, calling it the *mystery of our godliness*, or the gospel and truth. His use of truth in 3:15 (cf. 2:4, 7; 4:3; 6:5; 2 Tim 2:15, 18, 25; 3:7; 4:4; Titus 1:1, 14) sets the Apostle off into articulating that truth. This *godliness* (*eusebeia*), which as we have observed points at socially respectable civilized piety, is then delineated in six brief lines, each of which could be expanded into a lengthy discussion since each is inside the heart of the apostolic gospel. He opens his articulation of the central lines of the gospel with *without any doubt*, which claims that this mystery entails a confession to be believed and held to.[226] It also speaks of each Christian's commitment to both the recognition of the *great* work of God in the person of Christ Jesus and the grace of Christ Jesus to empower them into a gospel-transformed person (1 Tim 1:13–16). Using the term *eusebeia* with the term *mystery* the Apostle indicates that the Christian church, whether as civilized piety (2:2), ecclesial ethics (3:9), or the confessional beliefs of the church (3:16), expresses its identity in forms based on the gospel of Jesus Christ, from incarnation to ascension.[227] There is a tendency to turn the gospel and the Christian faith into a message about salvation, but as with 1 Corinthians 15:3–5 so here: that faith is first and foremost about Jesus.

Each of the following lines is a statement about Jesus. In spite of some ingenious attempts to explain the order of the lines, that order is not immediately clear.[228] First, the order could be seen as chronological for lines 1–5 with line 6 seemingly about the ascension. Yet, line 2 appears to be about the resurrection (and ascension; cf. 1 Peter 3:18: "made alive in the Spirit"). Lines 4 and 5 are about the Pauline mission, while line 6 restates in our view line 2 (cf. 1 Peter 3:19?). Others think the order could be two sets of three lines (1–3, 4–6; so NRSV), the first three about his incarnation state and the second set of three lines about his exalted

---

[226] Marshall, *Pastoral Epistles*, 522.
[227] Towner, *Timothy and Titus*, 276–277, 284–285; Collins, *1 & 2 Timothy and Titus*, 107. Marshall says, "The author's aim is accordingly to establish the intrinsic link between the Christ-event and Christian existence." See Marshall, *Pastoral Epistles*, 499, 523. Mounce and Towner see this confession as the theological foundation for all of Paul's teaching about proper church behavior; see Mounce, *Pastoral Epistles*, 215, 231; Towner, *Timothy and Titus*, 270–271, 284.
[228] For a comprehensive overview of many of the options for how to group and understand these six lines, see Knight, *Pastoral Epistles*, 182–184. Also, Marshall, *Pastoral Epistles*, 500–503; Mounce, *Pastoral Epistles*, 215–218.

state. If one entertains the speculation of positing an early Christian tradition edited by the Apostle, one could argue that the mission lines (4, 5) are added by Paul, leaving a fairly straightforward chronology: incarnation, resurrection, ascension gaze, and ascension to glory. A third take is that there are three couplets that stand in comparison to one another: *flesh* and *spirit*, *angels* in heaven and *nations* on earth, and the *world* and heavenly *glory*. Rather than placing these pairs in juxtaposition, it may be better to see the integral and complementary relationship between each pair, such as line 1 leads into line 2,[229] line 3 is fulfilled by line 4 (especially if *angels* are taken to be the apostolic messengers, cf. Matt 24:31), and line 5 is completed by line 6. In this there is a rough chronology from Christ's birth to ascension similar to the hymn in Phil 2:5–11. Regardless, Hutson cuts to the chase when he says that this "poem is a collage that evokes the Christ story, with emphasis on resurrection."[230]

He was revealed in flesh (1): here his incarnation is in view and, as such, indicates an early Christian conviction of preexistence, with *in flesh* indicating the cosmic and historical reality of human nature (John 1:14; Rom 1:3; 1 Pet 3:18) where God revealed the Son. Next, *vindicated in spirit* (2): a reference to his resurrection as an act of God that makes right what had been wrong. This theme of vindication is part of the earliest gospel preaching (cf. Acts 2:23–24). The term *spirit* can refer either to human spirit[231] or more likely to the divine Spirit (cf. Rom 1:4; 8:11),[232] in which case it would be "by" the Spirit (NIV). Then *seen by angels* (3): this could refer to the descent into hell (1 Pet 3:19) or to Jesus in his incarnation or even in his ascension and refer then to the heavenly gaze of angels. On the other hand, the term behind *angels* can refer to human envoys of God and, if that is the case here, then this is the appearance of Jesus after his resurrection to the apostles.[233] The possibility of *angels* pointing us at human messengers might be indicated by the fact that *ophthe*, the word for *seen*, is used in the NT to refer to Jesus' resurrection appearances

---

[229] Towner, *Timothy and Titus*, 280–281.
[230] Hutson, 1–2 Timothy, Titus, 104.
[231] Marshall, *Pastoral Epistles*, 525–526.
[232] Gordon Fee, *God's Empowering Presence: The Holy Spirit in the Letters of Paul* (Peabody: Hendrickson, 1994), 761–768; Collins, *1 & 2 Timothy and Titus*, 109.
[233] A similar listing expounding the mystery is found in *Diognetus* 11:3, a second century Christian letter.

(Lk 24:31; Acts 13:31; 26:16; 1 Cor 15:5, 6, 7, 8).[234] Next, *proclaimed among Gentiles* (4) and *believed in throughout the world* (5) are summary statements of the Pauline mission, which takes us back to *mystery* 3:16, a favorite term of Paul for his mission. Finally, *taken up in glory* (6) refers to the ascension.

The faith is articulated in a series of lines that tell us the story of Jesus.

4:1–5 SIGNS OF THE TIME

That "mystery of our religion" expression of 3:16, which generated an articulation of the essential points of the faith, now generates more thoughts about the opponents of the gospel. Following this passage, the Apostle turns to more personal instructions for Timothy.

4:1 Now the Spirit expressly says that in later times some will renounce the faith by paying attention to deceitful spirits and teachings of demons,
2 through the hypocrisy of liars whose consciences are seared with a hot iron.
3 They forbid marriage and abstain from certain foods, which God created to be received with thanksgiving by those who believe and know the truth.
4 For everything created by God is good, and nothing is to be rejected, provided it is received with thanksgiving;
5 for it is sanctified by God's word and by prayer.

The false teachers of Ephesus (1:3–11, 18–20) are described here as ascetics (4:3).[235] The Apostle assigns the rise of apostasy in the church to an eschatological scenario revealed by the Holy Spirit (4:1), and anchors the false beliefs of the apostates in the spirit-world (4:1) that operates in the church through these false teachers (4:2–3). The antidote to the attractiveness of their asceticism is a creation theology (4:4–5). Everywhere the apostle Paul formed churches he encountered opposition. Most often his opponents tended to be his own Jewish contemporaries, both nonChristian and Christian converts,[236] and the finishing sections of the Book of Acts

---

[234] While recognizing these NT usages, most people tend to think that *angels* refer to nonhuman celestial beings, see Knight, *Pastoral Epistles*, 185; Marshall, *Pastoral Epistles*, 526–527.
[235] See Chapter 1, "Introduction," section "The Opponents of the Pastoral Epistles"; and "Closer Look" at 1:3–7, section "The False Teachers and Their Teachings."
[236] Marshall, *Pastoral Epistles*, 533.

(21–28) provide a good example. Even in Rome under house arrest Paul is described as countering rumors among Jews about his gospel mission. The asceticism of 1 Timothy 4:3 emerges from his Jewish opponents as well (see Col 2:16–23).

The Times

The eschatological scenario (*in later times*) of apostasy comes into play from Jesus (Mark 13), Paul (cf. Acts 20:29–31 with 2 Thess 2:1–12), and Revelation 2–3.[237] The language suggests these are failing Christians who are abandoning their faith.[238] The link to eschatology comes from *the Spirit* who *expressly says* this is to happen *in later times* (or "in the later seasons"). This idea of the Spirit speaking can be rendered generically – that *the Spirit* has been speaking from Moses through the prophets through Jesus and the apostles and pertains to the present time (of the author) – or it can be taken more particularly as a word from an early Christian prophet, perhaps Paul himself.[239] The warning about false teachers in the last days of the current age is similarly mentioned in 2 Timothy 3:1–9 and by the writer of Jude 17–19, and was a common theme in other Second Temple Jewish literature around the first century.[240] Early Christian eschatology lived on the edge of the fulfillment of God's grand narrative (cf. Heb 1:1–2), and this edge percolated a sense of imminence. Israel's prophets spoke of God's work in the world in much the same way, predicting the next event in terms of the last event. Limited knowledge, which also Jesus admitted (Mark 13:32), is not then about being wrong but about a rhetoric rooted in not knowing the specific time and date on which something would happen.[241]

---

[237] Knight, *Pastoral Epistles*, 188.
[238] I. Howard Marshall, *Kept by the Power of God: A Study of Perseverance and Falling Away* (Minneapolis: Bethany House, 1969); Scot McKnight, *A Long Faithfulness: The Case for Christian Perseverance* (Denver: Paraclete Press, 2013); Roger E. Olson, *Arminian Theology: Myths and Realities* (Downers Grove: IVP Academic, 2006).
[239] David E. Aune, *Prophecy in Early Christianity and the Ancient Mediterranean World* (Grand Rapids: Eerdmans, 1983); Ben Witherington III, *Jesus, Paul and the End of the World* (Downers Grove: IVP Academic, 1992); Thomas W. Gillespie, *The First Theologians: A Study in Early Christian Prophecy* (Grand Rapids: Eerdmans, 1994); Towner, *Timothy and Titus*, 288; Ellen F. Davis, *Biblical Prophecy: Perspectives for Christian Theology, Discipleship, and Ministry*, Interpretation (Louisville: Westminster John Knox, 2014).
[240] Collins, *1 & 2 Timothy and Titus*, 113; Mounce, *Pastoral Epistles*, 234.
[241] Scot McKnight, *A New Vision for Israel: The Teachings of Jesus in National Context* (Grand Rapids: Eerdmans, 1999), 138–139.

The Manifestations

The connection of v. 1 to v. 2 is tighter than some translations suggest: in the later times some will apostatize (or cause to apostatize) by becoming absorbed with *deceitful spirits and teachings of demons*, and this happens in those who have *consciences* that have been *seared* or ruined through false teaching. That is, a corrupted moral faculty rejects what God makes known to them. Whoever these people may be, they have infected the households for whom Timothy is now pastorally responsible.

In 4:3 the Apostle sketches some core heterodox teachings of the false teachers. They *forbid marriage*, or all sexual activity,[242] an expression of ascetic mark of spiritual fervor and they *abstain from certain foods*. Throughout Pauline literature there is an interplay between marriage and food practices, addressing both the proper and immoral forms based in creation and temple (Rom 13:11–15:13, 1 Cor 5–11; Col 2:16–3:11; cf. 2 Cor 6:14–7:1). This interaction of sex and food is echoed by other NT writers as well (1 Pet 4:1–11; 2 Pet 2; Rev 2:14, 20–23, 14:8–12, 18:1–19:10, 22:14–15; cf. Heb 13:1–19, Jas 1:12-18, Jude 1). Abstaining from both was a custom of various Second Temple Jewish and Greco-Roman communities.[243] These two human desires locked some to the physical world while asceticism disentangled them from the physical world to open connections with the spiritual world.[244] Towner points out that within other Pauline churches the theology concerning the proper place of food and sex was particularly connected to "Jewish tendencies and sensibilities, Spirit enthusiasm, [and] a too-realized view of eschatology,"[245] which could also be at play in the Ephesian churches.

The Apostle opposes these Ephesian apostates' form of asceticism even if in some circumstances he does approve of some forms of intentional

---

[242] Marshall, *Pastoral Epistles*, 541; Towner, *Timothy and Titus*, 293.

[243] Marshall, *Pastoral Epistles*, 533, 534–535; Witherington, *Letters and Homilies for Hellenized Christians*, 254. For a survey of the cosmic and cultural significance of sexual activity in classical antiquity, see Peter Brown, *The Body and Society: Men, Women, and Sexual Renunciation in Early Christianity* (New York: Columbia University Press, 2008); Kyle Harper, *From Shame to Sin: The Christian Transformation of Sexual Morality in Late Antiquity*, Revealing Antiquity 20 (Cambridge, MA: Harvard University Press, 2013). See also Collins' informative excursus "The Debate on Marriage and Food" in Collins, *1 & 2 Timothy and Titus*, 114–117.

[244] Dibelius and Conzelmann, *Pastoral Epistles*, 65–66; Marshall, *Pastoral Epistles*, 532–533, 533 n. 4.

[245] Towner, *Timothy and Titus*, 294.

restraint of desires (if temporary, if agreed upon, if not imposed on others). Many today push for ecological readings of Scripture, searching for anchors in the biblical text and 1 Timothy 4:4 fits the bill. Not only does the Apostle appeal to Genesis in speaking of God as creator, but the term used in v. 4 – *everything created by God is **good*** – is the LXX translation of the Hebrew *tov* in Genesis 1, where it is used for divine approval of divine acts, an approval rooted in divine aesthetics. Hence, it can be translated "excellence" or "beautiful." Food, then, is a gift of God (cf. Gen 1:29, 9:2–3). Those who trust God can eat God's gifts.[246]

God's excellent created order can be received by believers *with thanksgiving* (3, 4), that is, as a gift from God. They need not turn away from (Greek, *apoblētos*, "toss away") any food, whether kosher or not. Jewish prayer life entailed constant prayers of thanksgiving, so it is likely that this thanksgiving has in mind a blessing of God in partaking of food (Mark 8:6). The theological anchor for receiving all food (cf. Acts 10) as God's gift is because *it is sanctified by God's word and* [mealtime] *prayer* (v. 5). In the term *sanctified* we may discover the presence of kosher theology, though some think this is about food offered to idols now being rendered holy in Christ through Christian mealtime prayers (1 Cor 8–10).[247] Jesus made all foods clean (Mark 7:19), Peter learns this in Acts 10, and Paul himself said the same (Rom 14:14). Food was a tension point in the Pauline mission. The Apostle says food is made clean *by God's word*, which refers routinely to the gospel, and therefore the food is sanctified by Christ (e.g., something like Mark 7:19) through the Spirit (e.g., Acts 10).

The Apostle here is not countering the false teachers' need for specific or mechanistic practice with a better Christian ascetic practice. His use in this paragraph of *Spirit*, *created*, and *God's word* reveals his creation theology (cf. 2:13–14). The Ephesians must learn from the Apostle how to recognize Satan's work seen in Genesis 3 – that is, a corruption of the good command of God (1 Tim 1:6–11) leading to food practices that inherently deny the goodness of God and his creation (4:3–5).[248] The Ephesians are called to overcome such demonic teaching by obeying the *Spirit* and should actively

---

[246] There is a dispute whether "everything created by God" in 1 Tim 4:4 includes marriage and sexual relations. For discussions, see Knight, *Pastoral Epistles*, 189–193; Collins, *1 & 2 Timothy and Titus*, 118, 119; Towner, *Timothy and Titus*, 296.
[247] Marshall, *Pastoral Epistles*, 545; Kelly, *Pastoral Epistles*, 96–97.
[248] Towner, *Timothy and Titus*, 296.

recognize the good gifts created by God to be *received with thanksgiving*, such as marriage and food.[249]

4:6–10 A GOOD SERVANT OF CHRIST

Back and forth go the eyes of the Apostle. He gazes at the opponents of the gospel mission in Ephesus and then speaks to Timothy about them and about the church, and then back to the opponents, and back to Timothy. Here he turns his attention once again to Timothy. The back and forth also pertains to one's character and in this context character is called *godliness* (4:7, 8) but the Greek term *eusebeia* refers to a broader idea, to socially respectable or civilized piety.[250] Such a character makes for a *good servant* (4:6) and an "excellent" (*kalos*) minister of the gospel. Over and over the Apostle urges Timothy to character formation (1:18–19; 6:11–14, 20).

4:6 If you put these instructions before the brothers and sisters, you will be a good servant of Christ Jesus, nourished on the words of the faith and of the sound teaching that you have followed.
7 Have nothing to do with profane and foolish tales. Train yourself in godliness,
8 for, while physical training is of some value, godliness is valuable in every way, holding promise for both the present life and the life to come.
9 The saying is sure and worthy of full acceptance.
10 For to this end we toil and suffer reproach, because we have our hope set on the living God, who is the Savior of all people, especially of those who believe.

The passage begins with personal words for Timothy that flow into a wider compass of teaching (4:6–7 leads to 4:8–10).

When the Apostle speaks here of *these instructions* he most likely refers to what has just been said about the opponents (4:1–5), which includes the claim that what God has made to be "good" (4:4, *kalos*) is to be embraced. That embrace makes for a *good servant* (4:6, again *kalos*; See Closer Look below), and here *good* is God's evaluation of a calling done according to

---

[249] Collins, *1 & 2 Timothy and Titus*, 112. Witherington points out that the creational theology that declares food a good gift from God is the same theology of 1 Corinthians that claims both marriage and food are created gifts by God; Witherington, *Letters and Homilies for Hellenized Christians*, 254–255.
[250] Hoklotubbe, *Civilized Piety*.

God's design. There is a softer sense of expectation in *put these instructions before*. Timothy is to continue his work of teaching and leading according to the apostolic gospel he has received, which entails opposing the false teachers but without using a heavy hand. The Apostle's use of *brothers and sisters* (NRSV's inclusive rendering of *adelphoi*) could be rendered "siblings."[251] Siblings frames Christian relationships in more intimate ways than "friends" and depicts the ecclesial gathering as a home and family.[252]

> A Closer Look: *Kalos* in the Pastoral Epistles[253]
>
> 1 Tim 1:8 Now we know that the law is good, if one uses it legitimately;
> 1 Tim 1:18 This charge I commit to you, Timothy, my child, in accordance with the prophecies made earlier about you, so that by following them you may fight the good fight,
> 1 Tim 2:3 This is right and is acceptable in the sight of God our Savior,
> 1 Tim 3:1 The saying is sure: whoever aspires to the office of bishop desires a noble task.
> 1 Tim 3:7 Moreover, he must be well thought of by outsiders, so that he may not fall into disgrace and the snare of the devil.
> 1 Tim 3:13 for those who serve well as deacons gain a good standing for themselves and great boldness in the faith that is in Christ Jesus.
> 1 Tim 4:4 For everything created by God is good, and nothing is to be rejected, provided it is received with thanksgiving;
> 1 Tim 4:6 If you put these instructions before the brothers and sisters, you will be a good servant of Christ Jesus, nourished on the words of the faith and of the sound teaching that you have followed.
> 1 Tim 5:10 she must be well attested for her good works, as one who has brought up children, shown hospitality, washed the saints' feet, helped the afflicted, and devoted herself to doing good in every way.
> 1 Tim 5:25 So also good works are conspicuous, and even when they are not, they cannot remain hidden.

---

[251] Scot McKnight, *Pastor Paul: Nurturing a Culture of Christoformity in the Church*, Theological Explorations for the Church Catholic (Grand Rapids: Brazos, 2019), 57–78.

[252] We stand with Marshall and others that this use of the term "brothers," in Greek *adelphoi*, is not limited to the male leaders mentored by Timothy; see Marshall, *Pastoral Epistles*, 548–549; Collins, *1 & 2 Timothy and Titus*, 120–121; Towner, *Timothy and Titus*, 303 and n. 2.

[253] See a discussion in Marshall, *Pastoral Epistles* 227-229.

> 1 Tim 6:12–13 Fight the good fight of the faith; take hold of the eternal life to which you were called and for which you made the good confession in the presence of many witnesses. **13** In the presence of God, who gives life to all things, and of Christ Jesus, who in his testimony before Pontius Pilate made the good confession, I charge you
> 1 Tim 6:18–19 They are to do good, to be rich in good works, generous, and ready to share, **19** thus storing up for themselves the treasure of a good foundation for the future, so that they may take hold of the life that really is life.
> 2 Tim 1:14 Guard the good deposit entrusted to you, with the help of the Holy Spirit living in us.
> 2 Tim 2:3 Share in suffering like a good soldier of Christ Jesus.
> 2 Tim 4:7 I have fought the good fight; I have finished the race; I have kept the faith.
> Titus 2:7 in all things, offering yourself as a model of good works and in your teaching offering integrity, gravity,
> Titus 2:14 He it is who gave himself for us that he might redeem us from all iniquity and purify for himself a people of his own who are zealous for good deeds.
> Titus 3:8 The saying is sure. I desire that you insist on these things, so that those who have come to believe in God may be careful to devote themselves to good works; these things are excellent and profitable to everyone.
> Titus 3:14 And let people learn to devote themselves to good works in order to meet urgent needs, so that they may not be unproductive.

A *good servant* is *nourished on the words of the faith and of the sound teaching* (4:6), which description is juxtaposed to failure of the false teachers with their "faith in lying spirits and demonic teachings" (4:1). The synonyms *words* and *teaching* are what Timothy has *followed* (a term evoking the Gospels' emphasis on discipleship), while the term *nourished* focuses on intentional personal growth in theology. These two terms for content (*words, teaching*) are modified by favorite terms in the PEs, *faith* and *sound*. Being *nourished* is an intentional activity, a continual and consistent practice of studying the Scriptures for a proper and *sound teaching* according to the apostolic understanding of the gospel (1:8–11; 2 Tim 3:15–17).

The good servant thus will *have nothing to do with* corrupted theology, here expressed in derogatory terms: *profane* (cf. 1:4–5) *and foolish tales.* Both point at not believing nonsense as well as not engaging in intellectual contests about foolish teachings, which in 1:4 were called "speculations."

There is also a connection here to the Apostle's contention with certain women in the Ephesian church (cf. 2:9–15, 5:13; 2 Tim 3:6).[254] In contrast, he tells Timothy in 4:7 to *train yourself in godliness*, that is "civilized piety." *Train yourself* reminds of v. 6's "nourished" only this time in an athletic register. While Jews often avoided the nakedness entailed in athletic training in Greek and Roman cities (including Tiberias),[255] the prevalent public athletic contests, including even in Jerusalem itself, allowed for images drawn from athletics to become common tropes (cf. Heb 5:14; 12:11). The good servant trains in *godliness*, not in physical competition nor in intellectual dominance, and in this way becomes a leader in the community of faith as an example of the good life.[256]

This all leads to another citation of a *saying* (4:9), quoted apparently from the Apostle's commonplace book: *while physical training is of some value, godliness* ["civilized piety"] *is valuable in every way* (4:8). The Apostle emphasizes what is eternal and effective, which means the physical has *some value* (Greek, *pros oligon*, "for a little while" or better "for some profit, value"). Does the Apostle have asceticism in mind with *physical training*, often enough connected to training as *askesis*, in mind or is this simply a comment about physical exercise in and of itself? We think it highly unlikely, after the tie to 4:1–5 in 4:6 itself, that the training of one's body is all he means. Asceticism as intentional somatic discipline (in 4:3 both sexual activity and foods are in view) is given a slight (*some value*) nod of affirmation here.[257] Regardless of that interpretation, *godliness* has *promise for both the present life and the life to come*. In providing a both-and the Apostle reveals that asceticism is not outright rejected but diminished in comparison to eternity. Christianity without life beyond death and without (to use the common term) heaven, is a Christianity without resurrection, which is – to put it bluntly – not Christianity at all.[258] Jesus and the Apostles are suffused with eschatological hope beyond this life.

---

[254] Witherington, *Letters and Homilies for Hellenized Christians*, 255–256.
[255] H. A. Harris, *Greek Athletics and the Jews*, Trivium Special Publications 3 (Cardiff: University of Wales Press, 1976).
[256] Witherington, *Letters and Homilies for Hellenized Christians*, 255.
[257] Kelly, *Pastoral Epistles*, 99–101; Towner, *Timothy and Titus*, 306–307. Contra Marshall, *Pastoral Epistles*, 552.
[258] N. T. Wright, *Surprised by Hope: Rethinking Heaven, the Resurrection, and the Mission of the Church* (New York: HarperOne, 2008); Scot McKnight, *The Heaven Promise: Engaging the Bible's Truth About Life to Come* (Colorado Springs: WaterBrook, 2015).

Verse 9, which is a footnote or a parenthetical remark, makes this "saying" contrasting somatic exercise and training in civilized piety[259] a teaching fit for all in the church of Ephesus: it is *worthy of full acceptance*, or "reception by all." The civilized piety to which the Apostle is calling Timothy and all in Ephesus is one that leads to Christian *hope* (v. 10), drawing out what was just said in v. 8b. *To this end* refers to the gospel mission in which Paul and his followers were engaged. The Apostle identifies with his audience in using *we toil and suffer reproach* but makes clear what is visible in every chapter of Paul's own life: persecution, discipline, hard labor, and the constant need for faithfulness as they carried on the gospel work (cf. esp. Col 1:24–2:5). He points out the need for this kind of effort and training *because we have our hope set on the living God*. There is no disjunction between *toil and labor*, common language for Christian missionary effort, and God's saving work.

This *God* is the *Savior of all people* (4:10), among whom are those who believe. This verse is the most appealed-to universalism text in the entire New Testament because the Apostle continues not with "i.e., those who believe" but *especially of those who believe*. The latter then is a subgroup of the former ("all people"). Most in the traditional camp think of the former (all humans) as the object of preaching and the latter as those who believe (cf. 1 Tim 2:3–5), or that *especially* does mean "i.e." or "that is" or "namely."[260] In which case *all people* refers only to believers. A second option could be that the false teachers are offering an exclusive gospel that is not universally available. The Apostle could then be countering that view with a claim about God's own universal love.[261]

We can muster a little more nuance along the lines of inaugurated eschatology. The Apostle's eschatological hope is the *promise for both the present life and the life to come*. The present realization of this *promise* is worked out in the *present life* in their civilized piety, their *godliness* (cf. Titus 1:1–3). Here is our suggestion then: God is the *Savior of all* humanity because the embodiment of *godliness* has come into the world as the mystery of civilized piety, namely, Jesus Christ (3:16). God is Savior *especially of those who believe* because Christians actively participate in

---

[259] For discussions of whether this saying refers to v. 8, to v. 8a and 8b or just 8a, or if it includes some or all of v. 10, see Marshall, *Pastoral Epistles*, 554.
[260] Marshall, *Pastoral Epistles*, 556; Knight, *Pastoral Epistles*, 203–204.
[261] Towner, *Timothy and Titus*, 311; Witherington, *Letters and Homilies for Hellenized Christians*, 257.

the civilized piety revealed and made possible in the redemption of Christ (3:15–16). This in-Christ civilized piety is a qualitatively different kind of *pietas* than the life of the world. Such concepts of active, intentional, and participatory salvation through faith are found throughout Paul as an embodied reality in the present.[262] God's work of salvation is intended to renew all creation, including all of humanity. However, participation in this inauguration of redemption is not passive but is instead an active embodiment of Jesus Christ's own civilized piety.[263] If one strives for a measure of consistency in the Pauline corpus one would have to argue then that faith producing civilized piety, or *godliness*, is necessary for salvation.

4:11–16 MINISTRY OF TEACHING

The discourse of the PEs moves back and forth from directly addressing either Timothy and Titus to speaking about or even to the congregations which they are to be leading. Here the Apostle turns directly to Timothy with a string of imperatives (asterisks in the text that follows). Once again character, which we have defined already as "goodness/excellence" or (in Hebrew, *tov*), emerges in 4:12 with *set the believers an example* as well as in 4:15's *Put these things into practice . . . so that all may see your progress* as well as in 4:16 with *Pay close attention to yourself . . . both yourself.* Timothy's personal progress in civilized piety is more important than his pastoral ministry because the latter flows out of the former.[264] The Apostle conceives of the pastor as someone whose life is exemplary, in which, to use the words of Parker Palmer, he is being told to "let your life speak,"[265] and out of such a life Timothy was to teach. The educational culture of the Greco-Roman world was one in which emulation was the key (e.g., Seneca, *Epistles* 6.5–6).[266]

---

[262] Michael J. Gorman, *Becoming the Gospel: Paul, Participation, and Mission*, The Gospel and Our Culture Series (Grand Rapids: Eerdmans, 2015); Nijay K. Gupta, *Paul and the Language of Faith* (Grand Rapids: Eerdmans, 2020).

[263] For a similar evaluation of v. 10 see Towner, *Timothy and Titus*, 309–312. For a pastoral reflection, Hutson, *1–2 Timothy, Titus*, 119.

[264] Dunn, "1–2 Timothy, Titus," 813–816.

[265] Parker J. Palmer, *Let Your Life Speak: Listening for the Voice of Vocation* (San Francisco: Jossey-Bass, 1999).

[266] Hutson, *1–2 Timothy, Titus*, 114–115.

4:11 Command and teach these things.
12 Let no one despise your youth, but set the believers an example in speech and conduct, in love, in faith, in purity.
13 Until I arrive, give attention to the public reading of scripture, to exhorting, to teaching.
14 Do not neglect the gift that is in you, which was given to you through prophecy with the laying on of hands by the council of elders.
15 Put these things into practice, devote yourself to them, so that all may see your progress.
16 Pay close attention to yourself and to your teaching; continue in these things, for in doing this you will save both yourself and your hearers.

The passage is a string of instructions and we will move from one imperative to another, beginning with the double-command to *command* and *teach* in 1 Timothy 4:11, with the former carrying the sense even of "order" (as in CEB, NIV). Such language reminds that this letter instructs Timothy with apostolic authority and directs him to lead the church in Ephesus. What are *these . . . things*? The previous paragraph's content.

In a culture like ours where relevance dominates, the third imperative (*let no one despise your youth*; 1 Tim 4:12) will be heard in precisely the wrong way. In our contemporary world the young leader is the hot-ticket item while the older leader is pushed off the platform as "old school." The classical world had a culture that valued age and wisdom (e.g., Proverbs, Sirach) so respecting youth was a challenge (cf. 1 Cor 16:10–11).[267] Timothy was young enough not to be considered an elder in a culture where elders ruled and would think of him as a "young whippersnapper." But what were the parameters of "youth" and "old" in the world of the PEs? It varied, but a general approximation would be that anyone under forty was a youth while anyone over fifty was old.[268]

> ### A Closer Look: Age
>
> **Josephus, Vita 9** Moreover, when I was a child, and about fourteen years of age, I was commended by all for the love I had to learning; on which account the high priests and principal men of the city came then frequently to me together, in order

---
[267] Towner, *Timothy and Titus*, 313–314.
[268] A good discussion can be found in Marshall, *Pastoral Epistles*, 239.

> to know my opinion about the accurate understanding of points of the law. (translation Whiston, updated)
> **m. Avot 5:21** He would say, "(1) At five to Scripture, (2) ten to Mishnah, (3) thirteen to religious duties, (4) fifteen to Talmud, (5) eighteen to the wedding canopy, (6) twenty to responsibility for providing for a family, (7) thirty to fullness of strength, (8) forty to understanding, (9) fifty to counsel, (10) sixty to old age, (11) seventy to ripe old age, (12) eighty to remarkable strength, (13) ninety to a bowed back, and (14) at a hundred – he is like a corpse who has already passed and gone from this world.

What earns respect, the Apostle instructs in v. 12, is lived theology – a life that speaks the gospel (*set the believers an example*), where *example* is a *tupos*, or a "type," a model, an example, a paradigm of civilized piety. As Jesus taught his disciples to follow him (Mark 1:16–20), so Paul himself urged imitating him (1 Cor 11:1), and thus he urges Timothy to become a model worthy of imitation. Moral development has always been more about emulation than information.[269] Five terms constitute this expected *example*, beginning with *speech*, which in Greek is nothing but *logos* (in "word") and will capture both casual conversation and public speaking (cf. 1 Tim 5:17; Tit 1:9), with suggestions of reason and logic.[270] The list continues with *conduct*, where once again we meet the emphasis on lived theology as a witness to the gospel, and such conduct is "civilized piety" (*eusebeia*).[271] Next comes *love* (see at 1:5) and *faith* (see at 1:2) as summary terms for Christian virtue. The last term for Timothy's exemplary life is *purity*, a cultic term expressing holiness (cf. 1 Pet 3:2), as in *1 Clement* 21:7: "let them display a character of purity, worthy of love" (Ehrman, LCL), but also includes the particular undertones of sexual chastity (made explicit in 5:2).[272]

The Apostle anticipates returning to Ephesus, but he says *until I arrive* (1 Tim 4:13; cf. 3:14–15) expend your energies on three things: *reading, exhorting, teaching*. The first is commonly translated as public or communal reading of scripture in gathered assemblies, as in the NRSV (*to the*

---

[269] Collins, *1 & 2 Timothy and Titus*, 128; Towner, *Timothy and Titus*, 314.
[270] Marshall, *Pastoral Epistles*, 561.
[271] Used also at Gal 1:13; Eph 4:22; Heb 13:7; James 3:13; 1 Peter 1:15, 18; 2:12; 3:1, 16; 2 Pet 2:7; 3:11.
[272] Towner, *Timothy and Titus*, 315–316; Knight, *Pastoral Epistles*, 206–207; Mounce, *Pastoral Epistles*, 260; Kelly, *Pastoral Epistles*, 104; Ward, *I & II Timothy and Titus*, 75.

public reading of scripture; so also NIV, with CEB having "public reading") but the Greek text only says "to reading." Gathering to hear someone read a text in the Greco-Roman and Jewish world (cf. Acts 13:15; 2 Cor 3:14) was common so it is natural for Paul to instruct his churches to read his letters publicly (Col 4:16; 1 Thess 5:27).[273] Once one comprehends that such reading is the public and communal reading of Scripture then one understands that the *exhorting* and *teaching* are probably pastoral instructions based upon what has been read (cf. 2 Tim 3:16–17). It should be noted that the purpose of *reading* the Scriptures is more than to provide information for *exhorting* and *teaching* but also to form a narrative framework by which Christians appropriate an ecclesial identity.[274] What was being read would have been our Old Testament and early apostolic writings, including a Gospel or two as well as Paul's own letters.[275]

Mentioning reading, exhorting, and teaching prompts the Apostle to remind Timothy not to *neglect the gift that is in you*, presumably the gift of teaching that his youthful propriety may have chosen not to exercise or which was silenced somewhat by elders.[276] This *gift* is a charism (cf. 1 Cor 12–14) *given to* him *through prophecy with the laying on of hands by the council of elders*. Here we encounter an ecclesiology, both charismatic-pneumatological as well as structural-ecclesial. Prophecies were uttered over or about Timothy by early Christian Spirit-inspired prophets (cf. Acts 13:1–3) as Paul (cf. 2 Tim 1:6) and the *elders* pressed their hands upon him (cf. Acts 6:6; 8:16–19; 9:12, 17; 13:3; 19:6) and so dispensed the Spirit to him. Recognized, educated, and spiritually formed leaders are those responsible for administering gifts to the next generation of teachers. Less is said than is practiced in ecclesiastical bodies today but there is more said here than is often taught or practiced among some. What is absent here is any sense of authority; what is present is a Spirit-based and ecclesially shaped dispensing of a gift to a young man.[277]

---

[273] Brian J. Wright, *Communal Reading*.
[274] For a good overview of the importance of this function of public reading as a practice, see Towner, *Timothy and Titus*, 317–321, 318 n. 29.
[275] Witherington, *Letters and Homilies for Hellenized Christians*, 258–259.
[276] Marshall, *Pastoral Epistles*, 564.
[277] For a good discussion of the evidence, Marshall, 565, 567–569. See also Mounce, *Pastoral Epistles*, 263; Kelly, *Pastoral Epistles*, 106.

Timothy's observable behaviors are to indicate *progress* in character formation (1 Tim 4:15; 2 Tim 3:9).[278] Apart from which Paul's gospel cannot be understood.[279] It is most probable that what Timothy is to *put ... into practice* includes both his behaviors and his gift exercised when reading, exhorting, and teaching. There is tension in the New Testament between hiding one's Christian practices (Matt 6:1-18) and doing things visibly before others as a way of witnessing to the gospel of Christ (5:13-16; Mark 12:41-44; here).

Noticeably again, the Apostle turns to Timothy's personal development in the next imperative: *pay close attention to yourself* (1 Tim 4:16). It seems facile to distinguish here between development in theological understanding in contrast with development in character since the two are indistinguishable.[280] Timothy's own behavior bolsters and displays his faithful *teaching* of the gospel, which leads to a redemption able to *save* both himself and those who obey his pastoral care, his Ephesian *hearers* (cf. 2 Clem 19).[281] The term *hearers* of the gospel carries a strong nuance of obedience and participation as a disciple (Matt 13:1-23, 28:18-20; Rom 10:5-21; cf. 2 Tim 2:14).[282] While Timothy's *teaching* includes the power to *save* his Ephesian *hearers* from the false teachers' teachings,[283] ultimately salvation here refers to final redemption (cf. 2:15; esp. 1 Peter 1:5; 2:2).[284] Such a warning tempers and limits the universalism doxology of the Apostle in 4:10 by recognizing Timothy's fundamental role in mediating, or at least maintaining, the salvation of others. We encounter once again the fact that the common early Christian sense of redemption was not quite so certain as is found in some circles of Christianity today.

5:1-16 OLDER FOLKS AND WIDOWS

The Apostle's teachings impress us since they are from someone pastoring from afar but still covering a variety of seemingly up-to-date topics.

---

[278] There is also a possible connection to how Stoics talked about their philosophical progress in virtue development by the Apostle's use of the Greek term *proskopē* when referring to Timothy's *progress*; see Collins, *1 & 2 Timothy and Titus*, 131-132.
[279] David A. deSilva, *Transformation: The Heart of Paul's Gospel* (Bellingham: Lexham, 2014).
[280] *Contra* Marshall, *Pastoral Epistles*, 571.
[281] For a similar assessment, Collins, *1 & 2 Timothy and Titus*, 132.
[282] Mounce, *Pastoral Epistles*, 265.
[283] Witherington, *Letters and Homilies for Hellenized Christians*, 260.
[284] Towner, *Timothy and Titus*, 328.

Commentary on 1 Timothy

Nothing is more realistic and relevant than relationships (5:1–6:2), beginning with the older folks.

Older Folks

One of the Apostle's concerns is how to speak with seniors in the churches, a concern indicating more of a wisdom culture.

5:1 Do not speak harshly to an older man, but speak to him as to a father, to younger men as brothers,
2 to older women as mothers, to younger women as sisters – with absolute purity.

The Apostle's instructions here have to do with common decency or civilized piety, which decency requires social deference to seniors on account of their wisdom[285] (cf. Lev 19:32). Conduct worthy of public respect excludes carelessly shaming elders: *do not speak harshly*. Behind *speak to him* is the Greek term normally conveying the sense of encouragement (*parakaleo*; so CEB). Everyone is to be treated as family: an *older man* is therefore to be treated as a *father*, and younger males as *brothers*. Language derived from the family register is at the heart of the Pauline understanding of the church[286] and, as Paul Trebilco has explained,[287] will have connoted relations marked by love, harmony, cooperation, conflict, forgiveness, and some kind of reasonable hierarchy. Paul himself developed sibling and family relations in the direction of love, mutual growth, and boundaries, all with the sense that Jesus was the eldest Brother. While the same Greek term behind *older man* is found for an elder in 5:17 (*presbuteros*), most think its appearance in 5:1 is about male (and in 5:2 female) seniors in general.

As older men are to be considered fathers, so older women (*presbuteras*) are to be related to as *mothers* and younger women as *sisters*, with one important proviso: with sexual *purity* (cf. Titus 2:6). The NRSV's *absolute* is stronger than the Greek, which has *pas* and could be translated as "all" or as in the CEB with "appropriate respect." The Apostle nurtures civilized

---

[285] Dunn, "First and Second Letters to Timothy and the Letter to Titus," 819–820, 824.
[286] McKnight, *Pastor Paul*, 57–78.
[287] Paul Trebilco, *Self-Designations and Group Identity in the New Testament* (Cambridge: Cambridge University Press, 2012), 16–67.

piety absent of sexual impropriety.[288] These two verses are also guidance for the whole community.[289]

Widows

From the older men and older women the Apostle now turns to an especially serious concern for earliest Christianity, namely, the care of widows: who counts, who doesn't, and how should they be treated and evaluated. The details are fuzzy enough even if the general direction is clear: provision for widows is expected, but no one should take advantage of the church's support. Fuzzy details have led to numerous speculative scenarios for a variety of terms and social realities in this text, not least a discussion about an official "order" of widows.[290] A widespread Christian practice of benefaction, or compassion for those in need, was being challenged to find its own way. Not all widows could be supported by the resources the churches had at its disposal. Some have concluded that the percentage of women aged forty and over who were widows may have been as high as 40 percent.[291]

5:3 Honor widows who are really widows.
   4 If a widow has children or grandchildren, they should first learn their religious duty to their own family and make some repayment to their parents, for this is pleasing in God's sight.
   5 The real widow, left alone, has set her hope on God and continues in supplications and prayers night and day,
   6 but the widow who lives for pleasure is dead even while she lives.
   7 Give these commands as well, so that they may be above reproach.
   8 And whoever does not provide for relatives, and especially for family members, has denied the faith and is worse than an unbeliever.
   9 Let a widow be put on the list if she is not less than sixty years old and has been married only once;

---

[288] Witherington, *Letters and Homilies for Hellenized Christians*, 262.
[289] Collins, *1 & 2 Timothy and Titus*, 132-133, 134.
[290] Cohick and Hughes, *Christian Women in the Patristic World*, 67-69.
[291] For recent discussions of the social realities that could be at work, see Winter, *Seek the Welfare of the City: Christians as Benefactors and Citizens* (Grand Rapids: Eerdmans, 1994), 62-78; Winter, *Roman Wives, Roman Widows*, 123-140. We don't need to pose an order of widows, or at least an official list, over against the emphasis on benefactions.

10 she must be well attested for her good works, as one who has brought up children, shown hospitality, washed the saints' feet, helped the afflicted, and devoted herself to doing good in every way.
11 But refuse to put younger widows on the list, for when their sensual desires alienate them from Christ, they want to marry,
12 and so they incur condemnation for having violated their first pledge.
13 Besides that, they learn to be idle, gadding about from house to house, and they are not merely idle, but also gossips and busybodies, saying what they should not say.
14 So I would have younger widows marry, bear children, and manage their households, so as to give the adversary no occasion to revile us.
15 For some have already turned away to follow Satan.
16 If any believing woman has relatives who are widows, let her assist them; let the church not be burdened, so that it can assist those who are real widows.

In male-centered worlds widows are too often neglected. Without realizing their own aims both Judaism and Christianity formed practices to care for widows. Three forms of support are seen in this passage: (1) family support (5:3–8), (2) an apparently official church list of widows who were supported (5:9–10), and (3) perhaps wider family members caring for widow relatives (5:16). In what follows we will eschew the textual order and focus our comments by topic: first, real widows (5:3, 5–6, 9–10); second, families supporting widows (5:4, 7–8); third, instructions about younger widows (5:11–15) and, fourth, the Christian's obligation for widows in their family (5:16).

One theme shapes the whole: compassion. Christians are expected to care for others, especially family members, and that means especially the vulnerable widow. At work in this social condition was also the reality of a dowry, given by the bride's father to the groom, and upon the death of her husband, the dowry was retained by the widow. That dowry is not mentioned this text but we could assume the dowry had been used and the widows were now in need of relief and routine support.

Real Widows (5:3, 5–6, 9–10)

To *honor* a widow was to provide in a manner that respects her social status, as the term *honor* was a preeminent social category in the Roman world (cf. 1 Tim 6:1).[292] Such *honor* carried connotations and expectations of financial support (cf. 5:17). Care for the widow was a characteristic of Judaism (Ex 22:22; Deut 10:18; 14:29; 16:11, 14; 24:17, 19–21; 26:12–13; 27:19, etc.) and earliest Christianity (Acts 6:1–6). In Ephesus there were too many women requesting support and the Apostle's concern was for those who were *really widows* (better than the CEB's decision to flatten the expression to "truly needy"). The problem could have been a conflict between the ideal widow of the Apostle and actual widows, some of whom were younger and pushing for sexual abstinence.[293]

1 Timothy 5:9–10 defines what constitutes someone who *really* is a *widow*. The "real" widow is *left alone* (meaning "has no relatives")[294] and thus can *set her hope on God* and be devoted to a life of prayer, that is to *supplications and prayers night and day* (5:5). The verse strikes a tone of the widow wanting to spend her life this way, but the text will strike some as insensitive to the genuine problem of loneliness and depression among our widows today. A model of widows devoted to prayer is at work. For such holy women the church has responsibility because the God of the Scriptures has an eye out for widows.

Verse six attempts to unmask the *widow who lives for pleasure*, and the term used here (*spatalaō*) indicates material luxury (cf. James 5:5; LXX Ezk 16:49) more than sexual indulgences,[295] which luxury points us back to the ostentatious dress of some women (2:9). Connecting 1 Tim 2 to 1 Tim 5's widows, especially the young widows, permits the reader to enter into a more socially realistic context for both passages, especially the former.[296] Such an ostentatious widow, the Apostle announces, is really *dead* (1 Tim 5:6).

At 1 Timothy 5:9 we encounter a verb (*katalego*) that is translated something like the NRSV's *put on the list* in most English translations, and it seems to indicate there was a register of real widows who were then dispensed with goods and support. Next (5:9b–10) comes the qualifications for who is so registered:

---

[292] For the wider discussion, David deSilva, *Honor, Patronage, Kinship and Purity: Unlocking New Testament Culture* (Downers Grove: IVP Academic, 2000).
[293] Manabu Tsuji, "Zwischen Ideal und Realität: Zu den Witwen in 1 Tim 5.3–16," *NTS* 47 (2001): 92–104.
[294] Winter, *Seek the Welfare of the City*, 71.
[295] Towner, *Timothy and Titus*, 342.
[296] Towner, with support from Winter, makes a similar connection between the widow conversation of 1 Tim 5 to the wealthy women of 1 Tim 2; see Towner, 342. See too Elsa Tamez, *Struggles for Power in Early Christianity: A Study of the First Letter to Timothy* (Maryknoll, NY: Orbis, 2007).

Commentary on 1 Timothy

(1) *not less than sixty years old;*
(2) *has been married only once;*
(3) *she must be well attested for her **good works**,*
(4) *as one who has brought up children,*
(5) *shown hospitality,*
(6) *washed the saints' feet,*
(7) *helped the afflicted,* and
(8) *devoted herself to **doing good** ["works" should be present] in every way.*

Besides age, which is explained in part in the younger widows paragraph at 5:11–15, and being married but once, the fundamental characteristic is nothing less than civilized piety, here crystallized in #3's *good works*, which includes her family life, her hospitality, her compassion, and her *doing good* ["works" should be in the translation] *in every way* (5:10's #8). Numbers 3 and 8 then encapsulate the whole, though #3's *good* is a different Greek term (*kalos*, "excellent") than #8's (*agathos*). Both describe a generous person, who now has "earned the right" to receive generosity at the end of their gospel-conformed life.

The age of *no less than sixty*, a litote, suggests women who are both needy and who are probably beyond the ability to provide for themselves. It is less likely that this means beyond the age of remarriage. A parallel to elders and deacons then appears in *has been married only once* (cf. 1 Tim 3:2, 12). The NIV has "has been faithful to her husband" (similarly the CEB), suggesting this is more about faithfulness rather than the number of times married, and Marshall appeals for this view to Titus 1:6 (a "one woman kind of man"). But at the time a once-married woman, the *univira*, was a virtue connected to social respectability.[297]

As stated above, #3 and #8 encompass #4–7, with 4–7 making explicit what the Apostle means by "good/excellent works."[298] As stated above (on 3:1–7), excellent works describe a life lived consistent with God's good design and manifested in central virtues of the Jewish as well as Greco-Roman world (civilized piety): hence, justice, love, mercy, peace, compassion, and holiness. In this text the focus is on love, mercy, and compassion for one's family, the church, and the sick. A real widow is one who has the public and ecclesial reputation for goodness.

---

[297] On the *univira* ideal, see the discussion above, section 3.1–7 "Bishops." Collins contends that the Hebrew Bible's category for scriptural widows refers only to once-married women; see Collins, *1 & 2 Timothy and Titus*, 137.

[298] #'s 4–8 are aorists and #3 is a present participle, giving slightly more emphasis to #3.

Being good for a widow means that she *has brought up* [or *nurtured*] *children*, and the question arises: if she is a real widow, which could mean without children or grandchildren to care for her, what children are in view? Many suggest, rightly we think, orphans are in view.[299] Notice the connection of widows and orphans in James 1:27. Goodness is seen as well in that she has *shown hospitality* and *washed the saints' feet*, expressions of early Christian hospitality (3:2; also Rom 12:13; Heb 13:2).[300] Footwashing, often connected with the work of servants (John 13), was a social act of kindness for those entering one's home (e.g., Gen 19:2; Luke 7:36–50; 8:1–3). In this verse it may be a metaphor for menial service.[301]

Family Support for Widows (5:4, 7–8)

The Apostle advocates family support of widows because it is a *religious duty* which means the widow's family members must *learn* civilized piety. He focuses here on *children or grandchildren* but in v. 16 (perhaps, too, in v. 8) this will expand to *relatives* in a broader way, which echoes Jesus' warning about *korban* (Mark 7:9–13). Care for widows is a *repayment to their parents*. Ultimately, such repayment *is pleasing*, or "acceptable" and "receptive," *in God's sight*.

The Apostle reminds Timothy to teach these things so the church will be *above reproach*, another indicator of social respect (5:7). The gravity of these instructions becomes forceful in verse eight's generalizing admonition: *And whoever does not provide for relatives ... has denied the faith and is worse than an unbeliever*. One hears in these words not only the fifth commandment ("honor your father and your mother"; Ex 20:12) but the wisdom of generations about familial love and provision. The word behind *provide* indicates provision that is planned and in that provision the *faith* of the person becomes visible. Those who don't provide are like the *unbeliever*.

---

[299] Marshall, *Pastoral Epistles*, 595.
[300] Christine D. Pohl, *Making Room: Recovering Hospitality as a Christian Tradition* (Grand Rapids: Eerdmans, 1999); Amy G. Oden, ed., *And You Welcomed Me: A Sourcebook on Hospitality in Early Christianity* (Nashville: Abingdon, 2001); Andrew Arterbury, *Entertaining Angels: Early Christian Hospitality in Its Mediterranean Setting*, New Testament Monographs 8 (Sheffield: Sheffield Phoenix Press, 2005). Arterbury's study is especially valuable for its documentation of the social realities from ancient novels.
[301] Some suggest this mention of footwashing indicates an official service in the church, like baptism or eucharist; so Neudorfer, *1. Timotheus*, 195; Marshall, *Pastoral Epistles*, 597.

The implication of these instructions limited the number of widows eligible for the church's own resources. The apostle Paul's teaching in 2 Corinthians 8:13–15 on equality is at least echoed in the balancing of provision that Apostle probes in 1 Timothy 5:1–16.

Younger Widows (5:11–15)

Experience with some failure in how best to show compassion for widows leads to more instructions: the *younger widows* are not to be enrolled on the official register. There is a stricture here based on age, on *sensual desire* (5:11) and on their then *having violated their first pledge* (v. 12), or "the initial act of faith to follow Christ."[302] This suggests that widows on the list indicated their commitment to Christ, which commitment also implies a subsequent choice to remarry meant renouncing the faith. The age is certainly less than sixty (cf. 5:9), but this term *younger* probably indicates a younger age, perhaps the twenties and thirties. At any rate, they are still capable of having children (5:14).

There are issues here in translation. *Sensual desires*, a strong expression, describes for many a sexual desire for marriage that results somehow in abandoning the faith. Perhaps the widows want to get remarried to an unbeliever.[303] It is wise for us to admit there are unknowns and assumptions that do not lead to clarity for interpretation. We can say the language of the text is less about the sexual or marital *desire* than a yearning against Christ. It could be translated "whenever they have strong impulses against (*katastrēniaō*) the Christos they want to marry." To be sure, it is an odd expression, and could combine a desire for sexual relations with a desire to abandon Christ and proper Christian civilized piety.[304] Perhaps there are other echoes at work, too. Again, *alienate them from Christ* indicates apostasy, an expression too strong to refer only to violating a registered vow of celibacy. Thus, *their first pledge* to Christ was an official expression of the widow's total dependence on God (5:5). Being overcome by desire

---

[302] Marshall, 599–600. Knight believes this pledge to be one of dedicated religious life as a widow supported by the care of the Ephesian church (cf. 1 Cor 7:32–35). See Knight, *Pastoral Epistles*, 226–227, 228.
[303] Towner, *Timothy and Titus*, 351–352; Mounce, *Pastoral Epistles*, 291; Collins, *1 & 2 Timothy and Titus*, 141; Witherington, *Letters and Homilies for Hellenized Christians*, 270–271. Ward does not believe this desire must be categorized as sexual, rather he describes it as an overwhelming desire for marriage that distracts from or overrides their pledge to Christ, see Ward, *I & II Timothy and Titus*, 85.
[304] See Johnson, *1–2 Timothy*, 266.

for marriage, perhaps as an entrance into or a maintenance of a high-status social life, described in 5:13 as "gadding about," becomes a symbolic act of apostasy for a widow who *is dead* (5:6).[305] One might in this desire for such a life find another connection to the ostentatious women in 1 Timothy 2:9.[306]

The Apostle's teaching about the *younger widows* seems to unmask deeper issues than who is on a list and who is not, and it is deeper than only violating one's previous commitment to celibacy. He engages perhaps a new group of younger widows,[307] perhaps what is sometimes called "the new Roman woman,"[308] by speaking of *sensual desires* (5:11), being *idle* and *gadding about*, and being *gossips and busybodies*, which is unfolded into *saying what they should not say* (5:13). This register of terms may derive more from the hyperbole of polemics than from observations of behavior. In such a register this term points at a specific social movement of wealthy women. Being *idle* describes women who have sufficient funds not to work, and therefore women having no need of funds from the church, or perhaps *idle* is a description of women using church funds to do nothing. Such younger widows are using their idle time not for excellent works but instead they are engaging in meaningless, even devious, chatter (or intellectual conversations about false teachings). The last expression of v. 13, *saying what they should not say*, indicates that these younger widows expostulate false teachings (cf. Titus 1:11).[309] The term *they learn* in 5:13a lines up negatively with the positive in 2:11, where they are to learn the true faith. There is then more reason to think the women in need of learning in chapter two at least include the younger widows in chapter five.

His positive instruction for these young widows is that they are to *remarry, bear children, and manage their households* (5:14). Once again, this suggests a connection to chapter two's surprising ending with marriage and childbearing (2:15), which suggests to me that the false teachings include asceticism and the denial of the goodness of creation's gifts (4:3–5). To cease from the behaviors connected to the false teachings is to return to a more acceptable form of life: marriage, children, and proper household management. Paul does consider singleness or celibacy as one

---

[305] For a similar assessment, see Towner, *Timothy and Titus*, 350.
[306] Towner, 356.
[307] Marshall wants two groups: those of v. 11 and those of v. 13. See Marshall, *Pastoral Epistles*, 601–602.
[308] Winter, *Roman Wives, Roman Widows*, 123–140.
[309] Towner, *Timothy and Titus*, 354–355.

way of surrendering one's life to Christ (cf. 1 Cor 7:32–35) but marriage was customary. The words in our passage then conform to a Pauline theology of marriage (see 1 Cor 7), which inherently countered part of the Ephesian false teachings (4:3). Again, the theme of civilized piety is evoked in not giving *the adversary* an *occasion to revile* the emerging Christian community in Ephesus (cf. 3:7 especially). The adversary here is either some human opponent of the gospel or Satan, who appears in 5:15, and who has conquered some of the widows.

In fact, some of these younger widows *have already turned away to follow Satan* (5:15), another indication that they are alienating themselves from Christ in their decisions to marry. There becomes an interesting link here between these young widows, who might be the rich women challenging male leaders during the worship gathering in 2:12, and the false teachers who were promulgating demonic teachings about Scripture, including marriage (1:3–4, 6–7, 4:1–3).

Christian Support for Relatives Who Are Widows (5:16)

The attention now narrows to a *believing woman* who has *relatives who are really widows*, and she is to *assist* the real widows so that *the church not be burdened*. A *believing woman*'s faithfulness contrasts with the young widow who falls into judgment for turning away from Christ in 5:11–12 (cf. too 5:3, 4, 8). Towner suggests that, since caring for widows required resources, the *believing woman* belongs to the group of wealthy women being chastised in 1 Timothy 2:9.[310] Civilized piety entails a faithful Christian woman's marriage, childrearing, and managing a household as well as care for widows in one's wider family reach. The aim was to narrow the list to widows with genuine needs. By delineating between the kinds of situations widows face and giving guidance about how these different kinds of widows are to be cared for in the Ephesian church, the Apostle lays out a communal life that satisfies the cultural expectations of civilized piety and expresses the gospel (2:2–4).

---

[310] Witherington also sees wealth and status attributed to these believing and faithful women; see Witherington, *Letters and Homilies for Hellenized Christians*, 273.

> A Closer Look: Crucial NT References to Widows
>
> Mark 12:40 They devour widows' houses and for the sake of appearance say long prayers. They will receive the greater condemnation.
>
> Mark 12:42–43 A poor widow came and put in two small copper coins, which are worth a penny. **43** Then he called his disciples and said to them, "Truly I tell you, this poor widow has put in more than all those who are contributing to the treasury.
>
> Luke 2:37 [Anna] then as a widow to the age of eighty-four. She never left the temple but worshiped there with fasting and prayer night and day.
>
> Luke 7:12 As he approached the gate of the town, a man who had died was being carried out. He was his mother's only son, and she was a widow, and with her was a large crowd from the town.
>
> Luke 18:3 In that city there was a widow who kept coming to him and saying, "Grant me justice against my accuser." . . . **5** yet because this widow keeps bothering me, I will grant her justice, so that she may not wear me out by continually coming.
>
> Acts 6:1 Now during those days, when the disciples were increasing in number, the Hellenists complained against the Hebrews because their widows were being neglected in the daily distribution of food.
>
> 1 Cor 7:8 To the unmarried and the widows I say that it is good for them to remain unmarried as I am.
>
> Jas 1:27 Religion that is pure and undefiled before God the Father is this: to care for orphans and widows in their distress and to keep oneself unstained by the world.

5:17–25 SOME CHURCH INSTRUCTIONS

Instructions for groups in the church continue throughout chapter five, indicated by the word *honor* (5:3, 17). Not all of vv. 17–25 pertain to elders, but vv. 17–22 are for the elders. At v. 23 the Apostle turns to Timothy more directly and personal, while vv. 24 and 25 are more general.

- **5:17** Let the elders who rule well be considered worthy of double honor, especially those who labor in preaching and teaching,
- **18** for the scripture says, "You shall not muzzle an ox while it is treading out the grain," and, "The laborer deserves to be paid."
- **19** Never accept any accusation against an elder except on the evidence of two or three witnesses.
- **20** As for those who persist in sin, rebuke them in the presence of all, so that the rest also may stand in fear.

Commentary on 1 Timothy

21 In the presence of God and of Christ Jesus and of the elect angels, I warn you to keep these instructions without prejudice, doing nothing on the basis of partiality.

22 Do not ordain anyone hastily, and do not participate in the sins of others; keep yourself pure.

5:23 No longer drink only water, but take a little wine for the sake of your stomach and your frequent ailments.

5:24 The sins of some people are conspicuous and precede them to judgment, while the sins of others follow them there.

25 So also good works are conspicuous, and even when they are not, they cannot remain hidden.

Instructions *for* church leaders abound in 1 Timothy (cf. 3:1–13). The Apostle's first focus is on remuneration for those in pastoral leadership (5:17–18).

Remuneration

Once again, the term elder (*presbuteros*) was not as precise then as it is in churches today.[311] As stated at 5:1, the term there referred to older males but in 5:17 *elders* are older males in pastoral leadership in the assemblies of Ephesus. The *elders* [that is, the older males in the assembly] *who rule well* are to be remunerated with *double honor*. Some of these *elders* are involved in *preaching and teaching* while others are not but all seem to *rule*.[312] The NRSV's choice of *rule* could be improved. The NIV fills in more than one blank with "who direct the affairs of the church" while the CEB has "who lead well." The Greek term here is *proistemi*,[313] and literally means "stand in front" or "stand ahead," so the CEB's "leads" is a far more natural

---

[311] For one who imposes too much from a later period but remains nonetheless suggestive, see Stewart, *Original Bishops*.

[312] It is too hasty to collapse the terms elders here in 3:17 and bishops from 3:1 as referring to the same office or type of leader in the first-century churches. A consistent characteristic of elders is the term appearing as a plural, though this need not indicate multiple elders in a particular house church (4:14, 5:17; Titus 1:5). The bishop appears as singular in the PEs, mostly because it is a type of leader (3:1, 2; Titus 1:7), but occurs as a plural in Phil 1:1. It is possible that the bishop was chosen as a leader over particular responsibilities, and one should think at least of some financial oversight. Holding this more nuanced relationship between the elders and the bishops seems present in Ignatius of Antioch (Ignatius, *To the Ephesians* 4, 20). See Andrew D. Clarke, *A Pauline Theology of Church Leadership*, LNTS 362 (London: T & T Clark, 2008).

[313] See also at Rom 12:8.

equivalent. Both the NRSV and the NIV impose too much authority in the term itself. Leading *well* is accurate and describes leading in theology, evangelism, spiritual formation, and the overall task of pastoring a church. It is perhaps simplest then to think of the term *elders* referring to all older men, only some of whom are in pastoral leadership.[314]

The elders who are to lead well are engaged in the *labor* of the Word. In the twentieth century there have been attempts to distinguish *preaching and teaching* into completely separable gifts but the terms interpenetrate one another: teaching is preaching, and preaching is teaching. Furthermore, behind the NRSV's and NIV's *preaching* is *logos*, not a term more customarily translated with preaching (*kērussō, euaggelizomai*). It may be wiser to translate "especially the ones laboring in word and teaching," with the former a more encompassing term and the specific form of the "word" under consideration.

The elder who leads with excellence is worthy of *double honor*. Because of the citations in v. 18 from the Old Testament and one of the Gospels (Luke 10:7; Matt 10:10) one should think the Apostle learned this in the Jesus tradition even if Paul's ideas are in the neighborhood (Gal 6:6; 1 Cor 9:7–14; 2 Cor 8–9). In which case this is about financial reimbursement but some think *honor* is about social respect more than financial remuneration. Many think the term *honor* is not about a routine or regular payment but more of a specific, one-time gift.[315] Thinking more widely, the accusations against the elders in 1 Timothy 5:19 are most likely about money (cf. 6:5). The word *double* could refer to honor for age and financial benefit for teaching; it could be little more than a trope. Marshall sides with those who think it refers to a double-sized meal at the church meals![316] Some suggest the *double honor* refers to being given respect in the community and financials as well.[317]

Marshall's anchor here is first, a free but principled use of an Old Testament text (*You shall not muzzle* ... ; cf. Deut 25:4) that was itself a free-standing law, one that curbed the greed of farmers and that fed the beast, and the second comes from a word of Jesus (Luke 10:7; Matt 10:10). If "scripture" applies to both textual references, then it at least suggests

---

[314] Marshall, *Pastoral Epistles*, 610–611.
[315] Marshall, 612–613, who calls it an honorarium and cites others.
[316] Marshall, 613–615.
[317] Collins, *1 & 2 Timothy and Titus*, 144; Witherington, *Letters and Homilies for Hellenized Christians*, 273.

Jesus' words are seen as scripture, but some think it more likely that the quote from Deuteronomy 25:4 is "scripture" and the teaching from Jesus further supports the Apostle's instruction about the double honor.[318]

Respect

In 1 Timothy 5:19, the NRSV's *Never* is an overreach and can lead to serious misunderstandings. It is a simple prohibition. The NIV's "do not entertain" and the CEB's "Don't accept" are better. The requirement here emerges from respect of age, one's gifts, and a desire for protection against false accusations. This judicial practice pulled from the legal procedure of Israel in Deuteronomy 19:15 reveals again the Jewish education of the Apostle and the largesse of social logic early Christian churches received from their Jewish forebearers. The OT citation is encouraged by Jesus in Matthew 18 and is something of a quick-and-easy appeal (2 Cor 13:1). Though the requirement itself has been abused at times by those in authority, the instruction is wise: elders were and are at times vulnerable to false accusations and one is not to *accept*, which means here embrace as corresponding to facts and thus leading into levels of correction and discipline, such an *accusation* without evidence, that is, *unless it is confirmed by two or three witnesses*.[319] It is, however, a fact that many offenses by church leaders are not witnessed by any other person. In such cases, this text should be set aside.

Correction

This respect shown for the elders, however, doesn't entail assumption that all elders are always in the right. Instead, Timothy is to *rebuke* wayward elders *in front of everyone* (5:20; cf. Matt 18:15–20; 1 Cor 5:4–5).[320] The term *rebuke* entails instruction, correction, discipline (CEB) and reproof (NIV), and so has the sense of explaining the wrong. One suspects that behind the text is a policy that public leaders sinning publicly need to be

---

[318] Gordon Fee, *1 and 2 Timothy, Titus*, NIBC (Peabody: Hendrickson, 1988), 134; Towner, *Timothy and Titus*, 364.
[319] So also Deut 17:6; 19:15; Matt 18:6; 2 Cor 13:1.
[320] See Marshall, *Pastoral Epistles*, 618; Knight, *Pastoral Epistles*, 236. For one who believes this rebuke is for sinners generally, Collins, *1 & 2 Timothy and Titus*, 146–147.

acknowledged publicly.[321] While this is about disciplining an elder, the Apostle aims at deterrence: *so that the rest also may stand in fear*. Just what had been done by the elder is not explicit but 6:5's profiteering is the best candidate. Public correction must be exercised with wisdom and compassion because the temptation of many is revenge and that leads to humiliating and shaming rather than deepening holiness.

The Apostle reminds Timothy with strong language (v. 21a), language drawn from the heavenly law court,[322] that he is to perform such activities *without prejudice* (or deciding before listening to the accusations), *doing nothing on the basis of partiality* (v. 21). Leaders are to be examined fairly as churches are to pursue justice and truth-telling in every situation. The discipline is cosmic (*in the sight of God and Christ Jesus and the elect angels*; cf. 1 Cor 11:10; Eph 3:10; 1 Pet 3:18–22).

Ordination

What is in mind when the Apostle instructs Timothy to *ordain*? Marshall lays out the two basic options:[323] (1) ordination to any position within the community of faith or (2) the ordination of someone to be an elder (perhaps to replace the sinning elder of 5:20).[324] However, others suggest this is not ordination at all but the grace of forgiveness to reconstitute a repentant elder (v. 20).[325] However, the nonmentioning of repentance, the lack of a needed time period, as well as the rather strong *for those who persist in sin* (v. 20a), all count against this view. It's about Timothy ordaining someone into ministry. We must not imagine a service with all the heavyweight figures and features involved, including a liturgy and the eucharist and the presiding bishop and a pageantry-laden clericalism running straight through the whole. Having warned against imposing our context on this text, we should remember that our world derived ordination from texts like this. In particular, behind *ordain* is the Greek term for placing one's hands on someone as an act of blessing,

---

[321] Knight, *Pastoral Epistles*, 236; Towner, *Timothy and Titus*, 371; Witherington, *Letters and Homilies for Hellenized Christians*, 276. Some think this rebuke should happen in front of the elders instead of the church; see Dibelius and Conzelmann, *Pastoral Epistles*, 77; Kelly, *Pastoral Epistles*, 127.
[322] Marshall, *Pastoral Epistles*, 619–620.
[323] Marshall, 620–622.
[324] For replacement, see Towner, *Timothy and Titus*, 373.
[325] Kelly, *Pastoral Epistles*, 127–128.

consecration, and transmission (Acts 6:6; 8:17–19; 13:3; 19:6).[326] This is not, however, to be done *hastily*; rather, one must be tested and proven as gifted and faithful.

Alongside ordaining, Timothy is exhorted *not to*[327] *participate in the sins of others*, and one can infer this from any hasty ordination as well as the refusal or hesitation to correct wayward elders. *Not to participate* implies making a common life with such persons: to lay hands on someone is to approve, to bless who they are, and to participate in them.[328] This negative is followed by the positive: *keep yourself pure*, with *pure* focusing on the ordination of elders.

Wine

Verse 23's admonition to *take a little wine for the sake of your stomach* appears out nowhere and belongs to common friendship type letters. Perhaps *No longer drink only water* indicates Timothy had undertaken a vow to be a teetotaler and some recent stomach ailments give the Apostle authority to declare a dispensation from the vow. Perhaps, too, the *keep yourself pure* injunction of v. 22 precipitated thinking about alcohol since abstinence from alcohol was one common form of the pure life (cf. Numb 6). Perhaps as well the sins of the elder included alcohol abuse or that the instructions to leaders did not demand total abstinence (1 Tim 3:3, 8; Titus 1:7). What we know is that we don't know.

General Instruction

The prominent term in the moral axioms of 1 Timothy 5:24–25, which may well remind at least some of his readers of common morality in the Greco-Roman world,[329] is *conspicuous* or "obvious" (NIV, CEB; translating *prodelos*). The Apostle contrasts two forms of behavior: *sins* and *good works*. The *sins* accompany, if they do not escort, the sinners before God to face their inevitable judgment. Whether publicly known or unknown,

---

[326] Also Numb 8:10; 27:18–23; Deut 34:9.
[327] The Greek indicates a close tie to the previous instruction: hence, "and neither participate in the sins of others."
[328] See Towner, *Timothy and Titus*, 375; Witherington, *Letters and Homilies for Hellenized Christians*, 277.
[329] Teresa Morgan, *Popular Morality in the Early Roman Empire* (New York: Cambridge University Press, 2007).

their sins will become manifest before God (cf. Matt 10:26–33). On the other hand, *good works* often connotes public and therefore known benevolence. These *good works* attach themselves to their doers and so also *cannot remain* [ultimately] *hidden*. The implication, then, is that judgment is based on behavior, and good works survive divine scrutiny (Matt 25:31–46; Rom 2:6–11; Jas 2:14–26; Rev 22:10–16). In context, 1 Timothy 5:24–25 about what is known and not known provides help in discerning the character of potential elders.

6:1–2A INSTRUCTIONS FOR SLAVES

1 Timothy 5 instructs older men, widows, and leading elders while 1 Timothy 6 finishes off a section by instructing slaves. As such, 5:1–6:2 parallels Paul's "household regulations" in Colossians 3:18–4:1 and Ephesians 5:21–6:9 (cf. Titus 2:9–10; 1 Pet 2:18–25). As with most everything overlapping between other Pauline letters, there are similarities with differences.

6:1 Let all who are under the yoke of slavery regard their masters as worthy of all honor, so that the name of God and the teaching may not be blasphemed.
2 Those who have believing masters must not be disrespectful to them on the ground that they are brothers and sisters; rather they must serve them all the more, since those who benefit by their service are believers and beloved.

Many have diminished Greco-Roman and even Jewish slavery and slaves by overtly stating that the slavery of the Classical world was not the same as New World slavery, and therefore one should see the NT texts about slavery as closer to modern day employment. This fails the test of history. "Slavery by definition," a modern expert on ancient slavery observes, "is a means of securing and maintaining an involuntary labour force by a group in society which monopolises political and economic power."[330] The slaves about whom the Apostle speaks and who are addressed here, then, are involuntary laborers, they are owned and maintained for the profit of the master(s), and the owners have the power to secure, maintain, and abuse those they've enslaved. We deny truth when we pretend otherwise about

---

[330] Keith R. Bradley, *Slaves and Masters in the Roman Empire: A Study in Social Control* (New York: Oxford University Press, 1987), 18. See too the excursus by Huizenga, *1–2 Timothy, Titus*, 73–87.

ancient slavery. It is far more correct to admit that the Bible's authors did not see a moral problem with slavery in the Classical world than to pretend that ancient slavery was a gentler form of slavery.[331]

The phrase *under the yoke of slavery* conjures the image of a beast of burden, and this connects the slavery of this text with Aristotle's famous dehumanizing of slaves.[332] Aristotle said that some humans "are lifeless and others living" (*Politics* 1.2.4) and also that slaves are to be classed alongside instruments or tools: "the slave is an assistant in the class of instruments of action" (1.2.6). So a slave is "property" and thus "a human being belonging by nature not to himself but to another" (1.2.7). Perhaps most degradingly as well as influentially, Aristotle made slavery a part of nature itself: some are "by nature slaves" (1.2.13) and that "he is by nature a slave who is capable of belonging to another . . . and who participates in reason so far as to apprehend it but not to possess it" (1.2.13). Since the body is natural and some people are physically shaped by nature for slavery, then for Aristotle slavery is therefore "an institution both expedient and just" (1.2.15). The Apostle does not justify the existence of slavery as a natural part of God's good creation, but he offers a theological understanding of slavery that situates the slave within the household and, by doing so, the slave is given familial honor and dignity.[333]

Those under the yoke of slavery are instructed to *honor* those who own them. While the usage of *honor* connects to other lines in the letter (1 Tim 5:3, 17), here the Apostle digs new ground about how believing slaves are to behave. Such submission is civilized piety, glorifies God, and prevents the church's *teaching* from losing social respectability (6:1; cf. Tit 2:5, 9–10; 1 Pet 2:10–3:7). It is indeed possible that some slaves found a personal liberation in the gospel that engendered a desire and an expectation of greater freedom and equality in the world, and therefore the Apostle's words could be heard as designed to hold back any rebellion of Christian slaves in nonChristian households.[334] At times this restraining view hangs on the Apostle suggesting eventual manumission.[335]

---

[331] Scot McKnight, *The Letter to Philemon*, NICNT (Grand Rapids: Eerdmans, 2017), 6–29.
[332] Marshall, *Pastoral Epistles*, 629. It is quite unlikely these are slaves who were also elders, contra C. K. Barrett, *The Pastoral Epistles*, New Clarendon Bible (Oxford University Press, 1963), 82.
[333] Towner, *Timothy and Titus*, 388–389.
[334] Marshall, *Pastoral Epistles*, 627–628; Towner, *Timothy and Titus*, 379–380; Mounce, *Pastoral Epistles*, 325.
[335] Among others, see Towner, *Timothy and Titus*, 379.

Slaves are not to be *disrespectful* (6:2) because they are now *brothers and sisters* or mutual "siblings," which evokes the potent line of Philemon: "no longer as a slave, but ... a beloved brother" (Phm 16). The consistency of the gospel's transforming power may have planted a seed in the letter to Philemon and in 1 Timothy 6:2 that would eventually denounce slavery, but that seed did not bloom for centuries. As a sibling in Christ the slave is to *serve them* [masters] *all the more* because their masters are *believers and beloved*.[336]

The Christian sibling life widens the slave's motivation from one of mere submission into family relations.[337] The expression *benefit by their service*, or the produce of their labor (a paraphrase of *euergesia*; "doing good work" and benefaction), is ambiguous.[338] Terms like *benefit by their service* normally indicate what a dominant person does for the benefit of a dependent. That is, it could point readers to a public benefaction by the master. Most often in the ancient world such an expression about benefaction referred to divine or imperial beneficence for the sake of people.[339] Some, however, have suggested *their service* might be something slaves themselves could do[340] but most think the masters are the ones doing the good works. The NRSV's wording can thus be tweaked to "because they are faithful and loving – those [masters] who assist [the public sector][341] with benefit/ benefaction." Still, the Christian slave's civilized piety of honoring their masters in their labors alters the master–slave relationship and by working for the master slaves participate in public benefactions of the master.[342]

6:2B–10 FOR TIMOTHY

The Apostle turns to a wide range of instructions for Timothy in the rest of the letter (as at 5:23–25). This section bears a striking similarity to 1:3–20, and its concerns can be summarized once again as "goodness" (from the

---

[336] For discussion of options, Marshall, *Pastoral Epistles*, 632–633.
[337] Marshall, 632; Knight, *Pastoral Epistles*, 247.
[338] The Apostle, true to his civilized piety theme, draws on the benefaction and patronage systems at work: see Nathan Nzyoka Joshua, *Benefaction and Patronage in Leadership: A Socio-Historical Exegesis of the Pastoral Epistles* (Carlisle: Langham Monographs, 2018).
[339] Hoag contends this is about God the Benefactor; see Hoag, *Wealth in Ancient Ephesus and the First Letter to Timothy*, 131–160.
[340] Huizenga, 1–2 Timothy, Titus, 72.
[341] For a good discussion of the verb, Kidd, *Wealth and Beneficence*, 144–156.
[342] Hutson, *1–2 Timothy, Titus*, 139–140. Some would suggest the benefaction is entirely toward the slave in the form of food, clothing, and shelter. But *euergesia* is overstated for quotidian provisions for slaves.

Apostle's Jewish context, the Hebrew *tov*), as "civilized piety" or "godliness" (*eusebeia*), and as "wisdom" (*sophia*), but he keeps an eye on the false teachers as well. It is a hermeneutical mistake to turn these instructions into a list of timeless rules. The teachings of this letter are not the sum total of apostolic gospel teaching but are instead a proper manifestation of the gospel within Timothy's Ephesian context.

2b Teach and urge these duties.
3 Whoever teaches otherwise and does not agree with the sound words of our Lord Jesus Christ and the teaching that is in accordance with godliness
4 is conceited, understanding nothing, and has a morbid craving for controversy and for disputes about words. From these come envy, dissension, slander, base suspicions,
5 and wrangling among those who are depraved in mind and bereft of the truth, imagining that godliness is a means of gain.
6 Of course, there is great gain in godliness combined with contentment,
7 for we brought nothing into the world, so that we can take nothing out of it,
8 but if we have food and clothing, we will be content with these.
9 But those who want to be rich fall into temptation and are trapped by many senseless and harmful desires that plunge people into ruin and destruction.
10 For the love of money is a root of all kinds of evil, and in their eagerness to be rich some have wandered away from the faith and pierced themselves with many pains.

After a general exhortation (6:2b), the Apostle turns to contesting those who oppose that apostolic tradition (6:3–5) before reminding Timothy about the wisdom of contentment (6:6–10).

General Exhortation

The opening exhortation (*Teach and urge these duties*) looks back either to the entire letter's contents or to the entire previous section (5:1–6:2a, with 5:23–25 as a sidebar for Timothy) or to the focus on teaching elders (5:17–22, with a reprise of 5:21 at 6:2b). The NRSV's *duties* is more specific than a general Greek term, translated best as "these things" (*tauta*). Since "these things" is general it is unwise to find a narrower focus than the first two options. In light of the theme of the next section (6:11–16) "these things" probably refers to the whole letter's content and teaching.

The Importance of Defending Apostolic Teaching

Running through the entire letter are directives about how to deal with and rebut false teachers. So prevalent is this theme that one can be certain it is the *Sitz im Leben* for the letter itself. From *Teach . . . these duties* the Apostle, without a break, says *Whoever* (or "If someone") *teaches otherwise*. These two English words woodenly translate *heterodidaskaleō*. As sketched in section "Problems at Ephesus" at the Apostle's first usage of *heterodidaskaleō* (1 Tim 1:3), this term points to wrong interpretations of the Old Testament that end the rigors of the Mosaic law, to status issues, to asceticism, to the behavior of the wealthy, and to moral failures that lead people astray.[343]

A subtle term can be missed in the NRSV's phrase *does not agree*. The Greek word *proserchomai* means "to approach." The problem is not only what the false teachers teach but their dismissive and irreverent posture toward the truth of Jesus' and the apostles' teachings. To summarize that truth the Apostle says *the sound words of our Lord Jesus Christ and the teaching that is in accordance with godliness*. The first expression (*the sound words . . . Christ*) could well refer either to the words of Jesus or more generally to *words* that are consistent with the teachings of Jesus.[344] Since the Apostle quoted Jesus in the previous section (5:18), the former has more in its favor.[345] To be distinguished from the teachings/words of Jesus is *the teaching that is in accordance with godliness* (6:3), or more accurately as we have contended about this letter to Timothy, "in accordance with civilized piety." When the term *eusebeia* is translated as "godliness" (NRSV) it connotes a specific Christian virtue concerning the personal struggle to avoid sin, suggesting a different register from the Jewish world connected to the temple and the character of God.[346] On

---

[343] Collins, *1 & 2 Timothy and Titus*, 156; Witherington, *Letters and Homilies for Hellenized Christians*, 284.
[344] Marshall, *Pastoral Epistles*, 638–639; Mounce, *Pastoral Epistles*, 337.
[345] At various times the relationship of Paul to the teachings of Jesus has driven debate, without any strong consensus. For an orienting discussion, David Wenham, *Paul: Follower of Jesus or Founder of Christianity?* (Grand Rapids: Eerdmans, 1995).
[346] Jo Bailey Wells, *God's Holy People: A Theme in Biblical Theology* (Sheffield: Bloomsbury T&T Clark, 2000).

the other hand, "civilized piety" for *eusebeia* draws our attention to a different register. That is, to the kind of character and behavior by the person that comports with a good public reputation, one of the driving concerns of earliest Christianity in the Roman Empire. Furthermore, civilized piety draws us away from thinking exclusively from terms that would later become the Creed. We should avoid thinking exclusively here of theological content, as we find in 1 Corinthians 15:3–28 or 1 Timothy 3:16, and instead concentrate on teaching that promotes a civilized lived theology.[347] The Apostle has already used both *sound* and *teaching* (1 Tim 1:10) so, as Collins has said, "For the Pastor and his community, sound teaching does not stand alone. It leads to a way of life, identifiable patterns of appropriate behavior."[348]

That both orthodoxy and orthopraxy are at work in *the teaching* the Apostle wants Timothy to defend becomes clear in the battery of expressions in vv. 4–5. The false teachers anchor their ways in themselves (*conceited*, or "self-inflated"; see 2 Tim 3:4), they are wrong in their convictions (*understanding nothing*), they turn discussions into heated debates (*morbid craving for controversy* or the CEB's "sick obsession with debates"; cf. 1 Tim 1:4) and "word wars" or theological battles (*logomachia*). These character weaknesses create (*From these* . . .) v. 5's *wrangling* (or "brawling"; cf. 2:8) *among those who are depraved* (or "morally corrupt") *in mind*. This phrase captures the divisiveness of v. 4: *envy, dissension, slander, base suspicions*.[349] These graphic terms in v. 4 are used for the false teachers and are then anchored in their corrupted character in v. 5. There is a weariness toward intellectual pursuit that is often mocked by the educated as mere anti-intellectualism, but here the Apostle gives a pointed warning for those Christians engaging in biblical, philosophical, and theological strivings: the life of the mind must be strictly guarded according to the civilized piety of the gospel or it will plunge its crusaders into a morally corrupt existence.[350] These Ephesian false teachers are *bereft of truth*, another of the Apostle's favorite terms in the PEs (cf. 2:4).

---

[347] "But given that the false doctrine produces rather different results, and that the measurement of orthodoxy versus unorthodoxy is uppermost in mind, Paul probably appeals to the quality of life ('godliness') as the standard or proof of the authority of his teaching." See Towner, *Timothy and Titus*, 394–395.
[348] Collins, *1 & 2 Timothy and Titus*, 155.
[349] Witherington notes this vice list is similar to the one found in Rom 1:29–31; see Witherington, *Letters and Homilies for Hellenized Christians*, 284.
[350] Mounce, *Pastoral Epistles*, 338.

This broadside against the Ephesian false teachers lands exactly where the Apostle aims: their motive is profit, that is, they are *imagining*[351] *that godliness* ("civilized piety") *is a means of gain* (v. 5). Civilized piety is a pathway to the upper echelons of respectable, wealthy society and could thus provide social connections for these fraudulent teachers. Simony, which is one of the earliest sins the church had to address, was named after its originator, Simon Magus (Acts 8:14–24). The occurrence of this problem in Ephesus would not be the last time such teaching occurred in the church.[352]

Material Contentment

The Apostle's pastoral wisdom turns the false teachers upside down in order to shake out the money: *there is great gain in godliness* ("civilized piety") *combined with contentment*. The two terms, *godliness* and *gain*, are upended from their characteristic misuse by the false teachers. The *gain* is not financial abundance but instead *contentment*, rooted in the reality of final closure[353] that you can take nothing through the gate of death (v. 7).[354] The Apostle echoes the teachings of Jesus (v. 8: *food and clothing*; cf. Matt 6:19–34; 10:9–10; Lk 10:4; cf. too James 2:16). The translation "contentment" may suggest to readers something other than what the Apostle is intending to say. Using *autarkeia*[355] suggested something along the idea of "self-sufficiency" or "self-interested responsibility" but in this passage there is clearly an element of satisfaction in the sufficiency-in-God at work as well.[356] The differences in the translations lead to significantly different implications: if "contentment" is meant then we are talking about an attitude, temperament, and disposition (cf. 2 Cor 9:7-8; Phil

---

[351] The words "imagining" or "pretending" (Marshall, *Pastoral Epistles*, 643) for the Greek *nomizō* is not as likely as "thinking" or "supposing." Collins points out that *nomizō* refers to "creating a custom or making a law" (Collins, *1 & 2 Timothy and Titus*, 156), which might mean it is a subtle reference to the false teachers' inability to interpret the Mosaic law properly (1 Tim 1:7).

[352] Hoag, *Wealth in Ancient Ephesus and the First Letter to Timothy*, 161–193.

[353] Knight, *Pastoral Epistles*, 254. For references in Jewish, Greco-Roman, and Christian literature, Kelly, *Pastoral Epistles*, 136; Mounce, *Pastoral Epistles*, 342; Towner, *Timothy and Titus*, 399–400.

[354] As Marshall puts it, "temporality versus eternality," in Marshall, *Pastoral Epistles*, 646. See also his pp. 646–648 for an extensive (and insoluble) discussion concerning the grammar of v. 7. Also, Towner, *Timothy and Titus*, 400.

[355] In v. 8 the verbal form is used: *arkeō*.

[356] See Marshall, *Pastoral Epistles*, 644–645.

4:11–13);[357] if "self-sufficiency" is the meaning then we are talking about working with one's hands, providing for one's family, and taking personal responsibility (cf. 2 Thess 3:10–12; Eph 4:28).[358] Some in Ephesus, including widows, were taking advantage of Christian generosity (1 Tim 5:4, 16) and now we see the same posture by these false teachers, drawing us again into a connection. Both senses are at work here: a self-sufficiency along with a sufficiency in God.[359]

The false teachers, now brought into strong contrast, are in it for the dough because *they want to be rich* (v. 9).[360] This is not a condemnation of the wealthy per se, especially since Jesus, Paul, and the early church relied so much on rich benefactors, particularly wealthy women (Lk 8:1–3; Acts 16:14–15; Rom 16:1–2). So, the *want* is a judgment of the desire *to be rich*. Those who succumb to a desire for wealth will be trapped in sins that become systemic, and they therefore *plunge* [themselves] ... *into ruin and destruction*.[361] The Apostle knows that small sins lead to greater sins and greater sins ruin the character of the leader. The counter? Personal disciplines of transformation, like those already mentioned in 4:13–15, such as prayer and Bible study and Christian fellowship and sacrament and mission.

The Apostle ends with a fertile proverb: *the love of money is a root of all kinds of evil* (v. 10).[362] He once again connects bad character to disastrous results (as done in v. 9). Those infected with money-love will learn that such a love corrupts faith and character in a mutually reinforcing dynamic that eventually leads to apostasy. The *many pains* could be understood as pain in this life but may be a repetition for *ruin and destruction* (v. 9).

---

[357] For one holding to *autarkeia* as "contentment" as a Christian reversal of "self-sufficiency": Kelly, *Pastoral Epistles*, 136.

[358] See Collins, *1 & 2 Timothy and Titus*, 156–157.

[359] See Witherington, *Letters and Homilies for Hellenized Christians*, 285–286.

[360] Using the substantival participle as the subject gives a more vivid sense: "the ones wanting to be rich." Witherington makes a connection between "wishing to be rich" here in v.9 and "wishing to be teachers of the law" in 1 Tim 1:7, see Witherington, *Letters and Homilies for Hellenized Christians*, 287.

[361] For a similar take see Collins, *1 & 2 Timothy and Titus*, 158. The two nouns in Greek are *oletheros* and *apōleia*, nominal forms connected to two verbs that rhyme and intensify one another: *ollumi* and *apollumi*.

[362] Phrases similar about the love of money were common in both the Jewish and Greco-Roman world. See Towner, *Timothy and Titus*, 403.

6:11–16 FINAL WORDS FOR TIMOTHY

From an exhortation to contest the false teachers in Ephesus and their preoccupation with aggrandizing money from ministry, the Apostle turns more directly to address Timothy's own spiritual practices, a list of common Christian habits (cf. 2 Tim 2:22–25; 3:10) with the tenth, *to keep the commandment* (6:13–16), developed the most. He includes a doxology (6:16). Following these exhortations, the Apostle will return in 6:17–19 to a proper approach to money.

6:11 But as for you, man of God, [1][363] shun all this; [2] pursue righteousness, [3] godliness, [4] faith, [5] love, [6] endurance, [7] gentleness.

12 [8] Fight the good fight of the faith; [9] take hold of the eternal life, to which you were called and for which you made the good confession in the presence of many witnesses.

13 In the presence of God, who gives life to all things, and of Christ Jesus, who in his testimony before Pontius Pilate made the good confession, I charge you

14 [10] to keep the commandment without spot or blame until the manifestation of our Lord Jesus Christ,

15 which he will bring about at the right time – he who is the blessed and only Sovereign, the King of kings and Lord of lords.

16 It is he alone who has immortality and dwells in unapproachable light, whom no one has ever seen or can see; to him be honor and eternal dominion. Amen.

While we ought not to attribute the Aristotelian form of virtue ethics to the Apostle, one ought not deny the formative power of habits/practices.[364] Anyone wanting to be a *man of God*, or better, *human of God* (*anthrōpos*, used here, has a more general meaning than the limited *anēr*, meaning "man" or "male" or "husband", as used in 2:8, 12), can find wisdom in the Apostle's instructions. The expression recalls *ish Elohim* from the Hebrew Bible and thereby connects Timothy's role in Ephesus to some of Israel's noble mediators of God's Torah and prophecies.[365] One could think more

---

[363] Numbers in brackets are added for the commentary below.
[364] Dru Johnson, *Knowledge by Ritual: A Biblical Prolegomenon to Sacramental Theology*, Journal of Theological Interpretation Supplements 13 (Winona Lake: Eisenbrauns, 2016).
[365] See Deut 33:1; 1 Sam 9:6; 1 Kgs 13:1; 2 Kgs 1:9–13; 4:1.

widely still and find that this language refers to any person who walks the line of the gospel faithfully (see 2 Tim 3:17).[366]

The Apostle begins with a look back to the previous passage's illumination of the false teacher's motives and habits, and he sweeps them away with *shun all this* (6:11), or "flee from" or "run from." In 2 Timothy 2:22 he is told to "shun" but there it is "youthful passions," which then, like our passage, moves into positive habits as well as countering false teachers (2:22–26).[367] The negative command to run away turns into nine positive terms, beginning with the positive command to *pursue righteousness* (1 Tim 6:11).[368] This is the first instance of *righteousness* in the PEs,[369] a term inherited from the Jewish world (*tsedeq*) connoting moral conformity to a divine standard, that standard being the Torah. Thus, it means Torah observant.[370] The father of Jesus, Joseph, is an example of an observant person (Matt 1:19).[371] In that the standard shifts from Moses to the teachings of Jesus and also to apostolic ethical teachings, one should see *righteousness* here pointing to the ethical corollaries of the new age in Christ, and hence as nothing less than inaugurated righteousness (cf. Rom 8:3–4). In the PEs it is most often expressed as *eusebeia*, or "civilized piety," which unsurprisingly then appears as #3 in this list of habits: *godliness* (1 Tim 2:2; 3:16; 4:7–8; 6:3, 5, 6; 2 Tim 3:5; Titus 1:1). Righteousness and civilized piety are followed by [#4] *faith* (1 Tim 6:11), which points to a complex of personal trust in Jesus as Messiah, allegiance to him as Lord and king, and the faithful confession that now summarizes (3:16) of what is believed by those allegiant to King Jesus.[372]

Next [#5] comes *love*, and here one is hard-pressed not to notice that for both Jesus (Mark 12:28–32 pars) and Paul (1 Cor 13), love is the preeminent virtue, while in our passage it seems to fall behind the first four. It is not that Paul was obligated to place love first in every list, but his own words made love the preeminent ethic (e.g., Rom 12:9; 13:8, 10; Gal 5:6, 13, 22). Love is a rugged, affective commitment of presence and advocacy, as well as a mutual

---

[366] See a good sketch in Marshall, *Pastoral Epistles*, 656–657.
[367] See also other instances of "shun" at Matt 3:7; John 10:5; with Pauline usage normally about avoiding God's judgment: Rom 2:3; 1 Cor 6:18; 10:14; 1 Thess 5:3.
[368] Collins, *1 & 2 Timothy and Titus*, 162.
[369] Also at 2 Tim 2:22; 3:16; 4:8; Titus 3:5.
[370] Towner, *Timothy and Titus*, 409. Witherington agrees; see Witherington, *Letters and Homilies for Hellenized Christians*, 292. *Contra* Marshall, *Pastoral Epistles*, 658.
[371] Przybylski, *Righteousness in Matthew*.
[372] Bates, *Salvation by Allegiance Alone*; Matthew W. Bates, *Gospel Allegiance* (Grand Rapids: Brazos Press, 2019).

life shaped by Christoformity. The Apostle then turns to two more habits: [#6] *endurance*, or resilient allegiance to King Jesus, and [#7] *gentleness*, a word (*praüpathia*) that differs from the Greek terms commonly translated as "gentleness," which are *praüs* (see 1 Cor 4:21) or *epieikeia* (2 Cor 10:1). There is a common placement of [#6] *endurance* together with [#4] *faith* and [#5] *love* in the Apostle's virtue lists (Titus 2:2; cf. 1 Thess 1:3). These form a similar triad to the other Pauline trio of hope, faith, and love. In our passage the rare term *praüpathia* points at the moderating and subduing of passions, particularly the quarrelsome or violent passions of the false teachers.

The list shifts in form at the end from being single terms to #8, #9, and #10's use of phrases. In an intentionally ironic turn of phrase after [#7] *gentleness*, the concern about false teachers in 6:1–10 now becomes overtly combative: *fight the good fight of faith* (6:12). The term the Apostle plays with here is *agōnizomai* and *agōn*,[373] which come from the world of public athletic contests more than warfare or military language,[374] though the violence of a desperate struggle is always just lurking beneath surface of these terms (cf. 1:18; Jn 18:36; 1 Thess 2:2). At the end of his life the Apostle will say "I have fought the good fight" (2 Tim 4:7), which since it echoes 6:12, should be seen as having accomplished this very instruction. Timothy is called to *fight* all who would distort the gospel but his battle is contained by self-control and *gentleness* (1 Tim 6:11). This exertion leads to the goal of [#9]: *take hold of eternal life* (6:12). Such a goal is out of sync with contemporary progressivisms because the Apostle focuses on the future eschatological reality of *eternal life* while most progressive movements perceive the present world according to their expectations about the world's inevitable progress.[375] A life oriented toward God's future is not incompatible, and almost never has been perceived to be incompatible, with a life that is fully engaged in the present world.[376] Combining civilized piety with *take hold of eternal life* makes just that point.

---

[373] Collins points out that the Apostle employs a nearly identical phrase in 1 Tim 1:18 using the military terms *strateunē* and *strateian*, so similar in fact that many English translations translate both phrases as "fight the good fight," see Collins, *1 & 2 Timothy and Titus*, 163 n. 94.

[374] See esp. 1 Cor 9:25; also as a metaphorical usage in Luke 13:24; John 18:36; Col 1:29; 4:12; 1 Tim 4:10; 2 Tim 4:7. See the discussion of the terms in Marshall, *Pastoral Epistles*, 659.

[375] Trevor Hart and Richard Bauckham, *Hope Against Hope: Christian Eschatology at the Turn of the Millennium* (Grand Rapids: Eerdmans, 1999).

[376] For a similar perspective see Kelly, *Pastoral Epistles*, 141; Towner, *Timothy and Titus*, 411.

Such an eschatological orientation toward the future[377] kingdom is Timothy's calling and it shaped his *good confession in the presence of many witnesses* (6:12). What *good confession* means precisely is not clear: it may be a general profession of the faith (e.g., Rom 10:9-10) with its corollary of self-denial (and a possible glance backward and forward at the money issue for some leaders); it could be the confession made by Timothy in the face of persecution; or it could refer his baptism where he publicly agreed (*homologeō*) that Jesus is Israel's Messiah and Savior.[378] That Jesus too *made the good confession* and that he made it *before Pontius Pilate* (6:13; cf. Mark 15:1-15 pars.; also perhaps John 18:29-38[379]) favors *good confession* as a general confession of submission to the will of God (e.g., Rom 10:9-10).

The Apostle exhorts Timothy *in the presence of God*. The modification of God with *who gives life to all things* suggests he has martyrdom and resurrection in mind.[380] So, the Apostle says *I charge you ... to keep the commandment* (6:13-14). Which *commandment*?[381] It seems to be a more general summons to allegiance to the Lord to fulfill his calling as a gospel ministry than to any specific commandment. The Apostle instructs Timothy to perform this *commandment* as a habit *without spot or blame* until the Eschaton arrives (6:13), which is here described as *the manifestation of our Lord Jesus Christ*, which itself comes according to God's timetable (6:14). That manifestation (*epiphaneia*, not *Parousia*)[382] is an act of God (*which he [God] will bring about* and do so *at the right time*).

---

[377] The emphasis is future for the expression at 1 Tim 1:16; 6:16; 2 Tim 2:10; Titus 1:2; 3:7.
[378] Some think this derives from Timothy's ordination: Knight, *Pastoral Epistles*, 264-265; Witherington, *Letters and Homilies for Hellenized Christians*, 293. For baptism, see Marshall, 661; Kelly, *Pastoral Epistles*, 142; Ward, *I & II Timothy and Titus*, 111; Towner, *Timothy and Titus*, 412.
[379] Michael Gourgues contends 1 Tim 6:13 reflects the use of the Johannine tradition in both the witness and the "come into the world" (cf. 1 Tim 1:15) themes; cf. Michael Gourgues, "Jesus' Testimony before Pilate in 1 Timothy 6:13," *JBL* 135 (2016): 639-648. This would then support a later dating of 1 Timothy.
[380] See a similar expression at Luke 17:33.
[381] For discussions, see Marshall, *Pastoral Epistles*, 664-665. For the possible connection of "the commandment" to ordination, Collins, *1 & 2 Timothy and Titus*, 165; Witherington, *Letters and Homilies for Hellenized Christians*, 294.
[382] For an overview of Jewish and Hellenistic understandings of a divine appearance, see Towner, *Timothy and Titus*, 416-418. See also Rob van Houwelingen, "The Meaning of *epiphaneia* in the Pastoral Epistles," *JSPL* 9 (2019) 89-108. He argues 2 Timothy 1:10 (and 4:1, 8) emphasize incarnation because of context. Challenged by Dogara Ishaya Manomi, "Salvific, Ethical, and Consummative 'Appearances' in the Pastoral Epistles? A Response to Rob van Houwelingen," *JSPL* 9 (2019): 109-117.

Just as Christ Jesus' first appearance might have seemed like an arbitrary moment in the human perception of history but has been revealed as occurring at a precise moment of God's theological history (2:6; Eph 1:9–10), so too God *will bring about* the second appearance of Christ Jesus *at the right time*, not according to human perception of time or history but according to a divine calendar (cf. Acts 1:6–7; 2 Pet 3:8–9).[383] Accordingly, it is God the Father who receives a doxology in language not typically found in Paul's letters: *blessed and only Sovereign, the King of kings and Lord of lords* (6:15; cf. Deut 10:17). The doxology that follows, a doxology that continues with *It is he alone* (evoking God's oneness in Deut 6:4–8) *who has immortality . . . to him be honor and eternal dominion* (1 Tim 6:16). Much of this doxology reuses terms elsewhere in the letter (1:11, 17).[384] Some see in the terms at work in the doxology a critique of the imperial cult. The exuberant expressions of God's glory in terms of political power (cf. Rev 4:11, 5:13–14)[385] and especially since *immortality* is not used in Second Temple Judaism for God could suggest the Apostle grabbed onto descriptions of pagan gods and emperors.[386]

The description that God *dwells in unapproachable light* invokes a Jewish theology of God as creator (e.g., Psalm 104:2; James 1:17–18; 1 Pet 2:9–10; 1 John 1:5). The Apostle stresses the total otherness of God's nature from creation's, the God *whom no one has ever seen or can see*, because only by perceiving such a theology can Timothy begin to comprehend the kind of eternal life he is grasping and the life of civilized piety it creates.

6:17–19 FINAL WORDS ABOUT THE WEALTHY

After instructing Timothy on a proper Christian leader's gospel-based character in juxtaposition to those of the false teachers, the Apostle returns

---

[383] Similarly, Collins, *1 & 2 Timothy and Titus*, 166; Towner, *Timothy and Titus*, 420. Witherington notes that "manifestation" language was imperial cult language to refer to divine appointments of kings and emperors, which was already being countered by Second Temple Jews (e.g., 3 Macc 5:35). See Witherington, *Letters and Homilies for Hellenized Christians*, 295.

[384] For a comparisons of these sections, particularly the doxologies, see Collins, *1 & 2 Timothy and Titus*, 165–166; Mounce, *Pastoral Epistles*, 351–352.

[385] Kelly, *Pastoral Epistles*, 146; Mounce, *Pastoral Epistles*, 361; Collins, *1 & 2 Timothy and Titus*, 167.

[386] Towner, *Timothy and Titus*, 415, 418–419, 421; Witherington, *Letters and Homilies for Hellenized Christians*, 295–296.

to the theme of wealth that had been left off at 1 Timothy 6:10. However, this return changes focus from leaders desiring wealth to the wealthy in general within the assemblies of Ephesus. Perhaps the wealthy of 6:17–19 are yet another group alongside the groups of 5:1, 3, 17, and 6:1. It is simplistic to think everyone in the earliest Christian assemblies was poor and that they were uniformly opposed by, or even themselves opposed to, the rich. The reality of house churches and benefactors (e.g., Rom 16:1–2) indicate a measure of wealth in the communities (cf. James 2:6 with 4:13–5:6), and so instructions as we find here about the rich reveal that there were wealthy people in the movement. Perhaps then they are those using their own *pietas* to gain status in Ephesus.

6:17 As for those who in the present age are rich, command them not to be haughty, or to set their hopes on the uncertainty of riches, but rather on God who richly provides us with everything for our enjoyment.
18 They are to do good, to be rich in good works, generous, and ready to share,
19 thus storing up for themselves the treasure of a good foundation for the future, so that they may take hold of the life that really is life.

In the Jewish tradition there were two distinct, if not always easy to recognize, complementary teachings about wealth: the first saw wealth as God's blessing (Deut 28) while the second saw the accumulation of riches as a sign of rapaciousness, decadence, and injustice (Isa 58; Luke 6:20, 24; 12:16–21; 16:1–14; James 4:13–5:6).[387] The Apostle's words in 6:17 align with the tradition's teaching of blessed wealth but does so by challenging wealthy Ephesian Christians, who may be climbing the social ladder but who can also be public benefactors, to generosity in 6:18. These two traditions emerge in Israel's history during varying circumstances. Sometimes the first was needed and at other times the second. The modification of *rich* with *in the present age* both reminds the rich of their temporary privilege and sets them up for an orientation to the eternal (cf. 6:19).

Those *rich* already *in the present age* are probably different from "those who want to be rich" in 6:10, and because of this distinction, the Apostle is not addressing greed per se again. Instead, a group, the *rich*, are ordered

---

[387] Scot McKnight, "James in the Story," in Eric Mason and Darian Lockett, eds., *Reading the Epistle of James: A Resource for Students* (Atlanta: SBL Press, 2019), 161–175.

not to be haughty.[388] The word for *command*, in Greek *paraggelō*, could be translated "encouraged." Haughtiness describes social climbing and status mongering so typical of the male-dominated Greco-Roman world. Status in society – expressed with honors given, protected by jealousy, and aggrieved by shame – penetrated every facet of the first-century Roman Empire, and a desire for honor became a constant moral challenge for those following the Messiah of the cross (Phil 2:3–11). Neither were the *rich* to *set their hopes on* the materialism of this world because of *the uncertainty of riches* (1 Tim 6:17). The term translated *uncertainty* (Grk., *adēlotēs*) describes the unclear and capricious nature of economic systems and human relations to them. Since the future is unknown the *rich* are to put their hope *on God.* Why? Because this good and generous God, and here the language could echo Artemis and the emperor as the Great Benefactor, *richly provides us with everything for our enjoyment.* This last descriptor (*enjoyment*) connotes a sense of leisure and relaxation but not in a self-indulgent sense (Mk 2:27; cf. Ex 34:21; Ps 127:2). This idea of *enjoyment* also draws on the Jewish tradition of God's blessing of material provision: those who do God's will are blessed (Deut 28), a tradition Jesus employs for his mission-workers (Matt 6:19–34; 10:5–15) and which Paul himself taught (2 Cor 8–9). It could suggest equitable economic conditions (cf. 2 Cor 8:13–15).[389]

As the Apostle emphasized the uncertainty of riches and trusting in God, so he also exhorted Timothy to teach the rich to be generous. The term *to do good* is used repeatedly in the Pauline tradition for generosity for the poor.[390] God enacts generosity by giving the rains (Acts 14:17) and Jesus teaches generosity to his followers by imitation of God's goodness (Luke 6:9, 33, 35), as does Peter (1 Pet 2:15, 20; 3:6, 17). So, this expression of cultivating or working what is good (*tov* in Hebrew) indicates a character of goodness that does good in all things. The riches of the rich unravel injustice in the practices of benevolent generosity: *to be rich in good works.* Both *generous* ("distribution of what is good") and *ready to share* (*koinōnikos*) as well as *storing up* are from vocabulary registers about a life of compassion, relieving those in need, and generosity.[391] To whom are

---

[388] See Mounce, *Pastoral Epistles*, 368–369.
[389] For a good exploration of generosity here, Hoag, *Wealth in Ancient Ephesus and the First Letter to Timothy*, 217–226.
[390] Longenecker, *Remember the Poor*; McKnight, *Pastor Paul.*
[391] Acts 2:43–47; 4:32–34.

they encouraged to be generous? The text does not say exactly and one could easily slide into thinking that this generosity is for the community of faith alone but it is more likely that the absence of such language, and the fairly typical Jewish custom of caring for the poor in one's community, indicate a wider distribution than just the church's poor. The Apostle has already laid a rather structured social net to care for those in need: families are obligated to their household members (1 Tim 5:4, 8, 16) and there is some system for the leaders of the corporate church to provide for the most needy widows who lack families within the community of faith (5:5, 9–10). These *good works* could very well be public acts that would display the civilized piety of the church in Ephesus, and thus may echo "benefit by their service" in 6:2. However, this generosity on the part of the rich was not, and should not be viewed as, an economic theory to end all poverty but a temporary stopgap so the poor might find self-sustaining work (cf. 1 Tim 6:6).[392]

The *treasure* language of 6:19, borrowing as it does from the Jewish tradition as well as from Jesus (Matt 6:19–21; 19:21), suggests a kind of meritoriousness of eternal life that puts dents in some forms of a Christian theology of grace. However, once one admits the power of grace to transform and that all scenes of God's final judgment in the New Testament correlate one's works with one's final destiny, one sees that this language is perfectly compatible with redemption by grace.[393] Thus, the Apostle offers a way of salvation for the *rich*. They are to *take hold of life*, which is the eternal life of God – [real] *life* (6:19) – by participating in it through beneficial acts of *good works*, generosity, and sharing.[394] (It reminds thus of John the Baptist in Luke 3:10–14.) The Apostle's subtle shift from the outsider "them" to insider "us" language (*our enjoyment*, v.17) signals that the generosity of wealthy Christians is an issue for discipleship.[395]

This is then the Christian civilized piety that the Apostle lays down for the *rich*. If any group's actions will draw the attention of the Ephesian elites quickly it will be when some of their own begin to live the gospel by publicly caring for the impoverished and struggling beyond the

---

[392] Göran Agrell, *Work, Toil and Sustenance* (Lund: Håkan Ohlssons, 1976).
[393] See the exceptional study of David J. Downs, *Alms: Charity, Reward, and Atonement in Early Christianity* (Waco: Baylor University Press, 2016). On grace, again Barclay, *Paul and the Gift*.
[394] Marshall, *Pastoral Epistles*, 669.
[395] Towner, *Timothy and Titus*, 426.

expectations of their patron–client systems. The Christian rich are not merely using gifts for the poor as a measured display of extravagant wealth or for the benefit of some public honor. Instead, engaging in an extravagant generosity could very well jeopardize the *rich*'s public honor and their financial comfort (cf. 17, *enjoyment*). Such a willingness to *share* with the poor might be disgraceful for the Ephesian aristocracy, but the Apostle contends that such a gospel-based economic life is *storing up for them a good foundation for the* [eschatological] *future*. Indeed, these rich Christians are displaying the gospel through their generosity and sharing with the poor in ways that allows them to begin experiencing eternal life even in the present age.[396]

6:20–21 YET MORE FINAL WORDS FOR TIMOTHY

The Apostle now signs off on the letter with a return to instruct Timothy directly.

> **6:20** Timothy, guard the deposit entrusted to you. Avoid the profane chatter and contradictions of what is falsely called knowledge;
> **21** by professing it some have missed the mark as regards the faith. Grace be with you.

Two more instructions close the letter, the first summarizing the letter's focus on teaching the true gospel by opposing false teaching, and the second seemingly shaped by the common problem Paul himself experienced in every mission community he formed: endless debates that do not lead to spiritual formation. *Guard the deposit entrusted to you* refers to something deposited with him,[397] and here it refers to the gospel (cf. *the faith*, v. 21), to orderly church formation, and to civilized piety.[398] The language of "deposit" for the faith leverages the theme of wealth to invoke something more valuable.

The grammar of 6:20b suggests that the two verbs (*guard, avoid*) are not two coordinated instructions but the first (*guard*) is the instruction while the second (*avoid*) is a means or a form of guarding. Thus, it could be

---

[396] Towner, *Timothy and Titus*, 429.
[397] That *paradosis*, or "tradition," is not used here leads some to think a distinction from *parathēkē* (1 Tim 1:18; 2 Tim 1:12, 14; 2:2) is at hand, but the New Testament uses tradition often enough (cf. 2 Thess 2:15; 3:6; 1 Cor 11:2, 23; 15:1–8; Jude 3). The two terms are all but synonymous.
[398] Johnson, *1–2 Timothy*, 311.

translated as "guard by avoiding" or even "guard by turning away from." The Apostle began this letter by criticizing the false teachers for expending their energy in debates (1:3–4 speaks of "myths," and "genealogies," and "speculations"; 1:6 uses "meaningless talk"; cf. 5:4–5) that do not promote "love" (1:5) while those obsessed with intellectual wrangling wander from the faith (1:6). The same issue emerges here at the end of the letter: *some have missed the mark as regards the faith* (6:21) precisely because they are obsessed with *profane chatter and contradictions* (6:20). Timothy is expected to *guard* the apostolic gospel by learning to *avoid* wasting his time on the rival *knowledge* of the false teachers.[399]

The letter ends with a customary prayer: *grace be with you* (and I must say "And also with you"), but one can't use the customary *grace* without it carrying over some echo of God's grace in nascent Christian theology, particularly as a gift for empowerment. The *you* in the last line of the letter is a plural "you-all," indicating that while this letter was written to Timothy, such a letter was filled with apostolic instruction for the Ephesian church, and thus would be expected to be read to the whole community of faith.

---

[399] Towner, *Timothy and Titus*, 431–432, 434; Witherington, *Letters and Homilies for Hellenized Christians*, 299.

3 Commentary on 2 Timothy

This letter is not like 1 Timothy or Titus but is more like a farewell, at least in a traditional reading of 4:1–8, esp. vv. 6–8, and some would argue it is the last letter written by Paul himself. I am unpersuaded that the farewell theory has been overturned. More than two decades ago Séan Charles Martin compared the image of Paul in 2 Timothy with the roughly contemporary images of Moses and concluded that as Moses was depicted as a prophet, a lawgiver, and a suffering intercessor, so also was Paul as depicted in this letter.[1] One cannot deny some thematic connections even if one is not altogether convinced by Martin's approach. This is one of the several themes in 2 Timothy that distinguishes this letter from the other PEs, though differences tend to get exaggerated at times.

1:1–2 THE APOSTLE TO PASTOR OF PASTORS

The letter does not tell us where Paul is or where Timothy is, though many assume Timothy is in Ephesus. When the Apostle says in 1:15 that "all who are in Asia have turned away from me" and in 4:12 that he has sent Tychicus to Ephesus we get the suggestion Timothy is not in Ephesus. Which leaves us asking where Timothy is, and some at least suggest he's back home in Iconium.[2] Paul is in Rome (1:17).

1:1 Paul, an apostle of Christ Jesus by the will of God, for the sake of the promise of life that is in Christ Jesus,

1:2 To Timothy, my beloved child: Grace, mercy, and peace from God the Father and Christ Jesus our Lord.

---

[1] Séan Charles Martin, *Pauli Testamentum: 2 Timothy and the Last Words of Moses* (Tesi Gregoriana, Serie Teologia 18; Rome: Gregorian University Press, 1997).
[2] Hutson, *1–2 Timothy, Titus*, 160.

Letters began then as they do now with a well-wish of some sort, and as now so then: they show variations. The greeting of 2 Tim differs somewhat from that of 1 Tim in (1) the change of "command of God our Savior ..." to a more consistent Pauline introduction of "will of God" (cf. 1 Cor 1:1; 2 Cor 1:1; Eph 1:1; Col 1:1), (2) the addition of "for the sake of the promise of life," and (3) the shift from "loyal child in the faith" to "beloved child."[3] These are nuanced but not notable differences. (For what is similar see the Commentary on 1 Timothy.) The Apostle's mission is to form churches in his prescribed mission regions and to appoint his close associates to look after those churches while he presses onward. The implication is that this letter functions both as a personal letter and as a letter for other church leaders and churches under their pastoral oversight.[4] The plethora of names mentioned by Paul hints at this characteristic in the letter. There are two dozen names mentioned in 2 Timothy as compared to only three names in 1 Timothy.[5]

As in 1 Timothy, Paul describes his relationship to the audience as that of an *apostle* by the *will of God*, a phrase connected to a Jewish sense of piety. These terms both cast a divinely determined form to Paul's whole life[6] and also locate his ministry in God's redemptive mission for creation,[7] here expressed as *for the sake of the promise of life that is in Christ Jesus* (2 Tim 1:1). Paul's missionary work, including this letter, is consistent with this *promise of life*.[8] Much today has been made of the gospel of Jesus and the apostles as not being about going to heaven when we die, and this emphasis has been salutary, but one might then fail to emphasize a fundamental theme of the gospel: the new kind of life given in Christ that begins to transform believers now and leads into an endless life with God beyond death (cf. 1 Timothy 4:8).[9] This two-dimension redemption comes

---

[3] For discussions of comparisons and for the conversation about pseudonymity, see Marshall, *Pastoral Epistles*, 683–687.

[4] Knight, *The Pastoral Epistles*, 2008, 363. Witherington is not convinced the intention of the letter was to be read congregationally, see Witherington, *Letters and Homilies for Hellenized Christians*, 307.

[5] Collins, *1 & 2 Timothy and Titus*, 2002, 178.

[6] Collins, *1 & 2 Timothy and Titus*, 187–188; Towner, *Timothy and Titus*, 2006, 440.

[7] This then touches more on the *missio Dei*, on which see now John R. Franke, *Missional Theology: An Introduction* (Grand Rapids, MI: Baker Academic, 2020).

[8] The NRSV's "for the sake of" shapes *kat' epaggelian* with purpose, as does the CEB's "to promote," but the prepositional phrase is used for the measuring stick of Paul's mission. NIV has "in keeping with" is more accurate. Towner, *Timothy and Titus*, 2006, 441–442. Contra Marshall, *Pastoral Epistles*, 685–686.

[9] Mounce, *Pastoral Epistles*, 464.

to us *in Christ Jesus* because of his resurrection and ascension (cf. Titus 1:2).

The shift from "loyal child" in 1 Tim 1:2 (*gnēsiō teknō*) to "beloved child" in 2 Tim 1:2 (*agapētō teknō*) not only indicates the more intimate character of this letter, but the term *agapētō* also indicates an intimate friendship many modern (male) ears find uncomfortable. Which is why it retains archaic translations like the NRSV's "beloved," a term from a register of largely unused religious words. The NIV and CEB have "dear," which is underdetermined as well. The term means "the child I love."[10] The term *agapētos* is used frequently in Paul's letters (more than twenty times), which is multiplied if one adds the verbal form (*agapaō*). As such, the Apostle's *beloved child* knows Paul's love (cf. 1:4; 4:9, 21; for Comment, see 1 Tim 1:5).

The distinctive literary features of 2 Timothy lead many to see the letter as a kind of farewell address and thus an encouragement for Timothy and other leaders to carry on the gospel mission in accordance with the scriptures and in the sure hope of Christ Jesus' eschatological coming.[11] (For the greeting see Comment on 1 Tim 1:2).

1:3-7 THE APOSTLE PRAYS FOR TIMOTHY

A characteristic of many Pauline letters is an opening thanksgiving that tells us about his prayer life (cf. esp. Rom 1:8-12, and also 1 Cor 1:4-9; Phil 1:3-11; Col 1:3-12; 1 Thess 1:2-10; 2 Thess 1:3-12; Phm 4-7; and 1 Tim 1:12-17). The Apostle expresses gratitude for Timothy's *sincere faith* and prays for his *gift* of God to be re-ignited. We see also the centrality of family in early Christian formation in this brief introduction. As well, a personal pastoral key is tapped when Paul says *I long to see you.*

1:3 I am grateful to God – whom I worship with a clear conscience, as my ancestors did – when I remember you constantly in my prayers night and day.

---

[10] Is this a term of heir or successor? Some think so on the basis of Gen 22:1, 13, 16; Gal 3-4. For the more affective sense, Marshall, *Pastoral Epistles*, 686.

[11] Collins, *1 & 2 Timothy and Titus*, 181-185, 188. Collins does not believe this to be a point in favor of authentic Pauline authorship but an indication that it was written later by an author speaking fictively on behalf of their hero near death. Witherington recognizes the possibility of the letter being in the genre of a farewell testament, but strongly contests the idea in favor of seeing it as a paraenetic letter, see Witherington, *Letters and Homilies for Hellenized Christians*, 302-305.

1:4 Recalling your tears, I long to see you so that I may be filled with joy.
1:5 I am reminded of your sincere faith, a faith that lived first in your grandmother Lois and your mother Eunice and now, I am sure, lives in you.
1:6 For this reason I remind you to rekindle the gift of God that is within you through the laying on of my hands,
1:7 for God did not give us a spirit of cowardice, but rather a spirit of power and of love and of self-discipline.

Instead of using the common word "thanks" (*eucharisteō*), which is not found in the PEs,[12] the Apostle says "I have grace for God" (1 Tim 1:12). The Apostle's own practices of priestly veneration (cf. Rom 1:9; 12:1; 15:15–16; Phil 3:3) come from his heritage (cf. Phil 3:4b–6 and Acts 23:1): *as my ancestors did* (1:3), that Jewish heritage witnessed in the use of liturgical-sounding morality. By saying *with a clear* [or, clean] *conscience* (see Comments at 1 Tim 1:5), the Apostle means he venerates God consistent with his Jewish heritage as fulfilled in King Jesus, though the emphasis may be on his apostolic ministry.[13] It is likely that with *clear* the Apostle is providing his bona fides when others are accusing him of apostasy. The Apostle expresses gratitude for Timothy in his daily prayers, a routine that included daily recitation (*constantly*) of the *Shema*, the Ten Commandments, and something like what is now called the *Amidah* (e.g., Deut 6:4–9; Luke 2:37; Mark 12:38–42; *Did.* 8:3).[14]

The personal dimension of Paul's relationship with Timothy (see Comments in Chapter 1, "Introduction," section "A Sketch of Timothy's Life"), expressed here in both emotional and intimate terms, is a crucial element of their missionary work (Acts 20:36–38).[15] Timothy is a man of emotions as is Paul (*I long, tears, joy*), and emotions are in need of as much discipleship as behavior. The routine connection by many scholars is that this language belongs within the register of friendship, but this assumption requires moving at least a step or two beyond the text: Paul never refers to

---

[12] See 1 Tim 2:1; 4:3 for *eucharistia*. The term *charis* is used often: 1 Tim 1:2, 12, 14; 6:21; 2 Tim 1:2, 3, 9; 2:1; 4:22; Titus 1:4; 2:11; 3:7, 15.
[13] Marshall, *Pastoral Epistles*, 691; Collins, *1 & 2 Timothy and Titus*, 191; Mounce, *Pastoral Epistles*, 467, 468; Towner, *Timothy and Titus*, 448–449.
[14] "Night and day" is not hyperbole and neither is "constantly."
[15] Matthew A. Elliott, *Faithful Feelings: Rethinking Emotions in the New Testament* (Grand Rapids: Kregel, 2006); Towner, *Timothy and Titus*, 453.

his coworkers as friends (*philoi*). Instead, his language comes consistently from the family and sibling registers.[16]

Prayers stir his memory about Timothy, which in turn stirs memories of the source of Timothy's *sincere faith*: his mother, *Eunice*, and grandmother, *Lois*.[17] Here *sincere* means nonfraudulent and unhypocritical (cf. 1 Tim 1:5; Rom 12:9; 2 Cor 6:6) and *faith* refers to one's allegiance, faithfulness, and trust over time. This faith *lived first*, or "resided, inhabited," in his faith-mentors. These names are not known from the account in Acts of Timothy's joining up with the Pauline mission in Lystra (cf. 16:1–3), though 2 Tim 1:5 confirms the presence of faith in his maternal, not paternal, side. The mention of Timothy's religiously virtuous upbringing hints again at these letters' emphasis on civilized piety, the proper way to live as Christians within society (cf. 1 Tim 3:4–5, 15, 5:4; Titus 1:5–6). The Apostle expresses the progression of Christian identity: the apostolic gospel is consistent with the faith of Israel, the Jewish faith of Timothy's mother and grandmother was fulfilled by their acceptance of the gospel, and now the Apostle commends Timothy for genuinely embodying Israel's gospel-fulfilled faith.[18] Christian faith can be a heritage in community.

Because of Timothy's genuine faith (*For this reason*) the Apostle reminds his mentee to awaken with fire – *rekindle* – God's charism (1 Cor 12:6; Phil 2:13) that was distributed to him *through the laying on of my hands* (1:6; cf. 1 Tim 4:14 [elders, prophecy] and 1 Thess 5:19). While the act of pressing one's hands on a person, common to both Christian and nonChristian Jews, became the rite of ordination over time, here the emphasis – as it should be – is on giftedness, more than status or office. One could say this act does not *make* Timothy a minister but *authorizes* him as a Pauline coworker. Yet, it is only the most nonsacramental of theologians that could think the two – gift and office – are unrelated.[19] The gift originates with God but is authorized and passed on by the Apostle

---

[16] Trebilco, *Self-Designations and Group Identity in the New Testament*; McKnight, *Pastor Paul*.

[17] My mother, named after this Lois, passed to her eternal glory in the midst of writing this commentary. She was responsible in many ways for my faith.

[18] Similarly, Mounce, *Pastoral Epistles*, 467–468; Collins, *1 & 2 Timothy and Titus*, 2002, 192; Towner, *Timothy and Titus*, 450; Witherington, *Letters and Homilies for Hellenized Christians*, 310.

[19] Much has been made of the differences between 1 Tim 4:14 (elders) and our verse, suggesting a hierarchical pattern: from God through the Spirit and Christ to Paul, who passes it on to elders, who pass it on to Timothy. For discussion, Marshall, *Pastoral Epistles*, 697–698; Towner, *Timothy and Titus*, 458–459.

(cf. 1 Tim 5:22; 2 Tim 1:12-14). A position like that of Timothy or Titus in the people of God cannot be seized on one's own, but needs to be confirmed through apostolic leadership (see 1 Tim 2:12).

One can mirror-read 1:7's concern with *cowardice* and *power* as an indicator of Timothy's weak-kneed faith, or confidence, or calling, but there is no evidence of Timothy's weakness anywhere nor is a negation (*not ... a spirit of cowardice*) necessarily an indicator of the opposite. Neither timid nor cowardly squares with what we know about Timothy. Furthermore, the Apostle ties himself to Timothy as he identifies the gift as theirs (*to us*, v. 7).[20] The charism from God given to Paul and then passed on through him to Timothy promotes spiritual *power* and *love* and *self-discipline* (1:7). The connection of *power*, in the sense of witness (Luke 4:14), with *love* as well as *self-discipline* (cf. Titus 2:4, 6, 12) counters the abusive, authoritarian approaches to ministry one finds among too many ministers.

1:8-14 TIMOTHY AND THE APOSTLE

Though 1:7 does not specify what kind of *cowardice* the Apostle had in mind, the next paragraph does provide some clarification. I find it unlikely that Timothy was tempted to disconnect himself from public testimony about the Lord Jesus and association with the Apostle. Timothy was a man of confidence, and the next paragraph exhorts him to take his stand in public where he will encounter opposition. Encouragement to press on does not necessarily counter cowardice.

The passage begins with an exhortation to Timothy, connects that exhortation to the Lord, the Apostle, and the gospel, and then moves into a digression about the gospel which leads back to the Apostle, and then returns to Timothy. Thus, the structure is somewhat chiastic: Timothy – Apostle – gospel – Apostle – Timothy.

1:8 Do not be ashamed, then, of the testimony about our Lord or of me his prisoner, but join with me in suffering for the gospel, in the power of God,

---

[20] Similarly, Witherington, *Letters and Homilies for Hellenized Christians*, 314-315; Towner, *Timothy and Titus*, 455. Towner sees the "us" of v. 7 referring to all Christians rather than being an intimate identification of Paul and Timothy, see Towner, 461.

> 9 who saved us
> and called us with a holy calling,
>> not according to our works
>> but according to his own purpose and grace,
>>> and this grace was given to us in Christ Jesus
>>> before the ages began,
>>> 10 but it has now been revealed
>>>> through the appearing of our Savior Christ Jesus,
>>> who abolished death
>>> and brought life and immortality to light through the gospel.

> 11 For this gospel I was appointed a herald and an apostle and a teacher,
> 12 and for this reason I suffer as I do. But I am not ashamed, for I know the one in whom I have put my trust, and I am sure that he is able to guard the deposit I have entrusted to him.
> 13 Hold to the standard of sound teaching that you have heard from me, in the faith and love that are in Christ Jesus.
> 14 Guard the good deposit entrusted to you, with the help of the Holy Spirit living in us.

The central instruction for Timothy is found in 2 Timothy 1:8's call to faithful exercise of his gift. The term *ashamed* comes from the register of an honor–shame society instead of it being personal embarrassment.[21] Thus, we need to hear about loss of public status (Rom 1:16),[22] and this loss occurred because of one's known connection to *the testimony about our Lord* and a public allegiance to Jesus as king (see comments on 1 Tim 6:13),[23] which occurred for Timothy in his association with the crucified one.[24] Honor and shame in the first-century world entailed not only the individual's honor and shame but also the person's representation of the

---

[21] Dunn, "1–2 Timothy, Titus," 838–839; Towner, *Timothy and Titus*, 463.

[22] Bruce J. Malina, *Christian Origins and Cultural Anthropology: Practical Models for Biblical Interpretation* (Atlanta: John Knox Press, 1986); David A. deSilva, *Honor, Patronage, Kinship & Purity: Unlocking New Testament Culture* (Downers Grove: IVP Academic, 2000).

[23] Behind the translation "testimony" is *martus*, which came to mean martyr, but here refers to the one who sees or experiences something, speaks of it with frankness, and so also takes the risk of the witness to embody the truth by standing on its side. The term has a natural setting in the courtroom.

[24] Towner, *Timothy and Titus*, 464. Collins reminds that crucifixion was also for the lowest of criminals and runaway slaves, see Collins, *1 & 2 Timothy and Titus*, 198.

Commentary on 2 Timothy

community. Therefore, this encouragement pertains also to civilized piety as the public face of the church at Ephesus (cf. 1 Tim 2:2).[25] The earliest Christians were tested daily about their status in society and the Apostle's words shape the core of that test: are Christians *ashamed . . . about our Lord*, who was crucified and was a scandal in the Greco-Roman world? Are the coworkers like Timothy *ashamed . . .* [about] *me his prisoner*? The Apostle implores Timothy to reject such shame.[26] In a subversive turn of phrase Paul rejects that it is the power of Rome which hold him in chains. Rather, the Apostle is *his prisoner* (Eph 3:1; Phm 1, 9), referring to the ultimate rule of Christ Jesus as *Lord* over all things, so even the worst of circumstances can serve him.[27] The lordship of Christ Jesus, then, is the basis for Paul's exhortation to *join . . . in suffering for the gospel* and the recognition that the necessary resilience to do so only comes *in the power of God* (1:8; cf. 1:7; 3:5).[28] This should not be construed to mean suffering is something good or to be pursued. The *power of God* in the gospel is not that violence is redemptive, but rather the gospel redeems suffering and death.

The Gospel

Mentioning God in the context of suffering and the gospel provokes an origami-like set of lines (1:9–10) considered by many to be a creed in nascent Christianity. (I have reformatted the translation above to illustrate the unfolding of subordination.) The gospel, which is the declaration of who Jesus is in the context of Israel's story (1 Cor 15:1–28; 1 Tim 3:16), brings great benefits to those who believe. In brief, two main acts of God open these verses: *saved us, called us*. Salvation is the full-orbed event (2 Tim 3:15) of God's desire (1 Tim 2:4) to rescue sinners (1:15), and it is achieved by a Savior (1:1; 2:3, 2 Tim 1:10, etc.) who requires vigilance and allegiance (1 Tim 4:16; 2 Tim 2:10). Salvation also ushers the saved into God's mission – hence, in 2 Tim 1:9 *saved* is followed up with *called with* (or, "to") *a holy calling*. While this *holy calling* is one generally heard as a

---

[25] Collins, *1 & 2 Timothy and Titus*, 199.
[26] Towner, *Timothy and Titus*, 464–465.
[27] Knight, *Pastoral Epistles*, 373; Mounce, *Pastoral Epistles*, 480; Witherington, *Letters and Homilies for Hellenized Christians*, 317.
[28] The translation "relying" is paraphrastic as is the CEB's "depending." The Greek term is *kata* and means something consistent with or measured by. Hence, the NIV's "by the power of God" (cf. 2 Cor 8:3; Eph 3:7, 20; Heb 7:16).

communal life of holiness, the Apostle drills down the *holy calling* in Timothy's own pastoral mission in Ephesus (cf. 1 Tim 5:22; 2 Tim 1:6).

God was neither obligated to human *works* nor to redeem sinful humanity. Rather God's redemption is consistent with God's *own purpose and grace*. God's work reveals his character nowhere more than in the face of Christ Jesus (1:10; Eph 1:9–10). A larger framing of such a divine plan is echoed in Romans 8:18–39, along with chapters 9–11 (also Eph 1:11; 3:11). One dividing line in modern studies about the apostle Paul is over the meaning of the phrase "works [of the Law]" and whether *works* here in 2 Timothy 1:9 is about those kinds of works of the Law, general good deeds enacted in a person's life,[29] or euergetism – public acts of benevolence for the common good of a city.[30] With the emphasis in the following verse on grace, one should probably hear in *works* those "works of the Law" that gave Jews a sense of elective status and distinction by separation,[31] which seems to be present in some of the false teachers' misuse of the law (cf. 1 Tim 1:3–11), if *works* lines up more with public euergetism then social status is in view. For Paul, salvation and calling are not the result of a person's status or merit, since as divinely good gifts given to a sinful humanity, they are incongruous with the merit of the one who receives them (cf. Eph 2:8–9).[32] The term *grace* then unfolds to reveal the place of grace, *in Christ Jesus* (cf. 2 Cor 5:19), as well as the time when that *grace* was given,[33] *before the ages began* (cf. Eph 1:4). So, this eternally antecedent act of God's predestining grace pours into human history *through the appearing of our Savior Christ Jesus*. Jesus's own accomplishment is then unfolded to show what is meant by *Savior*: he *abolished death* and *brought life and immortality*, all brought *to light* and enacted through the *gospel* itself.[34] Paul declared that nonbelievers cannot perceive the wisdom and power of the gospel on account of their darkened mind (1 Cor 2:1–16; Eph

---

[29] Marshall, *Pastoral Epistles*, 705.
[30] Winter, *Seek the Welfare of the City*.
[31] James D. G. Dunn, *The New Perspective on Paul*, rev. ed. (Grand Rapids: Eerdmans, 2008).
[32] Barclay, *Paul and the Gift*.
[33] In "was given" (1:9), we encounter a dramatic expression for how the Apostle views God's elective grace. As Marshall states (706–707), Christ must here be preexistent and, though redemption is not experienced until after Christ's incarnation, it is clearly "given" before creation and given "in Christ Jesus." But see James D. G. Dunn, *Christology in the Making: A New Testament into the Origins of the Doctrine of the Incarnation*, 2d ed. (Philadelphia: Westminster John Knox, 1989), 237–238.
[34] The common translation "brought" life (NRSV, NIV, CEB) could be better translated "illumined" or "revealed" life. So Marshall, *Pastoral Epistles*, 708.

Commentary on 2 Timothy

4:17-19), even though they are able to apprehend the contours of God's presence (Rom 1:19-20; cf. Acts 17:27). That dim candle becomes the brilliant sun revealed to all in the appearance of the divine Son (1 Cor 4:1-6; cf. Acts 17:30-31).[35]

The Apostle and Timothy

God *appointed* the Apostle to a mission defined by three terms: *herald, apostle, teacher* (1:11; similar to 1 Tim 2:7, see Comments there). The first term concentrates one's attention on announcing a message (cf. 1 Tim 2:7; 3:16; 2 Tim 4:2, 17; Titus 1:3), the second on being commissioned by Jesus (see Comment at 1 Tim 1:1), and the third on catechism (1 Tim 1:10; 2:7; 4:1, 6, 13, 16; 5:17; 6:1, 3; 2 Tim 3:10, 16; 4:3; Titus 1:9; 2:1, 7, 10). The word *herald* draws us back to *gospel* in 2 Tim 1:8 and 1:10,[36] but all three overlap, since all three focus on Christ Jesus himself.[37] The Apostle's mission often led to suffering but paradoxically such suffering is a sign of being on God's side (1:8; e.g., Gal 4:21-31). He willingly suffers *for this reason*: he is *not ashamed* of the gospel (1:12, cf. 1:8; Rom 1:16).

The Apostle clarifies his confidence and lack of being shamed: *for I know the one in whom I have put my trust.*[38] The language has been interpreted in various ways. For some the Apostle speaks here of God entrusting a deposit to Paul.[39] However, it is more likely that the Apostle entrusts something (himself, his ministry and its future) to God or Christ.[40] His ground of confidence then is profoundly personal: God, or Christ, can

---

[35] On the importance of the language of appearance, savior, and light; Collins, *1 & 2 Timothy and Titus*, 203-204.
[36] Witherington, *Letters and Homilies for Hellenized Christians*, 319.
[37] Towner, *Timothy and Titus*, 474; Ward, *I & II Timothy and Titus*, 153-154; Knight, *Pastoral Epistles*, 2008, 377; Scot McKnight, *The King Jesus Gospel: The Original Good News Revisited* (Grand Rapids: Zondervan, 2016).
[38] Who is "the one"? For God: Kelly, *Pastoral Epistles*, 165; Knight, *Pastoral Epistles*, 2008, 379; Mounce, *Pastoral Epistles*, 487; Towner, *Timothy and Titus*, 475. For Christ Jesus: Ward, *1 & 2 Timothy & Titus*, 155; Marshall, *Pastoral Epistles*, 710.
[39] Marshall, *Pastoral Epistles*, 710-711; Collins, *1 & 2 Timothy and Titus*, 211; Towner, *Timothy and Titus*, 475-476.
[40] One could think that, in light of the same words *tēn parathēkēn mou* (lit., "my deposit") in vv. 13-14, the Apostle has entrusted this deposit to Timothy. But the actors in these verses and v. 12 are not the same. The "God/he/Christ is able to guard my deposit" language of v. 12 differs from the "you guard the deposit" of vv. 13-14. See Witherington, *Letters and Homilies for Hellenized Christians*, 320.

protect this redemption until the judgment day ushering in the Age to Come (cf. Matt 25:14–30; Luke 19:11–27).

The Apostle's life is exemplary for Timothy (1:13–14), both in what he teaches (1:13; cf. 1:9–10) and in how he teaches (1:13b–14a), which itself is sustained by *the help of the Holy Spirit*. The dual exhortation of 1:8 was *do not be ashamed* and *join with me in suffering*, and now in 1:13–14 we find another dual exhortation: *Hold to the standard of sound teaching*, or better yet, "have a model [or "epitome"] of healthy words" (cf. 1 Tim 1:16), which is to be performed – not merely affirmed – *in the faith and love that are in Christ Jesus*. The apostolic teaching was learned, not by simple acquiescence but by watching Paul.[41] This apostolic *standard of sound teaching* stands in direct juxtaposition to those false teachers and their demonic teaching in Ephesus, which Timothy is charged with addressing (1:3).[42] The second part of the dual exhortation comes next: *Guard the good deposit entrusted to you*, indicates that the Apostle sees himself as passing on the gospel and its mission to a successor, Timothy. If mission involves evangelism, the forming of communities into God-honoring churches, then it requires both teaching the gospel's truths and guarding what is foundational from corruption. Yet these two actions happen only by the energy of God at work through the Spirit *living in us*.[43]

There is an interlinked working between God, Christ Jesus, and the Holy Spirit in this section. So much so that we might today recognize an early trinitarian theology. While God is the one who has saved us according to his purpose and grace (1:9), Paul is quick to call Christ Jesus our savior and the manifestation of God's grace and purpose (1:10), tightly binding the divine work of salvation between the two. The Holy Spirit's indwelling presence (1:14) is cast as the guarding presence in the present moment of "him" who is able to guard the course of the gospel until the eschaton (1:12),[44] whether "him" is God or Christ Jesus, and it is also the empowering presence of God necessary to reject the public shame of suffering for the gospel in love and faith (or allegiance) to Christ Jesus, just like the

---

[41] Towner, *Timothy and Titus*, 478; Witherington, *Letters and Homilies for Hellenized Christians*, 320–321.
[42] Towner, *Timothy and Titus*, 477–478.
[43] Witherington, *Letters and Homilies for Hellenized Christians*, 321.
[44] Towner, *Timothy and Titus*, 479.

Apostle (1:8, 12–13).[45] In these verses Paul gives a robust, theological encouragement to Timothy as one who is entrusted as a successor of the apostolic gospel,[46] even though he will suffer for it. The gospel mission is enveloped within God's own divine life, from eternity into history. It is given by God, manifest in Christ Jesus, and empowered through the Holy Spirit. Suffering and death cannot be a failure for those who are entrusted with the gospel because suffering and death have already been swallowed up by the story of the gospel in the resurrection life and incorruptibility revealed in it – so live the gospel without shame or fear!

1:15–18 RECEPTION AND RESPONSE

The personal details modern interpreters so often long to know come to the surface in this passage in ways rarely seen, and when this passage is combined with 2 Timothy 4:9–21 we are able to sketch a reasonable scenario for the letter. The Apostle is in Rome (1:17) defending himself for charges lodged against him in Jerusalem. Those charges were examined in Caesarea by two Roman authorities but he appealed as a citizen to Caesar (4:16; cf. Acts 21:27–28:31).

Timothy is in Ephesus and the Apostle wants him to come to Rome with Paul's coat, books, and parchments (2 Tim 4:9, 13, 21). It is likely late summer or autumn (4:21). Anyone allied with Paul at a defense before Nero could be indicted for complicity and this may well have led to desertions by *all who are in Asia*, that is, by everyone (1:15; 4:16; cf. 4:4), including Phygelus and Hermogenes, as well as Demas (1:15; 4:10, 16). Others have moved on, perhaps for reasons of ministry, including Crescens and Titus (4:10). At what appears to be a subsequent appearance in court, though scholarship varies here on timing, we learn of the courageous presence (at some time during Paul's imprisonment) of the Ephesian Onesiphorus (1:16–18). At the time of this letter Luke was the only one present (4:11). The phrase *when he arrived in Rome* (1:17) indicates the visitations occurred in Rome.

In spite of abandonment and opposition by a man named Alexander (4:14–15; cf. 1 Tim 1:20; Acts 19:33–34), the Lord sustained the Apostle and he seems to have escaped condemnation (2 Tim 4:17–18). Receiving a report from at least Onesiphorus about Ephesus, the Apostle sends

---

[45] Towner, 466.
[46] Towner, 466–467.

greetings in 2 Timothy to Prisca, Aquila, and the household of Onesiphorus (4:19). Timothy learns that Erastus is in Corinth, Trophimus in Miletus, and Paul sends greetings from those with him in Rome: Eubulus, Pudens, Linus, Claudius and the siblings of faith (4:20–21). Such is the context for 2 Timothy 1:15's word about those who have refused to stand alongside the Apostle in his trial before Caesar.

1:15 You are aware that all who are in Asia have turned away from me, including Phygelus and Hermogenes.
16 May the Lord grant mercy to the household of Onesiphorus, because he often refreshed me and was not ashamed of my chain;
17 when he arrived in Rome, he eagerly searched for me and found me
18 – may the Lord grant that he will find mercy from the Lord on that day! And you know very well how much service he rendered in Ephesus.

Ministry is accompanied with disappointments, some of which are bitter betrayals. When the Apostle was most vulnerable to the caprice of Rome some of his closest associates from *Asia* desert him, including two about whom we know nothing: *Phylegus and Hermogenes* (1:15). That the Apostle mentions their names suggests his pain and perhaps his judgment on their allegiance to the Lord, the very allegiance already brought to the fore in this second letter (1:7, 8, 12).[47] He reminds Timothy of such disappointments (*You are aware*, or "you know"). An enduring and faithful allegiance to Christ when threatened with suffering is perhaps the Apostle's most prized virtue.

When deserted in a crucial moment, one's most loyal companions can rise to the occasion, and one such person does just this: *Onesiphorus* (1:16). Imprisonment, unlike our day, was not where the accused were sent after a verdict against them but where the accused were housed until the trial. By and large, prison personnel did not provide food and clothing for the imprisoned.[48] They were instead dependent upon friends and family, and in this case one of Paul's coworkers provides for him: *he often refreshed me* probably refers to such necessary provisions. As Paul has declared that he is not ashamed, and as he has exhorted Timothy not to be ashamed (1:8, 12), so he informs the Ephesian Christians that their own Onesiphorus *was not ashamed of my chain* (1:16). Traveling from Ephesus to *Rome, he eagerly searched for me and found me* (1:17). We

---
[47] Towner, 481.
[48] Similarly, Witherington, *Letters and Homilies for Hellenized Christians*, 324.

learn from Acts 28:16 that Paul was in house arrest and received guests and preached the gospel (28:17-28) for "two whole years at his own expense" (v. 30). The comfort of friends like Onesiphorus prompts the Apostle to pray, or perhaps only wish, twice,[49] first that the Lord will grant mercy to *the household* and then he wishes that the man himself may *find mercy on that day* (2 Tim 1:18). Perhaps the man has since died, in which case this could be a prayer for the dead,[50] and that is why his wish is for the *household*. Mercy here seems to mean, in the first instance, God's blessing on the present life while the second sense is divine approbation at the final judgment. The Apostle then reminds the Ephesian church of *how much service* [Onesiphorus] *rendered* there, especially to Timothy.

The Apostle's paragraph touches on loyalty, a virtue that has the capacity to override other virtues if wrongly oriented. In some church settings pastors demand loyalty to "the brand" and to their particular, local church over doing what is right – like facing sexual allegations, financial corruption, and power abuse. In such cases loyalty becomes a vice that covers up truth, preventing confession and the fresh discovery to grace, forgiveness, reconciliation, and healing.[51]

2:1-7 METAPHORS OF MORALITY

In the first chapter the Apostle explored thanksgiving and the need for Timothy not to be ashamed and, if necessary, to suffer for Christ. Among these there is also the importance of holding firm to the essentials of the faith. At the beginning of chapter two the Apostle, after summing up 1:6-14 with three verbs (*be strong, entrust, share in suffering*), explores three metaphors of morality.[52] (Each of these are also found in 1 Corinthians 9.) He uses these three metaphors as a way of pressing home

---

[49] In both 1:16 and 1:18 the verb "grant" translates an optative, which is more along the line of a wish than a prayer. So Marshall, *Pastoral Epistles*, 720-721.

[50] Affirmed by many, for example Kelly, *Pastoral Epistles*, 171; Collins, *1 & 2 Timothy and Titus*, 2002, 217. But of late rebutted: cf. Marshall, *Pastoral Epistles*, 720. See also Towner, *Timothy and Titus*, 484-486; Mounce, *Pastoral Epistles*, 497-498.4

[51] Matthew D. Hockenos, *A Church Divided: German Protestants Confront the Nazi Past* (Bloomington: Indiana University Press, 2004); Matthew D. Hockenos, *Then They Came for Me: Martin Niemöller, the Pastor Who Defied the Nazis* (New York: Basic Books, 2018); Scot McKnight and Laura Barringer, *A Church Called Tov: Forming a Goodness Culture That Resists Abuses of Power and Promotes Healing* (Carol Stream: Tyndale Momentum, 2020), 159-174.

[52] For an exceptional study of popular morality and its various expressions, Morgan, *Popular Morality*. Huizenga explores the masculinist tones at work in 2 Timothy 2;

the importance of allegiance to Christ, and again draws on their intimate relationship with the term "my child" (2:1–7).

2 Tim 2:1 You then, my child, be strong in the grace that is in Christ Jesus,
2 and what you have heard from me through many witnesses entrust to faithful people who will be able to teach others as well.
3 Share in suffering like a good soldier of Christ Jesus.
4 No one serving in the army gets entangled in everyday affairs; the soldier's aim is to please the enlisting officer.
5 And in the case of an athlete, no one is crowned without competing according to the rules.
6 It is the farmer who does the work who ought to have the first share of the crops.
7 Think over what I say, for the Lord will give you understanding in all things.

The first word is *You*, and it is emphatic: *You*, Timothy, unlike the deserters of 1:15–18, are on a different path, the path of allegiance. The instructions to *be strong* (2:1),[53] actually a passive *endunamou* is better as "be strengthened" or "be empowered" by God and to *entrust* in the next verse are then explored with three metaphors: soldier (2:3–4), athlete (2:5), and farmer (2:6; cf. 1:11–14). Each of these concentrates on sticking to one's particular calling. The Apostle concludes with a pastoral observation that the Lord will confirm it all to Timothy.

The term *child* (2:1), which is not patronizing but endearing, appears to be the Apostle's preferred term for those whom he has mentored.[54] To *be strong* in this context means to be faithful like the soldier, the athlete, and the farmer, and the locus of this empowerment is *in the grace that is in Christ Jesus*.[55] One might infer that the Apostle is referring with *grace* to undeserved favor but in this context *grace* more likely points Timothy to

---

1–2 Timothy, 106–114. She roots her observations in Jennifer A. Glancy, "Protocols of Masculinity in the Pastoral Epistles," in Stephen D. Moore, and Janice Capel Anderson, eds., *New Testament Masculinities* (Semeia Studies 45; Atlanta: SBL, 2004), 235–264. In addition to these, Jennifer Larson examined attacks on Paul's masculinity and how he responded by rejecting customary norms of masculinity; see Jennifer Larson, "Paul's Masculinity," *JBL* 123 (2004): 85–97.

[53] Some connect 1:8–14 back to Moses and Joshua, and this would bring to the fore divine empowerment in such texts as Deut 3:28; 31:7. I owe this observation to Phil Towner.
[54] Notice 1 Tim 1:2, 18; 2 Tim 1:2; 2:1; Titus 1:4. The NIV takes liberty here to translate "son" in each of these references.
[55] The voice is passive instead of middle (see 1:6).

his calling, the charism of being a missioner in the gospel to the nations, which itself is part of what Christ is doing in the world.[56] That Timothy's calling is in view becomes clear in 2:2's resumption of 1:13-14 and attention to *what you have heard from me* (cf. 1:13) *through many witnesses*. Paul's missional theology was not just direct instruction but came to Timothy by way of other (undefined) coworkers who confirm his teaching; some suggest this means in the presence of other witnesses.[57] The missionary work of the Apostle always seems to have occurred in groups rather than just one-on-one sessions with the Apostle, who urges him to *entrust* or "present" this instruction to *faithful people*,[58] that is, to those whom he knows align with the Apostle's mission and faith.[59] Such persons are *able to teach others as well* (2:24; cf. 1 Tim 3:2, Tit 1:9). Here we see, like the opening to *m. Avot* 1:1, a chain of transmission, though it is hardly to be equated with apostolic succession of the later church traditions.[60] Inherent to good pastoring is mentoring others into the pastoral calling, and wise mentoring has a conservative side to it – namely, holding to and passing on the strong traditions of the church.

To be strong and to entrust (2:1, 2) takes on a special context in 2 Timothy, namely, the calling to be empowered to pass on the truth of the gospel in the face of opposition, but Timothy is not alone: *Share in the suffering*, or "co-suffer," is yet another exhortation and one of the many "co" terms used by Paul (1:8). While one might think the metaphor of *soldier* (cf. Phm 2) will emphasize courage in the face of such suffering, so popular in typical moral discourse, the Apostle turns it toward allegiance so that *of Christ Jesus* becomes possessive (Jesus' soldier). Allegiance is explored further in *No one ... gets entangled in everyday affairs* (2:4), or civilian life,[61] because the soldier's calling is to *please the enlisting officer* and go where he is told to go and do what he is told to do. To be a *good*, or

---

[56] Marshall, *Pastoral Epistles*, 724.
[57] For discussion, Marshall, 725.
[58] Knight's conviction that only males are in view is as tendentious as it is grammatically unnecessary. There is no wider Greek term than *anthrōpoi*, "humans," and Greek masculine plurals often include women. See Knight, *Pastoral Epistles*, 391.
[59] Towner, *Timothy and Titus*, 490-491.
[60] For a wise statements to this effect, see Marshall, *Pastoral Epistles*, 726-727. See also Collins, *1 & 2 Timothy and Titus*, 2002, 220; Kelly, *Pastoral Epistles*, 174; Mounce, *Pastoral Epistles*, 504-505.
[61] Collins notes that even through the AD second-century Roman soldiers were not allowed to marry or conduct any business outside of their prescribed service, see Collins, *1 & 2 Timothy and Titus*, 221. See also Marshall, *Pastoral Epistles*, 728-729.

"excellent" (*kalos*), soldier of Christ Jesus then is characterized by a singlemindedness to spend one's life pleasing his Lord, and this very observation sends us back to 2:1's *grace that is in Christ Jesus* to see Christ as the agent of grace that empowers Timothy.

The metaphor of a professional *athlete* (2:5) shifts Timothy's instructions from the soldier's devotion to the athlete *competing according to the rules*, but one should not see too much difference between what is said about the soldier from the athlete. As a soldier's "rules" please the officer and as Timothy is to please King Jesus, so the athlete disciplines himself not to cheat but to achieve the goal, since he surely competes for the prize and doesn't want disqualification.[62] Timothy would well have known the thrill of competition. In every major city in the Pauline mission existed stadiums and regular competitions. Since our passage is about Timothy's calling, we could infer from the reasonable similarity of the metaphorical use of soldiers and athletes that the "rules" of the apostolic mission are reducible to one: do what king Jesus says.

The *farmer* has a similar metaphorical suggestion: the one *who does the work*, that is, the one who faithfully labors in the field, is the one who qualifies for receiving the crop first or the first portion of the crop (2:6).[63] In fact, the language is stronger: "it's necessary for the laboring, hardworking[64] farmer first to receive the fruit" is another translation.

While these three metaphors explore different domains of language, a synthesis of them is clear: stick to the task and the reward will be yours. I. Howard Marshall sees the synthesis in slightly different terms: "the need for commitment and the readiness for acceptance of a demanding way of life by the Christian leader."[65] Reduced to the basics, the first is about surrender to one's leader, the second about following the rules, and the third about working hard. All three also include receiving a reward for one's effort. The Apostle, finally, invites Timothy to spend time pondering these metaphors and, in so doing, the Apostle is confident the Lord will make clear to Timothy his next steps (2:7).

---

[62] H. A. Harris, *Greek Athletes and Athletics* (Bloomington: University of Indiana Press, 1966); Michael B. Poliakoff, *Combat Sports in the Ancient World: Competition, Violence, and Culture, Sport and History* (New Haven: Yale University Press, 1987); Stephen G. Miller, *Ancient Greek Athletics* (New Haven: Yale University Press, 2004).

[63] The term "first" (*proton*) is ambiguous; for discussion of options, none of which are compelling, Marshall, *Pastoral Epistles*, 730.

[64] The participle *kopiōnta* is adjectival.

[65] Marshall, *Pastoral Epistles*, 728.

2:8–13 THE GOSPEL IN CONFESSIONAL LINES

The Apostle has concentrated his instructions on being faithful in both doing what Jesus has called him to do in the face of status-degrading shame and suffering, as well as on believing the apostolic gospel (e.g., 2 Tim 1:8, 13–14; 2:1–7). The "standard of sound teaching" (1:13), the "good treasure" (1:14), "the things passed to faithful people" (2:2) – all that he had heard from the Apostle and his coworkers in the mission – now become a set of confessional lines.

2 Tim 2:8 Remember Jesus Christ, raised from the dead, a descendant of David – that is my gospel,

9 for which I suffer hardship, even to the point of being chained like a criminal. But the word of God is not chained.

10 Therefore I endure everything for the sake of the elect, so that they may also obtain the salvation that is in Christ Jesus, with eternal glory.

11 The saying is sure: <u>If we have died with him</u>, we will also live with him; (1)

12 if <u>we endure</u>, we will also reign with him; (2) if we deny him, he will also deny us; (3)

13 if <u>we are faithless, he remains faithful</u> – (4) <u>for he cannot deny himself</u>.

The gospel itself is articulated in 2:8 and preaching that gospel is the Apostle's cause of suffering (2:9). Suffering is an opportunity to walk in the way of Christ (2:10) as a saying of the early church puts into memorable form (2:11–13). Christoformity expresses the core of the Christian life.[66] Christoformity forms the substructure, infrastructure, and structure of the apostolic theory of Christian living. To follow Jesus is to follow in the way of Jesus, and the way of Jesus is living for others, dying, and being vindicated by God.

---

[66] Michael J. Gorman, *Cruciformity: Paul's Narrative Spirituality of the Cross*, new ed. (Grand Rapids: Eerdmans, 2020); Michael J. Gorman, *Inhabiting the Cruciform God: Kenosis, Justification, and Theosis in Paul's Narrative Soteriology* (Grand Rapids: Eerdmans, 2009); Michael J. Gorman, *Becoming the Gospel: Paul, Participation, and Mission* (Grand Rapids: Eerdmans, 2015); Michael J. Gorman, *Participating in Christ: Explorations in Paul's Theology and Spirituality* (Grand Rapids: Eerdmans, 2019); McKnight, *Pastor Paul*.

The Gospel Articulated

Remember exhorts Timothy to take Jesus as his example of fidelity, courage, and victory in the face of suffering. The term means more than "recall" as it entails an instruction to embody what one recalls. The "standard of sound teaching" (1:13) is the gospel, which comes to expression in one person (Jesus; 2:8a) and two events in his life (raised, descended; 2:8bc). Although perhaps understated because it appears only as a prepositional phrase, the *gospel* is the standard for sound teaching. At 2:8d the NRSV's *that is my gospel*[67] translates *kata to euaggelion mou*, with the preposition *kata* nuanced into "that." This preposition (*kata*) indicates standard and measure, that is, that something is "consistent with" something else. Thus, Jesus as Messiah, Jesus as raised, and Jesus as descended from David are the gospel that measures true teaching. There is a shift in 2 Timothy away from the consistent polemic against false teachers found in 1 Timothy. The use of *my* with *gospel* would naturally challenge any different gospel taught by the false teachers but the emphasis here is on the alignment of Paul with the authentic apostolic gospel (cf. 1 Cor 15:1–28; Rom 1:3–5).[68]

It has become a commonplace in Christian thinking to merge "Christ" with "Jesus" and make the former if not his surname at least a name. This has recently been defeated: an emerging consensus is that "Christ" is an honorific or title for "Jesus" and thus "Jesus the king" or "Jesus the Messiah" or even "Jesus the Christ" are the best approaches,[69] and a recent study by Joshua Jipp has put all of this emerging consensus into a theology of the New Testament.[70] At the core of Christian theology is a confession that Jesus is the Lord, Jesus is the king, Jesus is the Messiah/Christ. The Acts of the Apostles can reduce the gospel to one word, namely, Jesus or his honorific: Acts 8:35; 11:20; 17:18; 18:5, 28; 19:13; 20:20–21; 28:23, 31.

---

[67] NIV has "This is my gospel" (similar to CEB); the ESV has "as preached in my gospel." The term "preached" is an interpretive addition. A similar expression is found at 1 Tim 1:11. Both "that" and "this" are equally justifiable translations of the preposition in this context.

[68] Dunn, "1–2 Timothy, Titus," 843.

[69] Matthew V. Novenson, *Christ among the Messiahs: Christ Language in Paul and Messiah Language in Ancient Judaism* (New York: Oxford University Press, 2012); Matthew V. Novenson, *The Grammar of Messianism: An Ancient Jewish Political Idiom and Its Users* (Oxford: Oxford University Press, 2017); Joshua W. Jipp, *Christ Is King: Paul's Royal Ideology* (Minneapolis: Fortress, 2015).

[70] Joshua W. Jipp, *The Messianic Theology of the New Testament* (Grand Rapids: Eerdmans, 2020).

Hence, the gospel is the story of Jesus and is not reducible to the saving benefits, whether the benefit is salvation, justification, or redemption. No, the gospel is Who Jesus is and from that emerges What he accomplishes, which comes into objective reality in what the Father does as a result of what Jesus did and what happened.[71] Thus, in our text the events in the life of Jesus, which terms may echo Romans 1:3–4 or (more likely) standard Christian summations, are two-fold: (1) *raised from the dead*, which must imply his crucifixion, and (2), a very Jewish way of framing Christology, *a descendant of David* (2:8bc). As is seen at times in the sermons in the Acts of the Apostles, the gospel is rooted in the vindicating resurrection of Jesus (e.g., Acts 2:23–24; 4:10; 10:39–40; 13:28–30; 17:31). To say Jesus has Davidic ancestry is to tell the story of Israel's anticipation of a coming, saving Messiah.

The Gospel and Suffering

The Apostle suffers because of this Jesus-gospel – the *for which* could be "in which" or even "in whom" – and his suffering is *even to the point of being chained like a criminal* (2:9). No doubt such a phrase brings to light his current imprisonment as he awaits trial under charges of being a dangerous *criminal* against Roman society, an imprisonment much more serious than the house arrest noted at the end of Acts.[72] He may be chained but his gospel continues to flourish (cf. Acts 28:20, 23–31). As Paul preached and taught at his workplace[73] so he does the same whether free or chained, allowing the obstacle of suffering to become a means of actually promoting the gospel itself.

The Apostle uses his imprisonment to show how suffering forms his own discipleship: *therefore*, or "because of the gospel of King Jesus," *I endure everything* (2 Tim 2:10). The Apostle endures *for the sake of the elect* (cf. Col 1:23–2:3), the people of God, here designated with a general term for those who are in Christ, namely, *the elect*.[74] The long-term goal, as is the case from Matthew through Revelation, is life in the Age to Come, or

---

[71] McKnight, *King Jesus Gospel*; Matthew W. Bates, *The Hermeneutics of the Apostolic Proclamation: The Center of Paul's Method of Scriptural Interpretation* (Waco: Baylor University Press, 2012); Bates, *Salvation by Allegiance Alone*.
[72] Witherington, *Letters and Homilies for Hellenized Christians*, 331–332.
[73] Ronald F. Hock, *The Social Context of Paul's Ministry: Tentmaking and Apostleship* (Minneapolis: Fortress, 2007).
[74] For discussion, Marshall, *Pastoral Epistles*, 737.

eternal life: *so they may obtain the salvation that is in Christ Jesus, with eternal glory*. This highlights the now and not yet of inaugurated eschatology and that salvation is past, present, and future.[75] There is no suggestion that Paul's own suffering is bringing redemption to others (cf. Col 1:24). Rather, what is in view is his commitment to the King Jesus gospel that brings the benefits of redemption. This is a similar theological defense that Paul uses for his ministry in 2 Corinthians 4. The Christian embodiment of the gospel life of King Jesus, especially by leaders, is meant to be an encouragement for believers as the grace of the resurrection increases within people of God and demonstrates God's gospel as a kingdom invitation to all nations until eternity is unveiled (4:13–18).[76]

A Sure Saying

To bolster his case the Apostle turns to a *sure* and therefore authoritative confession[77] that expresses the Christoformity of living the way of Jesus – in his death and his resurrection (2:11–13).[78] Four simple conditions are laid out and are enumerated in the translation above at the end of the lines. The tenses are marked in the translation (double underline for aorist, single underline for present, dashed underline for future[79]). Three of these four conditions have conclusions, the first two are positive (*we will also live with him, we will also reign with him*; cf. Matt 19:28 par. Luke 22:30) while the third has a negative implication: a denial of Christ means *he will also deny us* (2 Tim 2:12b). The first, *if we have died with him*, sounds like Romans 6:8's sacramental union with Christ Jesus in baptism, while the third concerning the consequences of denial could derive from Matthew 10:32–33 (par. Luke 12:8–9). The fourth phrase has a surprising twist and seems to show that these lInes are from a hymn: one expects *if we are*

---

[75] Eloquently explicated throughout G. B. Caird, *New Testament Theology*, ed. L. D. Hurst (Oxford: Clarendon Press, 1994); Ben W. Witherington III, *Biblical Theology: The Convergence of the Canon* (New York: Cambridge University Press, 2019).

[76] Witherington, *Letters and Homilies for Hellenized Christians*, 334; Marshall, *Pastoral Epistles*, 738; Towner, *Timothy and Titus*, 504–506.

[77] For discussion, Marshall, *Pastoral Epistles*, 326–330.

[78] There is much discussion about fragments of early Christian hymns in Pauline letters, as well as hymns themselves (e.g., Phil 2:6–11; Col 1:15–20), and this carries over to 2 Tim 1:11–13. Discussions revolve around origins, which bits are prior to this letter, and its theology independent of this text. For a brief summary, Marshall, 732–733.

[79] The completion of the lines with the present tenses of 2:13 turns attention toward a more vivid implication for Timothy's behavior.

faithless to be followed by "He will be faithless" but that becomes a theological problem so the Apostle twists it to be *he remains faithful for he cannot deny himself* (2:13ab; cf. 1 Tim 1:12). The last phrase, *he cannot deny himself*, actually returns to the third condition of 2:12b. Jesus is utterly reliable in the face of potential human faithlessness.[80] Yet, it would be going too far to cast this absolute faithfulness by Jesus as referring to a concept like the eternal preservation of the saints in some forms of Reformed theology. This would render the hymn internally inconsistent because of v. 12's confession of reciprocal denial. Rather, *he [Jesus] remains faithful* to his own gospel-life in times of pressure. Though many had failed to be faithful in Israel's history before Jesus and undoubtedly many after would not remain allegiant to him, the resurrection vindicates Jesus' eternal faithfulness as the long-awaited Davidic messiah who brings salvation to his people – *he cannot deny himself*.

The first two conditions (*If we have died, if we endure* in 2 Tim 2:11b–12a) express Christoformity. Timothy is reminded that co-dying with Christ means co-living and being resilient under suffering leads to co-ruling with Christ. Christoformity, to create some words, is bioformity, didaskoformity, cruciformity, and anastasiformity: conformity to his life, to his teachings, to his death, and to his resurrection (cf. Rom 8:29). For Paul, the discipleship of the Christian life is King Jesus' very life embodied in the Christian communal life in the power of the Spirit (Gal 2:20; Eph 1:18–23, 2:4–7; Phil 3:10–11; cf. 2 Cor 2:14–16). Our participation in the gospel does not mean that suffering redeems us, but rather the suffering of the elect in Christ Jesus is redeemed by the gospel on the road to the Age to Come, since victorious resurrection always awaits the faithful on the other side of their cruciform deaths (Phil 3:8–11; cf. Rev 6:9–11, 12:10–11, 13:9–10). Yet, there is a requirement: the second half of these conditional statements correlate with consistency to the first: those who die, live; those who endure, rule. But those who deny Jesus when pressed (2 Tim 2:13a has "disbelieve" or "anti-believe" and is probably apostasy; e.g., Acts 17:6–8) and refuse to stand with the assemblies of Christ in Ephesus[81] will be rejected by Christ at the final judgment. There is a moral rigor connected to genuine discipleship in the Pastorals, often noted by us by the term civilized piety, that can irritate the confidence of the morally lax, but it is a

---

[80] Marshall, *Pastoral Epistles*, 741–742.
[81] Trebilco, *The Early Christians in Ephesus from Paul to Ignatius*.

teaching straight through the Bible.[82] Union with Christ prompts pervasive, grace-empowered Christoformity.

2:14–26 FIVE COMMANDS

Timothy now hears a list of five commands (underlined) for his pastoral work in Ephesus: reminding (2:14), doing one's best to present oneself before God (2:15), avoiding profane chatter (2:16–21), shunning youthful passions (2:22a), pursue righteousness (2:22b), and having nothing to do with controversies (2:23–26). This passage sounds like the end to a Pauline letter, but there will be two more chapters after this long paragraph of commands for Timothy. There is also a renewed interest on the opponents, creating parallels with 1 Timothy.

2 Tim 2:14 <u>Remind</u> them of this, and warn them before the Lord that they are to avoid wrangling over words, which does no good but only ruins those who are listening.
  15 <u>Do your best</u> to present yourself to God as one approved by him, a worker who has no need to be ashamed, rightly explaining the word of truth.
  16 <u>Avoid</u> profane chatter, for it will lead people into more and more impiety,
  17 and their talk will spread like gangrene. Among them are Hymenaeus and Philetus,
  18 who have swerved from the truth, saying resurrection has already occurred. They are upsetting the faith of some.
  19 But God's firm foundation stands, bearing this inscription: "The Lord knows those who are his," and, "Let everyone who calls on the name of the Lord turn away from wickedness."
  20 In a large house there are utensils not only of gold and silver but also of wood and clay, some for special use, some for ordinary.
  21 All who cleanse themselves of the things I have mentioned will become special utensils, dedicated and useful to the owner of the house, ready for every good work.
  22 <u>Shun</u> youthful passions and <u>pursue</u> righteousness, faith, love, and peace, along with those who call on the Lord from a pure heart.

---

[82] Marshall, *Kept by the Power of God*.

23 Have nothing to do with stupid and senseless controversies; you know that they breed quarrels.
24 And the Lord's servant must not be quarrelsome but kindly to everyone, an apt teacher, patient,
25 correcting opponents with gentleness. God may perhaps grant that they will repent and come to know the truth
26 and that they may escape from the snare of the devil, having been held captive by him to do his will.

There does not appear to be an ordered argument here but rather a context-shaped set of instructions that are as rooted in the Pauline experience as they are specifics in Ephesus itself. I have ordered the passage by the five imperatives.

Remind

The opening command in 2:14, *remind*, is tied to a subordinating adverbial expression that is translated in the NRSV as *warn*, as if the two are coordinate imperatives. They are not. Timothy is to *remind* the assemblies of Ephesus about what they already know by *warning* or "clearly witnessing" (see 1 Tim 5:21) to the assemblies of Ephesus and refusing to engage in verbal fisticuffs over subject matters that have no substance. The intensive concern about verbal controversies comes to the surface again in the third and sixth imperatives of this section (*avoid* 2:16–21, *have nothing to do with* 23–26). The Apostle's command is given special emphasis in that Timothy is to remind his people *before the Lord*, that is, as accountable to God. The issue at hand, *wrangling over words* (or "not to word-war"), as will be clear in 2:23, are arguments about "stupid and senseless" topics that "breed quarrels" (2:26).[83] His concern is topic (perhaps myths and genealogies; cf. 1 Tim 1:4) and result: *does no good but only ruins those who are listening* (2:14). That which *ruins* other Christians refers to the issues of verbal wars that destroy or abominate a person's faith and practice, and therefore is very much along the line of what Paul called tripping stones (cf. Rom 14–15). It is possible this ruinous teaching is about the resurrection having already occurred in 2 Tim 2:16–18. This would mean Timothy is being told to ignore such fights

---

[83] Towner sees this warning as a deterrent from using the same verbal or teaching tactics as the false teacher, more than an avoidance of conversation about contested topics; see Towner, *Timothy and Titus*, 518.

because they are patently ridiculous to Christian theology, and he should effectively shun (cf. 2:22) such an unfruitful and dangerous topic from discussion within the community of faith.[84]

Do Your Best

Do your best, or seriously commit to *present yourself to God as one approved by him* (2:15), is a general Christian ethical exhortation for Timothy the Pastor. In this context, the exhortation retains the refraining from word-wars. Instead of engaging in hostile debates, Timothy is to work hard to be approved by God. Noticeably, the Apostle summarizes this *approved*-by-God status as being a *worker* who is socially not accepted. Such a gospel teacher works diligently at *rightly explaining the word of truth*. The relationship of *word* to *truth* is part of *rightly explaining*. It is either the "word about truth" or the "word that is truth." Most interestingly, the term *rightly explaining* refers to cutting a straight (unswerving, faithful) path toward a goal.[85] These are not then simply generalized ethics, but specific instructions for Timothy facing serious opposition to the gospel in Ephesus. His calling is to embody and teach the gospel.

Avoid Profane Chatter

Back again to the problem of war-words (2:16–21). There are word pictures in 2:16: (1) the word *Avoid* translates a term that literally could be translated "stand around or outside" (cf. Titus 3:9), (2) *chatter* translates what could be envisioned as "hollow voicing" (cf. 1 Tim 6:20), and (3) *profane* points to populist discourse. This is about the opinionated yacking of the uninformed who think they can take on the deeper truths. The problem here is that such hollow yacking promotes *impiety*, or as we have been translating throughout the PEs, "uncivilized piety," indicating the social disrespect shown to the assemblies for such *chatter*. Even more, the impact of the yackers on others *will spread* (or "advance") *like gangrene* (2:17a). This not only about the false teachers' behavior but an evaluation of the dangerous nature of their teaching.[86] The inner heart of the Letter of James is about control of the tongue by those designated as teachers and

---

[84] Knight, *Pastoral Epistles*, 410; Collins, *1 & 2 Timothy and Titus*, 2002, 234–235.
[85] Marshall, *Pastoral Epistles*, 748–749.
[86] Towner, *Timothy and Titus*, 524–525.

one of the major themes is the dramatic impact of vile speech (3:1–4:12). In an era of social media where the algorithms are designed to maximize outrage the terms of this passage take on added force.[87]

The Apostle names two of the yackers: *Hymenaeus and Philetus* (2:17b), and he describes them as those *who have swerved from the truth*, contending for an over-realized eschatology, that is, that the (general) resurrection has in fact already occurred as a spiritual event,[88] perhaps at one's baptism.[89] One sees similar issues with resurrection in Athens (Acts 17:32), Corinth (1 Cor 15:12), and Thessalonica (2 Thess 2:2).[90] Hymenaeus is attached to Alexander in 1 Timothy 1:20 as those whom the Apostle "handed over to Satan" because of their blasphemy. Their gangrene overturns *the faith of some* (2 Tim 2:18). Jesus, too, warned of impacting others in ways that destroy allegiance (Matt 18:6–7), and we are reminded again of Paul's image of stumbling (Rom 14:13; 16:17; 1 Cor 8:13; 2 Cor 11:29). The Apostle's admonishment to *Avoid* this *profane chatter* is not just for Timothy but it is to be practiced also by the whole church in Ephesus.[91]

The Apostle reminds Timothy that God's work sustains by reusing in 2 Tim 2:19 two Old Testament texts (Numb 16:5; Isa 26:13). The first concerns God's judging perception of who is truly allegiant, and the second those whose confession is matched by holiness. What is noticeable about 2 Tim 2:19 is its opening: *God's firm foundation stands* and on this foundation, the Apostle imagines, is written an *inscription*. The image of a *foundation* was used in 1 Timothy 6:19 for the allegiant life but a similar expression was used for the church at 1 Tim 3:15. The syntax permits other interpretations, including God himself being the foundation ("The firm foundation of God himself") or Christ, the apostles and prophets (Eph 2:20–21; cf. Rev 21:14).

The Apostle in 2 Tim 2:20 uses a metaphor for how Timothy must intentionally participate in God's work by turning away from wickedness.

---

[87] See my essay "The Pastor and Social Media," in S. McKnight, and Daniel M. Hanlon, eds., *Forming a Wisdom Culture in the Local Church* (Eugene: Wipf & Stock, 2021), 248–273.
[88] That the resurrection faith is an embodied reality has been argued extensively by N. T. Wright, *The Resurrection of the Son of God*, The New Testament and the Question of God 3 (Minneapolis: Fortress, 2003). This or a similar heresy might be connected later to the Samaritan Gnostic named Menander as mentioned by Irenaeus (*Haer.* 1.23.5). See Kelly, *Pastoral Epistles*, 184–185; Witherington, *Letters and Homilies for Hellenized Christians*, 337.
[89] Ward, *I & II Timothy and Titus*, 174.
[90] See the extensive discussion of options in Marshall, *Pastoral Epistles*, 751–754.
[91] Marshall, *Pastoral Epistles*, 750.

He begins with a general statement that *In a large house* there are different types of *utensils* for different usages (2 Tim 2:20; cf. 2 Cor 4:7). The house is likely the church just as in 1 Tim 3:15. Here, *special* and *ordinary*, which expresses well the meaning of *timia* compared to the ESV's more wooden "honorable," does not refer primarily to the value of the utensils as *gold*, *silver*, or *wooden*. Rather, purpose determines the value of the vessel.[92] If the purpose is to impress others, then gold and silver items make sense to use, but a mallet would be made of wood, not precious metal. Paul states that *all who cleanse themselves of the things I have mentioned*, pointing back to *iniquity* or "unrighteousness" in 2 Tim 2:19 and possibly all these ruinous beliefs in Ephesus, are able to *become special utensils* because God will consecrate them *for every good work* (2:21). The point is not that special types of people inevitably will be used as leaders for the churches,[93] rather those who actively *cleanse themselves* (cf. 2:15) will simultaneously be *dedicated* by God as a consecrated vessel to accomplish God's *good work*. God makes his people fit to accomplish his desires in his creation and for his gospel (cf. 1 Tim 1:12–16). Still, Christian transformation is an intentional participation with God in the holy life. This metaphor drives home the Apostle's OT quotations in 2 Tim 2:19: trust God will do his work in us, his people, while we faithfully reject wickedness.

Shun Youthful Passions

The fourth imperative (2:22), *shun* (or "flee from"), does not stand alone in that the fifth imperative ("pursue" below) has a clarifying conjunction (*de*) rather than a strong adversative. Hence, the NRSV's and NIV's coordinative "and," while the ESV chooses a stronger adversative ("Run away from ... Instead, pursue righteousness"). The two are tied together whether one uses "and" or "instead." Timothy, to be imitated by all pastors, is to flee from *youthful passions*. The CEB's "adolescent" carries the right tone, though the term "adolescent" has a social history in postmodern Christianity[94] unlike anything in first-century Ephesus. The term *youthful* might suggest recklessness but this is not Timothy's tendency. It is more

---

[92] Towner, *Timothy and Titus*, 539.
[93] Witherington, *Letters and Homilies for Hellenized Christians*, 339.
[94] Thomas Bergler, *The Juvenilization of American Christianity* (Grand Rapids: Eerdmans, 2012); Thomas E. Bergler, *From Here to Maturity: Overcoming the Juvenilization of American Christianity* (Grand Rapids: Eerdmans, 2014).

likely that "youthful passions" here are both a generalized expression, perhaps especially angled at sexual immorality (1 Tim 6:9; 2 Tim 3:6; Titus 2:12; 3:3), and aimed at such passions occurring in the immature (cf. 2 Tim 3:6; 1 Tim 5:11).

Pursue Righteousness, Etc.

The contrasting orientation in life to "youthful desires" is a typical set of terms from Paul: *righteousness, faith, love, and peace*. The term *righteousness* is too easily connected with the term holiness (*hagios*) and disconnected from its roots in Torah: the term refers to behaviors that conform to the Torah, which becomes behaviors that conform to Jesus' ethical vision and what can be generally reduced to life in the Spirit (Matt 5–7; Gal 5:16–26; see Comment at 1 Tim 6:11). *Faith*, as has been mentioned numerous times, can refer to the initial act of truth, to ongoing trust as allegiance, and be a summary statement of the gospel (the faith). Here we are to see faithful allegiance.[95]

Formationally central to Jesus, to Paul, and to John was *love* (see Comment at 1 Tim 1:5). Less prominent is *peace* (cf. 1 Tim 1:2; 2 Tim 1:2; Titus 1:4), which occurs exclusively in the salutations of the Pes apart from this one exception. To exhort the Pastor to be peaceful is to be a peacemaker when needed, a word-war avoider, a person marked by civilized piety, and someone who is formed by and nurtures the reconciliation of disagreeing and warring parties.[96] Those marked by these four virtues will nurture cultures of *tov* (goodness) and *charis* (grace) and so witness to a different way of life, and in the Roman Empire this will mean not chasing the splendors and self-intoxicating glories of the *cursus honorum* but instead the life marked by service to others. That is, Christoformity.[97] Such persons will be in communion with *those who call on the Lord from a pure heart* (2:22), with an emphasis on the term *pure*, or we could say

---

[95] For an extensive study, Teresa Morgan, *Roman Faith and Christian Faith: Pistis and Fides in the Early Roman Empire and Early Churches* (New York: Oxford University Press, 2015).
[96] Willard M. Swartley, *Covenant of Peace: The Missing Peace in New Testament Theology and Ethics* (Grand Rapids: Eerdmans, 2006).
[97] Gorman, *Becoming the Gospel*, 2015; McKnight, *Pastor Paul*, 147–168.

"kosher" (cf. 1 Tim 1:5). Such pure-hearted persons, which Kierkegaard famously described as willing one thing,[98] are marked by these four virtues.

Have Nothing to Do with Controversies

Back to war-words. The first, third, and sixth imperatives are devoted to avoiding verbal wars with others. That the Apostle returns to this indicates both the presence of verbal battles in the assemblies of Ephesus – all illustrated by various groups of Christians evidently forming in Ephesus, most of which seem to have been coagulating around how integrated the Christian was to be with the dominant culture[99] – as well as the importance of controlling one's tongue for those called to pastor churches. From these letters it seems likely that the issues were about economics, politics, public religion (civilized piety), food offered to idols, and cultic worship of the emperors.

As detailed at 2:14, the Apostle describes in similar terms the verbal fisticuffs as *stupid and senseless controversies,* or "moronic and uninstructed disputes." Of course, the false teachers saw themselves as educated.[100] They are a problem *because* they *breed quarrels* (2:23). The value of addressing issues and false teaching is revealed in the outcome of the conflict.[101] Again, the Apostle's wisdom is to *have nothing to do* with such word-wars. The expression refers to an act that is polite enough to be seen as excusing oneself or simply walking away.

The Apostle now turns toward Timothy with character traits of *the Lord's servant* (2:24). Here they are: (1) *not quarrelsome,* (2) *kindly to everyone,* (3) *an apt teacher,* (4) *patient,* and (5) *correcting opponents with gentleness* (2:24–25). Brief comments about each: (1) not to be quarrelsome is not to engage in the word-wars (2:14, 23, and 24) that all use the image of warring (*machē*). Instead, Timothy (2) is called to be peaceful by being gentle with *everyone,* and this again reveals the public nature of these virtues. The call to civilized piety calls for Christian social skills. Characteristically, every pastor is expected (3) to be capable of teaching the gospel and catechizing the newly baptized, which is also a requirement

---

[98] Sören Kierkegaard, *Purity of Heart Is to Will One Thing: Spiritual Preparation for the Office of Confession* (New York: Harper & Row Torchbooks, 1956).
[99] Trebilco, *The Early Christians in Ephesus from Paul to Ignatius.*
[100] Towner, *Timothy and Titus,* 545; Mounce, *Pastoral Epistles,* 534.
[101] Ward, *I & II Timothy and Titus,* 181.

for the bishop or overseer of 1 Timothy 3:2. The pastor is also (4) to be *patient* because the scriptures are "for reproof, for correction, and for training in righteousness" so the mature person is "equipped for every good work" (3:16–17). Any pastor knows that the process of growing into Christian maturity takes time and therefore requires patience on the part of the catechist. Involved as well is (5) dealing with those who strongly oppose[102] the gospel in a gentle manner rooted in the hope that this too will be transformed by the "reproof" and "correction" of scripture (3:16).

Why? The opponents, about whom the Apostle has spared few words from his insult bag, just might *repent and come to know the truth* (2:25). The Apostle believes that no one is outside the powers of God's grace to redeem. The focus of all rebuke is the further Christlikeness of any in the care of Timothy.[103] If redemption occurs *they may escape from the snare of the devil* (2:26). In these last five words we are given an indication of a constant malevolent influence (cf. 1 Tim 1:20, 2:14, 3:7, 4:1).[104] Like Revelation, the cosmology of the Apostle is thick: at work in the world is the *devil*, who accuses and aims at death for all humans, and the devil is accompanied by his minions of evil. The Apostle explains that their opponents here are *held captive* by the devil *to do his will*, but even so he believes they are fully responsible for false teachings and practices.

3:1–9 ANALYSIS OF APOSTASY

While the end of 2 Timothy 2 sounds like a segue into the letter's closing, the Apostle now steps back to provide an eschatological, indeed prophetic, explanation of the apostasy Timothy will encounter (3:1–9), which is nothing less than a shopping list of at least eighteen behaviors in the "last days" of "distressing times" (3:2–4, enumerated below, but one might add two more in vv. 6, 8). This prophecy is followed up with an appeal to the Apostle's own life of escape (3:10–11) and the inevitability of suffering (3:12) and wickedness (3:13), and this is accompanied with an appeal for Timothy to remain faithful to the scriptures (3:14–17).

---

[102] The word is forceful in Greek: *anti-dia-tithēmi*, thoroughly laid against someone or something.
[103] Mounce, *Pastoral Epistles*, 536; Witherington, *Letters and Homilies for Hellenized Christians*, 340.
[104] Towner, *Timothy and Titus*, 550–551.

3:1 You must understand this, that in the last days distressing times will come.
2 For people will be [1] lovers of themselves, [2] lovers of money, [3] boasters, [4] arrogant, [5] abusive, [6] disobedient to their parents, [7] ungrateful, [8] unholy,
3 [9] unfeeling, [10] implacable, [11] slanderers, [12] profligates, [13] brutes, [14] haters of good,
4 [15] treacherous, [16] reckless, [17] swollen with conceit, [18] lovers of pleasure rather than lovers of God,
5 holding to the outward form of godliness but denying its power. Avoid them!
6 For among them are [19] those who make their way into households and captivate immature women, overwhelmed by their sins and swayed by all kinds of desires,
7 who are always studying yet never able to recognize truth.
8 As Jannes and Jambres opposed Moses, so these people, of corrupt mind and counterfeit faith, also [20] oppose the truth.
9 But they will not make much progress because, as in the case of those two men, their folly will become plain to everyone.

The Apostle begins by anchoring vices they have observed that pertain to *the last days* (2 Tim 3:1), which also draws on a Jewish perception of moral decline as time on earth comes to its closure (Revelation 6–19).[105] For the Jewish Christians of the New Testament, *the last days* have been inaugurated by the coming of King Jesus and the outpouring of the Holy Spirit (1 Tim 4:1; cf. Acts 2:16–17, Rom 16:25–27; Heb 1:1–2; 1 Pet 1:20–21; James 5:3 Jude 17–19).[106] A revealing feature of the last days is moral decay.

A Vice List for Ephesus

No two lists of virtues or vices in the New Testament are the same (cf. 1 Tim 1:8–10). This list of vices (or traits of uncivilized piety) can be compared and contrasted with the characteristics of bishops/overseers and deacons (1 Tim 3:1–13; Titus 1:5–9), with the expectations he has for Timothy (particularly 2 Tim 2:15–17), or with other vice lists in the

---

[105] Witherington, *Letters and Homilies for Hellenized Christians*, 348.
[106] Knight, *Pastoral Epistles*, 428–429; Witherington, *Letters and Homilies for Hellenized Christians*, 349.

New Testament (Gal 5:19–21; Rom 1:29–32). There are many ancient corollaries, such as Aristotle's famous virtue list as well as those found in Theophrastus's thirty bad character types, which is nothing if not a comedic excursion through distinct character types of mostly upper-class male citizens in fourth-century BCE Athens. Theophrastus, student of both Plato and Aristotle (who gave Tyrtamus the name Theophrastus, which means "one who speaks like a god"), a polymath with over 200 books, was the successor to Aristotle as head of the Peripatos school, a position he held with distinction for some three decades. The well-known analytical approach of the peripatetics involved observation and classification. His *Characters*, which influenced moral teaching for centuries, and one should not exclude even John Bunyan's *Pilgrim's Progress* from this history, provides an insight into good character by poking fun at bad character. Plutarch was later to define Theophrastus's approach to humor as "a concealed rebuke for error" that leads someone who hears his character sketch to fill in "mentally on his own what is missing" in that character (Plutarch, *Table Talk* 2.1.4).[107] We provide a list of both Theophrastus and Aristotle in the Closer Look below. Vice lists were "crafted for oral presentation, so that repetition of sounds and other rhythmic devices sharpened the impact."[108]

Character matters to the Apostle, so any lists or discussions of character will always counter bad character traits (as in Theophrastus, though our text is absent of humor). So the Apostle now counters such a list with eighteen vices, which appear to be mostly random. We need to consider the opposite of vices to apprehend the traits of Christian civilized piety.

There is no space to examine in detail each trait so we offer brief observations. [1] Those who are *lovers of themselves* (2 Tim 3:2) either don't love God first or, more likely, don't love others (Mark 12:29–32) and are, hence, at least somewhat narcissistic, while [2] *lovers of money*, for the Apostle a core vice (1 Tim 6:10), are in contrast to those who love God, others, and virtue instead of material abundance. Those who are [3] *boasters* assume and exaggerate the fairly common expectation in the Roman Empire of pride in one's accomplishments and the requisite expectation of declaring so, and they are not unlike [4] the *arrogant*, or those who love high status recognition as a way of making themselves

---

[107] From Pertsinidis, *Theophrastus' Characters*, 46.
[108] Towner, *Timothy and Titus*, 552–553. In agreement, Witherington, *Letters and Homilies for Hellenized Christians*, 349–350.

A Closer Look: Character in Theophrastus of Eresos[109]

1. Dissembling	11. Obnoxiousness	21. Petty ambition
2. Flattery	12. Bad timing	22. Ungenerous
3. Idle chatter	13. Overzealousness	23. Fraudulence
4. Boorishness	14. Absent-mindedness	24. Arrogance
5. Obsequiousness	15. Grouchiness	25. Cowardice
6. Shamelessness	16. Superstition	26. Authoritarian
7. Garrulity	17. Griping	27. Rejuvenation
8. Rumormongering	18. Mistrust	28. Slander
9. Sponging	19. Squalor	29. Pro-scoundrels
10. Penny-pinching	20. Bad Taste	30. Chiseling

A Closer Look: Virtues of Aristotle[110]

	Deficiency	The Mean	Excess
1.	Coward	Courage	Rash
2.	Unable to feel	Temperance	Intemperance
3.	Lack of generosity	Generosity	Profligacy
4.	Pettiness	Magnificence	Vulgarity
5.	Pusillanimity	Magnanimity	Vanity
6.	Unambitious	Good ambition	Bad ambition
7.	Passivity	Gentleness	Irascibility
8.	Self-deprecation	Truthfulness	Boastfulness
9.	Boorishness	Wit	Buffoonery
10.	Quarrelsomeness	Friendliness	Obsequious
11.	Bad-tempered	Friendliness [same as 10]	Flatterer
12.	Shameless	Polite	Bashful
13.	Spitefulness	Righteous indignation	Enviousness

---

[109] The labels of these "characters" are, with only slight revision to help them fit in the lists, from J. Rusten, and I. C. Cunningham, *Theophrastus: Characters* (LCL 225; Cambridge, MA: Harvard University Press, 2002). Also J. Diggle, *Theophrastus' Characters*, Cambridge Classical Texts and Commentaries 43 (Cambridge: Cambridge University Press, 2004). See also Paul Millett, *Theophrastus and His World* (Cambridge Classical Journal Supplement 33; Cambridge: Cambridge Philological Society, 2007); Sonia Pertsinidis, *Theophrastus' Characters: An Introduction*, Routledge Focus on Classical Studies (New York: Routledge, 2018). Problematic for reading Theophrastus' *Characters* is the condition of the text, and Pertsinidis is not alone in excluding as secondary the prologues, epilogues, and the banal definitions. I could not move on without mentioning a worthy, and more fun, successor to Theophrastus in LeRoy Koopman's *Guide to Ecclesiastical Birdwatching* (Glendale: Regal, 1973).

[110] This is from the Introduction to *Theophrastus: Characters*, 14, but was of course expounded at length in Aristotle's *Nicomachean Ethics*. Translations are mostly theirs with some of my own.

manifest as superior. The Apostle next moves to [5] *abusive*, which in Judaism (1 Tim 1:13) carries the sense of blaspheming God, while in the Roman world and in this context has more to do with antisocial, rude, or uncivilized public behavior, such as insulting others.[111] At the opposite pole to "abusive" is reverent piety and especially in the PEs civilized piety.

The vices from #6 through #14 (2 Tim 3:2-3), minus #11, all are negations and begin in Greek with an *alpha-privative*, the English equivalent being "un" or "a" or "in" as *un*clean or *a*moral *or in*validate. [6] Those who *are disobedient to parents* (3:2) recalls the law (Deut 21:18) but the term translated *disobedient* conveys the sense of someone who is *unpersuaded* and even *unpersuadable*, and hence recalcitrant and repudiating one's parents. The Apostle envisages a Christian life in which obedience to parents is expected in childhood as seen in the Household Regulations (Col 3:20; Eph 6:1-3). However, a child's availability and consideration of their parents never abates in adulthood. The person who is [7] *ungrateful* could also put a label on the one who lacks grace in dealing with others and needs to learn how to be gracious and forgiving, while [8] *unholy* is not a translation of the typical Jewish concept of holiness (*hagios*) as usefulness for God's work but translates *anosios*, which often has the sense of disregarding or disrespecting the proper religious order God has instituted among men.[112] In 1 Timothy it is used for those in need of the law's revelation (1 Tim 1:9). Marshall contends that this is the one religious term in the list, but we must observe that religion was as public as it was private, if not more so, and had to do with social obligation. To be *anosios* comports well with civilized piety. The opposite of "unholy" in the Pes is *eusebeia*, civilized piety, which we see the Apostle working towards in 2 Tim 3:5. The translation *unfeeling* for [9] in 2 Timothy 3:3 describes unsympathetic and the unempathic person. This word, *astorgoi*, is opposite of the rarely used Greek word for love, *stergō*, which indicates the natural love that develops between husbands and wives, parents and children, siblings, and close-knit communal relationships. They are *inhuman* because they lack the natural compassion, mercy, and commiseration for those with a family connection. A similar sense is found in [10] *implacable*, which could be "heartless" (as it is in the NRSV's Rom 1:31) or unwilling to reach out one's hand of agreement. They refuse to allow forgiveness or reconciliation (cf. Matt 6:14-15). [11] A term used for the accuser, or

---

[111] Collins, *1 & 2 Timothy and Titus*, 247.
[112] Knight, *Pastoral Epistles*, 431-432.

Satan, or transliterated as "devil," *slanderers* (1 Tim 3:11; Titus 2:3) paints a person as one having the accusing, criticizing finger-pointer, thus, as hypercritical. The Christian community is called to love one another, not to judge one another, and to speak kindly (James 4:11–12). After [11]'s interruption of the negations, the Apostle speaks of [12] *profligates*, that is, those who have no grip on their own life – hence, unfiltered mouth, unconquered passions, and unbridled behaviors. The opposite is self-control and being filled with the Spirit (Gal 5:23; Eph 5:18). The term [13] *brutes* comes as a shock, but it also appears in Titus 1:12 as a mark of the Cretans and indicates an uncultivated, undomesticated, uncivilized barbarian. Again, the counter is a civilized and respectable public person (*eusebeia*). Next is [14] a word formed on its roots: *a* + *philos* [love] + *agathos* [good], which literally refers to those who don't love what is good. While "the good" is key a philosophical term for the Greek about the divine structure of nature, for the Jew it further indicates one of the Bible's most comprehensive moral terms (*tov*) of wisdom for how to live well within God's creation.

The terms seem to descend into Dante's inferno because [15] *treacherous*, which could easily be translated as "betrayers" (a term connected with Judas [Mark 3:19] and murder [Acts 7:52]), is the direct opposite of faithful, trustworthy, and honest. The image of falling over, which describes the drunken, the impulsive, and [16] the morally *reckless* is not unlike those described in Roman satires of Juvenal or in Petronius' *Satyricon*, not least in the tipsy behaviors in his feast of Trimalchio. Its alternative is a measured, controlled, moderate life. An honor and status society, as Rome was in spades, is fueled by the ambitious and those [17] *swollen with conceit*, which suggests persons puffed up and filled with desire for high status recognition (cf. 1 Tim 3:6; 6:5). This sort of ambition is put into comedy in Luke 14:7–14. Every agora in the Empire was populated by such persons, and its opposite is the paradoxical virtue of humility (Phil 2:6–11). Such self-important individuals are often [18] *lovers of pleasure*, a term made up of *philos* and *hedomai* (from which we get hedonism). It is not that God-lovers don't find pleasure in loving God[113] but that this form of *pleasure* is entirely sensual and fueled by social status (cf. Titus 3:3), hinting once more at the presence of sexual immorality. In the next verse (2 Tim 3:5) the Apostle reveals he has in mind those who

---

[113] One thinks of "Theophilus" in Acts 1:1, a name built on the adjective in 2 Tim 3:4.

have an outward form of godliness [or civilized piety], which means their religiosity seeks social approval and habituates itself to social custom but by openly *denying its power* they reject the godliness that shapes both the form and practice of the community of faith (1 Tim 3:14–16). The NRSV's decision to add "outward" is perhaps mistaken. The expression is "having a form of civilized piety" (as in NIV) and does not refer to hypocritical behaviors designed to mask disingenuous intentions (cf. Matt 6:1–18) but the promotion of a misguided style of genuine spirituality (1 Tim 1:6–7; 2 Tim 2:25–26) and rejection of the apostolic teaching (1 Tim 5:14–15, 6:3–5, 9–10, 20–21; 2 Tim 3:3–4).[114]

The Apostle has but one term in response to this list of eighteen vices: *Avoid* such persons! Turn from them to God and to a civilized piety of which God approves. One can see this as walking away from such persons or it could refer, in a more extended sense, to preventing such persons from infecting the assemblies in Ephesus.

It appears the apostle is not yet done, so one should count two more vices: [19] *those who make their way into households* (2 Tim 3:6), or who infiltrate the house churches (cf. Gal 2:4), and those who [20] *oppose the truth* (3:8). In v. 6 then the Apostle turns from a more general listing of vices to some specifics about (yet again) the false teachers one will face in Ephesus. There are two features of their practice – the home invasions[115] and their invasions with false teaching. This, then, is not unlike 1 Timothy 5:11–15's description of young widows and their false teaching. It is most unlikely that the Apostle, however, is referring generally to widows or women in 2 Timothy 3:6–9 for in fact these *women* are the victims of false teaching. The act of the false teachers here is to *captivate* (Rom 7:23 vs. 2 Cor 10:5) with their manipulative and strong-armed, even forceful approach.[116] In the former version of the NRSV the Apostle labels such women with the term *silly*, an interpretive move without evidence. The updated edition changed this to *immature*. The Greek term is a diminutive of women, hence "little" *women*, so the updated edition along with the CEB's "immature" is a better translation, as what is diminutive here is the women's theological capacity to reject false teachings.

---

[114] Marshall, *Pastoral Epistles*, 775; Knight, *Pastoral Epistles*, 432–433; Towner, *Timothy and Titus*, 560–561.
[115] The CEB has "slither into households" at 2 Tim 3:6.
[116] Witherington, *Letters and Homilies for Hellenized Christians*, 351–353.

The result is that these immature women are *overwhelmed by their sins and swayed by all kinds of desires, who are always studying yet never able to recognize the truth* (2 Tim 3:6b–7). This could suggest, if one assumes the same groups as in 1 Timothy 5 on the basis of similar descriptions of sins, that the women, who take the brunt of criticism in 1 Timothy, have been duped by male false teachers and so challenge or balk at the overseer's teaching of the apostolic gospel (1 Tim 2:12; see notes there).[117] If 1 Timothy 2:11 emphasizes a woman listening-to-learn as is also the case for Timothy in 2 Timothy 3:14, then 2 Timothy 3:7 suggests a listening-without-learning. These mistaken women are *always being instructed*, or apprenticed, but never become individuated into gospel *truth*. The terms used for where they never arrive – *can never arrive at a knowledge of the truth* – could suggest a focus on conversion rather than catechism.[118] The terms used are not clear, but what is clear is that this true knowledge leads into a life among the people of God, while the knowledge peddled by these false teachers leads into sin and away from the apostolic faith (cf. 1 Tim 6:20–21).

From his large basket of examples that could be taken from the OT, the Apostle pulls out two paradigmatic names of opponents to covenant truths: *Jannes and Jambres*, the two Egyptian sorcerers who are named not in the OT itself but over time acquire names (cf. Exod 7:8–13).[119] They have become for the Apostle paradigms of those who [20] *oppose the truth*, and the false teachers fail to embrace the truth because of a *corrupt mind and counterfeit faith* (2 Tim 3:8). Their mind, not being illuminated by the truth of Scripture or the gospel, is degraded or depraved (cf. Titus 1:15). Their faith is *counterfeit*, or nongenuine, rejected, or unapproved (2 Tim 3:5; Titus 1:16). The Apostle's term here suggests these false teachers are somehow connected to the gospel community but for the Apostle they are not genuine believers or approved teachers, though some had been before (1 Tim 1:20; 2 Tim 2:16–18). There is something about the apostolic gospel that is unsatisfying to them and they believe it needs to be reworked to more relevantly address the needs of Ephesian Christians.[120] These false teachers are the opposites of Timothy, who is approved and teaches truth (2 Tim 2:15).

---

[117] Towner, *Timothy and Titus*, 561–562.
[118] Towner, 563.
[119] See CD 5:17–19; Targum Neofiti to Exodus 7:11–12 does not have these names but Targum Pseudo-Jonathan does add them, and adds the names as well at Exodus 1:15. For further explanation, see Towner, 563–564.
[120] Towner, *Timothy and Titus*, 567–568.

With *mind* and *faith* it is not entirely clear if the Apostle is speaking about the women who have been led astray by the false teachers in 2 Timothy 3:8 or about the distorted faculties of the false teachers. The next verse's first half – *But they will not make much progress, . . . their folly will become plain* is compared with the *folly* "of those" (NRSV's *everyone* is too encompassing; so too NIV). The CEB is more accurate with "like those others." It's possible that "those others" could be the false teachers but the more common reading is that "those others" refers to *Jannes and Jambres*, which would mean the whole of 3:8–9 is focused on the false teachers.[121] Appealing to their coming social humiliation, the Apostle says their *folly*, or "ignorance" and lack of knowledge, *will become plain*. Such an expression refers to the public manifestation of their false teaching, and the "public" here is at least within the assemblies of Ephesus.

3:10–17 A CHARGE FOR TIMOTHY

There are three nodes then to the instruction of this letter: the Apostle's life as a model, the desired behavior of Timothy, and the regrettable behaviors of the opponents. He now turns to address Timothy.

2 Tim 3:10 Now you have observed my teaching, my conduct, my aim in life, my faith, my patience, my love, my steadfastness,
11 my persecutions and my suffering, the things that happened to me in Antioch, Iconium, and Lystra. What persecutions I endured! Yet the Lord rescued me from all of them.
12 Indeed, all who want to live a godly life in Christ Jesus will be persecuted.
13 But wicked people and impostors will go from bad to worse, deceiving others and being deceived.
14 But as for you, continue in what you have learned and firmly believed, knowing from whom you learned it,
15 and how from childhood you have known the sacred writings that are able to instruct you for salvation through faith in Christ Jesus.
16 All scripture is inspired by God and is useful for teaching, for reproof, for correction, and for training in righteousness,

---

[121] Marshall, *Pastoral Epistles*, 779–780; Dibelius and Conzelmann, *Pastoral Epistles*, 116–117.

17 so that everyone who belongs to God may be proficient, equipped for every good work.

The Apostle reminds Timothy of his own behavior (3:10–11), which turns into a generalizing principle (3:12), the reason for the principle (3:13, summarizing 3:1–9), proposes behavior for Timothy (3:14), and then reminds him of the foundation of scripture (3:15–17).

The Apostle's Example

The opening verb deserves a sharper translation than the NRSV's *observed*, a translation of the word *parakoloutheō*, which could be more accurately expressed as "followed alongside" in the sense of mentoring by personal accompaniment (cf. 1 Tim 4:6; 2 Cor 6:3–10).[122] The Apostle lists nine of his own witnessed-by-Timothy virtues that are worthy of imitation. He begins with (1) *my teaching* and (2) *my conduct*, or "my way of leading a life" or "my guidance." Education was by emulation in both Jewish and Christian ethics. That connection of life and teaching is why nothing undermines one's teaching like hypocrisy (cf. Matt 6:1–18; 23). Next comes (3) *my aim in life*, a single term in Greek expressing Paul's mission (cf. Rom 15:25–33; Acts 21:7–22:30), otherwise stated as the mystery of the gospel (Col 1:21–2:7). As is nearly always the case with the *pistis* word group, the sense of (4) *my faith* fluctuates from the singular act of trust, to faithfulness and allegiance, to the body of beliefs (see Comment at 1 Tim 1:2). Here the second sense is in view because it refers to a pattern of life. Faith's sense of allegiance merges quite naturally into (5) *my patience* as well as into (7) *my steadfastness* (number six immediately below). Any pondering of a combination of (2), (3), (4), (5), and (7) leads to a perception of the Apostle's sense of persevering faith, or what some today would call the circularity of grace, which means that grace once received becomes an agent of promoting grace in a person's life.[123] The terms "patience" and "steadfastness" speak of the Apostle's rugged commitment to King Jesus in the face of opposition, and it is in this sense that (6) *my love* comes to the

---

[122] Witherington, *Letters and Homilies for Hellenized Christians*, 356; Kelly, *Pastoral Epistles*, 198. Marshall diminishes the significance of imitation in this verb but he doesn't fail to bring such a theme to the fore in the list of nine virtues to follow. See Marshall, *Pastoral Epistles*, 783–786.

[123] Barclay, *Paul and the Gift*.

surface here: love's affection and emotion promotes as well a committed and embodied faithfulness to God (see Comment at 1 Tim 1:5).

All of these observable character traits promoted his "steadfastness" in the midst of opposition, expressed in 2 Tim 3:11 as (8) *my persecutions* and (9) *suffering*. He reminds Timothy of the events that had occurred in *Antioch, Iconium, and Lystra* (Acts 14:1–20), which included verbal attacks against his gospel preaching with Barnabas, a plot to stone them, a flight, the seeming attempt to pronounce the two gospelers to be divine figures, more opposition from the Jewish side, and a severe stoning that convinced the attackers they had been killed. This was only the beginning of a life of *persecutions* and *suffering*, catalogued in 2 Corinthians 11:16–12:10 and often personally witnessed by Timothy (2 Tim 3:10). But he reminds Timothy that *the Lord rescued me from all of them* (2 Tim 3:11) – but not without lasting marks (Gal 6:17). One look at Paul would have revealed a broken and bruised body full of energy for the gospel mission. The Apostle connects virtue to *persecutions* and *suffering*, drawing this list into the theme of Christoformity (2 Tim 1:8–12). Timothy is called to imitate Paul, who is imitating Christ, which means imitating Paul is imitating Christ (1 Cor 11:1; cf. 1 Cor 4:14–17; 1 Tim 1:2; 2 Tim 1:2).[124]

A Principle for Ministry

All who want to live a godly life in Christ Jesus will be persecuted (2 Tim 3:12) has been the experience of countless Christians through the ages. The Apostle combines *godly life*, which we have consistently maintained means "civilized piety" in the sense of a publicly lived and professed faith, with *in Christ Jesus*, which means that publicly acceptable life is not watered down into a new syncretism but is oriented clearly toward the Lord of all. Those *who want to live* a life of Christian civilized piety, even into the midst of persecution, are the exact opposites of those who merely hold to the form of such godly life together while denying its power (3:5). The Ephesus church had its own history but one can say that from its inception and into the second century one of its biggest temptations – seen in Acts, in the Pastorals, in Revelation and in the letter of Ignatius – was cultural

---

[124] Towner, *Timothy and Titus*, 574–577; Witherington, *Letters and Homilies for Hellenized Christians*, 357.

compromise.[125] An allegiant witness to Jesus in Ephesus led to persecution, which is why the Apostle writes that *all* Christians will meet opposition. One might wonder about the agency of the term *want*, which translates a vivid participle: "the one wanting to" or "the one choosing to." Daily, *all* the followers of Jesus in Western Asia Minor faced public scrutiny, status diminishment, economic hardship, and at times physical persecution for their allegiance to King Jesus (cf. Matt 16:24–28). Daily they had to choose to face the heat.

The Reason for the Principle

Verse thirteen may well suggest opposition from insiders. Paul's first label, *wicked people*, is general but it is narrowed in definition by the next term, *impostors* or "charlatans," and that second term suggests the *wicked* are fraudulent insiders, likely with an eye to those scheming their way into women's households (3:6).[126] As the Apostle made clear in 2 Tim 3:1, such apostasy and fraudulence are signs of the "last days" and "distressing times," and some details of moral decline are given in 3:2–9. More about this moral decline is found in 3:13 with *from bad to worse, deceiving others and being deceived*. The image of deception hints again at insiders infecting the assemblies. However, this doubled expression could be an emphatic way of speaking of the depth of deception.[127]

Instructions for Timothy's Behavior

In the context of the Apostle's own resilience and with moral collapse through deception occurring in both society and church, the instructions for Timothy are rather simple: *continue in what you have learned and firmly believed* (3:14). The word *continue*, *menē* in Greek, carries the force of a steadfast faithfulness to what he has *learned* and *believed*. His learning, or being apprenticed in the way of Christ, and believing in the sense of

---

[125] A full study can be found in Trebilco, *The Early Christians in Ephesus from Paul to Ignatius*.

[126] The word for *imposter*, *goēs* in Greek, originally meant "sorcerer," which may increase the side glance at the false teachers who were compared to Jannes and Jambres in 2 Tim 3:8.

[127] So Marshall, *Pastoral Epistles*, 787; Towner, *Timothy and Titus*, 578–579.

becoming fully convinced,[128] is all a part of the process that makes up conversion. For Timothy this process goes all the way back to his mother and grandmother and includes the gift given to him (1:5; cf. 1 Tim 1:18). This process culminates here in a tradition or teaching having been officially entrusted to Timothy (1 Tim 4:13–16, 6:20; 2 Tim 1:13–14) by the Apostle's specific reminder. The validity of the apostolic gospel is linked to a person: *knowing from whom* [plural] he *learned it*. Paul knows of those who have not continued, like John Mark (Acts 15:36–41) as well as Phygelus and Hermogenes (2 Tim 1:15).

The Foundation for the Instructions

Faithful continuance is rooted in Timothy's past instructions because *from childhood* he has *known the sacred writings* (cf. 1:5), a common way to refer to the Old Testament among Greek-speaking Jews. Exactly what Jewish education looked like in first-century Palestine is quite difficult to discern but knowing what it looked like in the diaspora (Timothy was from Lystra) is even more difficult. What we do know is that Jewish parents nurtured their children into a kind of Torah observance fit for life among the pagan nations (cf. 1 Tim. 1:8–11). While they learned mostly by imitation from watching and listening to their parents (primary socialization; 1 Cor. 4:15 strongly links imitation and parenthood), they also learned from teachers and from synagogue teachings (secondary socialization), much of which no doubt was consistent with their parents.[129] However his education occurred, Timothy learned about *the sacred writings*.

The Apostle lays a foundation for what Christians would form into a doctrine of scripture. His words are *all scripture* – meaning these Old Testament scriptures – *are able* (empowered) *to instruct you for salvation through faith in Christ Jesus* (3:15). The gospel-centeredness of the Apostle means he fully endorses the Old Testament as an instrument, even a means, of transformation as fulfilled *in Christ Jesus*, leading to a

---

[128] Grk., *pistoō*, not *pisteuō*, so that "firmly believed" is only partly accurate. The NIV has "become convinced of" and CEB "found convincing" are better. For discussion, Marshall, *Pastoral Epistles*, 787–788.

[129] William V. Harris, *Ancient Literacy* (Cambridge: Harvard University Press, 1989); Hengel, *The Pre-Christian Paul*; James L. Crenshaw, *Education in Ancient Israel: Across the Deadening Silence*, Anchor Bible Reference Library (New York: Doubleday, 1998); Michael Owen Wise, *Language and Literacy in Roman Judaea: A Study of the Bar Kokhba Documents* (New Haven: Yale University Press, 2015).

redemption *through faith*. It is entirely reasonable to think of *faith* here as the faithfulness of the risen Christ.[130]

The foundation for spiritual formation for Timothy points to *all scripture*,[131] which is (1) *inspired by God* and (2) *is useful* for a four-fold process of transformation:[132]

for teaching,
for reproof,
for correction,
and for training in righteousness,

and this process has an aim: to produce Christians who are habituated *for every good work* (3:16–17). We begin with a repetition: this is about the Old Testament (cf. Rom 15:4) and only derivatively about the New Testament.[133] The diminishment of the Old Testament in seminaries,[134] in preaching, and in ordinary Christian Bible reading must learn to face this text more honestly.[135] We may learn to read it backwards and then

---

[130] David J. Downs, "Faith(fulness) in Christ Jesus in 2 Timothy 3:15," *JBL* 131 (2012): 143–160; David J. Downs and Benjamin J. Lappenga, *The Faithfulness of the Risen Christ: Pistis and the Exalted Lord in the Pauline Letters* (Waco: Baylor University Press, 2019), 4–10.

[131] There is a grammatical debate that is not soluble simply by examining grammar. Is this "every individual scripture that is God-spirited is profitable?" or "all scripture is God-spirited?" or "every scripture is God-spirited?" The evidence does favor "scripture" (a singular in Greek) meaning an individual scripture (verse, passage; cf. Rom 4:3) even if Gal 3:8, 22 are almost certainly singulars referring to more than a single scripture. Nonetheless, the singular leans in the direction of an individual scripture reference. Since the term *pas* can mean "all" or "every," the problem with the singular "scripture" may be solved: if every scripture in the whole of the Scriptures is in view, then "all Scripture" (NRSV, NIV) or "every scripture [meaning all]" (CEB) are reliable translations. For a detailed breakdown, see Knight, *Pastoral Epistles*, 444–448; Mounce, *Pastoral Epistles*, 565–570; Towner, *Timothy and Titus*, 585–590.

[132] One might reasonably see a chiasmic structure in Greek if one thinks of the first letter of the terms, though one has to fudge a bit for the fourth: *didaskalia, elegmos, epanorthōsis,* [training in] *dikaiosunē*. Or one could see a chiasm in teaching/training and reproof/correction (Marshall, *Pastoral Epistles*, 795).

[133] John Goldingay, *Do We Need the New Testament? Letting the Old Testament Speak for Itself* (Downers Grove: IVP Academic, 2015); John Goldingay, *Reading Jesus's Bible: How the New Testament Helps Us Understand the Old Testament* (Grand Rapids: Eerdmans, 2017). Some think the term "scripture" includes the Gospels or even some of Paul's letters; see Knight, *Pastoral Epistles*, 447–448.

[134] Dale B. Martin, *Pedagogy of the Bible: An Analysis and Proposal* (Louisville: Westminster John Knox Press, 2008).

[135] Brent A. Strawn, *The Old Testament Is Dying: A Diagnosis and Recommended Treatment* (Grand Rapids: Baker Academic, 2017).

forwards, but we must read the Old Testament if we want to square ourselves with Jesus and the apostles.[136]

A second consideration is the expression *inspired by God*, which translates the neologism *theopneustos*, a term that surely means "God-spirited" or "God-breathed" or "God-inspired." The Spirit of God is behind, in, and through the Old Testament, requiring a hermeneutic that knows how to read the scriptures well.[137] Jews believed the Torah was given by God on Mount Sinai. The Torah was buttressed and supplemented over time by the ancient Israelites and Second Temple Jews with what we call the historical books, the writings, and the prophets, which became seen as part of Israel's scriptures. In addition, Jews knew that even Torah needed clarification if it was to be practiced well so there was the development of *halakot*, or rulings that explicated Torah. These rulings were eventually put in writing in the *Mishnah* and *Tosefta*, which drew commentary and story in the Jerusalem and Babylonian Talmuds. All this is to say that if the scriptures are to be properly interpreted, then they must be regularly read and then explained within the people of God.[138] Therefore, Christians are justified in believing the term *theopneustos* speaks of God's presence through the Spirit in the creation and interpretation of the scriptures, including the early Christian appropriation of the Old Testament and the church's wisdom over time to buttress and supplement the scriptures with the Gospels (1 Tim 5:18), Acts, the letters, and Revelation. The early Christians had clearly begun to discern this spiritual quality of inspiration *by God* within their own teachings and scriptures concerning the gospel even in the first century (cf. 2 Pet 1:21, 3:14–16).

---

[136] Richard B. Hays, *Echoes of Scripture in the Letters of Paul* (New Haven: Yale University Press, 1993); Richard B. Hays, *Reading Backwards: Figural Christology and the Fourfold Gospel Witness* (Waco: Baylor University Press, 2014); N. T. Wright, *The New Testament and the People of God*, Christian Origins and the Question of God 1 (Minneapolis: Fortress, 1992).

[137] Kevin J. Vanhoozer, *The Drama of Doctrine: A Canonical-Linguistic Approach to Christian Theology* (Louisville: Westminster John Knox, 2005); John Goldingay, *Biblical Theology: The God of the Christian Scriptures* (Downers Grove: IVP Academic, 2016); Witherington III, *Biblical Theology*.

[138] Towner, *Timothy and Titus*, 584. Josephus (*Ag. Ap.* 1:38–42) explains the Jewish concept of scripture's inspiration by God as (1) receiving the texts from the proper religious authority, referring to both formation and catechesis, (2) confession of the texts as divine revelation, and (3) faithfulness to embody these texts even to martyrdom. The Apostle expresses all three of these same characteristics: the first in 3:14, the second by the assumed faith in the confessional phrases *sacred writings* and *inspired by God* in 3:15–16a, and the third in expected affective motivation they generate in 3:16b–17.

Because the scriptures are "God-spirited" they are also *useful*, a term that in 1 Timothy 4:8 describes civilized piety and excellent works in Titus 3:8. The term inserts the "So what?" question into theological conversation. The Spirit empowerment of scripture, when read well and absorbed into the heart and mind, promotes character development. The scriptures (1) teach the reader or listener God's will, they (2) are useful for *reproof* or convicting a person of falling short in "teaching" and "conduct"(cf. 3:10), (3) for *correction* or nothing less than straightening a person out, and (4) they are profitable *for training in righteousness*, with the emphasis of "training" or exercising a person into spiritual fitness to do God's will.[139] The Apostle balances orthodoxy (*teaching, reproof*) and orthopraxy (*correction, training*) with the goal of a lived *righteousness*.

It is worth stating that for many teachers reading books about the Bible substitutes for reading the Bible itself, but it is the Bible alone that is spoken of as *inspired* and able to accomplish this kind of *training*. This training, the Apostle clarifies, transforms *everyone*[140] (lit. "the man of God," similarly in 1 Tim 6:11) who listens attentively to become *equipped for every good work* (cf. 2 Tim 2:21). Being *equipped for every good work* further explains *training in righteousness* and has the sense of apprenticing someone so they become capable of acts of service and goodness in the public arena (hence, "good works" and "civilized piety" are connected terms in the Pes).[141]

4:1–5 A CHARGE CONTINUED

The Apostle's personal and charge-like instructions to Timothy continue with two sets of instructions all shaped around Timothy's calling (4:2, 5). In the next passage the Apostle reshapes this passage somewhat by presenting himself as the model for Timothy to follow (4:7–8, 9–18). As has been the case from the front end of the letter, there is triangular movement: from the Apostle to Timothy to the opponents to Timothy to the Apostle.

---

[139] On righteousness, Przybylski, *Righteousness in Matthew*.
[140] Grk., literally is "God's human," a generalizing term that is best translated *everyone* (NRSV) or "person who belongs to God" (CEB). It could be a more narrowly defined special "man of God," such as the leader of the church; see Johnson, *1–2 Timothy*, 421; Towner, *Timothy and Titus*, 593; Witherington, *Letters and Homilies for Hellenized Christians*, 361–362. The NIV's "servant of God" is too narrowly focused.
[141] Collins, *1 & 2 Timothy and Titus*, 265; Towner, *Timothy and Titus*, 594; Witherington, *Letters and Homilies for Hellenized Christians*, 361–362.

Commentary on 2 Timothy

His talking "to" is also a talking "about" so the leader will be prepared for the challenges.

4:1 In the presence of God and of Christ Jesus, who is to judge the living and the dead, and in view of his appearing and his kingdom, I solemnly urge you:
2 proclaim the message; be persistent whether the time is favorable or unfavorable; convince, rebuke, and encourage, with the utmost patience in teaching.
3 For the time is coming when people will not put up with sound teaching, but, having their ears tickled, they will accumulate for themselves teachers to suit their own desires
4 and will turn away from listening to the truth and wander away to myths.
5 As for you, be sober in everything, endure suffering, do the work of an evangelist, carry out your ministry fully.

These instructions are in two sets: (1) five or six instructions of a solemn commitment before God (4:1–2), and (2) the eschatological expectation that there will be a growing diminishment of faithful orthodoxy, which is to be met by Timothy's being faithful in proclaiming the word of God (4:3–5). Some have wondered if this passage may not reflect credal words given at baptisms or at "ordinations" of bishops, elders, and deacons (cf. 1 Tim 1:18–19; 4:14).

Some Instructions for Pastors

Because King Jesus will return as the impartial judge of both *the living and the dead*, the Apostle ramps up the solemnity of the instructions: *In the presence of God and of Christ Jesus*. The Apostle depicts himself here, as he did in 1 Timothy 5:21 and in 2 Tim 2:14, standing in God's presence, making Timothy accountable to God (cf. Matt 18:18–20). The Apostle binds Timothy's present pastoral actions to the eschatological scrutiny of Christ. These instructions in vv. 1–2 are more than encouragements; they are solemn mandates.

The apostle's mandates in 4:2 are a staccato-like set of five, perhaps six, separable dimensions of the pastoral task:

(1) *Proclaim the message*
(2) *Be persistent whether the time is favorable or unfavorable*

(3) *Convince*
(4) *Rebuke*
(5) *Encourage*
(6) [all these] *with the utmost patience in teaching.*

One is immediately reminded by this list of the previous passage's language about how the scriptures are God-breathed and useful (3:16), though the terms here are not identical to the terms there. The instructions here are similar enough to make one think Timothy's six calls to action in 4:2 concern expounding scripture (cf. too Titus 2:15).

To *proclaim the message*, or "announce the word," includes but is not reducible to evangelism (see 4:5). The word behind *message* is *logos*, which is used in the Pes for the preeminent gospel saying (1 Tim 1:15), the nobility of the "bishop" (3:1), "God's word" (4:5; 5:17; 2 Tim 2:9, 15; Titus 1:3, 9; 2:5), the "words of the faith" (1 Tim 4:6), for the saying about physical exercise (4:9), for "speech" (4:12), the "sound words of our Lord Jesus Christ" (6:3), the "sound teaching" of the Apostle (2 Tim 1:13), for "talk" (2:17), for the "message" (4:2, 15), the "sound speech" (Titus 2:8), and for a "saying" about "eternal life" (3:8). The greatest number of these references is to the "word of God" which is the proclamation of the truth of the gospel. This phrase is connected to, but not limited to, the words of scripture. One should probably see in our passage's *proclaim the message* the idea of expounding the truth that is found in those scriptures. The second instruction, *be persistent . . .*, may remind yet again of the importance of resilient allegiance to one's gospel calling but the verb, literally "stand over," here suggests a "superintending" of eager leadership more than resilience. Perhaps it is best to think of hovering around waiting for any opportunity that may afford itself, *whether the time is favorable or unfavorable.*

The third, fourth, and fifth seem to be knotted to one another. To hover over the opportunities to proclaim the word entails more than the one task of either preaching or teaching: it involves the consummate pastoral tasks of persuasion (*convince*), pointing out failure (*rebuking*) as well as exhorting or consoling (*encourage*). Timothy's pastoral context requires each of these pastoral actions, and these words are able to carry much harsher meanings, such as "expose" (1 Tim 5:20; cf. Eph 5:11), "judge," and "implore" and thus can be easily misused by an authoritarian leader. Because of the potential abuse of power the Apostle adds an important restraint – "do all of these" *with the utmost patience in teaching.* The NIV's "with great patience and careful instruction" indicates two different modes of performing the previous five instructions.

Some More Instructions for Pastors

The instructions in 4:1–5 are warranted on the basis of an eschatology shaped both by the coming judgment as well as the rise of apostasy and theological decline (4:3–4).[142] What the Apostle says of false teachers in 4:3–4 he said in 1 Timothy 4:1–5, and that passage might shed light on the concrete realities in mind in 2 Timothy 4:3–4. They are marked by four traits: they opposed faithful gospel teaching, they find their own sources of authority, they refuse the truth, and they wander off into mythological ideas. Such false teachers resist *sound teaching* because they want to hear what they want to hear (see also 1 Tim 1:10; Titus 1:9; 2:1). They want doctrines that *suit their own desires*, or that tickle their ears – an image of pleasure, not curiosity[143] – as something novel they alone comprehend.

Christian theology has a conservative impulse: it conserves the gospel and resists what counters its truths. The opponents are people who *turn away from listening to the truth and wander away to myths* (cf. 1 Tim 1:4, 6; 4:7; Titus 1:14).[144] Some today seek to save the term "myth" by pointing out that it was a meaning-making narrative seeking to offer some revelation of truth. While this might have been true, Greeks and Romans in the first century often spoke of myths as unhistorical tales that offered moralistic lessons, like fables and parables. Paul believes that the apostolic gospel is a historically manifested reality inherently opposite of a myth (2 Tim 4:4).[145] Instead of turning to the faithful teachers of the gospel – elders and bishops who have been tested as faithful – they pile up or *accumulate for themselves teachers* who will teach what they want to hear, his terms for what we call "church shopping."

Unlike the false teachers – *As for you*, Timothy is expected to do four more things in addition to the six in the first set of instructions (2 Tim 4:5):

(7) *Be sober*
(8) *Endure suffering*
(9) *Do the work of the evangelist*
(10) *Carry out your ministry fully*.

---

[142] Witherington III, *Jesus, Paul and the End of the World*; Ben W. Witherington III, *New Testament Theology and Ethics*, 2 vols. (Downers Grove: IVP Academic, 2016).
[143] So Matthijs den Dulk, "No More Itch (2 Tim 4.3)," *NTS* 64 (2018): 81–93.
[144] For the teaching of the opponents, see Chapter 1, "Introduction", section "The Opponents in the Pastoral Epistles."
[145] Collins, *1 & 2 Timothy and Titus*, 2002, 270–271; Towner, *Timothy and Titus*, 605; Witherington, *Letters and Homilies for Hellenized Christians*, 365.

Sobriety indicates a moral and theological conservation of the gospel that simultaneously has the courage to face opposition (1 Thess 5:6, 8; 1 Pet 1:13; 4:7; 5:8). The Apostle's second instruction here, *endure suffering*, indicates suffering at the hands of these false teachers and the society. His third instruction about the *work of an evangelist* is a calling apparently only a few had in the early church (cf. Acts 21:8; Eph 4:11).[146] Nowhere is there an imperative in the New Testament calling everyone to be an evangelist, though each is to be ready as a witness and each is to support the work of those called to evangelism. It is not possible to know from this text if the Apostle is thinking along the lines of Ephesians 4:11, that someone has the gift of evangelism, or if he thinks Timothy's ministry needs to include evangelistic work.

If Timothy abides in these instructions he will be one who completely accomplishes (NRSV: *carry out*) his service to God or perhaps more accurately, to be "fully assured about his ministry." The term translated "carry out" has the sense of being fully assured in other texts (Luke 1:1; Rom 4:21; 14:5; Col 4:12), while later in this chapter (2 Tim 4:17) the sense may be more along the line of fully accomplished, though even there "fully assured" makes sense too. As the text moves next into Paul's statements about his own impending martyrdom, *carry out your ministry fully* includes a solemn note of succession.

4:6–18 PERSONAL DETAILS

One of the elements of letter writing informed recipients of news about the letter writer, and this is what this passage before us does. Historians comb over such passages to glean bits of information for reconstructing the biographical details about Paul's life. Portions like these press the claims of pseudonymity into deliberate falsification or at least deliberate fiction designed to give an appearance of historical reality.[147]

---

[146] John P. Dickson, *Mission-Commitment in Ancient Judaism and in the Pauline Communities*, WUNT 2 159 (Tübingen: J. C. B. Mohr (Paul Siebeck), 2003); John Dickson, *The Best Kept Secret of Christian Mission: Promoting the Gospel with More Than Our Lips* (Grand Rapids: Zondervan, 2013).

[147] For discussions see David G. Meade, *Pseudonymity and Canon: An Investigation into the Relationship of Authorship and Authority in Jewish and Earliest Christian Tradition* (Grand Rapids: Eerdmans, 1987); Armin Baum, "Pseudepigraphy," in Scot McKnight, Lynn H. Cohick, and Nijay K. Gupta, eds., *Dictionary of Paul and His Letters*, 2nd ed. (Downers Grove: IVP Academic, 2022), 877–882.

4:6 As for me, I am already being poured out as a libation, and the time of my departure has come.

7 I have fought the good fight; I have finished the race; I have kept the faith.

8 From now on there is reserved for me the crown of righteousness, which the Lord, the righteous judge, will give me on that day, and not only to me but also to all who have longed for his appearing.

9 Do your best to come to me soon,

10 for Demas, in love with this present world, has deserted me and gone to Thessalonica; Crescens has gone to Galatia, Titus to Dalmatia.

11 Only Luke is with me. Get Mark and bring him with you, for he is useful in my ministry.

12 I have sent Tychicus to Ephesus.

13 When you come, bring the cloak that I left with Carpus at Troas, also the books, and above all the parchments.

14 Alexander the coppersmith did me great harm; the Lord will pay him back for his deeds.

15 You also must beware of him, for he strongly opposed our message.

16 At my first defense no one came to my support, but all deserted me. May it not be counted against them!

17 But the Lord stood by me and gave me strength, so that through me the message might be fully proclaimed and all the Gentiles might hear it. So I was rescued from the lion's mouth.

18 The Lord will rescue me from every evil attack and save me for his heavenly kingdom. To him be the glory forever and ever. Amen.

Beginning with nothing less than a prediction of his own death (and martyrdom), an affirmation of his own faithfulness, and an expectation of future reward (4:6–8), the Apostle turns to the quotidian, if anything can be that in this man's end-of-life situation (4:9–18). The passage moves in and out of details and betrayals and fidelities, all wrapped up in a claim once again that the Lord has been with him. Perhaps most of all we encounter here a moving farewell by the Apostle.[148]

---

[148] Dunn, "1–2 Timothy, Titus," 859–860. Some have argued Paul was confident of being released to carry out further mission; see, e.g., Prior, *Paul the Letter-Writer*, 91–165; Craig A. Smith, *Timothy's Task, Paul's Prospect: A New Reading of 2 Timothy* (New Testament Monographs 12; Sheffield: Sheffield Phoenix Press, 2006).

The Apostle Facing Death

That the Apostle – *As for me* contrasts with *As for you* in 4:5 – is facing death means Timothy and others must carry on the work, and to do that Timothy needs to be reminded once again of the Apostle's faithfulness and future reward (4:6–8; cf. 1 Tim 1:12–20; 2 Tim 1:11–12; 2:8–13). The Apostle's affirmation of his own faithfulness is as Jewish as the Psalms, as it runs against the grain of Protestant sensibilities.

The Apostle depicts[149] his life as a *libation*, or drink offering (NIV), but it does not on its own indicate his death.[150] However, the connection of *libation* with *departure*, along with the obvious implication of his death in vv. 7–8[151] does suggest that the drink-offering imagery describes the total surrender of himself to death (cf. Phil 2:17). The apostle Paul lived with death hanging over his life for much of his missionary career, but there is a resignation here to his imminent death. The *departure,* he says, *has come* and one could translate as "the departure is superintending," even hovering over his situation.

Three snappy sentences summarize it all: (1) *I have fought the good fight*, (2) *I have finished the race*, and (3) *I have kept the faith* (4:7); the first two drawn from registers of competition and the third from the Jewish sense of observance of the Torah. The first is general and could be translated in a general sense: "I have contested/competed in the beautiful contest" (cf. 1 Tim 6:12). The second phrase, typical enough for Paul (Phil 2:16; 3:13–14; Acts 20:24), refers to the spectacular races in public athletic events, the arenas for which are found in archaeological sites from the Roman era, and their nature was running straight down an arena to a pole only to take a sharp turn for the return, which led to strategic cutting off of one's competitors.[152] The third phrase shifts registers from competition to a life of faithfulness before God. The Apostle uses himself as a model for Timothy, so the natural register for this third "I have" statement should be the exhortations to faithfulness (e.g., 3:10–4:5). What is *kept* are both the beliefs and practices of the Christian life, which we contend is often referred in the Pastorals by term "godliness," meaning a publicly witnessed

---

[149] The use of the present tense "I am ... being poured out" makes the act vivid for Timothy, and the "already" intensifies the vividness.
[150] Towner, *Timothy and Titus*, 610; Witherington, *Letters and Homilies for Hellenized Christians*, 368.
[151] Especially with *From now on*, or better yet, "All that remains" or "Finally" in 4:8.
[152] Harris, *Greek Athletes and Athletics*; Harris, *Greek Athletics and the Jews*.

Christian civilized piety.[153] There is no self-adulation in declaring *I have kept the faith*, since he will later point out that he was empowered by the presence of King Jesus (2 Tim 4:17), or as Ronald Ward put it, "He kept it because he himself was kept (John 17:11–15; 1 Thess 5:23)."[154] Part of the hope that encourages our present faithfulness is the assurance of honor bestowed by God to his people in celebration of dedication and service (1 Tim 6:17–19; cf. Matt 25:14–30).

Apostolic Christianity was anastasicentric, meaning resurrection centered. The resurrection transformed life with God by working backward into the entire story of Israel, turning Friday's crucifixion into Sunday's Easter. That event generated hope for those experiencing suffering and such a hope is on full display in 2 Timothy 4:8. He knows, now melding the competition and faithfulness register of terms, that he will receive a *crown of righteousness* because of his fidelity to God according to the gospel as expressed in 4:7, and he knows too that *the Lord will give* that crown to him and *also to all who have longed for his appearing*. The word *reserved*, in Greek *apokeitai*, refers to the honor and reward given by kings and emperors to their loyal servants who fulfill their service (cf. 2 Tim 4:5).[155] The phrase "crown of righteousness" is probably an epexegetical expression, so it could be understood as "the crown that is righteousness," but also could be "a crown caused by a life of righteousness (or doing God's will)." The "crown of boasting" in 1 Thessalonians 2:19, the "crown of life" in James 1:12, the "crown of glory" in 1 Peter 5:4 and Revelation 2:10 suggest the first option. There is, however, an emphasis in what follows on what the Apostle and others have done to be rewarded with such a crown: *to all who have longed for his appearing*. This hope, a theological constant of the early Christian faith (cf. 1 Cor 15:23), becomes a central tenet of the ecumenical creeds.[156]

The Apostle Reflecting on Faithfulness

At 4:9 the Apostle's words take on typical language from letters, and if one were to argue the letter is pseudonymous, it is here that the letter begins to

---

[153] Similarly Towner, *Timothy and Titus*, 613–614.
[154] Ward, *I & II Timothy and Titus*, 211. Similarly, Knight, *Pastoral Epistles*, 460–461.
[155] Kelly, *Pastoral Epistles*, 209.
[156] The Old Roman Creed, the Apostles' Creed, the Nicene Creed, and the Athanasian Creed.

take on a sense of forgery because of the details. Furthermore, the presence of friends (Eubulus, Pudens, Linus, Claudia) with the Apostle in 4:21 is in tension with the seeming loneliness in 4:9, 11.[157]

Their close relationship prompts Paul to urge Timothy to make a commitment *to come* to him as *soon* as possible (cf. Titus 3:12). The reason for such a request is that the Apostle is alone (cf. 2 Tim 4:11): in 4:10 we learn that *Demas* has *deserted* (4:16) the Apostle and returned to *Thessalonica*, and the Apostle informs Timothy of what sounds like the man's apostasy or at least unfaithfulness: *in love with this present world*. Demas has been a companion of Paul's in Western Asia Minor (Col 4:14; Phm 24) but, unlike those who "love" the appearing of the Lord (2 Tim 4:8), he now loves *this present world* (1 Tim 6:17). The language used here is reminiscent of the abandonment of John Mark, shortly mentioned in this passage, an abandonment of Paul's ministry but there is no reason to think it describes an apostasy.[158] Demas is to be contrasted with *Crescens* and *Titus* (4:10).[159] That Titus has gone to Dalmatia may well suggest his ministry in Crete had been completed by the writing of this second letter to Timothy (Titus 1:5).

Two more names now: *only Luke is with me*, no doubt the author of Luke-Acts is in mind and the companion of Paul, possibly also the writer of this letter as well, which emphasizes again the loneliness of the Apostle. He also wants Timothy to bring *Mark* to come be at his side (2 Tim 4:11), and it is noticeable that this (John) Mark is one who deserted Paul's mission and over whom Paul and Barnabas split (Acts 13:13; 15:36–41). This man, who had once abandoned the mission (in Paul's eyes; Acts 15:38) evidently reconciled with the Apostle (Col 4:10–11; Phm 24) and continues to be *useful* (cf. Phm 11). The one who was courier for Colossians and Philemon, one can presume, *Tychicus* (Col 4:7; cf. Acts 20:4; Eph 6:21), was *sent to Ephesus* (2 Tim 4:12), though many think this is an epistolary aorist and thus is seen as present. In which case, Tychicus could be the courier of 2 Timothy and would perhaps replace Timothy in Ephesus. The oddity is that *to Ephesus* suggests a different place than the direction of this letter, and thus perhaps Timothy is not in Ephesus. (Titus 3:12 says Tychicus may be sent to Crete, though it is unclear from where.)

---

[157] For a reasonable response, see Marshall, *Pastoral Epistles*, 812–813.
[158] Towner, *Timothy and Titus*, 622–623.
[159] It remains a possibility that Crescens' *Galatia* could be "Gaul" (as in some early mss) as Spain was the direction of Paul's mission (cf. Rom 15:24).

Requesting provisions or items for needs to be met is a typical feature of ancient letters, and here the Apostle asks Timothy to pick up his poncho-like *cloak* on his way through *Troas* and he also requests him to bring the *books, above all the parchments* (2 Tim 4:13).[160] It is likely he is talking about scrolls, and by *parchments* smaller codices.[161] We do not know if these are "books, that is parchments" or two separate kinds of items, though the former is more likely, nor do we know what was inscribed on these materials. It is fun to imagine that these are either the Apostle's notebooks or some copies of his previous letters.

The tone shifts in 2 Tim 4:14 by bringing up an *Alexander* again (1 Tim 1:20), this time *the coppersmith*, but he, like "Demas" of 2 Tim 4:9, is someone who may have fallen from the faith, and whatever occurred – *did me great harm*, perhaps in Troas. The paragraph is thus run through with the theme of faithfulness and unfaithfulness and offers a typical warning (4:14b). That the Apostle then says *You also must beware of him* suggests this Alexander is in Ephesus, and at least may make one think of Acts 19:33. With the imprecatory statement against Alexander, *the Lord will pay him back for his deeds*, the Apostle declares a dire truth about the man's fate while trusting in God's justice (Ps 49:24–26, 63:1–6; Isa 46–51; Rom 2:6–11, 12:19–21; 1 Thess 4:1–8; 2 Thess 1:5–12).[162]

The presence of the Lord in Paul's imprisonment and especially his trials comes now to the surface. *At his first defense* traditionally describes a trial. Was this the one in Jerusalem, which led to Caesarea, as we read about the various occasions in Acts 21:27–26:32? Or the one before Caesar in Rome, which is hinted at the end of Acts (28:16–31)? (In which case, is there a coming second defense implicit in 2 Timothy?) Or is this *first defense*, as many would contend, the first in a two-part trial: a hearing and a verdict? Whichever it may have been, Paul was alone: *no one came to my support* (4:16). The Roman Christians did not come to Paul's defense so he forgives them for this brotherly unfaithfulness.[163] If we tie this to Paul's time in

---

[160] It is too far a stretch to interpret the "cloak" and "parchments" as referring to the establishment of an apostolic succession in the form of Elijah to Elisha based solely on the assumption of the Pastoral's pseudepigraphal authorship, *contra* Collins, *1 & 2 Timothy and Titus*, 283–284. See Witherington, *Letters and Homilies for Hellenized Christians*, 379 n. 328.
[161] Marshall, *Pastoral Epistles*, 819–821.
[162] Towner, *Timothy and Titus*, 631–633; Ward, *I & II Timothy and Titus*, 218; Mounce, *Pastoral Epistles*, 593–594; Collins, *1 & 2 Timothy and Titus*, 285.
[163] Ward, *I & II Timothy and Titus*, 219–220. I am indebted to Justin Gill for the questions that follow.

Caesarea Maritima, are we to ask if Paul was abandoned in Caesarea and Rome? Does an affirmative answer here haunt his loneliness theme?

Here we find the moment about which this letter has already spoken with clarity: suffering is sometimes the calling of the followers of King Jesus and so Timothy is exhorted to suffer like Christ (and the Apostle). Sadly, *all deserted me* (cf. 4:10) is Paul's laconic description. In Christian grace he leans toward mercy for them because he knows how challenging these moments of martyrdom can be (*May it not be counted against them!*). If everyone abandoned Paul as Jesus was himself abandoned, that same Jesus was with him! This *Lord* empowered him (1 Tim 1:12; 2 Tim 2:1; Phil 4:13) – as Jesus told the missioners (Matt 10:16–20) – *so* the gospel mission, the heart of Paul's own mission (Col 1:24–2:5), could be sustained for all the nations (2 Tim 4:17). Perhaps he is suggesting that he would be released to carry on with the mission or, more likely, that he perceives his witness before the authorities in Rome to be his opportunity to tell the world about Jesus. Which is exactly how the trials as well as his imprisonment in Rome are described in Acts 21–28! Either way, by such abandonment and Christ's own presence with him, Paul is reembodying the gospel before all who might witness it. The Apostle's confidence has no boundaries, and suggests that the first release (2 Tim 4:17's *rescued from the lion's mouth*)[164] leads him to think he'll always be released: *The Lord will rescue me from every evil attack* (4:18) expresses a faith that is anastasicentric. Thus, *save me for his heavenly kingdom* is one kind of "rescue", though it must be perceived by the gospel hope of resurrection. That confession of the power of God to extend the mission and *save* him leads the Apostle to an epistolary doxology.[165]

4:19–22 LETTER ENDING

The Apostle Paul's letters often contain greetings like 2 Timothy 4:19, 21 (e.g., Rom 16:3–16; 1 Cor 16:19–20; 2 Cor 13:12; Phil 4:21–22; Col 4:10–17; 1 Thess 5:26; Titus 3:15; Phm 23–24), just as they fill in other details

---

[164] Probably a general reference to the mixture of demonic, imperial, or violent power, drawing on Jewish language and imagery of the nations as animals in God's creation, as reflected in Ps 22:21, Daniel, and 1 Pet 5:8, and probably not an indirect indicator of Nero personally. See Marshall, *Pastoral Epistles*, 825; Collins, *1 & 2 Timothy and Titus*, 286; Witherington, *Letters and Homilies for Hellenized Christians*, 380.

[165] Thus, Rom 1:25; 9:4–5; 11:33–36; 16:25–27; 2 Cor 11:31; Gal 1:3–5; Eph 3:20–21; 4:4–6; Phil 4:20; 1 Tim 1:17; 6:13–16.

Timothy may want to know (2 Tim 4:20) or that the Apostle wants him to know or emphasize again (4:21). The ending is also typical of letters and particularly what we know of Paul's letters (1 Cor 16:23–24; 2 Cor 13:13; Gal 6:18; Eph 6:23–24; Phil 4:23; Col 4:18; 1 Thess 5:28; 2 Thess 3:18; 1 Tim 6:21; Titus 3:15; Phm 25). These endings often provide a bit of information valuable for reconstructing the life of Paul and his coworkers, but they are also a manifestation of pastoral care. The suggestion often made that there is a contradiction between the apparent loneliness of 4:9–12 and the presence of friends in 4:21 is no more likely a contradiction for Paul than for a pseudonymous writer, and probably less so for Paul himself.

4:19 Greet Prisca[166] and Aquila, and the household of Onesiphorus.
20 Erastus remained in Corinth; Trophimus I left ill in Miletus.
21 Do your best to come before winter. Eubulus sends greetings to you, as do Pudens and Linus and Claudia and all the brothers and sisters.
22 The Lord be with your spirit. Grace be with you.

Prisca and Aquila are the Apostle's most peripatetic friends: they can be found in Pontus and Rome (Acts 18:2), as well as in Corinth (18:1) and Ephesus (18:19) and back to Rome (Rom 16:3–4), and here they appear again in 2 Timothy 4:19 – evidently once again in Ephesus. Their ministry involved risking their lives (Rom 16:3–4) and teaching (Acts 18:1–3, 24–28). That *Prisca* is mentioned first is more likely based on her higher status than anything else. *Onesiphorus*, according to 2 Tim 1:16, is an example of faithfulness under pressure.

Travel and personal details are assumed by the author and Timothy but not always known to us. An *Erastus* was sent with Timothy to Macedonia in Acts 19:22, and an *Erastus* had high status in Corinth according to Romans 16:23, and in our text the same name is used for someone who *remained in Corinth*, and all this suggests this is the same coworker. The name is uncommon[167] so the inscription of an Erastus in Corinth, datable to the New Testament period, suggests the same person, though some still dispute

---

[166] Her name is used by Paul but the diminutive "Priscilla" by Luke in Acts.
[167] T. A. Brookins, "The (In)Frequency of the Name 'Erastus' in Antiquity: A Literary, Papyrological, and Epigraphical Catalog," *NTS* 59 (2013): 496–513. Many do claim it is common; e.g., Marshall, *Pastoral Epistles*, 828.

his identity.[168] We don't know why Erastus stayed home but we know why *Trophimus* (Acts 20:4; 21:29) was not present with Paul: he was sick.

Again (2 Tim 4:9), the Apostle urges Timothy to come visit Paul, this time saying *before winter* (4:21) and this suggests the letter was written in the late Summer or Fall,[169] to which is added the greetings from *Eubulus, Pudens, Linus,* and *Claudia,* in fact, from *all the brothers and sisters.*

As the Lord was with Paul in his trials (4:17–18), so he prays for the Lord to be with Timothy, *The Lord be your spirit*, as he ministers the gospel under pressure in Ephesus. Knowing this letter is to be read before the whole assembly, the Apostle then sends a farewell, *Grace be with you*, to the whole Ephesian church he knows has been listening to his encouragement of their pastor.[170]

---

[168] Longenecker, *Remember the Poor*, 236–239.
[169] Kelly, *Pastoral Epistles*, 222.
[170] Towner, *Timothy and Titus*, 655–656; Witherington, *Letters and Homilies for Hellenized Christians*, 382.

4 Commentary on Titus

1:1–4 THE APOSTLE TO TITUS FOR THE ASSEMBLIES IN CRETE

1:1 Paul, a servant of God and an apostle of Jesus Christ, for the sake of the faith of God's elect and the knowledge of the truth that is in accordance with godliness,

1:2 in the hope of eternal life that God, who never lies, promised before the ages began –

1:3 in due time he revealed his word through the proclamation with which I have been entrusted by the command of God our Savior,

1:4 To Titus, my true child in the faith we share: Grace and peace from God the Father and Christ Jesus our Savior.

This letter is written from a city in western Greece, Nicopolis (3:12). Its opening, with its customary anticipation of themes in the body of the letter as well as its Pauline-type greeting, varies somewhat in substance from the other PEs. In this greeting the Apostle[1] identifies himself as a *servant of God* as well as an *apostle* (1 Tim 1:1; 2 Tim 1:1). In each of the three PEs the identification of the author is followed by a *kata* prepositional phrase (1 Tim 1:1: "by the command"; 2 Tim 1:1 "for the sake of the promise"), though the NRSV translates 2 Timothy's with "for the sake of" as it does for Titus 1:1 (*for the sake of*). This prepositional phrase provides the standard by which the mission God gave to the Apostle is measured, that is by *faith* and *knowledge*. Yet another prepositional phrase appears *in the hope* (1:2), which is then restated in 1:3 before he gets to the address and the greeting (1:4).

---

[1] For a discussion of the opening of the letter as consistent with Paul himself, see Marshall, *Pastoral Epistles*, 112–113.

Servant and Apostle

To translate *doulos* with "servant" (NRSV, NIV) misses the social evocation of a "slave" (CEB). The term *doulos* is used for household slaves in the PEs (1 Tim 6:1; Titus 2:9) and as a metaphor for gospel workers (2 Tim 2:24; Titus 1:1). The term connects the Apostle both with ordinary Christians (cf. Rom 6:16–20; 1 Cor 7:21–23)[2] and with notable leaders in both Israelite (Ps 104:26, 42) and Christian history (James 1:1). As such, a *slave of God* is one captured by God for the gospel. In this context, then, *doulos of God* is tantamount to *apostle of Jesus Christ* (see Comments at 1 Tim 1:1). As the greeting moves from Father-God to Christ Jesus (1:4), so the Apostle's callings originate in both Father and Son. The Apostle is not pulling rank but instead connecting Titus to the mission of God. Paul is but one link in the chain of *the faith* they *share* "according to the common faith" (cf. 1 Jn 1:1–4).

His calling is consistent with[3] *the faith of God's elect* as well as *the knowledge of the truth* that is itself consistent with *godliness*, or in this Commentary, "civilized piety."[4] In v. 1 *faith* is the content of what the community believes and is called to sustain (Titus 1:4, 13; 2:2; 3:15; cf. also 1 Tim 1:2; 3:9, 13; 4:1, 6; 5:8; 6:10, 21), the community here defined as *God's elect* (2 Tim 2:10), that is, those who are genuine believers but the term also evokes Israel as God's elect.[5] The *faith* here is comprehended in other terms such as *knowledge of the truth*, or "perception"[6] *of the truth* (cf. 1 Tim 2:4; 2 Tim 2:25; 3:7; see Comments on 1 Tim 2:4), but this *truth* is shaped by the kind of public profession of faith that is faithful to the gospel, which must be embodied in one's life and publicly visible.[7] Truth and life are to be harmonious, each witnessing the other.[8]

The Apostle's calling is measured by the faith, that is the knowledge of truth, and it is *in the hope of eternal life*,[9] and this will not have been just the Apostle's own conviction of life after death but a comprehensive vision

---

[2] Murray J. Harris, *Slave of Christ: A New Testament Metaphor for Total Devotion to Christ*, New Studies in Biblical Theology 8 (Leicester: Apollos/InterVarsity, 1999).
[3] Marshall, 119–120, sees this as purpose as does Towner, *Timothy and Titus*, 664, 666–667.
[4] Hoklotubbe, *Civilized Piety*.
[5] LXX: 1 Chron 16:13; Ps 105:6, 43; 106:5; Isa 43:20; 65:9.
[6] Perhaps a conversion term as in 1 Tim 2:4.
[7] Collins, *1 & 2 Timothy and Titus*, 304; Mounce, *Pastoral Epistles*, 379–380.
[8] Similarly, Towner, *Timothy and Titus*, 668.
[9] This prepositional phrase is parallel then to 1:1's "for the sake of"; so Marshall, *Pastoral Epistles*, 123–124; also NIV 2011. On eternal life, see Comments on 1 Tim 1:16; the

rooted in the resurrection and confidently expectant of the victory of God over all evil. Such a *hope* of salvation is rooted in the faithfulness of God: *God, who never lies, promised*. The Christian hope is rooted in God's promise given long ago (1 Tim 4:8; cf. 1 Jn 1:5–7), not scientific evidence of a post-mortem consciousness.[10] The promise proclaimed in the gospel no doubt fulfills all the promises to the people of God in the Old Testament but God's gospel is even more archaic as it was given from *before the ages began* (1 Tim 4:16; 2 Tim 1:8–10; cf. Eph 1:4; Heb 1:1–4; Jn 1:1–18; 1 Jn 1:1–3). As such, this *eternal life* is not merely the regaining and extension of human life against entropy but it is also God's own life, filled with his goodness and indestructability, infused into our resurrected bodies.[11] This promise is reaffirmed in Titus 1:3. Though *before the ages began*[12] is sometimes read as connected to *revealed* in v. 3, "before the ages began" finishes off v. 2 and a new sentence begins in 1:3. The term *revealed* has its object in "his word" (cf. 1 Tim 4:5; 2 Tim 2:9, 15) and this becomes apparent *through* the Apostle's gospel *proclamation with which* the Apostle has *been entrusted* (1:3). The revelation occurred *in due time*, or in "its own seasons," which could be seen as another shorthand expression for the early Christian sense of history and eschatology, say, as seen in Galatians 4:4's "fullness of time."[13]

What was *promised before the ages began* God revealed, or better yet, "made visible,"[14] at the right time was *his word through the proclamation*, which could be translated "his word in the kerygma," namely, the verbal announcement of Jesus as God's long awaited Davidic son, the Messiah, who conquered death and is coming again (2 Tim 1:9–10, 2:8).[15] It was the heart of Paul's mission to be *entrusted* with this kerygma as a result of *the command of God our Savior* (Titus 1:3; cf. 2 Tim 1:1's "by the will of God"). God's own gospel about King Jesus proves his own character of truth and

---

sense in Judaism was the Age to Come, which to be sure was eternal, but forever-ness was not the sole emphasis.

[10] C. F. D. Moule, *The Meaning of Hope: A Biblical Exposition with Concordance*, Facet Books 5 (Philadelphia: Fortress, 1963).

[11] Towner, *Timothy and Titus*, 669.

[12] This could mean before time began or from creation on, the former most likely: see Marshall, *Pastoral Epistles*, 126. The point is that God has it all planned.

[13] Oscar Cullmann, *Christ and Time: The Primitive Christian Conception of Time and History*, 3rd reprint edn. (Eugene: Wipf & Stock, 2018); Witherington, *Jesus, Paul and the End of the World*.

[14] Jerome D. Quinn, *The Letter to Titus*, AB 35 (New York: Doubleday, 1990), 25, 69. It is not the same as "reveal" (*apokaluptō*), though components of their meanings overlap. See Rom 16:26; Col 1:26.

[15] Jipp, *Messianic Theology*.

faithfulness. As such the gospel draws out OT themes of God's covenant. He is tapping once again in the PEs on the importance of fidelity to the divinely authorized gospel and its mission and what gives them both value is salvation (1 Tim 1:1; 2:3; 4:10; 2 Tim 1:10; Titus 1:4; 2:10, 13; 3:4, 6). We should note that God and Jesus are interchangeable as *Savior*.

True Son

The letter is sent to *Titus* who is described as Paul's *true child in the faith we share*. The appeal to loyalty is too often abused by authoritarian pastors in churches, and the Greek term behind it, *gnēsios*, has better translations than the older NRSV, which had "loyalty," like "true" (NRSVue, ASV, NIV, CEB) or "genuine" (2 Cor 8:8; 1 Tim 1:2). The legitimacy of Paul's authority comes from *the command of God* and through him is passed to his *true child*, Titus. *Gnēsios*, often designating a father's legitimate biological son, also was used to emphasize true paternity in a proper Jewish way of life.[16] Paul has become the father of Titus through intimate discipleship concerning how to embody the faith they *share* (2 Tim 1:1; cf. 1 Cor 4:14–17),[17] which expresses their mutual familial obligations to one another.[18] The Apostle was surrounded by coworkers who were his companions, his students, and who were at times his teachers as well.[19] Such persons became authentic representatives of the gospel mission, that is, of *the faith we share*, or "the common faith" (Titus 1:4).[20] What is "common" about this *faith* here is the gospel itself (1 Cor 15:1–8), which Paul traditioned to others as it came to him. His greeting is common too (Rom 1:7; 1 Cor 1:3; see Comments on 1 Tim 1:2).

1:5–9 PASTORS FOR THE PEOPLE

The first order of pastoral oversight for Titus in Crete is to form a council of elders in each town and, like in 1 Timothy 3:1–7 (cf. 5:17–20), the

---

[16] Collins, *1 & 2 Timothy and Titus*, 316–117.
[17] Witherington, *Letters and Homilies for Hellenized Christians*, 105.
[18] Towner, *Timothy and Titus*, 674–675.
[19] F. F. Bruce, *The Pauline Circle*, reprint edn. (Eugene: Wipf & Stock, 2006); Best, *Paul and His Converts*. A series of books on his social network has a volume on Titus: Ken Stenstrup, *Titus: Honoring the Gospel of God*, Paul's Social Network: Brothers and Sisters in Faith (Collegeville: Liturgical Press, 2010).
[20] Quinn, *The Letter to Titus*, 72.

Apostle provides a list of character traits. Again, consideration of Theophrastus' list of characters and Aristotle's virtues provides comparison to what the Apostle thinks is virtuous (see Closer Look at 2 Tim 3:1–9). That this list, numbered for easier reference, begins the letter suggests this was the most important task at hand. That this passage is immediately followed by one about false teachers (Titus 1:10–16) indicates the elders are the frontline safeguard against bad theology.

1:5 I left you behind in Crete for this reason, so that you should put in order what remained to be done and should appoint elders in every town, as I directed you:

1:6 someone who is [1] blameless, [2] married only once, [3] whose children are believers, [4] not accused of debauchery and [5] not rebellious.

1:7 For a bishop, as God's steward, must be [1] blameless; must not be [6]arrogant or [7] quick-tempered or [8] addicted to wine or [9] violent or [10] greedy for gain,

1:8 but he must be [11] hospitable, [12] a lover of goodness, [13] self-controlled, [14] upright, [15] devout, and [16] restrained,

1:9 holding [17] tightly to the trustworthy word of the teaching, so that he may be able both [18] to exhort with sound instruction and [19] to refute those who contradict it.

The Plan

The Apostle opens with a clarification of purpose: *for this reason*, he says, *I left you behind*[21] *in Crete* to straighten out the assemblies in various communities on Crete – a place known for many villages – and to do that meant forming a council of spiritual mentors. The chronology of Paul's letters is hard enough to figure out, but when one adds a letter (Titus) without many details and those details that are given are capable of explanation in a number of chronologies, placing the time of this letter becomes mostly guesswork. What is clear is the assignment: First, to *put in order what remained to be done* indicates the Apostle had probably been on

---

[21] It is possible the term *apoleipō* ("left behind") means "deployed." The implications of this expression if the letter is pseudonymous are explored narratologically by John W. Marshall, "'I Left You in Crete': Narrative Deception and Social Hierarchy in the Letter to Titus," *JBL* 127 (2008): 781–803. His approach appeals to an authorial sense of dominance throughout.

Crete and had *left*, and that when leaving some tasks had not yet been completed.[22] Or perhaps the condition of the assemblies had fallen apart due to false teaching and the mission work needed to be shored up with new elders/bishops. Therefore, the Apostle wants Titus to straighten things out, a more literal and picturesque translation of the Greek term (*epidiorthoō*). The theological challenges on Crete are pointed out in Titus 1:10–16 and that text is followed up with "teach what is consistent with sound doctrine" (2:1). One element not yet done is to *appoint elders in every town*, and the Apostle indicates he had previously instructed Titus to do this (*as I directed you*).

In this text *elder* and *bishop* apparently refer to the same group (1:5 and 1:7, with *gar* opening v. 7, indicating a reason for the previous[23]). The overlap seems present also in Acts 20:17 and 20:28 but especially in 1 Peter 5:1–2.[24] To adapt the descriptions written up in the Comments at 1 Timothy 3:2, the term bishop is found in the New Testament at Philippians 1:1 and Acts 1:20; 20:28 for some noticeable ministry in a local church, and it points us to a spiritual task. This shift from a specific plural group to a more generic singular term with *elders* to *bishop*[25] is a similar syntactical move employed by the Apostle in 1 Timothy 2:9–12 with "women" to "woman" (see comments there). Pastoral ministry, whether the term is bishop, elder, or pastor, is as varied as it is complicated: those in one's assembly will more or less shape what that pastoral task will involve, while the fundamental calling to be a pastor/overseer/elder will also shape the relationship with the assembly.[26]

The term *elder* has to do with a wisdom culture respecting age, while *bishop*, or overseeing, has more to do with function. This functional aspect is seen in the term *God's steward* as the Greek word, *oikonomos*, refers to the person chosen and empowered by the father of the household, the

---

[22] Marshall, *Pastoral Epistles*, 151.
[23] V. 7 is abrupt and anacoluthic, and it oddly repeats a term (*blameless*) already used, and it changes from *elders* to *bishop*. Accordingly, some think this is the start (or at least use) of a second list. One could suggest, too, that after 1:6's *blameless* the Apostle clarifies what he means by *blameless* through v. 6 and then resumes his point at the opening of v. 7. Some see this abrupt language as an indication of an interpolation, see Dibelius and Conzelmann, *Pastoral Epistles*, 1972, 132–133. Though others reject the idea of interpolation, see Kelly, *Pastoral Epistles*, 231–232.
[24] Marshall, *Pastoral Epistles*, 149.
[25] Ward, *I & II Timothy and Titus*, 240; Knight, *Pastoral Epistles*, 291; Marshall, *Pastoral Epistles*, 159, 160; Mounce, *Pastoral Epistles*, 390; Towner, *Timothy and Titus*, 686.
[26] For a lengthy explanation, Marshall, *Pastoral Epistles*, 170–181.

paterfamilias, to administer the household (cf. 1 Tim 3:4–5, 15). The two terms (elder, bishop) appear to be referring to the same group of leaders, with their common ministry involving hospitality, teaching, taking care of the church folks, and being a public presence of civilized piety. The term *appoint* suggests for some a more authoritarian, top-down model of forming a council of *elders/bishops*.[27] The Greek term is *kathistēmi* and can suggest a more organic "establish" or "institute," either translation implying the recognition of someone's giftedness. At least one model of leaders being formed is Acts 6:1–6 where the deacons were chosen from among faithful men already serving the community of faith, a pattern that could be operative in Crete. Titus' role may be less the one deciding who is worthy to lead and more the role to approve, establish, and instruct into leadership those already doing the work of Paul's gospel mission. That *elders* is plural (*bishop* is singular at 1:7) leads some to think Titus formed a plurality of elders in each city,[28] but the language may mean a number of elders over a number of cities.

The List

The qualifications for an elder/bishop combine character and competency.[29] Spiritual mentors are to be theologically educated (#s 17–19) and, if one counts terms, even more they are to be marked by moral formation and character (#s 1–16).

This list contains seventeen or nineteen items compared with fourteen in 1 Timothy, with the following comparative list showing the similarities and differences. (Items #4, 5 may refer to the elder's children not the elder.) Tistus's list is on the left, 1 Timothy's on the right, and I have taken some liberties to connect the two with generally similar virtues. The language of Titus shows four basic divisions: positives (#1–4), negatives (#5–10), positives (#11–16), ministries of the word (#17–19).

---

[27] For discussions, see Comments on 1 Tim 3:2 and 5:1–2.
[28] Fee, *1–2 Tim, Titus*, 21–22.
[29] Dunn, "1–2 Timothy, Titus," 864–865.

Titus 1:6-9	1 Timothy 3:1-7
1. Blameless (vv. 6, 7)[30]	1. "above reproach"
2. Married once[31]	2. Married once
3. Children believe	3. Manages household
4. [Not accused of debauchery]	
5. [Not rebellious]	
6. Not arrogant (v. 7)	4. "not a recent convert ... puffed up"
7. Not quick-tempered	5. See #10 in this list
8. Not addicted to wine	6. "not a drunkard"
9. Not violent	7. "not violent but gentle"
10. Not greedy for gain	8. "not a lover of money"
11. Hospitable (v. 8)	9. Hospitable
12. Lover of goodness	
13. Self-controlled	10. Same term: "temperate" in 1 Tim 3:2
14. Upright	
15. Devout	
16. Restrained	
17. Holding tightly to the word (v. 9)11. Apt teacher[32]	
18. Exhort with sound instruction	
19. Refute opposers of 18.	

Eleven similar virtues, eight different for Titus and four different for 1 Timothy, are found in these lists. Clearly, though both are kicked off similarly (1 Tim 3:2; Titus 1:7), there was no official list, and this matters for how the text is read and how it is used in many churches today for composing an official list for the qualifications of elders/bishops (and deacons). While overlaps are very clear – who could not include Titus's #s 17–19, for instance? – these lists illustrate that character is what matters most and these are character traits of a spiritual mentor who is shaped by *tov*, or goodness (see Comments at 1 Tim 3:1–7). In the context of the PEs the list sketches various components of civilized piety and the opening [1] *blameless* is about reputation, and it is repeated with *bishop* in Titus 1:7. (On Titus's #s 1, 2, 3, 6, 7, 9, 10, 11, 13, and 17, see Comments at 1 Tim 3:1–7).

---

[30] See Comments at 1 Tim 3:10.
[31] A much disputed term; see Comments at 1 Tim 3:12 and the extensive discussion in Marshall, *Pastoral Epistles*, 155–157.
[32] Not in Titus: Sensible, respectable, not quarrelsome, thought of well by outsiders.

Some take #4 and #5 to be about the children of the elders, not about the elders themselves,[33] while others see them about the elders.[34] Here's an alternative translation: "Having allegiant children not in the category of dissolution or disorder." The expression [4] *not accused of debauchery* (NIV: "not being wild"; CEB: "self-indulgence") is semi-legal language for a person who has committed *asōtia*, a term general enough to include public drunkenness, disturbance, indulgent in body and luxurious living as well as gluttony – in other words, a prodigal (cf. Luke 15:13; Eph 5:18; 1 Pet 4:4). The term [5] *an-hypotaktos*, translated in the NRSV with *not rebellious* (similar in CEB), with "disobedient" in the NIV, has the sense of someone who is disorderly in society or anarchic (cf. Titus 1:10; 1 Tim 1:9).

That the *elder/bishop* is to be a [12] *lover of goodness* evokes the Hebrew term *tov* and its various Greek nuances of excellence, goodness, and beauty (in character) and thus points to an exemplary leader.[35] The terms [14–16] *upright, devout, and self-controlled* span the cultural worlds of the Apostle: they can be either Jewish or Greco-Roman or both,[36] the term *upright* having the sense of one who is Torah observant and also just.[37] There is a connection, too, with justification (*dikaiosunē*; cf. 3:5, 7). *Devout* has considerably different senses: for the Jew it connotes a life in accordance with Torah and halakah, the *tzaddik* or the *chasid*, while in the Greco-Roman world it is more about publicly respectable piety and cultic worship, hence not far from *eusebeia*, or civilized piety. The last term, *engkratēs* is a preeminent virtue in the Greco-Roman world. It refers to a person's control of one's desires, appetites, and passions, especially in regards to food and sex.

The "apt teacher" of 1 Timothy 3:2 is unfolded in Titus 1:9's three-fold instructions: the *bishop/elder* is to have a tight grip on *the word*, that is, of the message about God's redemption in King Jesus, which becomes canonized in Scripture (cf. 1:3) and the Nicene Creed.[38] The teacher's calling then is to be faithful to the gospel of Paul and the apostles (cf. Titus 1:9, 11; 1 Tim 2:7; 4:11; Rom 6:17; 12:7; 16:17; 1 Cor 12:28–29; Eph 4:11; Heb 6:2).

---

[33] Kelly, *Pastoral Epistles*, 231; Ward, *1 & 2 Timothy & Titus*, 239–240; Knight, *Pastoral Epistles*, 290; Marshall, *Pastoral Epistles*, 158–159; Collins, *1 & 2 Timothy and Titus*, 322; Towner, *Timothy and Titus*, 682–684; Witherington, *Letters and Homilies for Hellenized Christians*, 111.
[34] Mounce, *Pastoral Epistles*, 389.
[35] Marshall, *Pastoral Epistles*, 163.
[36] Mounce, *Pastoral Epistles*, 391; Towner, *Timothy and Titus*, 684–685.
[37] Towner, 689–690.
[38] McKnight, *The King Jesus Gospel*.

As one who is faithful, unlike those about to be described in 1:10–16, the *bishop/elder* is *to exhort with sound instruction*, which is a major theme of the PEs (cf. 1 Tim 1:10; 6:3; 2 Tim 1:13; 4:3; Tistus's 1:13; 2:1, 2), and to be theologically alert enough and courageous enough *to refute*, or convince, the opponents of that *sound doctrine*.[39] One thinks then of the creed-like statements of 1 Timothy 3:16 and 2 Timothy 2:8–13.

Titus' list contains some negations of vices (#s 4, 5, 6, 7, 8, 9, and 10) and touches upon the famous list of characters in Theophrastus (cf. his #6, 9, 11, 19, 21, 23, 24, 26, 29). When one turns to Aristotle's more complete list from deficiencies to the golden mean to the excesses, one can observe #s 1, 2, 3, 4, 5, 8, 10, 11, and 12. What stands out for the Pauline lists is their Jewish rootedness and morality (Titus #s 2–4, 8–15) and their appropriateness for the one mentoring in the Christian faith (#1, 11, 13–15, 17–19). Distinctions aside and not minimized, the virtues of Titus 1:6–9 are also about respectable public life that would intentionally and properly interact within the communities of Crete and hence exhibit not only a private religious goodness, *tov*, but also cultivate civilized behavior.[40]

We circle back to the purpose above: these virtues are needed, these vices eliminated, and are what are necessary for a leader to be able to keep things in order (Titus 1:5). Titus will be able to establish these sorts of *elders/bishops* and move on with confidence that the assemblies scattered on Crete will carry on a faithful witness to the Lord Jesus.

1:10–16 TROUBLEMAKERS ON CRETE

Descriptions of the Apostle's opponents are rarely charitable but "charitable" has become a term fashionable for civil societies formed with tolerance. Such was not the way of the ancient world[41] so the descriptions in this paragraph express rhetorically pointed disagreements, yea, denunciations.[42] Marshall calls the language here "extremely harsh"[43] and

---

[39] Towner, *Timothy and Titus*, 692–693.
[40] See also Gal 5:22–26 and Col 3:12–17 for other sortings of Christian virtues.
[41] Luke Timothy Johnson, "The New Testament's Anti-Jewish Slander and the Conventions of Ancient Polemic," *JBL* 108 (1989): 419–441; Witherington, *Letters and Homilies for Hellenized Christians*, 117–118.
[42] Richard J. Mouw, *Uncommon Decency: Christian Civility in an Uncivil World*, 2nd edn. (Downers Grove: IVP, 2010); William Keith and Robert Danisch, *Beyond Civility: The Competing Obligations of Citizenship* (University Park: Penn State University Press, 2020).
[43] Marshall, *Pastoral Epistles*, 192.

Huizenga accuses the author of ethnic bigotry and racism.[44] Hoklotubbe examines this passage through the lens of the discourses of subjugated groups forming their identity over against "inscribed opponents," that is, Judeans and barbarians filled with superstitions.[45]

The polemic fits with other polemical moments in the PEs (1 Tim 1:3–11, 18–20; 4:1–7; 6:3–10; 2 Tim 2:23–26; 3:1–9; Titus 3:8–11). Because of these troublemakers Titus is to form a council of elders/bishops (Titus 1:5–9) or, put differently, a council of theologically alert and morally formed pastors who can nurture a Christ-following civilized identity.[46]

1:10 There are also [1] many rebellious people, [2] idle talkers and [3] deceivers, especially those of [4] the circumcision;

1:11: they must be silenced, since they are [5] upsetting whole families by teaching for sordid gain what it is not right to teach.

1:12 [6] It was one of them, their very own prophet, who said, "Cretans are always liars, vicious brutes, lazy gluttons."

1:13 That testimony is true. For this reason rebuke them sharply, so that they may become sound in the faith,

1:14 not paying attention to Jewish myths or to commandments of those who reject the truth.

1:15 To the pure all things are pure, but to the [7] corrupt and [8] unbelieving nothing is pure; their very minds and consciences are corrupted.

1:16 They [9] profess to know God, but they [10] deny him by their actions; they are [11] detestable, [12] disobedient, [13] unfit for any good work.

There is an assortment of thirteen descriptors of the opponents Titus will encounter on Crete and whom he is to resist and instruct in the hope of transformation. I have numbered them for easier reference. Descriptions of the troublemakers (1:10, 11b–12, 15–16) are interspersed with instructions for Tistus's pastoral approach to them (1:11a, 13–14). Are these troublemakers Jewish opponents of the gospel? Are they Jewish believers like those at Galatia or even Rome who are seeking to impose Torah observance on gentiles? Or is the group of opponents large, including Jewish opponents?

---

[44] Huizenga, *1–2 Timothy, Titus*, 138–144.
[45] T. Christopher Hoklotubbe, "Civilized Christ-Followers among Barbaric Cretans and Superstitious Judeans: Negotiating Ethnic Hierarchies in Titus 1:10–14," *JBL* 140 (2021); 369–390.
[46] Similarly, Ward, *I & II Timothy and Titus*, 243; Towner, *Timothy and Titus*, 694–695.

The evidence is not one-sided[47] but it leans in the direction of Jewish troublemakers who exercise influence after the work of Paul but within the church,[48] and such persons seek full conversion of gentiles to Torah observance (cf. 3:9).[49] One should not suppose that the false teaching on Crete is identical to that at Ephesus, but we have good reasons to think these opponents were at one time part of the messianic community.

The Troublemakers

That there are *many* who oppose the gospel mission of the Apostle matches what Luke says about Paul in various cities in the Book of Acts. On Crete they are [1] *rebellious* (see Comments at 1 Tim 1:9; Titus 1:6), or anarchic with respect to the apostolic gospel and the traditions then forming, and they are also [2] *idle-talkers*, a term used but once in the NT meaning people whose content in speech is meaningless, hollow, and useless (see 1 Tim 1:6). Titus 3:9's "worthless" is a cognate. Their speech pattern for the Apostle also includes another once-in-the-NT term, [3] *deceivers*, and this because they are not captured by the truth of the gospel (cf. the cognate at 1 Tim 2:14 for Eve's deception). The Apostle's concern seems once again to be Jewish opponents, though the opening term here (*especially*, translating *malista*) seems to indicate a group within a larger group:[50] [4] *especially those of the circumcision*. Though used but once in the PEs, this is a common term for Paul's polemic (cf. Rom 2:25–29; 3:1, 30; 4:9–12; 15:8; 1 Cor 7:19; Gal 2:7–9, 12; 5:6, 11; 6:15; Eph 2:11; Phil 3:3, 5; Col 2:11; 3:11; 4:11). Everywhere Paul went he created theological and social status disturbance for his fellow Jews.[51]

It is not clear if the Apostle is addressing *especially the circumcision* in v. 11's *they must be silenced* or if *they* is the larger group of opponents, probably the latter (for more on this instruction, see the section below "Instructions for Titus"). The reason for this is that [5] *they are upsetting whole families* or, better yet, "whole households" in the sense of collapsing

---

[47] Titus 1:12 does not immediately suggest a Jewish Christian group.
[48] Towner, *Timothy and Titus*, 695.
[49] Marshall, *Pastoral Epistles*, 192.
[50] Marshall prefers a translation like "namely," and thus not referring to a group within a group; see Marshall, *Pastoral Epistles*, 195.
[51] For one discussion, Jerry Sumney, *Identifying Paul's Opponents: The Question of Method in 2 Corinthians*, reprint edn., Bloomsbury Academic Collections. Biblical Studies: The Epistles (London: Bloomsbury Academic, 2015).

faith (cf. 1 Tim 5:13; 2 Tim 2:18). The opponents are at work in the intimate settings of the assemblies, and their teachings are shaped for avaricious profit (Titus 1:11; cf. 1 Tim 6:5), with *sordid* used elsewhere by Paul for publicly shameful behaviors (1 Cor 11:6; 14:35; Eph 5:12). Their greed is complicated by what they teach, and greed is a big problem for the Apostle at this time (cf. 1 Tim 6:5, 17–19), and Paul himself was sensitive about this topic (cf. 1 Cor 9).[52] His description of the opponents is brief with *what it is not right to teach* but at v. 14 he speaks of their *Jewish myths and commandments*. One can speculate what these *myths* might be, but we are probably safer to assume it could refer to speculative theology buttoned down with orders on how to follow such a theology (cf. 1 Tim 4:1–5; Col 2:16–19 for something along this line). Pastors should take note that Titus isn't being directed to begin an inquisition into or against every opinion held by the Cretan Christians, rather he and the elders he appoints are called to address bad beliefs as they manifest disruption and antigospel practices into the communal life of the churches.[53]

Epimenides, here called *their very own prophet*,[54] uttered words used by the Apostle for [6] the shameful behaviors of the opponents (my translation):

Cretans are always falsifiers,
Bad beasts,
Workless guts.

The *liars* of the NRSV ties into v. 10's *deceivers* but the term is a trope for the Cretans for claiming Zeus was buried on their island,[55] the *vicious brutes* illustrating verbal denunciation by labeling opponents as animals (cf. Dan 7 to Rev 12–13), while *lazy gluttons* may well describe the one who wants to eat without laboring for one's food – a workless person who is little more than the gut. In other words, a moocher, a freeloader, a sponger. Language like that by one of their own is turned by the Apostle against the

---

[52] Greed is a common complaint about the Cretans; on which Marshall, *Pastoral Epistles*, 198 n. 126. See also McKnight, *Pastor Paul*, 149–152.
[53] Marshall, *Pastoral Epistles*, 191, 196; Towner, *Timothy and Titus*, 696–698; Witherington, *Letters and Homilies for Hellenized Christians*, 120–121.
[54] Referring here to Epimenides, *Cretica* 1–4. For a description from ancient sources as well as the actual source for this quotation, Marshall, *Pastoral Epistles*, 199–203.
[55] Hutson, *1–2 Timothy, Titus*, 221–222. To be a Cretan (*krētizein*) was to be a liar, and this fits with other ethnic group or national stereotypes and thus was at times equally dangerous.

opponents and, because *that testimony is true,* the Apostle wields a powerful word-weapon (1:13a).

The instructions for Titus will be covered in the next section, so we turn now to v. 15's rather sudden but clear distinguishing of the two groups: one is *pure,* for whom all things are pure (cf. Mark 7:14-15; Rom 14:14, 20; 1 Tim 4:5) because they are pure in Christ, and the other is [7] *corrupt* and [8] *unbelieving,* or unfaithful. With at least one eye on the "circumcision" opponents, Paul uses the term *pure,* which could be translated "clean," and had to evoke kosher food and kosher morality for a Jewish audience (1 Tim 4:3-5).[56] The alternative is just as Jewish: *corrupt* could be translated as "soiled" or "polluted" or "defiled." Their theology and their practice, indicated in *minds and consciences,* are polluted. The Apostle's concerns are not just their teachings but also their behaviors. This is clear in Titus 1:16's [9] *They profess to know God but* [10] *they deny him by their actions,* or "works" (cf. 2 Tim 3:5), and this must refer to rejecting God's good creation and the foods he provides (cf. 1 Tim 4:1-5). There is an assumption by the Apostle that knowledge of God is glimpsed in the life of the Christian (cf. 2 Tim 3:12; 1 Jn 3:4-10).[57] His final words are damning denunciations: [11] *detestable,* [12] *disobedient,* [13] *unfit for any good work* (same Greek term as *actions*). The term *detestable* is yet another term that evokes Jewish prophetic denunciation of pagan immoralities and idolatries, while [12] could speak more about the opponents being "unpersuaded" and perhaps even "unpersuadable." Thus, the opponents are *unfit,* that is, unapproved after being tested (2 Tim 2:15). They are not recognized for civilized piety, which is expected for the Christians on Crete.

Instructions for Titus

Stepping back to 1:13b-14 to hear what Titus is being called to do, it is not clear if the Apostle is addressing *especially the circumcision* in v. 11a's *they must be silenced* or if *they* is the larger group of opponents, probably the latter. There is good evidence for a number of Jewish communities on Crete (cf. Acts 2:11 and Josephus, *Antiquities* 17.327). That some of them were converted to belief in Jesus is indicated in Acts 2:11, though what became of such persons no one knows and neither ought we to connect

---

[56] Jonathan Klawans, *Impurity and Sin in Ancient Judaism* (New York: Oxford University Press, 2004); Knight, *Pastoral Epistles,* 301-302; Towner, *Timothy and Titus,* 706-707.
[57] Towner, 709-710.

them to the troublemakers. To *silence*, or "stopper the mouth," requires that the space in which they are causing the troubles is controlled by the Christian leaders, which suggests the house churches on Crete, again leading us to think the opponents are Jewish Christians. The Apostle instructs Titus to *rebuke them sharply* (1:13), and *sharply* has the sense of cutting with a knife, but denunciation is not the point of this strong rhetoric. Rather, the Apostle wants to believe these opponents *may become sound in the faith* (cf. 2 Tim 2:24–26), terms we've already seen in Titus (see Comments on terms at 1:1, 9). That this is not simply powering up over opponents and shutting them down is indicated both here and in 3:10–11. Once again the Jewish nature of the opponents emerges: *not paying attention to Jewish myths or to commandments of those who reject the truth* (1:14), with *myths* being more than legends and fables but a Pauline term for false teachings shaped by misleading interpretations of the Torah (Titus 3:9; cf. 1 Tim 1:3–4, 6–7, 8) that lead to bad, at least unChristian, behaviors.[58] The NRSV's choice to translate "humans" with "those who" blunts an evocation of Jesus' criticism of human traditions (Mark 7:1–20; also Col 2:22).[59] The difference in character between the elders Titus is to appoint and these troublemakers is on display.[60]

2:1–10 INSTRUCTING THE HOUSEHOLDS

The agenda for Titus on Crete is to "put in order" and to "appoint elders" (1:5), the latter task requiring appropriate character (1:6–9), and the reason for these instructions is the presence of false teachers disrupting entire households (1:10–16). Titus is to silence and to rebuke such persons. The Apostle then turns to a more positive task, namely, instructing the believers in how to live (2:1–10), and to do this he makes use of a common approach: what looks like a household code (Col 3:18–4:1; Eph 5:21–6:9; 1 Pet 2:10–3:7) concerned more with ages than with one's status (though the

---

[58] Some see an early kind of Jewish Christian Gnosticism being addressed here too, see Kelly, *Pastoral Epistles*, 236; Mounce, *Pastoral Epistles*, 396. There is strong pushback against glimpses of Gnosticism; Marshall, *Pastoral Epistles*, 196–197; Towner, *Timothy and Titus*, 697.
[59] Towner, *Timothy and Titus*, 705; Collins, *1 & 2 Timothy and Titus*, 335.
[60] Witherington, *Letters and Homilies for Hellenized Christians*, 127.

words for *slaves* is about status),[61] particularly those members of the household who would be considered subordinate – the elderly, women, the young, and slaves.[62] The household was the context for most of earliest Christianity and thus ethics were framed by the ordering of a household.[63] One can ponder what differences occur when one moves ethics framed by a household to ethics framed by individualism or various other social structures.

2:1 But as for you, teach what is consistent with sound instruction.
2:2 Tell the older men to be temperate, serious, self-controlled, and sound in faith, in love, and in endurance.
2:3 Likewise, tell the older women to be reverent in behavior, not to be slanderers or enslaved to much wine; they are to teach what is good,
2:4 so that they may encourage the young women to love their husbands, to love their children,
2:5 to be self-controlled, chaste, good managers of the household, kind, submissive to their husbands, so that the word of God may not be discredited.
2:6 Likewise, urge the younger men to be self-controlled
2:7 in all things, offering yourself as a model of good works and in your teaching offering integrity, gravity,
2:8 and sound speech that cannot be censured; then any opponent will be put to shame, having nothing evil to say of us.
2:9 Urge slaves to be submissive to their masters in everything, to be pleasing, not talking back,
2:10 not to stealing, but showing complete and perfect fidelity, so that in everything they may be an ornament to the teaching of God our Savior.

Titus 2 instructs Titus to teach the truth (2:1) by speaking directly to various groups in the households on Crete, in particular, to *older men* (2:2), *older women* (2:3–5), *younger men* (2:6), Titus himself (2:7–8, picked up again at 2:15), and *slaves* (2:9–10). Though starting with *teach what is consistent with sound doctrine*, what follows is not an exposition on the content of *sound* or "healthy" *doctrine* but a teaching on behaviors. The

---

[61] Marshall, *Pastoral Epistles*, 231–236. Some question whether these are truly household codes or merely something similar; e.g., Witherington, *Letters and Homilies for Hellenized Christians*, 130–132, 133.
[62] Witherington, 132.
[63] Towner, *Timothy and Titus*, 714–716; Collins, *1 & 2 Timothy and Titus*, 345; Witherington, *Letters and Homilies for Hellenized Christians*, 130.

Apostle assumes Titus knows the content of healthy teaching and seeks to encourage a proper embodiment of it.[64] The most common word is *sophron*, translated "prudence" and "self-control" and used for each of the groups addressed except the slaves (2:2, 4, 5, 6; cf. v. 12). The term expresses a vision for civilized piety, a social respectability that is both taught and transcended by a life of Christoformity.[65]

Instructions for Titus (2:1, 7–8)

We begin with Tistus's (*But as for you*) assignment for the households on Crete. The Apostle orders him not so much to *teach* (NRSV, NIV), but to "speak" (CEB: "should talk") what fits with healthy (*sound*; cf. 1 Tim 1:10; 6:3; 2 Tim 1:13; 4:3; Titus 1:9, 13; 2:1, 2) *teachings*. It is unwise to equate what the Apostle has in mind with the Nicaean Creed and the solas of the Reformation or any major church confession, but what is said here is consistent with that sort of gospel tradition. Consistency with the gospel (1 Cor 15:1–8; 1 Tim 3:16; 2 Tim 2:8–13) mattered then and matters now.

The Apostle instructs Titus again in 2:7-8 to be marked by *sound speech* in v. 8. These verses begin with the instruction to *show yourself in all respects a model of good works* (2:7a). *In all respects* continues from 2:6 and is not a new sentence (CEB;[66] *contra* NRSV, NIV). Education is as much if not more emulation than it is information[67] so the Apostle exhorts Titus to become a *tupos* (model, example, paradigm) as he tells Timothy (1 Tim 4:12).[68] Here he is to be exemplary when it comes to *good works*, which when used affirmatively in the NT means publicly observable acts of benevolence and compassion (cf. Matt 5:16; 11:2, 19; 26:10 with Eph 2:8–10 with 1 Tim 2:10; 5:10; 6:18; 2 Tim 3:17; Titus 2:14; 3:1, 8, 14).

As is so often the case in the PEs, gospel-anchored teaching comes to the fore: *in your teaching show integrity, gravity, and sound speech* (Titus 2:7–8a), or "integrity, respect, not knowably wrong with a healthy word."

---

[64] Towner, *Timothy and Titus*, 717, 718–720; Kelly, *Pastoral Epistles*, 239; Marshall, *Pastoral Epistles*, 238; Mounce, *Pastoral Epistles*, 413.
[65] Hoklotubbe, *Civilized Piety*.
[66] Marshall, *Pastoral Epistles*, 253; Quinn, *Titus*, 123. Hutson thinks the Apostle may have put it between the instructions, so it works with both the end of v. 6 and the beginning of v. 7; Hutson, *1–2 Timothy and Titus*, 230.
[67] Copan, *Saint Paul as Spiritual Director*, 59–72; Hood, *Imitating God in Christ: Recapturing a Biblical Pattern*.
[68] Mounce, *Pastoral Epistles*, 413; Collins, *1 & 2 Timothy and Titus*, 344; Towner, *Timothy and Titus*, 731; Witherington, *Letters and Homilies for Hellenized Christians*, 140.

The term *integrity* here refers to a lack of corruption and decay,[69] whereas the term *gravity* (NIV, CEB: "seriousness") also has the sense of a respectful manner and, as with the case of other terms, evokes civilized piety and public reputation (1 Tim 2:2; 3:4). Sound teaching that *cannot be censured* perhaps carries unnecessarily some legal connotations: "knowably wrong" is perhaps a better rendering. All of this is done with an eye on how to conduct oneself over against one's opponents and maintain a good public reputation in the Cretan cities. The one who teaches like this will *put to shame*, that is defeat, the ideas of *the opponent* of the gospel because they will have *nothing evil to say* of those so conducting themselves.[70] A similar concern with publicly observable behavior and public reputation, all for the sake of the gospel mission, is at work in 1 Peter 2:11–3:7.

Instructions for Older Men (2:2)

One might wonder if "elders" (the office) are in view yet again, but in light of the vocabulary (*presbutēs* not *presbuteros*; cf. Phm 9) and 2:3's concern with *older women* we can be assured that he has seniors rather than authorities in mind, and this reflects a culture that believes sages hold an essential place within communal life to provide wisdom.[71] How old? Someone nearing the age of fifty if not sixty years old would be one calculation, but for others in the Classical world "old" began at forty! These sages should be *temperate* or sober in both alcohol consumption and morality; *serious* or socially respectful to others and personally respectable; *self-controlled*, which is a term from the register of wisdom; and *sound in faith* or "healthy in the faith," which could suggest that theological fidelity is not just the work of those holding the offices of elders and bishops and deacons, but when combined with the next two moral virtues, the term *faith* probably here speaks of faithfulness as a Christian characteristic generally expected of all. In addition, they are to be characterized by *love* (Comments 1 Tim 1:5) and *endurance* or resilience through stress (Comments 1 Tim 6:11). Each of these terms is characteristic of the PE's general moral vision of socially respectable, Christian civilized piety (cf. 1 Tim 6:11; 2 Tim 3:10). The terms here are found in the lists for elders,

---

[69] Collins, *1 & 2 Timothy and Titus*, 344.
[70] Towner, *Timothy and Titus*, 734.
[71] McKnight and Hanlon, eds., *Wise Church*.

Commentary on Titus

bishops, or deacons in 1 Timothy 3 and Titus 1, but faith and love are combined with hope to form the classic gospel virtue triad (1 Cor 13:13).

> **A Closer Look: What Makes a Person "Old"?**
>
> Solon, then, reckons the life of man by the aforesaid ten weeks of years. And Hippocrates the physician, says that there are seven ages: those of the little boy, the boy, the lad, the young man, the man, the elderly man, the old man, and that these ages are measured by multiples of seven, though not in regular succession. His words are: "In man's life there are seven seasons, which they call ages, little boy, boy, lad, young man, man, elderly man, old man. He is a little boy until he reaches seven years, the time of the shedding of his teeth; a boy until he reaches puberty, i.e. up to twice seven years; a lad until his chin grows downy, i.e. up to thrice seven years; a young man until his whole body has grown, till four times seven; a man till forty-nine, till seven times seven; an elderly man till fifty-six, up to seven times eight; after that an old man" (Philo, *On the Creation of the World* 105, LCL; Colson and Whitaker).

Instructions for Older Women (2:3–5)

As at 1 Timothy 3:11 the Apostle follows "older men" with *older women*, and once again a major theme is civilized piety that they both embody and teach to *younger women* (Titus 2:4). The *older women* are given a list of perhaps four character manifestations so they can teach *younger women* seven more virtues. All eleven are no doubt applicable to all women.

The *older women* are to be "sacred" in an observable, socially respectable manner (*reverent in behavior*), terms that often describe those fit for the activity and dignity of a priest in a temple (cf. 1 Tim 2:10).[72] As examples they are *not to be slanderers* (1 Tim 3:11; 2 Tim 3:3) or *enslaved to much wine*, which was a common moral challenge in the ancient world (and again today).[73] Noticeably, they are instructed to be teachers: *teach what is good*. Some restrict this from being a teaching office on the basis of 1 Timothy 2:12 in the Pauline churches,[74] that constricts women teaching

---

[72] Marshall, *Pastoral Epistles*, 243–244; Mounce, *Pastoral Epistles*, 410; Towner, *Timothy and Titus*, 723.
[73] Witherington, *Letters and Homilies for Hellenized Christians*, 137.
[74] Kelly, *Pastoral Epistles*, 240; Knight, *Pastoral Epistles*, 307; Mounce, *Pastoral Epistles*, 410.

in 1 Timothy 2:12 until they are morally and theologically formed. While it is true that they are teaching *younger women* in Titus 2:3, and this pericope is not expounding specifically on the teaching office but is focused on age-based social duty as noted above, the text does not explicitly prohibit them from exercising their sage influence towards anyone but younger women.[75] They are to *teach what is good* or what is "excellent" and "beautiful," again an example of the forcefulness of the Hebrew term *tov* as a moral and ethical pursuit in the Jewish tradition (e.g., Amos 5:14–15).

Such teachings then are to wisen the *younger women* to embody seven virtues in their households.[76] They are to be "man lovers" and "children lovers" (Titus 2:4), both of which are nouns pointing to greatly esteemed virtues in both the Greco-Roman and Jewish cultures.[77] As with the "older men," the younger women are to be *self-controlled*[78] (cf. 1 Tim 2:9) and *chaste,* another cultic word used in the sense of devoted to God (1 Tim 5:22). When spoken about women both terms stressed sexual purity.[79] When it comes to their households, illustrating that the wife ran the household (cf. 1 Tim 5:14), they are to be *good managers of the household* and *kind*. This kindness, the word being "good"[80] in Greek, is a character trait likely connected to *submissive to their husbands*, which has been both abused and misunderstood. The term is connected to social order in one's household as the wife orders herself in relation to her husband, and this will not mean to do whatever he says or that the man is to dominate. Instead, it has to do with being the kind of woman that relates to her husband in an orderly, socially respectable manner. As Peter told his churches, this is to be done for the sake of the gospel, here *the word of God* (cf. 1 Tim 5:14; 6:1; Titus 2:10; 1 Pet 2:12; 3:1). The younger women are to embody the gospel sufficiently so that the gospel is not blasphemed, insulted, or *discredited*. Discrediting the gospel seems to have been a

---

[75] Similarly, Witherington, *Letters and Homilies for Hellenized Christians*, 138.
[76] Towner, *Timothy and Titus*, 724.
[77] Marshall, *Pastoral Epistles*, 247–248; Collins, *1 & 2 Timothy and Titus*, 342; Towner, *Timothy and Titus*, 726.
[78] The NRSV chooses to translate this Greek term *sōphrōn* as *prudent* for the older men in v. 2 but *self-controlled* for the younger women in v. 5! The NIV has "self-controlled" for both usages. The difference is due to the dynamic application of the Greek term for different groups of people; see Witherington, *Letters and Homilies for Hellenized Christians*, 135–136.
[79] Towner, *Timothy and Titus*, 724; Collins, *1 & 2 Timothy and Titus*, 342; Kelly, *Pastoral Epistles*, 241; Ward, *1 & 2 Timothy and Titus*, 253; Marshall, *Pastoral Epistles*, 248; Mounce, *Pastoral Epistles*, 411.
[80] Marshall, *Pastoral Epistles*, 248–249.

Commentary on Titus

special concern for the "subordinate" member of these household regulations because of the rumor of insubordination and anarchism supposedly launched by the liberating instructions for the subordinate member.[81]

Instructions for Younger Men (2:6–7a)

Not much is said to the *younger men*: they are *to be self-controlled* like the "older men" (2:2; translated in the NRSV as *prudent*) and to the "younger women" (2:5). This word was often used to curb male sexual desire[82] but, as stated above, these men are to be *self-controlled* "in all respects," including their sexual desires.

Instructions for Slaves

Finally, the Apostle turns to *slaves* in the household. Every time one sees this term in the New Testament one needs to repeat this definition by a well-known Canadian expert on ancient slavery: "Slavery by definition is a means of securing and maintaining an involuntary labour force by a group in society which monopolises political and economic power."[83] The all-too-common suggestion that New World slavery was much worse than Roman slavery is both historically mistaken and insensitive: a slave is a slave is a slave. A slave is a body owned, and owned bodies are whom the Apostle turns to next.[84] The *slaves* are *to be submissive* – again meaning living an orderly life in an ordered household – to *their own masters* (2:9), and the hardest words here evoke much pain in our culture: *in* all things, though this would not include known sinful behavior.[85] The NRSVue has *to be pleasing* while the NIV softens it to "try to please them," though "try" is not technically present. A simple wooden translation is "good-pleasers," and this connects to what comes next: *not talking back*, or not to contradict. Not only they are instructed to submit and to please but now their voices are silenced. Such was the way of slavery, to which the earliest

---

[81] See especially Ben Witherington III, and G. Francois Wessels, "Do Everything in the Name of the Lord: Ethics and Ethos in Colossians," in Jan G. van der Watt, ed., *Identity, Ethics, and Ethos in the New Testament*, BZNW 141 (Berlin: De Gruyter, 2006), 303–333; Witherington, *Letters and Homilies for Hellenized Christians*, 132–133; Marshall, *Pastoral Epistles*, 246, 250; Towner, *Timothy and Titus*, 714.
[82] Towner, *Timothy and Titus*, 730; Ward, *I & II Timothy and Titus*, 254.
[83] Bradley, *Slaves and Masters*, 18.
[84] McKnight, *Philemon*, 6–29.
[85] Mounce, *Pastoral Epistles*, 415; Towner, *Timothy and Titus*, 738.

apostles were more or less blind even as they were working out a redemptive way of treating slaves as siblings in Christ! (Philemon). Hutson suggests Paul "hedges" when it comes to slavery "with principles that undermine the position of the master."[86] There can be no doubt that Paul's fundamental concepts of equality in Christ pave an avenue against slavery, though Paul did not walk that path.

Slaves were notorious for theft, so the Apostle makes use of that stereotype: *not stealing* (2:10). Thus, a slave eating when she shouldn't, working on the side for extra money, or laying aside some of the master's funds for his own use would be examples. The aim is not the economy of the slaveowner but to *showing complete and perfect fidelity*, which could be translated "exhibiting every allegiance [in doing] good." This translation suggests two elements of the slave's behaviors: allegiance as well as doing good. The NIV has "to show that they can be fully trusted" but almost erases the term "good." Loyalty far too often tends toward eliding what is good. Once again civilized piety, seen by others, becomes a witness to the gospel's peacefulness, which is precisely what the Apostle says next: this makes the *teaching about God our Savior attractive* (2:10). The word *attractive* translates a word that means to adorn or decorate (see 1 Tim 2:9; 1 Pet 3:5) so that one might think here of a slave decorating the doctrines about God's redemption by living a good life, noticeable as it would be to others. Such gospel goodness provides a dignity and importance to the Christian slave's life that his status in the world did not.[87]

2:11–15 THE HOUSEHOLD'S REDEMPTIVE FOUNDATION

One of the most attractive forms of framing Christian ethics today is virtue ethics, which comes to us through Aristotle and then Aquinas and now expressed in any number of variations. The essence of virtue ethics is habits done in a manner that become character-forming, which is undoubtedly a partial insight into how moral character actually is formed. In fact, the virtues mentioned here are highly valued and greatly encouraged in the Greco-Roman world and were also esteemed by the piety and wisdom culture of Second Temple Hellenistic Judaism.[88]

---

[86] Hutson, *1–2 Timothy, Titus*, 144.
[87] Ward, *1 & 2 Timothy and Titus*, 257–258; Marshall, *Pastoral Epistles*, 258, 261; Collins, *1 & 2 Timothy and Titus*, 347; Towner, *Timothy and Titus*, 739.
[88] Marshall, *Pastoral Epistles*, 269.

Virtue ethics, however, isn't Christian until God's empowering grace in Christ through the Spirit redeems them, and then it is not truly virtue ethics but Spirit-prompted living into Christoformity![89] The household code of Titus 2:1–10 is founded, not on habit-forming-character, but on redemption in Christ. This redemption, when combined with such habits, can be transformative of both a person's character and the community in which they are transformed (similar in 3:1–7). Our passage, which some contend is rooted in earlier traditions and even a baptismal tradition,[90] clarifies redemption in Christ (2:11–14), and then finishes with a one-verse reminder to instruct the Cretan assemblies concerning what the Apostle has so far said (2:15). These instructions widen the audience to all, and not to one specific group in the household.

2:11 For the grace of God has appeared, bringing salvation to all,
2:12 training us to renounce impiety and worldly passions and in the present age to live lives that are self-controlled, upright, and godly,
2:13 while we wait for the blessed hope and the manifestation of the glory of our great God and Savior, Jesus Christ.
2:14 He it is who gave himself for us that he might redeem us from all iniquity and purify for himself a people of his own who are zealous for good deeds.
2:15 Declare these things; exhort and reprove with all authority. Let no one look down on you.

The most immediate prompt for 2:11's turn to redemption is the household code section concluding in 2:10, which reminded the slaves that their behavior could be an "ornament to the doctrine of God our Savior." This passage then articulates the content of "the doctrine of God" and it moves quickly: 1) the foundation of grace is stated (2:11a), 2) grace's effects are clarified (2:11b, 12a, 12b), 3) the time during which the effects of grace are at work (2:13), and 4) God's whole work in Christ Jesus is restated in 2:14.

Foundation of Grace

Grace has been reduced in Christian theological circles at times to simplicities: G̲od's r̲iches a̲t Christ's e̲xpense. It has also been reduced to "pure" or

---

[89] Similarly, Towner, *Timothy and Titus*, 740; Witherington, *Letters and Homilies for Hellenized Christians*, 143.
[90] Marshall, *Pastoral Epistles*, 263–265.

"sheer" grace in such a manner that humans seemingly have no responsibility, and thus cease being agents in the redemption God works. The recent studies by John Barclay, however, have thrown open a large window of light on the topic.[91] He has concluded that grace has six "perfections": 1) superabundance, emphasizing the lavishness and permanence of God's gift in Christ; 2) singularity, pressing into service the conviction that God's attitude is purely that of grace; 3) priority, that the gift is given before the one receiving initiates; 4) incongruity, where the emphasis falls on the giving of the gift without regard to the receiver's status or worthiness; 5) efficacy, the power the gift has upon the recipient as an agent; and 6) non-circularity, where the receiver is not engaged in reciprocal giving relations with the giver. Paul emphasizes the incongruity of the gift and the receiver, but other themes are present in Pauline theology too: there is superabundance, priority, as well as efficacy. A Pauline theology of grace requires each to play its part in soteriology, and the exegete will seek which elements are in play in each appearance of the word "grace."

This leads to Titus 2:11's *For the grace of God has appeared*, and it doesn't "fit" any of the above specifically because it encompasses all of them! Put differently, *grace* becomes an agent and bestows the gift itself, namely God's act of love for humans in Christ to rescue them. The word *appeared*, a term used in a similar way for the manifestation of "goodness and loving kindness" in 3:4, is connected to similar terms (*phainō* and *epiphaneia* and *phaneroō* are cognate). It here refers to the appearing of Christ incarnate (1 Tim 3:16; 6:14; 2 Tim 1:10; 4:1, 8; Titus 2:13) and the message about him (Titus 1:3).[92] In light of the effects of grace to follow, *grace* here has the sense of gift, redemption, and efficacy in transformation in this present world.[93]

Effects of Grace

One sees three effects of God's Agent Grace appearing: *salvation* (2:11b), *training us to renounce* ... (2:12a) and *to live lives* (2:12b). The

---

[91] Barclay, *Paul and the Gift*; John M. G. Barclay, *Paul and the Power of Grace* (Grand Rapids: Eerdmans, 2020). Barclay does not see as tight a connection of Paul to the author of the PEs, which means "grace" in the PEs would be seen as a development after Paul. His perfections can be used heuristically in the PEs.

[92] Marshall, *Pastoral Epistles*, 287–296; Collins, *1 & 2 Timothy and Titus*, 350–351; Towner, *Timothy and Titus*, 745.

[93] Witherington, *Letters and Homilies for Hellenized Christians*, 142.

manifestation of grace is connected to God and Jesus *bringing salvation*, since both are depicted as Savior (1:3; 2:10; 3:4 with 2 Tim 1:10; Titus 1:4; 2:13; 3:6). The NRSV's *bringing* is implied, and it could be simpler as "which means" or even appeared "with" redemption, or one could just have a more brusque tone: "Grace ... has appeared, deliverance for all humans." Many have paused long over *to all* or "for all humans" (2:11). Some think this stresses the extension of salvation to all the groups mentioned in 2:2–10[94] while others see grace overcoming the Jew and gentile divide in the typical Pauline sense, but the macroscopic nature of this expression (cf. 3:2 and 1 Tim 2:1, 4; 4:10) suggest those kinds of limitations don't apply here. Rather, it is 1 Tim 4:10 that best explains what is in the Apostle's mind: God is "Savior of all people" and that is followed by "especially for those who believe." The limitation here then is not with God's grace or with grace's provision but with human agents not choosing to embrace this grace.

The second effect is *training us to renounce impiety and worldly passions* (2:12a). Behind *training* is *paideuō* conveying the sense of instruction, mentoring, and disciplining (1 Tim 1:20; 2 Tim 2:25; cf. 1 Cor 11:32; 2 Cor 6:9; Heb 12:5–11) with the goal to transform the uneducated into the civilized.[95] Grace is the instructor here and grace's effect is transformation out of sin, here concretized as *impiety* (or, "uncivilized piety"), that is socially disrespectful behaviors, and *worldly passions*, which will be detailed some in Titus 3:3. The language is subtle: the Apostle's concern for transformation concerns desires (*epithumia*; 3:3) and these desires are described negatively as *worldly*, or "worldly-decorated." The term is not simply "world" (*kosmos*) but *kosmikos*, which refers to adorning oneself with what pleases the *kosmos*.

The third effect is *to live lives that are self-controlled, upright, and godly* (2:12b) – or prudent, righteous/just, and with civilized piety. These are three of the four cardinal virtues of the Hellenistic world.[96] Here the idea is to live *in the present age* (picked up in 2:13) a life that is very much like what the Apostle has instructed for elders/bishops in 1:6–9 but is especially found in Tistus's version of the household regulations in 2:2–10. A Christian's public life is to embody "prudence" to provide wisdom, to

---

[94] Knight, *Pastoral Epistles*, 319.
[95] Towner, *Timothy and Titus*, 747–748.
[96] Towner, 749. The missing fourth virtue being "manliness" or *andreia* in Greek, see Marshall, *Pastoral Epistles*, 271.

embody "righteousness/justice" to enact God's truth, and thus it embodies "civilized piety" in the family, city, and empire. The term *godly* (or civilized piety) opened the letter (1:1) and has remained a strong theme throughout (and in the PEs generally).

Time for Grace to Do Its Work

The *present age* of 2:12 is now opened up as the time awaiting the final Epiphany,[97] or what is often called the Second Coming or Parousia. Earliest Christianity inherited from Second Temple Judaism a strong tension between the now and not yet, this age and the age to come, between the first advent of Christ and his second, and all ethics were constrained by this tension.[98] It is a period of the kingdom being present but not yet consummated with fullness.[99] The return of Christ is here given two expressions: *the blessed hope and the manifestation of the glory of . . . Jesus Christ* (2:13), with *blessed* applying perhaps to both *hope* and *manifestation* [epiphany]. Imminency, or the expectation that King Jesus would return soon, was alive and well when Titus was written, though its intensity has been overdrawn at times.[100] The term *blessed* points to God's blessing of humans at the total redemption of creation, of humans experiencing that redemption with a glorious happiness, and therefore *hope* for such a glory is a *blessed* reality as it brings into the present moment a joy rooted in the gospel-assured future (Matt 5:3–12; Luke 6:20–26).[101]

Deserving of some attention is the grammar of Titus 2:13's *our great God and Savior, Jesus Christ*, which has been rendered by some as (1) *our great God and* (2) *[our] Savior, Jesus Christ*, yet others have made it about glory (*the glory of our-God-and-Savior, Jesus Christ*), while others have rightly shown that this is one person: *our great-God-and-Savior*, namely,

---

[97] Towner, *Timothy and Titus*, 750.
[98] Witherington, *Letters and Homilies for Hellenized Christians*, 151.
[99] George Eldon Ladd, *A Theology of the New Testament*, ed. Donald A. Hagner, rev. edn. (Grand Rapids: Eerdmans, 1993). For ethics, this tension has been updated and expanded in Witherington III, *NT Theology and Ethics*.
[100] Marshall, *Pastoral Epistles*, 272; Witherington, *Letters and Homilies for Hellenized Christians*, 144.
[101] Marshall, *Pastoral Epistles*, 272–274; Mounce, *Pastoral Epistles*, 425; Towner, *Timothy and Titus*, 751–752.

Jesus Christ.¹⁰² Earliest Christianity soon recognized Jesus along with the Father as one God,¹⁰³ and recent studies have opened up fresh insights into a Pauline sense of Trinity.¹⁰⁴

Foundation and Effects Restated

This Jesus-as-God *gave himself for us* summarizes the redemption themes already present from 2:10 on and leads to the theme of grace's power to transform, which is the restatement of the three effects in 2:11b–12: *redeem us from all iniquity and purify for himself a people of his own who are zealous for good deeds*. Early Christian soteriology is on display here: God's act of redemption in Christ liberates (in an exodus sense; *lutroō*; cf. Exod 6:6; Mark 10:45 and Luke 24:21; 1 Pet 1:18) a people from enslavement to sin, that is covenant-breaking (*anomia* as "lawlessness" is connected to Torah) and "cleanses" (a *kosher* morality) them into a life of *good deeds*, or "beautiful works," this latter expression once again rising to the level of civilized piety as a life noted by public benevolence and respect.¹⁰⁵

God's work through King Jesus faithfully fulfills the promises made to Israel and by this grace both invites all into the people of God and empowers the redeemed to embody the gospel. King Jesus' salvation here must be understood in terms as intentionally selfless love, vicarious, liberating, expiatory, and communally representative,¹⁰⁶ with the goal not merely to remove sin but even to transform into Christlikeness.¹⁰⁷

---

[102] These options are discussed at length in Marshall, *Pastoral Epistles*, 276–282; Mounce, *Pastoral Epistles*, 426–431. See especially Murray J. Harris, *Jesus as God: The New Testament Use of Theos in Reference to Jesus* (Grand Rapids: Baker, 1992), 173–185.

[103] Larry W. Hurtado, *Lord Jesus Christ: Devotion to Jesus in Earliest Christianity* (Grand Rapids: Eerdmans, 2003); Larry W. Hurtado, *How on Earth Did Jesus Become a God? Historical Questions about Earliest Devotion to Jesus* (Grand Rapids: Eerdmans, 2005); Richard Bauckham, Jesus and the God of Israel: *God Crucified* and Other Studies on the New Testament's Christology of Divine Identity (Grand Rapids: Eerdmans, 2008); James D. G. Dunn, *Did the First Christians Worship Jesus? The New Testament Evidence* (Louisville: Westminster John Knox, 2010).

[104] Wesley Hill, *Paul and the Trinity: Persons, Relations, and the Pauline Letters* (Grand Rapids: Eerdmans, 2015); Matthew W. Bates, *The Birth of the Trinity* (New York: Oxford University Press, 2016).

[105] Towner, *Timothy and Titus*, 763–766.

[106] Collins, *1 & 2 Timothy and Titus*, 2002, 354–355; Towner, *Timothy and Titus*, 759–761.

[107] Witherington, *Letters and Homilies for Hellenized Christians*, 144–145.

Summing It All Up

What the Apostle has been telling Titus to do from 1:5 on is now recaptured in three terms in 2:15: *declare*, or more likely "say" or "speak" as in 2:1, *exhort* and *reprove*. He is to do these with the strength of the Apostle behind him and thus *with all authority*, or with a sense of aligning folks into an orderly, Christian way of life.[108] That he will be opposed is why he must add *Let no one look down on you*, or what might be a more picturesque sense, "Don't let anyone think around you or go behind closed doors about you or think they can go above you." This last sentence in the passage reminds of 1 Timothy 4:12 and the Apostle may well be thinking of Titus 2:6's counsel to "younger men."

3:1–11 CIVILIZED PIETY

Titus 3:1 resumes this letter's version of the household regulations (2:2–10).[109] If we see 2:15 as a summary of the regulations in 2:2–10, then 2:11–14 clarifies the foundation for those regulations. The Apostle now turns to conduct for all of the believers in their public life and within those instructions clarifies again the redemptive foundation of civilized piety (3:4–8). These final instructions can be summarized as a civilized piety[110] anchored in the redemption of Christ.

Titus 3:1 Remind them [1] to be subject to rulers and authorities, [2] to be obedient, [3] to be ready for every good work,
2 [4] to speak evil of no one, [5] to avoid quarreling, [6] to be gentle, and [7] to show every courtesy to everyone.
3 For we ourselves were once foolish, disobedient, led astray, slaves to various passions and pleasures, passing our days in malice and envy, despicable, hating one another.
4 But when the goodness and loving kindness of God our Savior appeared,
5 he saved us, not because of any works of righteousness that we had done, but according to his mercy, through the water of rebirth and renewal by the Holy Spirit.
6 This Spirit he poured out on us richly through Jesus Christ our Savior,

---

[108] Towner, *Timothy and Titus*, 768.
[109] Witherington, *Letters and Homilies for Hellenized Christians*, 154.
[110] Hoklotubbe, *Civilized Piety*.

Commentary on Titus

7 so that, having been justified by his grace, we might become heirs according to the hope of eternal life.
8 The saying is sure.
   I desire that you insist on these things, so that those who have come to believe in God may be careful to devote themselves to good works; these things are excellent and profitable to everyone.
9 But avoid stupid controversies, genealogies, dissensions, and quarrels about the law, for they are unprofitable and worthless.
10 After a first and second admonition, have nothing more to do with anyone who causes divisions,
11 since you know that such a person is perverted and sinful, being self-condemned.

After a list of general seven moral exhortations for Titus to give to the Cretans (3:1–2), the Apostle reminds the assemblies on Crete that they were once sinners themselves, trapped in seven vices (3:3), but that they have been delivered from that immoral life. Their salvation is by God's grace, not works done beforehand to ingratiate themselves to him, and the Spirit has been *poured out* on them to transform them for *the hope of eternal life* (3:4–8a). Redemption's reminder leads to further instructions for Titus to establish for the assemblies (3:8b–11).

Seven Reminders (3:1–2)

Seven reminders, numbered above, are given to Titus to pass on to the assemblies, implying of course that he will be marked by these same virtues. Once again, if one compares this list with the virtues and characteristics of either Aristotle or Theophrastus, the distinctive nature of Christian virtue rises to the surface while also indicating the kind of life that will be socially, publicly respectable on Crete. Similar instructions for how to live a public life are found elsewhere in the NT (cf. Rom 12–13; 1 Tim 2:1–2; 1 Pet 2:11–3:7). That Titus is to *remind them* indicates they have already been instructed in these matters. These instructions are as much about survival as they are a strategy of influence or tactic of subversion.[111]

---

[111] Towner, *Timothy and Titus*, 769. Marshall sees four basic ideas: subjection to authorities, readiness for good works, nonaggression, and showing patience; see Marshall, *Pastoral Epistles*, 300–304.

The first is the reminder [1] to live an orderly life by being *subject to rulers and authorities*, whoever they might be (3:1) and regardless of any temptation to anarchy (1:6, 10) as Cretans were known to be unruly.[112] This instruction fits one common early Christian strategy found also in Romans 13:1–7 and 1 Peter 2:11–12. Namely, a good public life will be more beneficial for the Christian movement,[113] but one should not limit these instructions to strategy alone (cf. 1 Tim 2:1–4). A good public life can subvert the ways of the Empire and thus be both a way of being "in" but not "of" the Empire.[114] They are also [2] to consent willingly (*to be obedient*), that is, to be people who can be persuaded by the authorities. In short, Christians are to be good citizens of the society they live within, without capitulating to anything that would deny the gospel in belief or public practice.[115] In their public life the Cretan believers are also [3] to *be ready* to participate (when and if possible) in public benevolence, for this is the evocation of *every good work* (cf. Rom 13:3; 1 Pet 2:11–12, 14–15).

While 3:1 is more concerned with how the Christians were to participate at the more elite levels of civic life, 3:2 speaks to relationships with others within normal day-to-day civic life. Hence, their speech – and here one thinks especially of the letter of James – [4] is *to speak evil of no one* but this translation, like that of the CEB ("they shouldn't speak disrespectfully"), is too general. The NIV's "to slander" better reflects the Greek term here as it is *blasphēmeō*, which evokes blasphemy of God and degrading insults of others.[116] Public, verbal insults of others, perhaps rulers, are in view. Thus, they are [5] *to avoid quarreling*, or to be "non-warriors" or not to be "word-warriors" (3:9; also 2 Tim 2:23–24; further at Rom 12:18; Col 3:15; James 1:19–21; 3:13–18; 4:1–2). One thinks, too, of its opposite, that is, being a peacemaker (Matt 5:9).[117] Instead of using degrading speech and fostering a warrior mentality, Christians are [6] *to be gentle*, and we should note that #s 5 and 6 are also together in the instructions for bishops (1 Tim 3:3). The idea is to be a reconciler. The final virtue reveals the social consciousness of the Apostle for the Cretans in full bloom, something

---

[112] Witherington, *Letters and Homilies for Hellenized Christians*, 155.
[113] Collins, *1 & 2 Timothy and Titus*, 357.
[114] Michel de Certeau, *The Practice of Everyday Life*, trans. Steven Rendall (Berkeley, CA: University of California Press, 1984), xix, 34–39; Towner, *Timothy and Titus*, 771–772.
[115] Witherington, *Letters and Homilies for Hellenized Christians*, 155–156.
[116] The term is used thirty-four times in the NT and in the PEs at 1 Tim 1:20; 6:1; Titus 2:5; 3:2.
[117] Swartley, *Covenant of Peace*.

Commentary on Titus

contrary to the rough Cretan stereotype: [7] *to show every courtesy to everyone* (3:2).[118] They are each to be personal exhibits of the widespread Christian virtue of "meekness" or *courtesy* in their public relations (see 2 Tim 2:25; cf. 2 Cor 10:1; Gal 5:23; 6:1; Eph 4:2; Col 3:12; James 1:21; 3:13; 1 Pet 3:16), a virtue exhibited and taught by Jesus himself (cf. Matt 5:5; 12:15–21).

Seven Vices (3:3)

Life as sketched for the Cretans is rooted in the new life found in Christ. The Apostle identifies with both Titus and the Cretans when he says *We ourselves were once* (3:3a), and a mutual personal narrative of conversion is what he has in mind. He has in mind here a stereotype of gentile pagan sinfulness (Gal 1:13–17; Rom 1:18–32; 6:20–22; 1 Cor 6:9–11).[119] Conversion across the board involves a context, some kind of crisis (not always "spiritual"), a quest for resolving the crisis, an encounter with an advocate for (in this case) the gospel about Jesus, a decision leading to commitment, and multidimensional consequences.[120] The Apostle's perception is that what was *once* the case is no longer true of them (cf. Col 1:21–22; 3:5–11) and in so saying he skips immediately to the consequences of conversion – a new way of life. All conversions, it has been said, are simultaneously apostasies from where one was previously, and where they were before comes to expression in (yet another) list of vices, also seven.

His angle on their past is retrospective, a backward reading of one's own narrative, and the revision of one's autobiography is the tell-tale sign of conversion.[121] Accompanying this reconstructed memory is the development of negative rhetoric about one's former allegiances, and so the Apostle sketches their past in strongly negative terms – from being *foolish* to actually *hating one another*. Such a retrospective narrative is rooted, too, in their new virtues and relationships in the assemblies of Paul's mission churches. His description of their past is both agential (*disobedient, hating one another*) and victimization (*led astray, slaves, despicable*).[122] Note another reference to

---

[118] Towner, *Timothy and Titus*, 773.
[119] Dibelius and Conzelmann, *Pastoral Epistles*, 147.
[120] Scot McKnight, *Turning to Jesus: The Sociology of Conversion in the Gospels* (Louisville: Westminster John Knox, 2002), 49–114.
[121] McKnight, *Pastor Paul*, 127–146.
[122] Towner, *Timothy and Titus*, 777.

slaves in such a short letter and again the mention of *passions* (cf. Titus 2:12). His vice list is shaped as much by his virtue list, one suspects, as by their actual behaviors in the past.

Redemption in Christ (3:4-8a)

The virtues of these early Christians are the work of God's grace (2:11), the Spirit (1 Tim 3:16; 4:1; 2 Tim 1:7, 14; Titus 3:5), and the mediation of Christ (3:6b). The passage is to be read with a proto-trinitarian lens. This formula-filled passage is not Romans 3:21-25, Philippians 2:6-11, or Colossians 1:13-20. And neither is it the soteriological scheme of the gospel in 1 Corinthians 15:1-8. The centrality of Spirit varies from the more cross-centered soteriology of other early Christian traditions and Pauline statements.

This redemption, which in 2:11 was called "grace," is here called the *goodness and loving kindness of God*, though both of these terms could be freshened up by the Cretan context as they are used at times for the emperor and rulers. The first term is *chrēstotēs* and is closer to graciousness than anything else, and thus sends us back to 2:11's "grace." This matters since God's graciousness is all about his revelation of incongruous grace in Christ (see Comments at 2:11). The second term, *philanthrōpia*, points to love for other humans,[123] which summarizes the virtues of 3:1-2's social behaviors. These two divine-human virtues *appeared* together, just as "grace appeared" at 2:11, and these launch into what may well be the use of an existing early Christian tradition (3:4b-7), which moves from the time, to the basis of redemption, to the redemption itself (*saved us*), to the agents and means, and to the consequences.[124]

The tradition (3:4) begins with the Originator and Patron[125] of *goodness, loving kindness*, and redemption: *God our Savior* (cf. Comments at 2:13). There is a possible hint of identity marking, since in the Roman Empire the emperors were considered saviors, so the use of *our Savior* (3:4, 6) implicitly demotes the emperors in favor of our Lord Jesus Christ and the Father.[126] The *Savior* delivers (*he saved us*; cf. 2 Tim 1:9-10) Christians

---

[123] Used only elsewhere in the NT at Acts 28:2.
[124] Marshall, *Pastoral Epistles*, 306-308.
[125] Witherington, *Letters and Homilies for Hellenized Christians*, 156-157.
[126] Towner, *Timothy and Titus*, 778-779; Witherington, *Letters and Homilies for Hellenized Christians*, 157.

not because of any works, which is deeply Pauline (e.g., Gal 2:16; Rom 3:20, 28), though with perhaps a different emphasis. Paul's normal emphasis with *works* is the boundary marking observances of food laws, sabbath, and circumcision – such *works* were the marks of identity for Jews in the diaspora[127] – but one has to ask if *works* here means those Jewish boundary markers or the acts of public benevolence as hinted at in 3:1–2. But notice that *works* is contained by ("in") *righteousness* (see Comments at 1 Tim 6:11; 2 Tim 2:22; 3:16), a preeminently Jewish term for right living with God and would possibly be at work in Titus on account of the opposition from Jews on Crete (cf. 1:10, 14; 3:9).[128] The incongruity of grace, however, is clearly in mind with the ending phrase indicating that God's grace is not dependent on anything *that we had done* (3:5).

God *saved us* in a measure consistent with *his mercy* (cf. "grace" at 2:11; Rom 12:1–2). Salvation in the New Testament is eschatological and one can speak reasonably of the three tenses of salvation as being past, present, and yet future (e.g., Eph 2:8; 1 Cor 1:18; Rom 8:18–39; 13:11; Col 3:1–4; Titus 2:11–13).[129] This *mercy* accompanies *the water of rebirth* and *renewal by the Holy Spirit*.

Debate has not only accompanied the readings of these expressions[130] but it has especially focused on 3:5's *water of rebirth*: does this refer to water baptism as a rite or is it a metaphor? Since this concerns how one is saved, the answer to the question does matter. The majority of scholars, both liturgically today and historically by tradition, believe the *water of rebirth* refers to water baptism,[131] pointing to such texts as 1 Corinthians 6:11 or Acts 2:38, and this majority interpretation is unmoved by the strong connection of salvation to baptism. After all, baptism is connected to union with Christ (Rom 6:1–14; Col 2:9–15), to Spirit and church reception (Acts 2:38; 1 Cor 12:13), and to the forgiveness of sin (Acts 2:38; 22:16; Gal 3:27; 1 Cor 6:11).[132] Other scholars, however, think this is a

---

[127] Dunn, *The New Perspective on Paul*.
[128] Towner, *Timothy and Titus*, 779–781.
[129] Caird, *New Testament Theology*, 118–135.
[130] Four options: (1) through a washing of rebirth and renewal which *is* associated with the Spirit; (2) through a washing of rebirth and renewal which *are* associated with the Spirit; (3) through a washing associated with the Spirit that brings rebirth and renewal; (4) through a washing of rebirth and through a renewal associated with the Spirit. The first is best and the language is adapted from Marshall, *Pastoral Epistles*, 316–322.
[131] E.g., Collins, *1 & 2 Timothy and Titus*, 365–366.
[132] Scot McKnight, *It Takes a Church to Baptize* (Grand Rapids: Brazos, 2018), 47–62.

spiritual washing (not a reference to baptism as a rite).[133] There is a distaste on the part of some to connect the rite of baptism to salvation, in spite of texts in the New Testament that make this connection. One needs merely to recognize that the Spirit working, and bodies going into water, are not incompatible actions, and neither does water baptism exclude a person's agential action of trust. Water baptism and Spirit baptism are connected. Two words, then, are used in 3:5 for redemption: *rebirth* (*palingenesia*; see Matt 19:28) and *renewal* (*anakainōsis*; Rom 6:1–11; 12:2), both of which are connected to early Christian-inaugurated eschatology as the launching of new creation (Rom 8). The emphasis is the consequences of God's saving work: humans are reborn and given a new life in new creation, and hence are to live a civilized piety according to a new family, people, and God.[134]

In this soteriologically loaded passage there is a lack of emphasis on the cross because the Spirit is the agent, not only in *renewal by the Spirit* but especially in 3:6's *This Spirit he poured out on us richly through Jesus Christ our Savior.*[135] Acts uses *poured out* for the Spirit at Pentecost (Acts 2:17, 18, 33), drawing on the coming of the Spirit as the fulfillment of the Messianic age,[136] and this has been done with superabundance (*richly*). There is here a clear Trinitarian network in redemption: God the Father saves and pours out, the Spirit is the agent, and Christ is the means. The Spirit rises in significance in this passage because of the theme of transformation. Consequences do, however, clearly flow from redemption. In v. 7 we read about the redeemed *having been justified by his* prior and incongruous *grace*,[137] which is a participial phrase that summarizes what was said in vv. 4–6 (cf. 2:11, 14). The consequence for the one *justified* (cf. 1 Tim 3:16) is to be newly born as *heirs* (Gal 3:23–4:7; Rom 8:17) consistent with *the hope of eternal life* (3:7). Such persons live now in light of the kingdom of God (cf. Col 1:13–14), what one scholar once called living "as if."[138]

---

[133] E.g., Marshall, *Pastoral Epistles*, 318; Witherington, *Letters and Homilies for Hellenized Christians*, 158–159, 160.
[134] Towner, *Timothy and Titus*, 789, 794; Witherington, *Letters and Homilies for Hellenized Christians*, 162.
[135] Fee, *God's Empowering Presence*, 777–784.
[136] Towner, *Timothy and Titus*, 783–786.
[137] Collins, *1 & 2 Timothy and Titus*, 363.
[138] A. E. Harvey, Strenuous Commands: The Ethic of Jesus (London: SCM, 1990).

The first sentence of 3:8, *This saying is sure*,[139] could refer back to the previous lines or anticipate the next verse, or perhaps it goes with both. The first option is preferred as 3:4–7 appears to be the use of an early Christian tradition (1 Tim 1:15; 3:1; 4:9; 2 Tim 2:11).[140] Its intent is to enhance the truthfulness (here) of what has just been said.

Final Instructions (3:8b–11)

What the Apostle has said from 1:5 on, or at least from 2:1 on (tied as 3:1–2 is to 2:2–10), when it comes to matters of behavior is all rooted in redemption and the Apostle wants no wavering from Titus on these things. For the Apostle, redemption moved a person out of one way of life and into another, a gospel-based civilized piety. That is, it is not just a moment in time but a life with consequences. Thus we are not surprised he ties the two together: those who have come to believe are to be people of good works, which again points to a civilized, public piety[141] that is profitable to everyone (or simpler, "to humans"). Such works are actually "beautiful" (*kalos*), that is, their impact on others is pleasing. (Others suggest these things refers not to good works but to the soteriological lines of 3:4–7.[142])

A civilized piety rooted in redemption (2:11–14; 3:4–7) requires that the Cretans also avoid public wrangling *about the law*, which again turns the tension in the assemblies toward verbal fisticuffs with Jews who either are not believers or who are imposing Torah observance on gentile believers.[143] Something similar was said at 1:10–16 (cf. 2 Tim 2:23–26). These debates are reduced to slogans: "moronic" or *stupid controversies, genealogies, dissensions, and quarrels about the law* and they are *stupid* and divisive because they are *unprofitable and worthless* for leading to civilized piety. The Old Testament, it should be recalled, is "profitable" when it is read well (1 Tim 1:8) and for the right purpose, namely, an education that transforms (2 Tim 3:16–17). Speculations from *genealogies* do not profit (cf. 1 Tim 1:4).

The Apostle now proceeds into church order: the divisive, faction-forming person (*hairetikos*, from which we get "heretic") is to be

---

[139] Marshall, *Pastoral Epistles*, 326–330.
[140] Towner, *Timothy and Titus*, 789; Witherington, *Letters and Homilies for Hellenized Christians*, 161.
[141] Towner, *Timothy and Titus*, 792.
[142] Marshall, *Pastoral Epistles*, 332–333.
[143] Witherington, *Letters and Homilies for Hellenized Christians*, 163.

admonished no more than twice (Matt 18:15-20) and then avoided, if not shunned by the whole community by excommunication (*have nothing more to do with*; cf. 1 Tim 1:20).[144] Qumran knows of this kind of discipline for a variety of unacceptable behaviors (1QS 6:24-7:25) and our passage reminds of 1 Corinthians 5's instructions to discipline the unrepentant and impenitent. Such a person, the Apostle informs Titus, is one who has turned away (*perverted*) or "twisted" (CEB), he or she is "sinning" (*sinful* is a verb in 3:11) and they are deconstructing themselves into *self-condemnation*.[145]

3:12-15 FINAL WORDS

The closing of the Pauline letters takes on a common pattern: travel plans, a general exhortation, some greetings, and a prayer for God's grace. For other closings, see Romans 15:14-33, 1 Corinthians 16:5-14, 2 Corinthians 13:1-11, Galatians 6:11-17, Philippians 4:10-20, 2 Thessalonians 3:13-15, and Philemon 21-22, while we find similar themes also in the PEs at 2 Timothy 4:9-18.

Titus 3:12 When I send Artemas to you, or Tychicus, do your best to come to me at Nicopolis, for I have decided to spend the winter there.

13 Make every effort to send Zenas the lawyer and Apollos on their way, and see that they lack nothing.

14 And let people learn to devote themselves to good works in order to meet urgent needs, so that they may not be unproductive.

Titus 3:15 All who are with me send greetings to you. Greet those who love us in the faith.

Grace be with all of you.

Travel Plans

The Apostle begins his closing with an indication of travel plans. *When I send Artemas ... or Tychicus* suggests they will relieve Titus and carry on the mission plans (1:5). At which time Titus can come to Paul, who is in *Actia Nicopolis*,[146] a city in Western Greece where the Apostle is wintering.

---

[144] Towner, *Timothy and Titus*, 797-799; Collins, *1 & 2 Timothy and Titus*, 369.
[145] Witherington, *Letters and Homilies for Hellenized Christians*, 163-164.
[146] Collins, *1 & 2 Timothy and Titus*, 371-372; Witherington, *Letters and Homilies for Hellenized Christians*, 164-165.

Thus, the letter is probably written in late summer or autumn.[147] This is near other locations for the Apostle's mission work (cf. Rom 15:19; 2 Tim 4:10). We do not know why the Apostle thinks Tistus's mission on Crete will end nor why he wants the latter to join him, though we know he will later be sent to on mission work to Dalmatia (2 Tim 4:10). There is a picture of Paul painted here that is more than simply the exuberant and wandering preacher; he has matured in some ways to become an administrator over other teachers as delegates with the authority and obligation to guide the Gentile churches in proper obedience to the faith (cf. Rom 1:5).[148]

The rather unpredictable nature of Paul's plans are known from 1 Corinthians 16:5–12 and this may be present in *when*, which could be translated "whenever" and that uncertainty is also present in *or* (before *Tychicus*). *Artemas* appears here only in the NT while *Tychicus* may have been the courier for Colossians and perhaps also Philemon (cf. Col 4:7; Eph 6:21–22; Acts 20:4; 2 Tim 4:12), though this last verse indicates Paul on other occasion had plans for him to be sent to Ephesus. There is a seriousness or urgency about the Apostle's directives here: *do your best* (3:12) is similar to *make every effort* (3:13; Greek *spoudazō* and *spoudaiōs*).

We know nothing about *Zenas the lawyer* but *Apollos* is well known, assuming it is the same person as the Jewish Christian evangelist from Alexandria (cf. 1 Cor 1:12; 16:12; Acts 18:24–19:10). The two are en route, and so Titus and the Cretan churches are to provide for them so they may carry on their trip: *and see that they lack nothing* (cf. 3 Jn 5–6).[149] That the first man is a *lawyer* could indicate that he was a Jewish convert and had become an expert in the law (cf. 3:9; also Luke 7:30; 10:25; 11:45–46; 11:52; 14:3), though some hold him to be a Roman jurist instead.[150] The closing of a letter often enough brings to light the name of the courier and it is as likely as not that these two traveling evangelists actually are themselves the couriers, who would then read the letter to Titus in a performative way.[151]

---

[147] Marshall, *Pastoral Epistles*, 341–342
[148] Marshall, *Pastoral Epistles*, 343; Collins, *1 & 2 Timothy and Titus*, 370; Towner, *Timothy and Titus*, 800.
[149] Towner, 801.
[150] Kelly, *Pastoral Epistles*, 258; Knight, *Pastoral Epistles*, 357; Marshall, *Pastoral Epistles*, 343; Towner, *Timothy and Titus*, 801–802.
[151] Bernhard Oestreich, *Performance Criticism of the Pauline Letters*, trans. Lindsay Elias and Brent Blum (Eugene: Cascade, 2016).

One More Instruction

Again the Apostle includes an exhortation *to devote themselves to good works* (3:8) and once again this will have pointed at the public actions of those with civilized behavior. These actions are by *people*, a feeble translation of *hoi hēmeteroi*, which means "our own"[152] usually referring to an exclusive relational group or, better yet, "our siblings" (also at 2 Tim 4:15; also Acts 26:5; Rom 15:4; 1 John 1:3; 2:2). These *people* are *to learn* through instruction (cf. 1 Tim 2:11; 5:4, 13) to do what Titus is being instructed to do for the two letter couriers: *to meet urgent needs*. Such a life of charitable deeds in their community, both to those within the faith (Gal 6:10; 1 Jn 3:17)[153] and to those outside the faith,[154] will make their lives "fruitful" (here translated too commercially as *unproductive*). Their formation in discipleship was to a formation in public action and not just private spirituality. The presence once again of civilized piety at the very end of the letter indicates the importance of this topic for the assemblies on Crete.

Greetings

Titus is being greeted by *all who are with* the Apostle (3:15), and the Apostle sends his greetings to *those who love us in the faith*. This is common to Paul's letters (e.g., Rom 16:16; Col 4:10, 12, 14; Phm 23), but it is not common for Paul to use *phileō* for love (only at 1 Cor 16:22).

The last expression, found at 1 Timothy 6:21 and also at 2 Timothy 4:22 (and 1 Cor 16:23-24; 2 Cor 13:13; Gal 6:18; Eph 6:23-24; Phil 4:23; Col 4:18; 1 Thess 5:28; 2 Thess 3:18; Phm 25), is a Christian prayer blessing to Titus and the Cretan churches reminding them of embodied grace:[155] *Grace be with all of you!*

---

[152] Collins takes v. 14 to be an encouragement of the Apostle through Titus to Zenas and Apollos specifically because in their continued missionary ventures they will meet hardships. Also, such a lesson will be overheard and should be learned by all Christians; see Collins, *1 & 2 Timothy and Titus*, 2002, 373.
[153] Witherington, *Letters and Homilies for Hellenized Christians*, 166.
[154] Longenecker, *Remember the Poor*.
[155] Towner, *Timothy and Titus*, 805.

Bibliography

Adams, Edward. *The Earliest Christian Meeting Places: Almost Exclusively Houses?* Rev. ed. New York: Bloomsbury T & T Clark, 2015.
Agrell, Göran. *Work, Toil and Sustenance.* Lund: Håkan Ohlssons, 1976.
Arterbury, Andrew. *Entertaining Angels: Early Christian Hospitality in Its Mediterranean Setting.* New Testament Monographs 8. Sheffield: Sheffield Phoenix Press, 2005.
Barclay, John M. G. *Paul and the Gift.* Grand Rapids, MI: Eerdmans, 2015.
———. *Paul and the Power of Grace.* Grand Rapids, MI: Eerdmans, 2020.
Barnett, P. W. "Apostle." In *Dictionary of Paul and His Letters* ed. G. F. Hawthorne and R .P. Martin, 45–51. Downers Grove, IL: IVP Academic, 1993.
Barr, Beth Allison. *The Making of Biblical Womanhood: How the Subjugation of Women Became Gospel Truth.* Grand Rapids, MI: Brazos, 2021.
Bates, Matthew W. *The Birth of the Trinity.* New York: Oxford University Press, 2016.
———. *The Hermeneutics of the Apostolic Proclamation: The Center of Paul's Method of Scriptural Interpretation.* Waco, TX: Baylor University Press, 2012.
———. *Salvation by Allegiance Alone: Rethinking Faith, Works, and the Gospel of Jesus the King.* Grand Rapids, MI: Baker Academic, 2017.
Bauckham, Richard A. *Jesus and the God of Israel: God Crucified and Other Studies on the New Testament's Christology of Divine Identity.* Grand Rapids, MI: Eerdmans, 2008.
———. "Pseudo-Apostolic Letters." *JBL* 107 (1988): 469–494.
Baum, Armin. "Pseudepigraphy." In *Dictionary of Paul and His Letters*, ed. Scot McKnight, Lynn H. Cohick, and Nijay K. Gupta, 2nd ed., 877–882: Downers Grove, IL: IVP Academic, 2022.
Berger, Peter L., and Thomas Luckmann. *The Social Construction of Reality: A Treatise in the Sociology of Knowledge.* New York: Anchor, 1967.
Bergler, Thomas E. *From Here to Maturity: Overcoming the Juvenilization of American Christianity.* Grand Rapids, MI: Eerdmans, 2014.
———. *The Juvenilization of American Christianity.* Grand Rapids, MI: Eerdmans, 2012.
Best, Ernest. "Paul's Apostolic Authority —?" *JSNT* 27 (1986): 3–25.
———. *Paul and His Converts. The Sprunt Lectures 1985.* Edinburgh: T & T Clark, 1988.
Bosch, David J. *Transforming Mission: Paradigm Shifts in Theology of Mission.* Maryknoll, NY: Orbis Books, 2011.
Bradley, Keith R. *Slaves and Masters in the Roman Empire: A Study in Social Control.* New York: Oxford University Press, 1987.
Brookins, T. A. "The (In)Frequency of the Name 'Erastus' in Antiquity: A Literary, Papyrological, and Epigraphical Catalog." *NTS* 59 (2013): 496–513.
Bruce, F. F. *The Pauline Circle.* Reprint ed. Eugene, OR: Wipf & Stock, 2006.
Caird, G. B. *New Testament Theology.* Ed. L. D. Hurst. Oxford: Clarendon Press, 1994.
Campbell, Douglas A. *Framing Paul: An Epistolary Biography.* Grand Rapids, MI: Eerdmans, 2014.
Certeau, Michel de. *The Practice of Everyday Life.* Trans. Steven Rendall. Berkeley: University of California Press, 1984.
Cohick, Lynn H. *Women in the World of the Earliest Christians: Illuminating Ancient Ways of Life.* Grand Rapids, MI: Baker Academic, 2009.

Cohick, Lynn H., and Amy Brown Hughes. *Christian Women in the Patristic World: Their Influence, Authority, and Legacy in the Second through Fifth Centuries.* Grand Rapids, MI: Baker Academic, 2017.

Collins, John N. *Diakonia: Re-Interpreting the Ancient Sources.* New York: Oxford University Press, 2009.

Collins, Raymond F. *I & II Timothy and Titus.* Louisville, KY: Westminster John Knox, 2002.

Copan, Victor A. *Saint Paul as Spiritual Director: An Analysis of the Concept of the Imitation of Paul with Implications and Applications to the Practice of Spiritual Direction.* Reprint ed. Paternoster Biblical Monographs. Eugene, OR: Wipf & Stock, 2008.

Corbier, Micheille. "Family Behavior of the Roman Aristocracy, Second Century B.C.–Third Century A.D." In *Women's History and Ancient History*, ed. Sarah B. Pomeroy, trans. Ann Cremin, 173–196. Chapel Hill: University of North Carolina Press, 1991.

Crenshaw, James L. *Education in Ancient Israel: Across the Deadening Silence.* Anchor Bible Reference Library. New York: Doubleday, 1998.

Cullmann, Oscar. *Christ and Time: The Primitive Christian Conception of Time and History.* 3rd ed. Eugene, OR: Wipf & Stock, 2018.

Dickson, John P *The Best Kept Secret of Christian Mission: Promoting the Gospel with More Than Our Lips.* Grand Rapids, MI: Zondervan, 2013.

Mission-Commitment in Ancient Judaism and in the Pauline Communities. WUNT 2 159. Tübingen: J. C. B. Mohr (Paul Siebeck), 2003.

Diggle, J. *Theophrastus' Characters*, Cambridge Classical Texts and Commentaries 43 Cambridge: Cambridge University Press, 2004.

Downs, David J. *Alms: Charity, Reward, and Atonement in Early Christianity.* Waco, TX: Baylor University Press, 2016.

Du Mez, Kristin Kobes. *Jesus and John Wayne: How White Evangelicals Corrupted a Faith and Fractured a Nation.* New York: Liveright, 2020.

Dunn, James D. G. *Christology in the Making: A New Testament into the Origins of the Doctrine of the Incarnation*, 2d ed. Philadelphia: Westminster John Knox, 1989, 237–238.

Did the First Christians Worship Jesus? The New Testament Evidence. Louisville, KY: Westminster John Knox, 2010

"The First and Second Letters to Timothy and the Letter to Titus: Introduction, Commentary, and Reflections." In *New Interpreter's Bible: A Commentary* 11, 773–880. Nashville, TN: Abingdon, 2000

Neither Jew nor Greek: A Contested Identity. Christianity in the Making 3. Grand Rapids, MI: Eerdmans, 2015.

The New Perspective on Paul. Rev. ed. Grand Rapids, MI: Eerdmans, 2008.

Elliott, Matthew A. *Faithful Feelings: Rethinking Emotions in the New Testament.* Grand Rapids, MI: Kregel, 2006.

Ellis, E. Earle. "Pastoral Letters." In *Dictionary of Paul and His Letters*, ed. Gerald F. Hawthorne, and Ralph P. Martin, 658–666. Downers Grove, IL: IVP Academic, 1993.

Fee, Gordon. *1 and 2 Timothy, Titus.* NIBC. Peabody, MA: Hendrickson, 1988.

God's Empowering Presence: The Holy Spirit in the Letters of Paul. Peabody, MA: Hendrickson, 1994.

France, R. T. *Women in the Church's Ministry: A Test-Case for Biblical Hermeneutics.* Didsbury Lectures. Eugene, OR: Wipf & Stock, 2004.

Franke, John R. *Missional Theology: An Introduction.* Grand Rapids, MI: Baker Academic, 2020.

Funk, Robert W. "The Apostolic *Parousia*: Form and Significance." In *Christian History and Interpretation: Studies Presented to John Knox*, ed. William R. Farmer, C. F. D. Moule, and Richard R. Niebuhr, 249–268. Cambridge: Cambridge University Press, 1967.

Gehring, Roger W. *House Church and Mission: The Importance of Household Structures in Early Christianity.* Peabody, MA: Hendrickson, 2004.

Glahn, Sandra L. "The First-Century Ephesian Artemis: Ramifications of Her Identity." *BibSac* 172 (2015): 450–469.

"The Identity of Artemis in First-Century Ephesus." *BibSac* 172 (2015): 316–334.

Goldingay, John. *Biblical Theology: The God of the Christian Scriptures.* Downers Grove, IL: IVP Academic, 2016

Bibliography

Do We Need the New Testament? Letting the Old Testament Speak for Itself. Downers Grove, IL: IVP Academic, 2015.
Reading Jesus's Bible: How the New Testament Helps Us Understand the Old Testament. Grand Rapids, MI: Eerdmans, 2017.
Goodman, Martin. *Mission and Conversion: Proselytizing in the Religious History of the Roman Empire.* New York: Oxford University Press, 1994.
Gorman, Michael J. *Becoming the Gospel: Paul, Participation, and Mission.* Grand Rapids, MI: Eerdmans, 2015.
Cruciformity: Paul's Narrative Spirituality of the Cross. New ed. Grand Rapids, MI: Eerdmans, 2020.
Inhabiting the Cruciform God: Kenosis, Justification, and Theosis in Paul's Narrative Soteriology. Grand Rapids, MI: Eerdmans, 2009.
Participating in Christ: Explorations in Paul's Theology and Spirituality. Grand Rapids, MI: Eerdmans, 2019.
Gundry, R. H. "The Form, Meaning, and Background of the Hymn Quoted in 1 Timothy 3:16." In *Apostolic History and the Gospel: Biblical and Historical Essays Presented to F .F. Bruce on His 60th Birthday*, ed. W. Ward Gasque and Ralph P. Martin, 203–222. Grand Rapids, MI: Eerdmans, 1970.
Hanson, A. T. *Studies in the Pastoral Epistles.* London: SPCK, 1968.
Harding, Mark. *Tradition and Rhetoric in the Pastoral Epistles.* Studies in Biblical Literature 3. New York: Peter Lang, 1998.
Harris, H. A. *Greek Athletes and Athletics.* Bloomington: University of Indiana Press, 1966.
Greek Athletics and the Jews. Trivium Special Publications 3. Cardiff: University of Wales Press, 1976.
Harris, Murray J. *Jesus as God: The New Testament Use of Theos in Reference to Jesus.* Grand Rapids, MI: Baker, 1992.
Prepositions and Theology in the Greek New Testament: An Essential Reference Resource for Exegesis. Grand Rapids, MI: Zondervan, 2012.
Slave of Christ: A New Testament Metaphor for Total Devotion to Christ. New Studies in Biblical Theology 8. Leicester: Apollos/InterVarsity, 1999.
Harris, William V. *Ancient Literacy.* Cambridge, MA: Harvard University Press, 1989.
Hart, Trevor, and Richard Bauckham. *Hope Against Hope: Christian Eschatology at the Turn of the Millennium.* Grand Rapids, MI: Eerdmans, 1999.
Harvey, A. E. *Stenuous Commands: The Ethic of Jesus.* Philadelphia: TPI, 1990.
Hatch, Edwin. *The Organization of the Early Christian Churches.* Reprint ed. The Bampton Lectures 1880. Eugene, OR: Wipf & Stock, 1999.
Hays, Richard B. *Echoes of Scripture in the Letters of Paul.* New Haven. CT: Yale University Press, 1993.
The Moral Vision of the New Testament: Community, Cross, New Creation, A Contemporary Introduction to New Testament Ethics. San Francisco: HarperOne, 1996.
Reading Backwards: Figural Christology and the Fourfold Gospel Witness. Waco, TX: Baylor University Press, 2014.
Hellerman, Joseph H. *The Ancient Church as Family.* Minneapolis, MN: Fortress, 2001.
Hengel, Martin. *Judaism and Hellenism: Studies in Their Encounter in Palestine in the Early Hellenistic Period.* Trans. John Bowden. 2 vols. Philadelphia: Fortress, 1974.
The Pre-Christian Paul. Trans. John Bowden. Philadelphia: Trinity Press International, 1991.
Hill, Wesley. *Paul and the Trinity: Persons, Relations, and the Pauline Letters.* Grand Rapids, MI: Eerdmans, 2015.
Hock, Ronald F. *The Social Context of Paul's Ministry: Tentmaking and Apostleship.* Minneapolis, MN: Fortress, 2007.
Hockenos, Matthew D. *A Church Divided: German Protestants Confront the Nazi Past.* Bloomington: Indiana University Press, 2004.
Then They Came for Me: Martin Niemöller, the Pastor Who Defied the Nazis. New York: Basic Books, 2018.
Hoklotubbe, T. Christopher. *Civilized Piety: The Rhetoric of Pietas in the Pastoral Epistles and the Roman Empire.* Waco, TX: Baylor University Press, 2017.

"The Pastoral Epistles." In *The State of Pauline Studies*, ed. Nijay K. Gupta, Erin Heim, and Scot McKnight. Grand Rapids, MI: Baker Academic, 2022.
Hood, Jason B. *Imitating God in Christ: Recapturing a Biblical Pattern*. Downers Grove, IL: IVP Academic, 2013.
Horsley, G. H. R. *New Documents Illustrating Early Christianity*. 3. Grand Rapids, MI: Eerdmans, 1983.
Huizenga, Annette Bourland *Moral Education for Women in the Pastoral and Pythagorean Letters: Philosophers of the Household*. NovTSup 147. Leiden: Brill, 2013.
――― *1-2 Timothy, Titus*. Wisdom Commentary 53. Collegeville, MN: Liturgical, 2016.
Hultgren, Arland J. "The Pastoral Epistles." In *The Cambridge Companion to St Paul*, ed. James D. G. Dunn, 141–155. New York: Cambridge University Press, 2003.
Hurtado, Larry W. *How on Earth Did Jesus Become a God? Historical Questions about Earliest Devotion to Jesus*. Grand Rapids, MI: Eerdmans, 2005.
――― *Lord Jesus Christ: Devotion to Jesus in Earliest Christianity*. Grand Rapids, MI: Eerdmans, 2003.
Hutson, Christopher R. *First and Second Timothy and Titus*. Paideia Commentaries on the New Testament. Grand Rapids, MI: Baker Academic, 2019.
Ilan, Tal. *Integrating Women into Second Temple History*. Peabody, MA: Hendrickson, 2001.
――― *Jewish Women in Greco-Roman Palestine*. Peabody, MA: Hendrickson, 1996.
Jipp, Joshua W. *Christ Is King: Paul's Royal Ideology*. Minneapolis, MN: Fortress, 2015.
――― *The Messianic Theology of the New Testament*. Grand Rapids, MI: Eerdmans, 2020.
Johnson, Emily Suzanne. *This Is Our Message: Women's Leadership in the New Christian Right*. New York: Oxford University Press, 2019.
Johnson, Luke Timothy. *The First and Second Letters to Timothy*. AB 35A. New Haven, CT: Yale University Press, 2001.
――― "The New Testament's Anti-Jewish Slander and the Conventions of Ancient Polemic." *JBL* 108 (1989): 419–441.
Joshua, Nathan Nzyoka. *Benefaction and Patronage in Leadership: A Socio-Historical Exegesis of the Pastoral Epistles*. Carlisle: Langham Monographs, 2018.
Karris, Robert J. "The Background and Significance of the Polemic in the Pastoral Epistles." *JBL* 92 (1973): 549–564.
Keener, Craig S. *Paul, Women, and Wives: Marriage and Women's Ministry in the Letters of Paul*. 2nd ed. Grand Rapids, MI: Baker Academic, 2004.
Keith, William, and Robert Danisch. *Beyond Civility: The Competing Obligations of Citizenship*. University Park, PA: Penn State University Press, 2020.
Kelly, J. N. D. *The Pastoral Epistles*. Reprint ed. BNTC. London: Adam & Charles Black, 1963.
Kidd, Reggie M. *Wealth and Beneficence in the Pastoral Epistles: A "Bourgeois" Form of Early Christianity?* SBLDS 122. Atlanta, GA: Scholars Press, 1990.
Kidson, Lyn M. "Pastoral Epistles." In *Dictionary of Paul and His Letters*, ed. Scot McKnight, Lynn H. Cohick, and Nijay K. Gupta, 2nd ed. Downers Grove, IL: IVP Academic, 2022.
――― *Persuading Shipwrecked Men: The Rhetorical Strategies of 1 Timothy 1*. WUNT 2.526. Tübingen: Mohr Siebeck, 2021.
Kierkegaard, Sören. *Purity of Heart Is to Will One Thing: Spiritual Preparation for the Office of Confession*. New York: Harper & Row Torchbooks, 1956.
Klauck, Hans-Josef. *Ancient Letters and the New Testament: A Guide to Content and Exegesis*. Waco, TX: Baylor University Press, 2006.
Klawans, Jonathan. *Impurity and Sin in Ancient Judaism*. New York: OUP, 2004.
Knight III, George W. *The Pastoral Epistles*. NIGTC. Grand Rapids, MI: Eerdmans, 1999.
Kroeger, Richard Clark, and Catherine Clark Kroeger. *I Suffer Not a Woman: Rethinking 1 Timothy 2:11–15 in Light of Ancient Evidence*. Grand Rapids, MI: Baker Academic, 1998.
Ladd, George Eldon. *A Theology of the New Testament*. Ed. Donald A. Hagner. Rev. ed. Grand Rapids, MI: Eerdmans, 1993.
Larson, Jennifer. "Paul's Masculinity," *JBL* 123 (2004): 85–97.
Legarreta-Castillo, Felipe de Jesús. *The Figure of Adam in Romans 5 and 1 Corinthians 15: The New Creation and Its Ethical and Social Reconfiguration*. Emerging Scholars. Minneapolis, MN: Fortress, 2014.

Bibliography

Levenson, Jon D. *The Love of God: Divine Gift, Human Gratitude, and Mutual Faithfulness in Judaism*. Princeton: Princeton University Press, 2016.
Levinskaya, Irina. *The Book of Acts in Its Diaspora Setting*. The Book of Acts in Its First Century Setting 5. Grand Rapids, MI: Eerdmans, 1996.
Levison, John R. *Portraits of Adam in Early Judaism: From Sirach to 2 Baruch*. Journal for the Study of the Pseudepigrapha, Supplement Series 1. Sheffield: JSOT Press, 1988.
Lewis, C. S. *The Four Loves*. New York: Harcourt Brace Jovanovich, 1960.
Loader, William. *The New Testament on Sexuality*. Grand Rapids, MI: Eerdmans, 2012.
Longenecker, Bruce W. *Remember the Poor: Paul, Poverty, and the Greco-Roman World*. Grand Rapids, MI: Eerdmans, 2010.
Longenecker, Richard N., ed. *The Road from Damascus: The Impact of Paul's Conversion on His Life, Thought, and Ministry*. Grand Rapids, MI: Eerdmans, 1997.
Macaskill, Grant. *Union with Christ in the New Testament*. New York: Oxford University Press, 2018.
Malina, Bruce J. *Christian Origins and Cultural Anthropology: Practical Models for Biblical Interpretation*. Atlanta, GA: John Knox Press, 1986.
Marsh, Charles, Peter Slade, and Sarah Azaransky, eds. *Lived Theology: New Perspectives on Method, Style, and Pedagogy*. New York: Oxford University Press, 2016.
Marshall, I. Howard. *Kept by the Power of God: A Study of Perseverance and Falling Away*. Minneapolis, MN: Bethany House, 1969.
———. *The Pastoral Epistles*. ICC. London: T & T Clark, 1999.
Martin, Dale B. *Pedagogy of the Bible: An Analysis and Proposal*. Louisville, KY: Westminster John Knox Press, 2008.
Martin, Séan Charles. *Pauli Testamentum: 2 Timothy and the Last Words of Moses*. Tesi Gregoriana, Serie Teologia 18. Rome: Gregorian University Press, 1997.
McKnight, Scot. *A Community Called Atonement*. Nashville, TN: Abingdon, 2007.
———. "*Eusebeia* as Social Respectability: The Public Life of the Christian Pastor." In *Rhetoric, History, and Theology: Interpreting the New Testament*, ed. Todd D. Still and Jason A. Meyers, 157–174. Lanham, MD: Lexington/Fortress Academic, 2021.
———. "Few and Far Between: The Life of a Creed." In *Earliest Christianity within the Boundaries of Judaism: Essays in Honor of Bruce Chilton*, ed. Alan J. Avery-Peck, Craig A. Evans, and J. Neusner, 168–186. Leiden: E. J. Brill, 2016.
———. *The Heaven Promise: Engaging the Bible's Truth About Life to Come*. Colorado Springs, CO: WaterBrook, 2015.
———. *It Takes a Church to Baptize*. Grand Rapids, MI: Brazos, 2018.
———. "James in the Story." In *Reading the Epistle of James: A Resource for Students*, ed. Eric Mason and Darian Lockett, 161–175. Atlanta, GA: SBL Press, 2019.
———. *Jesus and His Death: Historiography, the Historical Jesus, and Atonement Theory*. Waco, TX: Baylor University Press, 2005.
———. *The King Jesus Gospel: The Original Good News Revisited*. 2nd ed. Grand Rapids, MI: Zondervan, 2015.
———. *The Letter to Philemon*. NICNT. Grand Rapids, MI: Eerdmans, 2017.
———. *A Light among the Gentiles: Jewish Missionary Activity in the Second Temple Period*. Minneapolis, MN: Fortress, 1991.
———. *A Long Faithfulness: The Case for Christian Perseverance*. Denver, CO: Paraclete Press, 2013.
———. *A New Vision for Israel: The Teachings of Jesus in National Context*. Grand Rapids, MI: Eerdmans, 1999.
———. *Pastor Paul: Nurturing a Culture of Christoformity in the Church*. Theological Explorations for the Church Catholic. Grand Rapids, MI: Brazos, 2019.
———. *Turning to Jesus: The Sociology of Conversion in the Gospels*. Louisville, KY: Westminster John Knox, 2002.
McKnight, Scot, and Laura Barringer. *A Church Called Tov: Forming a Goodness Culture That Resists Abuses of Power and Promotes Healing*. Carol Stream, IL: Tyndale Momentum, 2020.
McKnight, Scot, and Daniel Hanlon, eds. *Wise Church: Forming a Wisdom Culture in Your Local Church*. Eugene, OR: Wipf & Stock, 2021.

McKnight, Scot, and Joseph B. Modica, eds. *Jesus Is Lord, Caesar Is Not: Evaluating Empire in New Testament Studies*. Downers Grove, IL: IVP Academic, 2013.

Meade, David G. *Pseudonymity and Canon: An Investigation into the Relationship of Authorship and Authority in Jewish and Earliest Christian Tradition*. Grand Rapids, MI: Eerdmans, 1987.

Miller, James D. *The Pastoral Letters as Composite Documents*. SNTMS 93. Cambridge: Cambridge University Press, 1997.

Miller, Stephen G. *Ancient Greek Athletics*. New Haven, CT: Yale University Press, 2004.

Millett, Paul. *Theophrastus and His World,* Cambridge Classical Journal Supplement 33; Cambridge: Cambridge Philological Society, 2007.

Mitchell, Margaret M. "New Testament Envoys in the Context of Greco-Roman Diplomatic and Epistolary Conventions: The Example of Timothy and Titus." *JBL* 111 (1992): 641–662.

Morgan, Teresa. *Popular Morality in the Early Roman Empire*. New York: Cambridge University Press, 2007.

———. *Roman Faith and Christian Faith: Pistis and Fides in the Early Roman Empire and Early Churches*. New York: Oxford University Press, 2015.

Moule, C. F. D. *The Meaning of Hope: A Biblical Exposition with Concordance*. Facet Books 5. Philadelphia: Fortress, 1963.

Mouw, Richard J. *Uncommon Decency: Christian Civility in an Uncivil World*. 2nd ed. Downers Grove, IL: IVP Academic, 2010.

Murphy-O'Connor, Jerome. *St. Paul's Ephesus: Texts and Archaeology*. Collegeville, MN: Liturgical, 2008.

Myers, Jason A. "Rhetoric from the *Rusticas*: In Search of the Historical Timothy and Implications for the Rhetoric of 1–2 Timothy." In *Rhetoric, History, and Theology: Interpreting the New Testament, ed.* Todd D. Still and Jason A. Myers, 179–200. Lanham, MD: Lexington/Fortress Academic, 2022.

Neff, Miriam. *From One Widow to Another: Conversations on the New You*. 2nd ed. Chicago: Moody, 2009.

Neudorfer, Heinz-Werner. *Der Erste Brief Des Paulus an Timotheus*. 2nd ed. Historisch-Theologische Auslegung: Neues Testament. Witten: SCM R. Brockhaus, 2012.

Novenson, Matthew V. *Christ among the Messiahs: Christ Language in Paul and Messiah Language in Ancient Judaism*. New York: Oxford University Press, 2012.

———. *The Grammar of Messianism: An Ancient Jewish Political Idiom and Its Users*. Oxford: Oxford University Press, 2017.

Oden, Amy G., ed. *And You Welcomed Me: A Sourcebook on Hospitality in Early Christianity*. Nashville, TN: Abingdon, 2001.

Oestreich, Bernhard. *Performance Criticism of the Pauline Letters*. Trans. Lindsay Elias and Brent Blum. Eugene, OR: Cascade, 2016.

Olson, Roger E. *Arminian Theology: Myths and Realities*. Downers Grove, IL: IVP Academic, 2006.

Palmer, Parker J. *Let Your Life Speak: Listening for the Voice of Vocation*. San Francisco: Jossey-Bass, 1999.

Payne, Philip Barton. *Man and Woman, One in Christ: An Exegetical and Theological Study of Paul's Letters*. Grand Rapids, MI: Zondervan, 2009.

Pertsinidis, Sonia. *Theophrastus' Characters: An Introduction*. Routledge Focus on Classical Studies. New York: Routledge, 2018.

Pierce, Ronald W., Rebecca Merrill Groothuis, and Gordon D. Fee, eds. *Discovering Biblical Equality: Complementarity Without Hierarchy*. 2nd ed. Downers Grove, IL: IVP Academic, 2005.

Piper, John, and Wayne Grudem, eds. *Recovering Biblical Manhood and Womanhood: A Response to Evangelical Feminism*. Westchester, IL: Crossway, 2012.

Pohl, Christine D. *Making Room: Recovering Hospitality as a Christian Tradition*. Grand Rapids, MI: Eerdmans, 1999.

Poliakoff, Michael B. *Combat Sports in the Ancient World: Competition, Violence, and Culture*. Sport and History. New Haven, CT: Yale University Press, 1987.

Porter, Stanley. *The Apostle Paul: His Life, Thought, and Letters*. Grand Rapids, MI: Eerdmans, 2016.

Prior, Michael. *Paul the Letter-Writer and the Second Letter to Timothy*. JSNTSup 23. Sheffield: Sheffield Academic Press, 1989.

Przybylski, Benno. *Righteousness in Matthew and His World of Thought*. SNTSMS 41. Cambridge: Cambridge University Press, 1981.

Quinn, Jerome D. *The Letter to Titus*. AB 35. New York: Doubleday, 1990.

Richards, E. Randolph. *Paul and First-Century Letter Writing: Secretaries, Composition and Collection*. Downers Grove, IL: IVP Academic, 2004.

Roloff, Jürgen. *Der Erste Brief an Timotheus*. EKKNT. Zürich/Neukirchen-Vluyn: Benziger/Neukirchener Verlag, 1988.

Rusten, J. and I. C. Cunningham, *Theophrastus: Characters* LCL 225; Cambridge, MA: Harvard University Press, 2002.

Sanders, E. P. *Judaism: Practice and Belief, 63 BCE–66 CE*. Minneapolis, MN: Fortress, 2016.

Paul and Palestinian Judaism: A Comparison of Patterns of Religion. Minneapolis, MN: Fortress, 2017.

Schüssler-Fiorenza, Elisabeth. *In Memory of Her: A Feminist Theological Reconstruction of Christian Origins*. New York: Crossroad, 1983.

deSilva, David A. *Honor, Patronage, Kinship & Purity: Unlocking New Testament Culture*. Downers Grove, IL: IVP Academic, 2000.

Transformation: The Heart of Paul's Gospel. Bellingham, WA: Lexham Press, 2014.

Smith, Craig A. *Timothy's Task, Paul's Prospect: A New Reading of 2 Timothy*. New Testament Monographs 12. Sheffield: Sheffield Phoenix Press, 2006.

Stanton, G. N. "Paul's Gospel." In *The Cambridge Companion to St Paul*, ed. James D. G. Dunn, 173–184. Cambridge: Cambridge University Press, 2003.

Staples, Jason A. *The Idea of Israel in Second Temple Judaism: A New Theory of People, Exile, and Israelite Identity*. New York: Cambridge University Press, 2021.

Stenstrup, Ken. *Titus: Honoring the Gospel of God*. Paul's Social Network: Brothers and Sisters in Faith. Collegeville, MN: Liturgical, 2010.

Stepp, Perry L. *Leadership Succession in the World of the Pauline Circle*. New Testament Monographs 5. Sheffield: Sheffield Phoenix Press, 2005.

Stewart, Alistair C. *The Original Bishops: Office and Order in the First Christian Communities*. Grand Rapids, MI: Baker Academic, 2014.

Strait, Drew J. *Hidden Criticism of the Angry Tyrant in Early Judaism and the Acts of the Apostles*. Lanham, MD: Lexington/Fortress Academic, 2019.

Strawn, Brent A. *The Old Testament Is Dying: A Diagnosis and Recommended Treatment*. Grand Rapids, MI: Baker Academic, 2017.

Sumney, Jerry. *Identifying Paul's Opponents: The Question of Method in 2 Corinthians*. Reprint ed. Bloomsbury Academic Collections. Biblical Studies: The Epistles. London: Bloomsbury Academic, 2015.

Swartley, Willard M. *Covenant of Peace: The Missing Peace in New Testament Theology and Ethics*. Grand Rapids, MI: Eerdmans, 2006.

Tamez, Elsa. *Struggles for Power in Early Christianity: A Study of the First Letter to Timothy*. Maryknoll, NY: Orbis, 2007.

Thornton, Dillon T. *Hostility in the House of God: An Investigation of the Opponents in 1 and 2 Timothy*. BBRSuppl 15. Winona Lake, IN: Eisenbrauns, 2016.

Towner, Philip H. *The Letters to Timothy and Titus*. NICNT. Grand Rapids, MI: Eerdmans, 2006.

Trebilco, Paul. *The Early Christians in Ephesus from Paul to Ignatius*. Grand Rapids, MI: Eerdmans, 2007.

Self-Designations and Group Identity in the New Testament. Cambridge: Cambridge University Press, 2012.

Twomey, Jay. *The Pastoral Epistles Through the Centuries*. Chichester, UK; Malden, MA: Wiley-Blackwell, 2008.

van Nes, Jermo. *Pauline Language and the Pastoral Epistles: Linguistic Biblical Studies*. Leiden: Brill, 2017.

Van Neste, Ray. *Cohesion and Structure in the Pastoral Epistles*. JSNTSup 280. London: T & T Clark, 2007.

Vanhoozer, Kevin J. *The Drama of Doctrine: A Canonical-Linguistic Approach to Christian Theology.* Louisville, KY: Westminster John Knox, 2005.
Volf, Miroslav, and Matthew Croasmun. *For the Life of the World: Theology That Makes a Difference.* Grand Rapids, MI: Brazos, 2019.
Ward, Ronald A. *Commentary on I & II Timothy and Titus.* Dallas, TX: Word, 1974.
Wells, Jo Bailey. *God's Holy People: A Theme in Biblical Theology.* Sheffield: Bloomsbury T & T Clark, 2000.
Wenham, David. *Paul: Follower of Jesus or Founder of Christianity?* Grand Rapids, MI: Eerdmans, 1995.
Westfall, Cynthia Long. *Paul and Gender: Reclaiming the Apostle's Vision for Men and Women in Christ.* Grand Rapids, MI: Baker Academic, 2016.
White, John L. *Light from Ancient Letters.* Foundations and Facets. Philadelphia: Fortress, 1986.
Wilson, S. G. *Luke and the Pastoral Epistles.* London: SPCK, 1979.
Winter, Bruce W. *Roman Wives, Roman Widows: The Appearance of New Women and the Pauline Communities.* Grand Rapids, MI: Eerdmans, 2003.
    Seek the Welfare of the City: Christians as Benefactors and Citizens. First Century Christians in the Graeco-Roman World. Grand Rapids, MI: Eerdmans, 1994.
Wise, Michael Owen. *Language and Literacy in Roman Judaea: A Study of the Bar Kokhba Documents.* New Haven, CT: Yale University Press, 2015.
Witherington III, Ben W. *Biblical Theology: The Convergence of the Canon.* New York: Cambridge University Press, 2019.
Witherington. *Jesus, Paul and the End of the World.* Downers Grove, IL: IVP Academic, 1992.
    Letters and Homilies for Hellenized Christians: A Socio-Rhetorical Commentary on Titus, 1–2 Timothy and 1–3 John. Downers Grove, IL: IVP Academic, 2006.
    New Testament Theology and Ethics. 2 vols. Downers Grove, IL: IVP Academic, 2016.
    Women in the Earliest Churches. SNTMS 58. Cambridge: Cambridge University Press, 1991.
    Women and the Genesis of Christianity. Ed. Ann Witherington. Cambridge: Cambridge University Press, 1990.
Witherington III, Ben W., and G. Francois Wessels. "Do Everything in the Name of the Lord: Ethics and Ethos in Colossians." In *Identity, Ethics, and Ethos in the New Testament*, ed. Jan G. van der Watt, 303–333. BZNW 141. Berlin: De Gruyter, 2006.
Wright, Brian J. *Communal Reading in the Time of Jesus: A Window into Early Christian Reading Practices.* Minneapolis, MN: Fortress, 2017.
Wright, N. T. *The New Testament and the People of God.* Christian Origins and the Question of God 1. Minneapolis, MN: Fortress, 1992.
    The Resurrection of the Son of God. The New Testament and the Question of God 3. Minneapolis, MN: Fortress, 2003.
    What Saint Paul Really Said: Was Paul of Tarsus the Real Founder of Christianity? Grand Rapids, MI: Eerdmans, 1997.
Yarbrough, Robert W. *The Letters to Timothy and Titus.* Pillar New Testament Commenary. Grand Rapids, MI: Eerdmans, 2018.

Scripture Index

Genesis
  1:29, 82
  2–3, 58
  2, 59
  2:7–8, 58
  2:7, 53
  3, 82
  3:13, 59
  3:16, 61
  3:20, 58
  9:2–3, 82
  19:2, 98

Exodus
  6:6, 209
  7:8–13, 162
  20:12, 98
  22:22, 96
  30:19–21, 47
  34:21, 122

Leviticus
  19:32, 93

Numbers
  6, 107
  16:5, 151

Deuteronomy
  6:4–8, 120
  6:4–9, 26, 42, 129
  10:17, 120
  10:18, 96
  14:29, 96
  16:11, 14, 96
  19:15, 105

  21:18, 159
  24:17, 96
  24:19–21, 96
  25:4, 104–5
  26:12–13, 96
  27:19, 96
  28, 121, 122

Job
  10:18, 61

Psalms
  22:9–10, 61
  28:2, 47
  49:24–26, 179
  63:1–6, 179
  71:6, 61
  104:2, 120
  104:26, 184
  104:42, 184
  127:2, 122

Proverbs
  1:2–7, 54

Isaiah
  26:13, 151
  46–51, 179
  58, 121
  66:9, 61

Jeremiah
  29:7, 40

Ezekiel
  16:49, 96

229

Daniel
7, 195

Amos
5:14–15, 202

Malachi
1:10–12, 47

Matthew
1:19, 117
5–7, 153
5:3–12, 208
5:5, 213
5:9, 212
5:13–16, 92
5:16, 199
6:1–18, 92, 161, 164
6:14–15, 159
6:19–34, 114, 122
6:19–21, 123
6:24, 70
10:5–15, 122
10:9–10, 114
10:10, 104
10:16–20, 180
10:26–33, 108
10:32–33, 146
11:2, 199
11:19, 199
12:15–21, 213
13:1–23, 92
13:22, 70
16:24–28, 166
18:6–7, 151
18:15–20, 105, 218
18:18–20, 171
19:21, 123
19:28, 146, 216
22:13, 71
23, 164
24:31, 78
25:14–30, 136, 177
25:31–46, 108
26:10, 199
26:14–16, 70
28:18–20, 92

Mark
1:16–20, 90
2:17, 33
2:27, 122
3:19, 160
7:1–20, 197
7:9–13, 98
7:14–15, 196
7:19, 82
8:6, 82
9:35, 71
10:35–45, 71
10:45, 42, 209
12:28–32, 26, 117, 129
12:29–32, 157
12:41–44, 92
13, 80
13:32, 80
14:10–11, 70
15:1–15, 119

Luke
1:1, 174
2:37, 129
3:10–14, 123
4:14, 131
5:17, 24
6:9, 122
6:13, 70
6:20–26, 208
6:20, 121
6:24, 121
6:33, 122
6:35, 122
6:45, 67
7:30, 219
7:36–50, 98
8:1–3, 98, 115
10:4, 114
10:7, 104
10:25, 219
11:45–46, 219
11:52, 219
12:8–9, 146
12:16–21, 121
14:3, 219
14:7–14, 160
15:13, 191
16:1–4, 121
19:10, 33
19:11–27, 136
22:3–6, 70

Scripture Index

22:30, 146
24:21, 209
24:31, 79

John
  1:1–18, 185
  1:9, 33
  1:14, 78
  12:4–6, 70
  13, 98
  17:11–15, 177
  18:29–38, 119
  18:36, 118

Acts
  1:6–7, 120
  1:20, 64, 188
  2:11, 196
  2:16–17, 156
  2:17, 65, 216
  2:18, 216
  2:23–24, 78, 145
  2:33, 216
  2:38, 215
  4:10, 145
  5:34, 24
  6:1–6, 71, 96, 189
  6:6, 91, 107
  7:52, 160
  8:14–24, 114
  8:16–19, 91
  8:17–19, 107
  8:35, 144
  9:1–29, 32
  9:12, 91
  9:17, 91
  10, 82
  10:39–40, 145
  11:20, 144
  11:30, 65
  12:25–14:29, 14
  13:1–3, 91
  13:1, 15
  13:3, 91, 107
  13:13, 178
  13:15, 91
  13:28–30, 145
  13:31, 79
  14:1–20, 165
  14:8–21, 14

14:17, 122
14:23, 65
15:2, 65
15:4, 65
15:6, 65
15:22–23, 65
15:36–41, 167, 178
16:1–3, 130
16:1, 13
16:3, 14
16:4, 65
16:13, 39
16:14–15, 115
17:6–8, 76, 147
17:14–15, 14
17:15, 14
17:18, 144
17:27, 135
17:30–31, 135
17:31, 145
17:32, 151
18:1–3, 181
18:1, 181
18:2, 181
18:5, 14, 144
18:19, 181
18:24–19:10, 219
18:24–28, 181
18:26, 55
18:28, 144
19:6, 91, 107
19:13, 144
19:21–22, 22
19:22, 14
19:23–27, 60
19:33–34, 3, 4, 137
19:33, 179
21–28, 180
20:1–6, 14
20:4, 13, 178, 182, 219
20:17–38, 22
20:17, 65, 188
20:20–21, 144
20:24, 176
20:25, 3
20:28, 64, 188
20:29–31, 80
20:36–38, 129
21–28, 80
21:7–22:30, 164

Acts (cont.)
  21:27–28:31, 137
  21:27–26:32, 179
  21:8, 174
  21:9, 55
  21:18, 65
  21:29, 182
  22:3–21, 32
  22:16, 215
  23:1, 129
  26:5, 220
  26:9–20, 32
  26:16, 79
  28:16–31, 179
  28:16, 139
  28:17–28, 139
  28:20, 145
  28:23–31, 145
  28:23, 144
  28:30, 139
  28:31, 2, 144

Romans, 9, 12
  1:1–7, 32
  1:3–5, 144
  1:3–4, 145
  1:3, 78
  1:4–5, 76
  1:4, 78
  1:5, 31, 219
  1:7, 21, 186
  1:8–12, 128
  1:9, 129
  1:16, 132, 135
  1:18–32, 213
  1:19–20, 135
  1:29–32, 157
  1:31, 159
  2:6–11, 108, 179
  2:25–29, 194
  3:1, 194
  3:21–25, 214
  3:20, 215
  3:28, 215
  3:29–30, 42
  3:30, 194
  4:9–12, 194
  4:21, 174
  5:12–14, 59
  6:1–14, 215

  6:1–11, 216
  6:16–20, 184
  6:8, 146
  6:17, 191
  6:20–22, 213
  7:16, 29
  7:23, 161
  8, 216
  8:3–4, 117
  8:11, 78
  8:17, 216
  8:18–39, 134, 215
  8:29, 147
  9–11, 134
  10:2, 32
  10:5–21, 92
  10:9–10, 119
  11:5, 55
  12–13, 211
  12:1–2, 215
  12:1, 39, 76, 129
  12:2, 216
  12:7, 55, 191
  12:9, 117, 130
  12:13, 69, 98
  12:18, 212
  12:19–21, 179
  12:19, 47
  13:1–7, 40, 212
  13:3, 212
  13:8, 117
  13:9, 26
  13:11–15:13, 81
  13:11, 215
  14–15, 149
  14:1, 47
  14:5, 174
  14:13, 151
  14:14, 82, 196
  14:20, 196
  15:4, 168, 220
  15:8, 194
  15:14–33, 218
  15:15–16, 129
  15:19, 218
  15:23–24, 3
  15:23, 3
  15:25–33, 164
  16:1–2, 74, 115, 121
  16:3–16, 180

Scripture Index

16:3–4, 181
16:16, 220
16:17, 151, 191
16:21, 14
16:25–27, 156
16:26, 20

1 Corinthians, 9
  1:1, 127
  1:3, 186
  1:4–9, 128
  1:12, 219
  1:18, 215
  2:1–16, 134
  2:16–17, 76
  3:5, 32
  4:1–6, 135
  4:2, 32
  4:14–17, 165, 186
  4:15, 167
  4:17, 14
  4:21, 118
  5–11, 81
  5, 218
  5:4–5, 105
  5:5, 38
  6:9–11, 213
  6:11, 215
  7, 101
  7:19, 194
  7:21–23, 184
  7:25, 32
  7:32–35, 101
  8–10, 82
  8:4–6, 42
  8:13, 151
  9, 139, 195
  9:7–14, 104
  11:1, 90, 165
  11:2–16, 56
  11:6, 195
  11:10, 106
  11:12, 58
  11:32, 207
  12–14, 91
  12:4–11, 55
  12:6, 130
  12:13, 215
  12:28–29, 191
  13, 117

13:13, 201
14:34–35, 56
14:35, 195
15:1–28, 133, 144
15:1–8, 186, 199, 214
15:3–28, 113
15:3–5, 77
15:5–8, 79
15:8–11, 32
15:12, 151
15:21–28, 30
15:23, 177
16, 3
16:5–14, 218
16:5–12, 219
16:10–11, 14, 89
16:10, 14
16:12, 219
16:14, 26
16:19–20, 180
16:22, 220
16:23–24, 181, 220

2 Corinthians, 9, 21
  1, 3
  1:1, 14, 127
  1:3–7, 21
  1:19, 14
  2:12–17, 15
  2:14–16, 147
  3:14, 91
  4, 146
  4:1–6, 32
  4:7, 152
  4:13–18, 146
  5:19, 134
  6:3–10, 164
  6:6, 129
  6:9, 207
  6:14–7:1, 81
  7:12–13, 15
  7:15, 15
  8–9, 15, 104, 122
  8:8, 186
  8:13–15, 99, 122
  8:23, 15
  9:7–8, 114
  10:1, 118, 213
  10:5, 161
  11:3, 53

2 Corinthians (cont.)
  11:16–12:10, 165
  11:23–2, 9, 9
  11:29, 151
  13:1–11, 218
  13:1, 105
  13:12, 180
  13:13, 181, 220

Galatians, 9, 12, 21
  1:11–24, 32
  1:13–17, 213
  2:1–10, 15
  2:1, 15
  2:3, 15
  2:7–9, 194
  2:9, 15
  2:10, 15
  2:12, 194
  2:16, 215
  2:20, 147
  3:20, 42
  3:23–4:7, 216
  3:27, 215
  3:28, 56
  4:4, 185
  4:21–31, 135
  5:6, 117, 194
  5:11, 194
  5:13, 117
  5:16–26, 153
  5:19–21, 157
  5:22, 67, 117
  5:23, 160, 213
  6:1, 213
  6:6, 104
  6:10, 220
  6:11–17, 218
  6:15, 194
  6:17, 165
  6:18, 181, 220

Ephesians, 21
  1:1, 127
  1:3–14, 21
  1:4, 134, 185
  1:9–10, 120, 134
  1:11, 134
  1:18–23, 147
  2:3, 47

  2:4–7, 147
  2:8–9, 134, 199
  2:8, 215
  2:11, 194
  2:19–3:7, 76
  2:20–21, 151
  3:1–6, 73
  3:1, 133
  3:9–10, 76
  3:10, 106
  3:11, 134
  4:2, 213
  4:4–6, 42
  4:11–16, 69
  4:11, 65, 174, 191
  4:17–19, 135
  4:28, 115
  4:31, 47
  5:11, 172
  5:12, 195
  5:18, 160, 191
  5:21–6:9, 108, 197
  6:1–3, 159
  6:21–22, 219
  6:21, 178
  6:23–24, 181, 220

Philippians
  1:1, 14, 64, 71, 188
  1:3–11, 128
  2:3–11, 122
  2:5–11, 78
  2:6–11, 160, 214
  2:8–11, 76
  2:13, 130
  2:14, 47
  2:16, 176
  2:17, 176
  2:19–23, 14
  2:19, 14
  2:22, 14
  3:3, 129, 194
  3:4–11, 32
  3:4–6, 129
  3:5, 194
  3:8–11, 147
  3:10–11, 147
  3:13–14, 176
  4:8, 73
  4:10–20, 218

Scripture Index

4:11–13, 115
4:13, 180
4:21–22, 180
4:23, 181, 220

Colossians
  1:1, 14, 127
  1:3–12, 128
  1:7, 71
  1:13–20, 214
  1:13–14, 216
  1:21–2:7, 164
  1:21–22, 213
  1:23–2:3, 145
  1:24–2:5, 73, 87, 180
  1:24, 146
  2:9–15, 215
  2:11, 194
  2:16–3:11, 81
  2:16–23, 80
  2:16–19, 195
  2:22, 197
  3:1–4, 215
  3:5–11, 213
  3:8, 47
  3:11, 194
  3:12, 213
  3:14, 26
  3:15, 212
  3:18–4:1, 108, 197
  3:20, 159
  4:7, 178, 219
  4:10–17, 180
  4:10–11, 178
  4:10, 220
  4:11, 194
  4:12, 174, 220
  4:14, 178, 220
  4:16, 91
  4:18, 181, 220

1 Thessalonians
  1:1, 14
  1:2–10, 128
  1:3, 118
  2:2, 118
  2:19, 177
  3:1–6, 14
  3:1–5, 14
  4:1–8, 179
  5:6, 174
  5:8, 174
  5:12–13, 64
  5:19, 130
  5:23, 177
  5:26, 180
  5:27, 91
  5:28, 181, 220

2 Thessalonians
  1:3–12, 128
  1:5–12, 179
  2:1–12, 80
  2:2, 8, 151
  3:10–12, 115
  3:13–15, 218
  3:18, 181, 220

1 Timothy
  1:1, 3, 31, 133, 135, 183, 184, 186
  1:2, 14, 37, 90, 128, 153, 164, 165, 184, 186
  1:3–20, 38, 110
  1:3–11, 37, 47, 79, 134, 193
  1:3–7, 10, 21
  1:3–4, 101, 125, 197
  1:3, 3, 10, 11, 14, 21, 23, 25, 33, 37, 39, 53, 112
  1:4–5, 33, 85
  1:4, 11, 23, 25, 29, 37, 58, 85, 113, 149, 173, 217
  1:5, 26, 27, 29, 37, 73, 90, 125, 128, 129, 130, 153, 154, 165, 200
  1:6–11, 82
  1:6–7, 11, 29, 101, 161, 197
  1:6, 37, 125, 130, 173, 194
  1:7, 11, 21, 24, 25, 26
  1:8–11, 11, 21, 25, 85, 167
  1:8–10, 156
  1:8, 197, 217
  1:9–10, 28
  1:9, 159, 191
  1:10, 28, 113, 135, 173, 192, 199
  1:10–11, 23, 53
  1:11, 28, 31, 33, 120
  1:12–20, 176
  1:12–17, 21, 31, 37, 42, 128
  1:12–16, 3, 152
  1:12–13, 69
  1:12, 31, 32, 129, 147, 180
  1:13–16, 77

1 Timothy (cont.)
  1:13–14, 32
  1:13, 31, 33, 159
  1:14, 27, 28, 31
  1:15–16, 33
  1:15, 31, 59, 133, 172, 217
  1:16, 31, 41, 136
  1:17, 5, 31, 120
  1:18–20, 10, 21, 79, 193
  1:18–19, 83, 171
  1:18, 3, 14, 118, 167
  1:19, 11, 25, 27, 28, 38
  1:20, 3, 4, 11, 22, 25, 137, 151, 155, 162, 179, 207, 218
  2:1–15, 52
  2:1–7, 39, 44
  2:1–4, 212
  2:1–3, 39
  2:1–2, 47, 76, 211
  2:1, 38, 39, 44, 51, 207
  2:2–4, 101
  2:2, 71, 77, 117, 133, 200
  2:3–6, 41
  2:3–5, 87
  2:3, 41, 133, 186
  2:4–7, 40
  2:4–6, 39
  2:4, 41, 59, 77, 113, 133, 184, 207
  2:5–6, 42
  2:6, 41, 120
  2:7, 3, 5, 32, 39, 42, 47, 77, 135, 191
  2:8–15, 44–62
  2:8–10, 53
  2:8, 39, 46, 47, 48, 51, 62, 69, 113, 116
  2:9–15, 11, 74, 86
  2:9–12, 188
  2:9–10, 12, 46, 59
  2:9, 48, 50, 51, 62, 71, 96, 100, 101, 202, 204
  2:10, 199, 201
  2:11–15, 46, 52, 55
  2:11–12, 56
  2:11, 29, 47, 51, 52, 53, 58, 59, 100, 162, 220
  2:12, 52, 54, 55, 59, 62, 101, 116, 131, 162, 201
  2:13–15, 70
  2:13–14, 58, 60, 82
  2:13, 53
  2:14, 55, 59, 155, 194
  2:15, 12, 26, 27, 28, 49, 53, 55, 59, 62, 100

3, 201
3:1–13, 103, 156
3:1–7, 62, 74, 97, 186, 190
3:1–5, 11, 25
3:1, 63, 64, 74, 172, 217
3:2, 69, 71, 72, 74, 97, 98, 141, 155, 188, 190, 191
3:3, 47, 73, 107, 212
3:4–5, 70, 130, 189
3:4, 29, 54, 64, 200
3:5, 64
3:6, 11, 25, 65, 68, 160
3:7, 70, 101
3:8–13, 4
3:8–10, 74
3:8–9, 38, 47
3:8, 69, 72, 74, 107
3:9–10, 74
3:9, 27, 37, 73, 74, 77, 184
3:10, 74, 170
3:11, 47, 73, 74, 160, 201
3:12, 97
3:13, 29, 184
3:14–16, 161
3:14–15, 3, 90
3:14, 76
3:15–16, 88
3:15, 76, 77, 130, 151, 152, 189
3:16, 21, 41, 73, 77, 87, 113, 117, 133, 135, 192, 199, 206, 214, 216
4:1–10, 10
4:1–7, 193
4:1–5, 83, 86, 195, 196
4:1–3, 53, 59, 101
4:1–2, 11, 25
4:1, 28, 79, 85, 135, 155, 156, 184, 214
4:2–3, 79
4:2, 27
4:3–5, 11, 25, 53, 55, 82, 100, 196
4:4–5, 79
4:3–4, 11, 25
4:3, 25, 77, 79, 80, 81, 101
4:4, 82, 83
4:5, 172, 185, 196
4:6–7, 83
4:6, 28, 73, 83, 85, 86, 135, 164, 172, 184
4:7–8, 11, 25, 83, 117
4:7, 58, 173
4:8–10, 83

Scripture Index

4:8, 127, 170, 185
4:9, 86, 87, 172, 217
4:10, 11, 25, 41, 43, 87, 92, 186, 207
4:11, 22, 89, 191
4:12, 3, 20, 26, 27, 28, 88, 89, 172, 199, 210
4:13–16, 167
4:13–15, 115
4:13, 90, 135
4:14, 3, 37, 130, 171
4:15, 88, 92
4:16, 59, 88, 92, 133, 135, 185
5, 108
5:1–6:2, 108
5:1–16, 99
5:1–2, 3
5:1, 65, 93, 103, 121
5:2, 90, 93
5:3–16, 12
5:3–8, 95
5:3, 95, 101, 102, 109, 121
5:4–5, 125
5:4, 95, 101, 115, 123, 130, 220
5:5–6, 95
5:5, 96, 99, 123
5:6, 70, 96, 100
5:7–8, 95
5:7, 22, 98
5:8, 28, 98, 101, 123, 184
5:9–10, 95, 96, 123
5:9, 96, 99
5:10, 97, 199
5:11–15, 95, 97, 161
5:11–13, 74
5:11–12, 55, 101
5:11, 69, 99, 100, 153
5:12, 99
5:13, 47, 55, 58, 86, 100, 195, 220
5:14–15, 161
5:14, 47, 55, 99, 100, 202
5:15, 24, 101
5:16, 95, 98, 115, 123
5:17–25, 102
5:17–22, 102, 111
5:17–20, 186
5:17–18, 103
5:17, 65, 90, 93, 96, 102, 103, 109, 121, 135, 172
5:18, 104, 112, 169
5:19, 65, 104, 105

5:20, 105, 106, 172
5:21, 111, 149, 171
5:22, 63, 107, 131, 134, 202
5:23–25, 110, 111
5:23, 3, 102, 107
5:24–25, 107, 108
5:24, 102
5:25, 102
6, 108, 184
6:1–10, 118
6:1, 96, 109, 121, 135, 202
6:2–10, 10
6:2, 67, 110, 111, 123
6:3–10, 11, 73, 193
6:3–5, 111, 161
6:3, 23, 112, 117, 135, 172, 192, 199
6:4–5, 11, 66, 113
6:4, 70
6:5, 77, 104, 106, 113, 114, 117, 160, 195
6:6–10, 111
6:6, 117, 122
6:7–10, 50
6:7, 4, 114
6:8, 114
6:9–10, 25, 73, 161
6:9, 115, 153
6:10, 4, 70, 115, 121, 157, 184
6:11–16, 37, 112
6:11–14, 83
6:11, 27, 47, 117, 118, 153, 170, 200, 215
6:12, 28, 73, 118, 119, 176
6:13–16, 116
6:13–14, 119
6:13, 22, 119, 132
6:14, 119, 206
6:15, 120
6:16, 116, 120
6:17–19, 50, 116, 121, 177, 195
6:17, 20, 22, 121, 122, 124, 178
6:18, 121, 199
6:19, 121, 123, 151
6:20–21, 10, 11, 38, 161, 162
6:20, 24, 37, 83, 124, 125, 150, 167
6:21, 24, 28, 73, 106, 124, 125, 181, 184, 220

2 Timothy
1:1, 3, 127, 183, 185, 186
1:2, 4, 21, 128, 153, 165
1:3, 4, 27, 31, 37, 73, 129, 136

2 Timothy (cont.)
  1:4, 4, 128
  1:5, 4, 14, 28, 130, 167
  1:6–14, 139
  1:6, 4, 91, 134
  1:7, 24, 27, 131, 133, 138, 214
  1:8–12, 165
  1:8–10, 185
  1:8, 4, 132, 133, 135, 136, 137, 138, 141, 143
  1:9–10, 133, 136, 185, 214
  1:9, 59, 133, 134, 136
  1:10, 20, 133, 134, 135, 136, 186, 206, 207
  1:11–14, 140
  1:11–12, 176
  1:11, 4, 32, 42, 135
  1:12–14, 131
  1:12–13, 137
  1:12, 135, 136, 138
  1:13–14, 136, 141, 143, 167
  1:13, 4, 27, 141, 143, 144, 172, 192, 199
  1:14, 136, 143, 214
  1:15–18, 140
  1:15, 4, 126, 137, 138, 167
  1:16–18, 4, 137
  1:16–17, 10
  1:16, 138, 181
  1:17–18, 4, 38
  1:17, 126, 137, 138
  1:18, 4, 139
  2:1–7, 140, 143
  2:1, 4, 140, 141, 142, 180
  2:2, 4, 141, 143
  2:3–4, 140
  2:3, 4
  2:4, 37, 141
  2:5, 29, 140, 142
  2:6, 140
  2:7–8, 199
  2:7, 142, 199
  2:8–13, 176, 192, 199
  2:8, 30, 143, 144, 145, 185, 199
  2:9, 4, 143, 145, 172, 184, 185
  2:10, 24, 59, 133, 143, 145, 184
  2:11–13, 143, 146
  2:11–12, 147
  2:11, 217
  2:12, 146, 47
  2:13, 27, 147
  2:14–26, 10
  2:14, 11, 92, 148, 149, 154, 171

2:15–17, 156
2:15, 77, 92, 148, 150, 152, 162, 172, 185, 196
2:16–21, 148, 149, 150
2:16–18, 149, 162
2:16, 11, 150
2:17, 11, 22, 150, 151, 172
2:18, 11, 77, 151, 195
2:19, 151, 152
2:20, 151, 152
2:21, 152, 170
2:22–26, 117
2:22–25, 116
2:22, 4, 27, 117, 148, 150, 152, 153, 215
2:23–26, 148, 149, 193, 217
2:23–24, 212
2:23, 11, 149, 154
2:24–26, 38, 197
2:24–25, 154
2:24, 141, 154, 184
2:25–26, 38, 161
2:25, 77, 155, 184, 207, 213
2:26, 25, 149, 155
3:1–9, 10, 80, 155, 164, 187, 193
3:1–7, 24
3:1, 156
3:2–9, 166
3:2–4, 155
3:2–3, 159
3:2, 70, 157
3:3–4, 161
3:3, 159, 201
3:4, 70, 113
3:5, 117, 133, 159, 160, 162, 165, 196
3:6–9, 161
3:6–7, 162
3:6, 86, 153, 155, 161, 166
3:7, 77, 162, 184
3:8–9, 4, 163
3:8, 24, 155, 161, 162, 163
3:9, 92
3:10–11, 4, 155, 164
3:10, 27, 116, 135, 165, 200
3:11–12, 4
3:11, 165
3:12, 155, 164, 165, 196
3:13, 155, 164, 166
3:14–17, 155
3:14–15, 4, 14
3:14, 164, 166
3:15–17, 85, 164

Scripture Index

3:16–17, 91, 155, 168, 217
3:15, 59, 133, 167
3:16, 135, 155, 172, 215
3:17, 117, 199
4:1–8, 126
4:1–5, 10, 173
4:1–2, 171
4:1, 206
4:2, 135, 170, 171, 172
4:3–5, 171
4:3–4, 11, 173
4:3, 30, 135, 192, 199
4:4, 24, 77, 137, 173
4:5, 170, 172, 173, 177
4:6–8, 4, 175, 176
4:7–8, 170, 176
4:7, 118, 176, 177
4:8, 177, 178, 206
4:9–21, 137
4:9–18, 170, 175, 218
4:9–12, 181
4:9, 4, 14, 128, 137, 177, 178, 179, 182
4:10, 4, 15, 137, 178, 180, 219
4:11, 4, 137, 178
4:12, 4, 126, 178, 219
4:13, 4, 137, 179
4:14–15, 4, 137
4:14, 179
4:15, 172, 220
4:16, 4, 137, 178, 179
4:17–18, 137, 182
4:17, 4, 135, 174, 177, 180
4:18, 4, 59, 180
4:19, 4, 138, 180, 181
4:20–21, 138
4:20, 4, 181
4:21, 4, 14, 128, 138, 178, 180, 181, 182
4:22, 220

Titus
  1, 201
  1:1–3, 87
  1:1, 77, 117, 183, 184, 197, 208
  1:2, 128, 183
  1:3, 135, 172, 183, 185, 191, 206, 207
  1:4, 4, 15, 20, 21, 153, 183, 184, 186, 207
  1:5–9, 15, 63, 156, 193
  1:5–6, 130
  1:5, 4, 10, 15, 65, 178, 188, 192, 197, 210, 217, 218

1:6–9, 192, 197, 207
1:6, 97, 212
1:7–9, 69
1:7, 26, 64, 65, 69, 73, 107, 188, 189, 190
1:9–16, 10
1:9, 30, 69, 90, 135, 141, 172, 173, 191, 197, 199
1:10–16, 15, 187, 188, 197, 217
1:10, 11, 24, 25, 191, 193, 212, 215
1:11–12, 193
1:11, 11, 25, 73, 100, 191, 193, 195, 196
1:12, 160
1:13–14, 193, 196
1:13, 184, 192, 196, 197, 199
1:14, 11, 25, 77, 173, 195, 197, 215
1:15–16, 193
1:15, 11, 25, 27, 162
1:16, 162, 196
2:1–10, 197, 205
2:1–8, 12
2:1, 135, 173, 188, 192, 198, 199, 210, 217
2:2–10, 207, 210, 217
2:2, 4, 27, 73, 118, 184, 192, 198, 199, 203
2:3–5, 198
2:3, 4, 55, 73, 160, 200, 202
2:4, 131, 199, 201, 202
2:5, 109, 172, 199, 203
2:6, 93, 131, 198, 199, 210
2:7–8, 198, 199
2:7, 135
2:8, 172
2:9–10, 108, 109, 198
2:9, 203
2:10, 135, 186, 202, 204, 205, 207, 209
2:11–14, 205, 210, 217
2:11–13, 215
2:11–12, 209
2:11, 41, 59, 205, 206, 207, 214, 215, 216
2:12, 131, 153, 199, 205, 206, 207, 208, 214
2:13, 20, 186, 205, 206, 207, 208, 214
2:14, 199, 205, 216
2:15, 172, 198, 205, 210
3:1–7, 205
3:1–2, 211, 214, 215, 217
3:1, 5, 199, 210, 212
3:2, 207, 212
3:3–7, 4
3:3, 153, 160, 207, 211, 213
3:4–8, 210, 211
3:4–7, 214, 217

Titus (cont.)
 3:4–6, 216
 3:4, 186, 206, 207, 214
 3:5, 59, 191, 214, 215, 216
 3:6, 20, 186, 207, 214, 216
 3:7, 191, 216
 3:8–11, 193, 211
 3:8, 172, 199, 217, 220
 3:9–11, 10, 11
 3:9, 11, 25, 150, 194, 197, 212, 215
 3:10–11, 197
 3:11, 218
 3:12–13, 15
 3:12, 4, 15, 178, 183, 219
 3:13, 15, 219
 3:14, 199
 3:15, 180, 181, 184, 220
 3:17, 220

Philemon, 204
 1, 14, 133
 2, 141
 4–7, 128
 9, 133, 200
 11, 178
 16, 110
 21–22, 218
 23–24, 180
 23, 220
 24, 178
 25, 181, 220

Hebrews
 1:1–4, 185
 1:1–2, 80, 156
 5:14, 86
 6:2, 191
 8:6, 42
 12:5–11, 207
 12:11, 86
 12:28, 31
 13:1–19, 81
 13:2, 98

James
 1:1, 184
 1:6–8, 47
 1:12–18, 81
 1:12, 177

1:17–18, 120
1:19–21, 212
1:21, 213
1:27, 98
2:6, 121
2:16, 114
3:1–412, 150–1
3:13–18, 212
3:13, 213
4:1–2, 212
4:8, 47
4:11–12, 160
4:13–5:6, 121
4:13–16, 121
5:3, 156
5:5, 96
5:14, 65

1 Peter
 1:5, 92
 1:13, 174
 1:18, 209
 1:20–21, 156
 2:2, 92
 2:9–10, 120
 2:10–3:7, 109, 197
 2:11–3:7, 200, 211
 2:11–12, 40, 212
 2:11, 37
 2:12, 202
 2:13–17, 40
 2:14–15, 212
 2:15, 122
 2:18–25, 108
 2:20, 122
 2:25, 64
 3:1, 202
 3:2, 90
 3:3, 50
 3:4, 51, 53
 3:5, 204
 3:6, 122
 3:16, 213
 3:17, 122
 3:18–22, 106
 3:18, 77, 78
 3:19, 77, 78
 4:1–11, 81
 4:4, 191

Scripture Index

4:7, 174
5:1-2, 188
5:1, 65
5:2, 64
5:4, 177
5:5, 65
5:8, 174

2 Peter
  1:21, 169
  2, 81
  3:8-9, 120
  3:14-16, 169

1 John
  1:1-4, 184
  1:1-3, 185
  1:3, 220
  1:5-7, 185
  1:5, 120
  2:2, 220
  3:4-10, 196
  3:17, 220
  4:7-10, 26

2 John
  1, 65

3 John
  1, 65
  5-6, 219

Jude
  1, 81
  17-19, 80, 156

Revelation
  2-3, 80
  2:10, 177
  2:14, 81
  2:20-23, 81
  4:11, 120
  5:13-14, 120
  6-19, 156
  6:9-11, 147
  12-13, 195
  12:10-11, 147
  13:9-10, 147
  14:8-12, 81

18:1-19:10, 81
21:14, 151
22:10-16, 108
22:14-15, 81

Extra Biblical Jewish, Greco-Roman, and Christian Literature

1 QS
  6:24-7:25, 218

Acts of Andrew (Latin)
  25:1-11, 62

Anthia and Habrocomes (or, *Ephesiaca*)
  1.2.5-6, 50
  1.3.1-2, 51

Letter of Aristeas
  45, 40

Aristotle
  Politics
    1.2.4, 109
    1.2.6, 109
    1.2.7, 109
    1.2.13, 109
    1.2.15, 109
  Ascension of Isaiah
    11, 62

2 Baruch
  72-74, 61
  73:7, 61

1 Clement
  2.7, 4
  5:6-7, 5
  5:7, 3
  21:7, 90
  60.4, 4
  61.2, 4

2 Clement
  19, 92

Clement of Alexandra
  Stromateis
    1.1, 5

Clement of Alexandra (cont.)
   1.9, 5
   1.10, 5
   4.7, 5
  Exhortation
   1, 5
  Didache
   8:3, 129
   15:2, 68
   15:10, 68

Eusebius
  Church History
   2.2.2, 6

Herodotus
  Histories, 66

Homer
  Iliad
   13.278–286, 66

Irenaeus
  Ag. Heresies
   1.23.4, 5
   2.14.7, 5
   3.1.1, 5
   4.16.3, 5
   5.17.1, 5

Josephus
  Against Apion
   2.202, 60
  Antiquities
   17:14, 68
   17:327, 196
  Bellum Judaicum
   1.477, 68
  Vita
   9, 89

Laudatio Turiae 68
Life of Adam and Eve
  25:1–4, 61–2

Mishnah
  Avot
   5:21, 90
  Odes of Solomon
   19:7–8, 62

Plato
  Republic, 66

Plutarch
  Table Talk
   2.1.4, 157

Polycarp
  Philippians
   4.1, 4
   5.2, 4
  Protevangelium of James
   11:17–20, 62

Semonides of Amorgos
  Poem on Women, 66

Seneca
  Epistles
   6.5–6, 88

Sirach
  25.15–26, 59

Tertullian
  Baptism
   17, 8

Theophrastus
  Characters, 66–7

Printed in the United States
by Baker & Taylor Publisher Services